ETHICS IN
U.S. GOVERNMENT

ETHICS IN U.S. GOVERNMENT

An Encyclopedia of Investigations, Scandals, Reforms, and Legislation

Robert North Roberts

GREENWOOD PRESS
Westport, Connecticut • London

Library of Congress Cataloging-in-Publication Data

Roberts, Robert North.
     Ethics in U.S. Government : an encyclopedia of investigations, scandals, reforms, and
legislation / Robert North Roberts.
          p. cm.
     Includes bibliographical references and index.
     ISBN 0–313–31198–6 (alk. paper)
     1. Political ethics—United States—Encyclopedias. 2. Political corruption—United
States—Encyclopedias. I. Title.
     JK468.E7 R556   2001
     973'.03—dc21   00–061699

British Library Cataloguing in Publication Data is available.

Library of Congress Catalog Card Number: 00–061699
ISBN: 0–313–31198–6

First published in 2001

Greenwood Press, 88 Post Road West, Westport, CT 06881
An imprint of Greenwood Publishing Group, Inc.
www.greenwood.com

Printed in the United States of America

The paper used in this book complies with the
Permanent Paper Standard issued by the National
Information Standards Organization (Z39.48–1984).

10 9 8 7 6 5 4 3 2 1

CONTENTS

INTRODUCTION

James Madison wrote in the *Federalist Papers* over 200 years ago, "If angels were to govern men, neither external nor internal controls on government would be necessary." Madison clearly understood that in the future the United States would face its share of political scandals. From Edmund Randolph's 1794 resignation as secretary of state to President Bill Clinton's January–February 1999 Senate impeachment trial, government ethics controversies have played an important role in the evolution of the national government.

From the 1789 swearing in of President George Washington to the 1828 election of President Andrew Jackson, the United States faced relatively few government ethics scandals. From 1828 to the passage of the Pendleton Act of 1883, the country saw an explosion in government ethics scandals brought about in large measure by the growth of the "spoils system" and the inability and unwillingness of government institutions to prevent a growing number of public officials from seeing government service as a rich opportunity to line their own pockets at the public expense. The post–Civil War period from the 1868 presidential election of Ulysses S. Grant to the end of the 1870s saw an unprecedented level of public corruption at the federal, state, and local level. Efforts to reform public institutions generally failed; however, a small group of reformers never lost hope in the restoration of honesty and integrity to government.

From the 1883 passage of the Pendleton Act, which established a new federal merit system through the Progressive Movement (1900–1920), the nation saw a transformation in government ethics. At the federal level, political parties gradually lost their stranglehold on government positions with the enactment of laws designed to protect federal employees from being forced to make campaign contributions or to participate in partisan political activities. The Progressive Era also saw the enactment of the first campaign finance laws prohibiting corporate campaign contributions to candidates for federal office and requiring limited campaign finance disclosure. Much like the war recovery years of the 1870s, the 1920s saw a significant slump in public service ethics as symbolized by the Teapot Dome scandal which saw Secretary of the Interior Albert Fall accept hundreds of thousands of dollars in bribes in return for leasing the right to pump oil for naval oil reserves located at Teapot Dome, Wyoming, and Elk Hills, California.

To a large degree, the stock market crash of 1929, the ensuing Great Depression, and World War II helped to ring out the excesses of the 1920s. The idealism of Franklin Roosevelt's New Deal and the Second World War crusade against Nazi Germany and Imperial Japan raised public expectations regarding the ability of government to successfully tackle the most difficult challenges that a nation might face, while striving to live up to a noble ethos.

Yet, by the early 1960s, a series of ethics controversies involving members of the Truman and Eisenhower administrations led to a consensus that to maintain public confidence in the objectivity and impartiality of government decision making, government institutions needed to adopt much tighter public ethics restrictions, especially as the power, discretion, and breadth of government rose. Through the 1960s, Congress and Presidents John Kennedy and Lyndon Johnson successfully tightened executive branch ethics rules. In 1971 Congress passed the Federal Election Campaign Act in an effort to control the escalating cost of running for federal office in the mass media age.

On August 9, 1974, President Richard Nixon resigned as the result of the Watergate scandal. Watergate ushered in a new era of reform. In 1974 Congress passed major amendments to the Federal Election Campaign Act and in 1978 Congress passed the Ethics in Government Act. From 1979 through the end of June 1999, twenty special prosecutors and independent counsels conducted investigations of alleged criminal conduct by high-level executive branch officials. Presidents Jimmy Carter, Gerald Ford, Ronald Reagan, George Bush, and Bill Clinton would face their share of public ethics controversies. And through the post-Watergate period, Congress continued to struggle with finding a way to slow the growing influence of money and special interest lobbying.

Ethics in U.S. Government: An Encyclopedia of Investigations, Scandals, Reforms, and Legislation provides a ready reference source on political ethics controversies, investigations and public ethics reforms throughout American history. In preparing the book, I made a conscious decision to devote a significant number of entries on individuals involved in ethics controversies that have taken place since the end of World War II. Readers must understand that the fact that an individual is dealt with in an entry does not indicate that the individual engaged in illegal or inappropriate conduct. It simply means that the individual became involved in a serious ethics controversy. Consequently readers must take care not to assume an individual engaged in wrongdoing as a result of a listing.

Throughout American history political scandals and political reform have helped to shape the nation's political system. Today the search continues for ways to protect public confidence in the integrity of government and the political process.

ACRONYMS

AEC	Atomic Energy Commission
BIR	Bureau of Internal Revenue
BOB	Bureau of the Budget
CAB	Civil Aeronautics Board
CIA	Central Intelligence Agency
CREEP	Committee to Re-Elect the President
CSC	Civil Service Commission
DAEO	Designated Agency Ethics Official
DNC	Democratic National Committee
EPA	Environmental Protection Agency
FBI	Federal Bureau of Investigation
FCPA	Federal Corrupt Practices Act
FEC	Federal Election Commission
FECA	Federal Election Campaign Act
FTC	Federal Trade Commission
GAO	General Accounting Office
GSA	General Services Administration
LDA	Lobbying Disclosure Act of 1995
NSC	National Security Council
OMB	Office of Management and Budget
OTS	Office of Thrift Supervision
RFC	Reconstruction Finance Corporation
RNC	Republican National Committee

RTC	Resolution Trust Corporation
SEC	Securities and Exchange Commission
TVA	Tennessee Valley Authority
USOGE	U.S. Office of Government Ethics

TIMELINE OF IMPORTANT EVENTS

1975	Secretary of State Edmund Randolph resigns after vigorously denying allegations that he accepted money from France to oppose a treaty with England.
1802	Allegation that Thomas Jefferson fathered a child with one of his slaves published.
1824	November 2: Presidential candidate Andrew Jackson wins the popular vote but fails to win a majority of electoral votes. The House elects John Quincy Adams as president after Henry Clay throws his support behind Adams in return for Adams appointing Clay as secretary of state.
1829	Andrew Jackson sworn in as president of the United States. Jackson expands the "spoils system," which makes political loyalty a qualification for government positions.
1834	March 28: The Senate votes 26 to 20 to censure President Andrew Jackson for directing Treasury Department officials not to make further government deposits into the National Bank.
1838	Samuel Swartwout, collector for the New York Customs House, flees to England with millions of dollars taken from customs receipts.
1852	Galphin Claim Controversy.
1856	Political corruption allegations regarding the presidential election campaign of Democratic presidential candidate James Buchanan.
1860	House Covode committee political corruption investigation of the administration of President James Buchanan.
1862	April 30: House votes to censure Secretary of War Simon Cameron for approving a number of fraudulent contracts related to the prosecution of the Civil War.

1863	President Abraham Lincoln suspends the right to Habeas Corpus.
1868	May 16: After Senate impeachment trial, President Andrew Johnson escapes being removed as president by one vote.
1869	September 24: Sudden collapse of gold prices led to investigation of whether President Grant and Grant family members assisted gold speculators James Fisk Jr. and Jay Gould to corner the gold market.
1872	September 4: The *New York Sun* alleges that the Union Pacific Railroad and Credit Mobilier company gave members of Congress the opportunity to purchase Credit Mobilier stock far below face value in an effort to prevent a congressional investigation of construction cost for the transcontinental railroad.
1873	February 27: House votes to censure Representatives Oakes Ames, R-Mass., and James Brooks, D-N.Y., for their role in the Credit Mobilier stock scandal.
1875	Secretary of Treasury Benjamin H. Bristow starts so-called Whiskey Ring investigation.
1876	February 24: A St. Louis, Missouri, U.S. District Court jury finds General Orville E. Babcock not guilty of participating in the Whiskey Ring tax fraud scheme. Babcock served as President Ulysses S. Grant's personal secretary. March 2: President Ulysses S. Grant accepts the resignation of Secretary of War William Belknap before Congress can begin impeachment proceedings against Belknap for accepting kickbacks. May 31: James Mulligan appears before a House committee and accuses Maine representative and former Speaker of the House James G. Blaine of allowing major railroads to bail him out of financial trouble. June 20: Secretary of Treasury Benjamin H. Bristow resigns his post to run for the 1976 Republican presidential nomination.
1883	January 23: President Chester A. Arthur signs the Civil Service Reform Act (Pendleton Act) into law.
1884	September 27: *Judge* publishes a front-page political cartoon of a baby reaching out his hands to Democratic presidential candidate Grover Cleveland crying, "I want my pa." The cartoon referred to an allegation that Cleveland had fathered an illegitimate child.
1905	December 5: In his annual message, President Theodore Roosevelt asks Congress to prohibit corporations from making contributions to any political committee.
1907	January 26: Congress passes the Tillman Act, which prohibits corporations and national banks from making political contributions to candidates for federal office.
1910	January 10: President William Howard Taft fires Chief Forester Gifford Pinchot.

1921   May 31: President Harding issues an executive order transferring man-agement of naval oil reserves from the Navy Department to the Interior Department.

1922   April 14: *Wall Street Journal* reports that Secretary of the Interior Albert Fall leased the Teapot Dome, Wyoming, oil field to Harry Sinclair's Mammoth Oil Company.

1923   March 4: Albert Fall resigns as secretary of the interior.
       August 2: President Warren Harding dies in San Francisco, California, after returning from an Alaskan vacation.

1924   President Calvin Coolidge nominates and the Senate confirms Owen Roberts and Atlee Pomerene as Teapot Dome Scandal special counsels.

1925   February 28: Congress passes the Federal Corrupt Practices Act.

1927   October 10: The Supreme Court upholds the cancellation of the Teapot Dome, Wyoming, and Elk Hill, California, naval oil and gas leases made by Secretary of the Interior Albert Fall to Edwin Doheny and Harry Sinclair.

1929   October 25: A U.S. District Court jury convicts former Secretary of Interior Albert Fall of accepting a bribe from Edward Doheny related to the Teapot Dome oil leases.

1939   August 2: Congress passes the Hatch Act, prohibiting most federal em-ployees from engaging in partisan political activities.

1949   August 30: General Harry Vaughan, military aide to President Harry Truman, testifies before Senate Committee investigation regarding alle-gations that he improperly allowed friends to use his office to obtain private business.

1951   September 27: President Harry S. Truman's message to Congress on ethics in government.
       October 15: Senate committee issues the report *Proposals for Improve-ment of Ethical Standards in the Federal Government, Including Estab-lishment of a Commission on Ethics.*

1952   April 4: Attorney General Howard McGrath fires Newbold Morris, spe-cial assistant to the attorney general. Morris had been appointed in Feb-ruary to oversee government cleanup campaign.
       September 23: Republican vice-presidential candidate Richard M. Nixon gives so-called "Checkers" speech, responding to allegations that he had misused campaign contributions to cover personal expenses.

1953   Bureau of the Budget enlists the services of Vice President and Director of First Boston Corporation Adolphe Wenzell to negotiate the Dixon-Yates contract.

1955   July 11: Attorney General Herbert Brownell Jr. announces President Ei-senhower's decision to cancel the Dixon-Yates contract.

1958   September 22: Sherman Adams, chief of staff to President Dwight David Eisenhower, resigns as the result of controversy over contacting federal regulatory agencies on behalf of friends.

1961   January 9: The Supreme Court upholds President Eisenhower's cancellation of the Dixon-Yates power contract because of the existence of a conflict of interest on the part of a part-time consultant used by the Bureau of the Budget to negotiate the contract in the case of *United States v Mississippi Valley Generating Co.*
                       January 22: President John F. Kennedy appoints an advisory panel on ethics in government.
                       May 5: President Kennedy issues Executive Order 10939, To Provide a Guide on Ethical Standards to Government Officials.

1962   October 23: President Kennedy signs into law a major revision of federal bribery and conflict of interest laws.

1963   September 9: An owner of a private vending machine company files suit against Bobby Baker, the secretary to the Senate majority leader, alleging that Baker had used his influence to obtain a vending machine contract for a defense plant in a company in which Baker held a financial interest.

1965   May 9: President Lyndon Johnson issues Executive Order 11222, Prescribing Standards of Ethical Conduct for Government Officers and Employees.

1966   January 5: A federal grand jury indicts Bobby Baker on fraud and tax evasion charges; a year later a federal jury convicts Baker of tax evasion.

1969   May 14: Associate Supreme Court Justice Abe Fortas resigns as the result of conflict of interest allegation.
                       July 16: Senator Edward Kennedy drives his car off a bridge located on Chappaquiddick Island; Mary Jo Kopechne dies in the accident.

1971   June 13: *New York Times* begins publication of parts of the Pentagon Papers leaked by Daniel Ellsberg.
                       September 3: G. Gordon Liddy and E. Howard Hunt lead a break-in to the offices of Daniel Ellsberg, a Los Angeles, California, psychiatrist.

1972   February 7: President Nixon signs into law the Federal Election Campaign Act of 1971.
                       February 15: Attorney General John Mitchell resigns to head President Nixon's Committee to Re-Elect the President (CREEP).
                       June 17: Five burglars arrested inside the office of the Democratic National Committee located in the Watergate complex planting bugging devices.

1973   January 30: G. Gordon Liddy and James McCord convicted of various offenses related to the Watergate break-in.
                       April 30: Nixon White House aides H. R. Haldeman, John Ehrlichman, and Attorney General Richard Kleindienst resign. Nixon fires White House Counsel John Dean.

May 18: Senate Watergate hearing begins.

May 18: Harvard law professor Archibald Cox accepts position as Watergate special prosecutor.

July 13: Former Nixon White House aide Alexander Butterfield tells Senate Watergate Committee about the existence of a White House taping system.

July 23: President Nixon refuses to turn over White House tapes to Senate Watergate Committee or Watergate special prosecutor Archibald Cox.

October 10: Vice President Spiro T. Agnew resigns as the result of allegations that he took kickbacks while serving as governor of Maryland during the 1960s.

October 20: In the so-called Saturday Night Massacre, President Nixon orders the firing of Watergate special prosecutor Archibald Cox.

November 1: President Nixon appoints Houston lawyer Leon Jaworski as the second Watergate special prosecutor.

1974   July 12: A U.S. District Court jury finds former Nixon White House aide John Ehrlichman guilty of conspiracy and perjury related to the September 1971 break-in at the office of Daniel Ellsberg's psychiatrist.

July 24: The Supreme Court orders President Nixon to turn over Watergate tapes to special prosecutor Leon Jaworski in the case of *United States v Nixon*.

August 9: President Nixon becomes the first president to resign.

September 8: President Gerald Ford pardons former president Nixon for Watergate-related offenses.

October 15: President Ford signs into law the Federal Election Campaign Act Amendments.

1976   January 30: Supreme Court hands down *Buckley v Valeo*, which finds key provisions of the Federal Election Campaign Act constitutional and unconstitutional.

1977   January 4: President-Elect Jimmy Carter announces new ethics guidelines for all high-level presidential nominees and appointees.

September 24: President Carter's director of Office of Management and Budget, Bert Lance, resigns to fight allegations that he had engaged in improper banking practices while heading a Georgia bank prior to becoming OMB director.

1978   October 26: President Carter signs into law the Ethics in Government Act.

1980   April 30: U.S. District Court jury acquits Bert Lance on nine counts of bank fraud.

August 4: Carter White House issues lengthy report denying any administration wrongdoing in the activities of Billy Carter, President Carter's brother, lobbying on behalf of the Libyan government.

October 2: House votes to expel Representative Michael Myers for his involvement in the FBI Abscam public corruption sting.

1982   June 24: Supreme Court rules in *Nixon v Fitzgerald* that the Constitution
            provides presidents of the United States with absolute immunity from
            civil suits for action taken in office.

1986   May 29: Whitney North Seymour Jr. receives an appointment as an
            independent counsel to investigate Michael Deaver, former chief of staff
            to President Ronald Reagan.
            December 19: Lawrence Walsh receives an appointment as the Iran-
            contra independent counsel.

1987   May 6: CIA Director William Casey dies in the midst of the growing
            Iran-contra investigation.
            December 16: A U.S. District Court jury finds former Reagan White
            House Chief of Staff Mike Deaver lying about lobbying; he is sentenced
            to 1,500 hours of community service and a $100,000 fine.

1988   June 29: The Supreme Court upholds the constitutionality of the inde-
            pendent counsel law in *Morrison v Olson*.

1989   January 25: President George Bush establishes President's Commission
            on Ethics Law Reform.
            March 9: By a vote of 53 to 47, the Senate rejects the former Texas
            Senator John Tower as President George Bush's secretary of defense due
            to allegations of a drinking problem.
            March 10: Release of *To Serve with Honor: Report of the President's
            Commission on Federal Ethics Law Reform*.
            April 12: President George Bush issues Executive Order 12674, Prin-
            ciples of Ethical Conduct for Government Officers and Employees.
            May 4: A U.S. District Court jury convicts Marine Colonel Oliver North
            on various charges related to the Iran-contra affair.
            May 31: Democratic Speaker of the House Jim Wright announces his
            decision to resign from Congress after a finding by the House ethics
            committee that Wright violated House ethics rules. Wright denied any
            intent to violate House ethics rules.
            November 28: President George Bush signs the Ethics Reform Act into
            law.

1990   April 16: Former Reagan White House National Security Advisor John
            Poindexter convicted of conspiracy, obstruction of justice, and perjury
            related to the Iran-contra affair.
            July 20: U.S. Court of Appeals for the District of Columbia reverses the
            convictions of Iran-contra figure Oliver North.
            July 26: House of Representatives votes to reprimand Representative
            Barney Frank for improperly using his office to help a male prostitute.
            November 15: Senate Keating Five Hearings, an investigation of the
            relationship of five U.S. Senators with Charles Keating, begins.

1991   September 1: U.S. Office of Government Ethics issues new Standards
            of Ethical Conduct for employees of the Executive Branch.
            November 16: Iran-contra conviction of former Reagan White House
            National Security Advisor John Poindexter reversed on appeal.

December 3: John Sununu, chief of staff to President George Bush, announces his decision to resign after extended controversy over Sununu's travel practices.

1992   March 8: Story appears in the *New York Times* that details the failure of the Whitewater land development.
            June 16: Former Secretary of Defense Caspar Weinberger indicted by a federal grand jury for obstructing the Iran-contra investigation.
            December 24: President Bush pardons Weinberger and five other Iran-contra figures.

1993   January 22: Attorney General nominee Zoe Baird withdraws her name from consideration as the result of controversy over her failure to pay Social Security taxes for undocumented employees.
            May 19: The White House fires seven longtime employees of the White House travel office.
            July 20: Deputy White House Counsel Vincent Foster commits suicide in a Washington, D.C., area park.
            August 4: Iran-contra independent counsel Lawrence Walsh submits his final report to the U.S. Court of Appeals for the District of Columbia.

1994   March 14: Associate Attorney General Webster Hubbell resigns.
            May 6: Former Arkansas state employee Paula Jones files suit against President Bill Clinton for an alleged sexual harassment incident on May 8, 1991.
            May 27: Supreme Court holds in *Clinton v Jones* that the Constitution does not permit President Bill Clinton to delay the sexual harassment lawsuit until after his term as president.
            August 5: Kenneth Starr receives appointment as the Whitewater independent counsel after President Clinton signs into law a new independent counsel law.
            October 3: Secretary of Agriculture Mike Espy resigns after allegations that he accepted improper gifts from businesses regulated by the Department of Agriculture.

1995   February 22: The Supreme Court, in *United States v National Treasury Employees Union*, finds unconstitutional a provision of the Ethics Reform Act of 1989 prohibiting all federal employees from accepting honorariums for giving speeches or writing articles.
            March 7: Oregon Republican Senator Robert Packwood announces his decision to resign from the Senate ethics committee after it finds strong evidence of sexual harassment of congressional staffers by Packwood.
            November 16: A federal jury acquits Billy R. Dale, the former White House travel office director, of embezzlement charges.

1996   April 28: President Bill Clinton testifies on videotape as defense witness in the Little Rock, Arkansas, trial of Jim Guy Tucker and James and Susan McDougal.
            May 26: A U.S. District Court jury convicts Tucker and the McDougals on fraud and conspiracy charges.

August 29: Dick Morris resigns as political consultant to President Clinton after a tabloid publishes a story of Morris's alleged relationship with a prostitute.

1997

January 21: Republican Speaker of the House Newt Gingrich accepts a House reprimand and agrees to pay a $300,000 fine for violating House ethics rules.

1998

January 12: Linda Tripp provides independent counsel Kenneth W. Starr with tapes of her conversations with Monica Lewinsky about Lewinsky's relationship with President Clinton.

January 16: Whitewater independent counsel Kenneth Starr receives authority to investigate possible criminal violations by President Clinton in an effort to conceal his relationship with Lewinsky.

January 17: President Clinton is deposed in the Paula Jones sexual harassment lawsuit.

March 8: James McDougal dies in federal prison.

March 19: Washington lawyer Carol Elder Bruce appointed as independent counsel to investigate whether Secretary of the Interior Bruce Babbitt lied to Congress regarding the reasons for the Interior Department's denial of gambling license to a Wisconsin Indian tribe.

April 1: U.S. District Court Judge Susan Webber Wright dismisses the Paula Jones sexual harassment lawsuit against President Clinton.

April 17: President Clinton testifies before the Monica Lewinsky grand jury.

May 26: Ralph I. Lancaster Jr. receives appointment as independent counsel to investigate whether Secretary of Labor Alexis Herman solicited a kickback while serving as a Clinton White House aide.

September 9: Whitewater independent counsel Kenneth Starr submits a report on his Monica Lewinsky investigation to the House.

December 2: A U.S. District Court jury finds former Agriculture Secretary Mike Espy not guilty of accepting $35,000 in illegal gratuities.

December 19: House approves two articles of impeachment against President Bill Clinton: perjury before a grand jury and obstruction of justice.

1999

February 12: After a Senate impeachment trial, President Clinton is found not guilty of perjury before the grand jury and obstruction of justice.

April 13: U.S. District Court Judge Susan Webber Wright finds President Clinton in contempt of court for giving false testimony in his deposition in the Paula Jones case.

June 30: Authority for the appointment of independent counsels expires after Congress fails to extend the independent counsel law.

September 7: Former Secretary of Housing and Urban Development Henry Cisneros pleads guilty to a single misdemeanor count of making false statements to the FBI regarding payments made to a former mistress.

October 13: Independent counsel Carol Elder Bruce ends investigation of Secretary of Interior Bruce Babbitt without obtaining any criminal indictments.

October 19: A special federal appeals panel appoints Robert W. Ray as the second Whitewater independent counsel.

2000   March 13: Whitewater independent counsel Robert Ray ends his investigation of the White House acquisition of FBI files of former Reagan and Bush administration appointees without seeking any indictments.
April 5: Independent counsel Ralph I. Lancaster Jr. ends investigation of Labor Secretary Alexis Herman without seeking any indictments.

2001   January 20: Independent Counsel Robert Ray ends Monica Lewinsky investigation after President Clinton agrees to a five-year suspension of his Arkansas law license and admits that he gave false testimony in the Monica Lewinsky scandal. However, President Clinton insisted he had not knowingly given false testimony.
January 20: President Clinton pardons 130 individuals.

A

ABSCAM INVESTIGATION. In the aftermath of the **Watergate scandal**, in 1976 the Department of Justice established a new **Public Integrity Section** within the Department's Criminal Division. At the same time, U.S. attorneys and the Federal Bureau of Investigation (FBI) significantly increased resources devoted to public corruption investigations and prosecutions. **Federal prosecutors** working for the Justice Department and U.S. Attorneys Offices relied heavily on the investigatory work of the FBI agents to develop the necessary evidence to indict local, state, and federal officials on public corruption charges. In addition to collecting evidence of possible illegal conduct, the late 1970s and early 1980s saw the FBI begin to make use of elaborate **stings** to gather evidence on public officials suspected of engaging in corrupt activities. The Abscam sting constituted the most publicized of the early FBI public corruption stings.

The origins of the Abscam sting had nothing to do with political corruption in Congress. During 1978 the FBI began an undercover operation in an effort to obtain stolen art work. FBI agents posed as fences interested in purchasing stolen art work and financial instruments. The FBI turned the focus of the undercover operation from stolen art work to political corruption after an informant told agents that he might be able to find a number of politicians willing to help the undercover agents with their problems for a fee.

As the sting unfolded, intermediaries acting on behalf of the FBI contacted a number of members of Congress. The intermediaries told the members of Congress that individuals representing the interests of wealthy Arabs wanted to meet with the members to help the Arabs with certain problems. At a series of videotaped meetings during 1979 and early 1980, the FBI agents, posing as the representatives of the wealthy Arabs, asked some members to help the Arabs obtain U.S. residency by introducing legislation permitting the Arabs to remain in the United States. The undercover FBI agents asked other members to help them obtain federal grants and gambling licenses. The FBI videotaped a number of members accepting cash after agreeing to help the Arabs with their problems. Early in 1980 a federal **grand jury** indicted Democrats John W. Jenrette Jr., S.C.; Raymond F. Lederer, Pa.; John M. Murphy, N.Y.; Michael J. Myers, Pa.; and Frank Thompson Jr., N.J. on various public corruption charges. The grand jury also indicted Republican House member Richard Kelly, Fla. Democrat senator Harrison A. Williams Jr., N.J., was the only senator indicted as the result of the Abscam sting. Between 1980 and the end of 1982, federal juries convicted all seven defendants on various criminal charges related to the affair. After losing appeals alleging that the FBI illegally entrapped them into accepting payments, the Abscam defendants subsequently served time in federal correctional facilities.

On October 2, 1980, the House voted to expel representative Michael Myers. He became the first member of the House to be expelled since the end of the Civil War. Representatives Jenrette and Lederer resigned in order to avoid being expelled. Despite the fact that Senator Harrison A. Williams fought through 1982 to keep his seat in Congress, he finally resigned after a vote by the **Senate Select Committee on Ethics** recommended his expulsion to the full Senate. Representatives Kelly, Murphy, and Thompson subsequently failed to gain re-election to their House seats.

Related Entry: Stings

SUGGESTED READINGS: Congressional Quarterly, *Congressional Ethics: History, Facts, and Controversy*, Washington, D.C.: Congressional Quarterly, 1992; James Q. Wilson, "The Changing FBI—The Road to Abscam," *Public Interest* (Spring 1990): 3–14.

ABSOLUTE OFFICIAL IMMUNITY DOCTRINE. In the 1959 landmark case of *Barr v Matteo*, 360 U.S. 564, the Supreme Court held that the Constitution prohibited individuals from bringing civil tort suits against public employees and officials for alleged injuries caused by the performance of discretionary acts by public employees and officials. The Supreme Court distinguished the discretionary acts of public officials from their mandatory duties. In the *Matteo* case, a federal administrator issued a press release indicating that a federal employee might be guilty of wrongdoing. The official subsequently sued the administrator for defamation of character. The high court argued that public officials needed absolute immunity from suits resulting from the performance of discretionary duties to free public officials to perform their official duties without fear of becoming the subject of civil tort suits. In other words the threat of being sued might deter some public officials from doing their duty as public servants.

Beginning in the early 1970s, a series of Supreme Court decisions sharply reduced the number of public employees and officials entitled to absolute official immunity from civil tort suits. In an effort to increase the accountability of public officials for injuries caused by their actions, the Supreme Court ruled that the vast majority of local, state, and federal officials are only entitled to qualified official immunity. Under the **Qualified Official Immunity Doctrine**, individuals may sue most administrative officials for rights violations if the administrative officials "knew or reasonably should have known" their actions would violate the constitutional or statutory rights of individuals. However, in the 1982 decision of *Nixon v Fitzgerald*, the Supreme Court ruled that the Constitution provides presidents of the United States with absolute immunity from civil suits arising from actions taken by a president while occupying the White House. On the other hand, in the 1997 case of **Clinton v Jones**, the Supreme Court held that the absolute immunity doctrine did not prohibit the federal courts from hearing a sexual harassment lawsuit brought by Little Rock, Arkansas, resident Paula Jones against Bill Clinton for conduct that took place prior to his election as president.

Current Supreme Court decisions hold that in addition to the president of the United States, the Constitution only provides judges and legislators and executive branch officials with judicial-like responsibilities with absolute immunity from civil tort suits. That immunity only applies to actions directly related to the performance of their official duties.

Related Entries: *Clinton v Jones* (1997); *Nixon v Fitzgerald* (1982)

SUGGESTED READING: "You Can't Sue the President," *Newsweek*, July 5, 1982, 80.

ADAMS, ARLIN. *See* HUD Scandal; Independent Counsel Investigations; Reagan Administration Ethics Controversies

ADAMS, SHERMAN (January 8, 1899–October 27, 1986). Chief of Staff for President Eisenhower, 1953–1958.

Sherman Adams served as President Dwight Eisenhower's chief of staff from the beginning of the Eisenhower administration, in January 1953, until his forced resignation during September 1958. Prior to assuming his White House position, Adams served as governor of New Hampshire. During the spring of 1958, an ethics controversy erupted over whether Sherman Adams had improperly contacted a number of federal regulatory agencies on behalf of New England industrialist Bernard Goldfine. During 1953 Goldfine had complained to Adams about being mistreated by the Federal Trade Commission (FTC). Late in 1953 Adams contacted the chairman of the FTC, Edward F. Howrey, about the FTC investigation. During 1956 Adams had asked a member of President Eisenhower's White House staff to contact the Securities and Exchange Commission (SEC) to determine the nature of SEC concerns with Goldfine's East Boston Company. The White House aide informed Adams that for a number of years the East Boston Company had failed to file required financial disclosure reports. Although Adams admitted making the contacts on behalf of Adams, he denied ever having asked either the FTC or the SEC to give Goldfine preferential treatment.

Media reports then surfaced that Goldfine had provided Adams with a number

Sherman Adams resigns as White House chief of staff, September 22,
1958. © Bettmann/CORBIS

of gifts and allowed Goldfine to pick up the $1,642.28 cost for Adams's stay
at the elegant Sheraton-Plaza Hotel in Boston. Besides admitting that he had
allowed Goldfine to pick up more than one hotel bill, Adams subsequently
admitted that Goldfine gave him an expensive vicuna coat and an expensive
oriental rug. Throughout the controversy Adams denied any relationship between his contacts and the gifts he received from Goldfine. More than anything
else, the appearance of a link between Goldfine's gifts and Adams's contacts
with the FTC and SEC created a firestorm for the Eisenhower administration.
Adams voluntarily appeared before a congressional investigatory committee in
an effort to defuse the controversy. He admitted making the contacts and accepting a number of gifts, but Adams forcefully denied any wrongdoing.

Extremely concerned about the impact of this scandal on Republican candidates for the House and Senate during the 1958 midterm congressional elections,
Republican Party leaders placed heavy pressure on President Eisenhower to
dismiss Adams. Republicans feared that the Adams affair might lead voters to
take their anger out on Republican congressional candidates. On September 23,
1958, Adams resigned his position as President Eisenhower's chief of staff to
return to private business in his home state of New Hampshire. In a strongly

worded resignation letter, Adams maintained that he "never influenced nor attempted to influence any agency, or any officer or employee of any agency in any case, decision, or matter whatsoever." Adams also blamed his situation on "a campaign of vilification" designed to destroy him "and in doing so embarrass the Administration and the President of the United States." In his letter accepting Adams's resignation, President Eisenhower expressed great regret over the decision of Sherman Adams to resign. "Your performance has been brilliant; the public has been the beneficiary of your unselfish work," wrote President Eisenhower. "I accept your resignation with sadness. You will be sorely missed by your colleagues on the staff and by the department and agencies of the government, with which you have worked so efficiently."

Although the Justice Department subsequently found that Adams had not violated any federal laws, the Adams controversy raised serious questions regarding the propriety of high-level federal officials contacting federal agencies on behalf of private citizens. Early in 1961 President John Kennedy began an ethics reform program designed to provide federal employees and officials with clearer guidelines between permissible and impermissible official conduct.

After returning to New Hampshire, Adams developed and ran the multimillion dollar Loon Mountain ski resort. On October 28, 1986, at the age of eighty-seven, Adams died of respiratory failure.

Related Entries: Eisenhower Administration Ethics Controversies; Gift Acceptance Prohibitions

SUGGESTED READINGS: David Frier, *Conflict of Interest in the Eisenhower Administration*, Ames: Iowa State University Press, 1969; Judith Martin, "Sherman Adams Fell from Grace and Hasn't Looked Back," *Washington Post*, May 22, 1977, H1; Richard Pearson, "Sherman Adams Dies; Was Eisenhower Aide," *Washington Post*, October 28, 1986, B7.

AGNEW, SPIRO T. (November 9, 1918–September 17, 1996). Vice President of the United States, January 1969–October 1973.

In a move that surprised many political observers, Republican presidential candidate Richard Nixon selected Maryland Governor Spiro T. Agnew to be his 1968 vice-presidential running mate. The Nixon campaign used Agnew to launch the strongest attacks against Democratic candidate Hubert Humphrey. Continuing throughout President Nixon's first term, the Nixon administration used Agnew to launch attacks against Nixon critics in the media and opponents of Nixon's Vietnam war policy. Vice President Agnew played a key role in the Nixon White House efforts to mobilize Nixon's so-called "silent majority." Despite Agnew's loyal service, President Nixon and members of Nixon's White House rarely consulted Agnew on significant policy matters.

The conduct that ultimately led to Spiro Agnew's October 10, 1973, resignation as vice president occurred before the 1968 election. From 1962 to 1967, Agnew served as county executive of Baltimore County in Maryland. From 1967 to 1969, Agnew served as the governor of Maryland. During 1970 the U.S.

Vice President Spiro T. Agnew. Bettmann/CORBIS

attorney for Maryland began an extensive investigation of public corruption in Maryland state and local government. By 1973 the investigation uncovered strong evidence that Agnew accepted bribes and kickbacks from government contractors while serving as governor of Maryland.

Armed with the evidence, **federal prosecutors** faced the difficult issue of whether the Constitution permitted the indictment of a sitting vice president or whether an indictment and criminal trial would have to wait until the House impeached Agnew and the Senate voted to remove him from office or the end of Agnew's term as vice president. Faced with a long and drawn out constitutional battle, federal prosecutors offered Agnew a deal that he accepted. Agnew agreed to resign as vice president, plead no contest to criminal tax evasion, pay a $10,000 fine, and serve three years' probation.

Agnew's resignation did not end his legal troubles. Maryland filed a civil suit to force Agnew to return the money he allegedly received in bribes and kickbacks. Nine years after resigning, Agnew paid the state of Maryland $248,735 in restitution. After resigning as vice president, Agnew moved to California and became a successful international business consultant. In the years following his resignation, Agnew continued to deny that he had broken any laws while serving as governor of Maryland. On September 17, 1996, Spiro Agnew died at the age of seventy-seven.

Related Entries: Federal Prosecutor; Nixon Administration Ethics Controversies

SUGGESTED READINGS: Spiro T. Agnew, *Go Quietly . . . Or Else*, New York: Morrow, 1980; "Agnew: Second Vice President in U.S. History to Resign," *CQ Almanac* (1973): 1054–1059; Richard M. Cohen and James Witcover, *A Heartbeat Away: The Investigation and Resignation of Vice-President Spiro T. Agnew*, New York: Viking Press, 1974.

AMES, OAKES. *See* Credit Mobilier Scandal

APPEARANCE OF IMPROPRIETY RULE. Throughout American history, local, state, and federal employees and officials have been subject to laws designed to prevent public officials from using their public positions for personal gain. During a large part of the nineteenth century, however, the growth of the **spoils system** and inadequate financial safeguards led to a massive increase in public corruption at the local, state, and federal level. From the passage of the **Pendleton Act of 1883** through the early 1960s, Congress and the U.S. Civil Service Commission gradually enacted new laws and tightened rules governing the behavior of career federal employees and officials in an effort to restore public confidence in the integrity of federal employees and officials. For instance Congress passed the Hatch Act of 1939 which prohibited the vast majority of federal employees from taking an active role in political campaigns.

Beginning in the early 1950s, reform efforts shifted to preventing financial conflicts of interest involving government employees and officials. Conflict-of-interest scandals involving members of both the Truman and Eisenhower administrations helped to intensify calls for tighter federal ethics regulations. In an effort to protect public trust in government, Presidents John Kennedy and Lyndon Johnson issued ethics directives that instructed executive branch employees and officials to avoid situations which might create the appearance of a financial conflict of interest between their public duties and personal financial affairs.

On May 8, 1965, President Johnson issued **Executive Order 11222** which included a new "appearance of impropriety" rule. The new rule directed all executive branch employees and officials to "avoid any action, whether or not specifically prohibited by subsection (a), which might result in, or create the appearance of (1) using public office for private gain; (2) giving preferential treatment to any organization or person; (3) impeding government efficiency or economy; (4) losing complete independence or impartiality of action; (5) making a government decision outside official channels; or (6) affecting adversely the confidence of the public in the integrity of the Government."

Through the 1960s and 1970s, the "appearance of impropriety" rule produced little controversy. Executive Order 11222 gave each federal agency and department considerable discretion in how they enforced federal ethics rules. The situation changed with the 1980 presidential election of Ronald Reagan. Between 1981 and 1989, more than one hundred Reagan administration officials or former Reagan administration officials found themselves subject to allegations of improper or illegal conduct. The **Reagan administration ethics controversies** touched off a vigorous debate over the fairness of the "appearance of impropriety" rule to federal employees and officials. In 1985, the **U.S. Office of Government Ethics** (USOGE) became the subject of strong congressional criticism for suggesting that the appearance of impropriety rule might be "aspirational" in nature. In other words Executive Order 11222 did not permit federal agencies to discipline federal employees and officials for violating the general appearance of impropriety standard. The controversy forced the USOGE to back down from this position.

On April 12, 1989, President George Bush issued **Executive Order 12674, Principles of Ethical Conduct for Government Officers and Employees**. The Bush ethics directive included a new appearance of impropriety rule that directed federal employees and officials "to endeavor to avoid any action creating the appearance that they are violating the law or ethical standards promulgated to his order." The decision to replace the word *shall* with *endeavor* was the Bush administration's attempt to protect federal employees and officials from unwarranted allegations of improper conduct.

Related Entries: Executive Order 11222; Executive Order 12674; Reagan Administration Ethics Controversies; U.S. Office of Government Ethics

SUGGESTED READINGS: Ronald Brownstein, "Agency Ethics Officers Fear Meese Ruling Could Weaken Conflict Laws," *National Journal*, March 23, 1985, p. 642; Executive Orders in Which OGE Have a Role: URL: *http: //www.usoge.gov*.

ARTHUR, CHESTER ALAN (October 5, 1830–November 18, 1886). President of the United States, 1881–1885.

Chester A. Arthur served as the twenty-first president of the United States from 1881 to 1885. Arthur's rise to the presidency began many years before as a loyal member of the New York State Republican Party. Early in his career as a lawyer, New York political power broker Roscoe Conkling became Chester Arthur's mentor. Through much of the nineteenth century, New York political leaders used their power to obtain federal government appointments to important federal positions. Appointments to the customs house of the Port of New York became some of the most sought after **patronage** positions. At the urging of New York Senator Roscoe Conkling, President Grant appointed Chester Arthur to the plum position as collector of customs for the port of New York in 1871.

The disputed **election of 1876** saw Republican **Rutherford B. Hayes** elected as President of the United States. Unlike President Grant, who had little stomach

Chester A. Arthur. Still Picture Branch, National Archives
and Records Administration

for serious political reform, President Hayes soon made clear that he did not intend to follow the patronage practices of his predecessors. Hayes announced his
support for civil service reform and took the bold step, in 1878, of dismissing
Chester Arthur as collector of customs for the Port of New York. This dismissal
touched off a war between Senator Conkling and President Hayes. Senator Conkling used his considerable power in Congress and the Republican Party to attempt
to force Hayes to restore Arthur to his position. In the end Hayes prevailed.

In 1880 the Republican Party nominated James A. Garfield as president and
Chester A. Arthur as vice president. Hayes had promised to only serve one term
as president. Throughout their political careers, neither Garfield nor Arthur had
shown any inclination to support political reform. Both strongly supported the
spoils system as vital to the survival of the Republican Party. On July 2, 1881,
Charles Guiteau, a disgruntled office seeker, shot President Garfield. On September 19, 1881, he died from his wounds. Chester Arthur immediately became
president of the United States.

The assassination had a profound impact on the American people and Chester
Arthur. Recognizing that many Americans blamed the assassination on the spoils

system, Arthur dropped his opposition to civil service reform and helped to push the **Pendleton Act** through Congress in 1883. The act established the first federal civil service system. Equally important the Arthur administration aggressively pursued corruption in a number of federal agencies and departments. Whether motivated by political concerns or a legitimate change of heart, President Arthur surprised many by becoming a supporter of civil service reform and other measures designed to reduce corruption in government programs.

Political necessity may have motivated Chester Arthur's transformation from a vocal defender of the "spoils system" to a supporter of civil service reform. Through the 1880s and 1890s, the Civil Service Commission made significant progress in ending **political assessments** of federal employees. However, by the end of the 1890s, unregulated campaign contributions replaced political assessments as the most serious political reform issue.

Related Entries: Hayes, Rutherford B.; Pendleton Act of 1883

SUGGESTED READING: Nathan Miller, *Stealing from America: A History of Corruption from Jamestown to Reagan*, New York: Paragon House, 1992, 243–250.

ASSESSMENTS. *See* Political Assessments

ASSOCIATION OF THE BAR OF THE CITY OF NEW YORK AND FEDERAL ETHICS REGULATION. Between 1950 and 1960, a series of public ethics controversies created serious problems for the administrations of Presidents Harry S. Truman and Dwight David Eisenhower. A series of congressional investigations raised serious questions about the effectiveness of federal ethics regulation. Early in 1960 the Association of the Bar of the City of New York issued a study entitled *Conflict of Interest and Federal Service*. Written at the height of the Cold War, the report stressed the importance of updating federal ethics laws and policies in order to reduce confusion over federal ethics regulations that deterred some individuals from accepting government positions. At the same time, the study urged the tightening of federal ethics rules to prevent federal employees and officials from using their public positions for personal financial gain. To improve the effectiveness of the federal ethics program, the study recommended that Congress update existing criminal prohibitions and that the White House issue new ethics regulations to establish clear rules governing the acceptance of gifts and honorarium by executive branch employees and officials, along with other matters that might weaken public trust in government. To help improve the effectiveness of federal ethics regulation, the report recommended supplementing criminal ethics prohibitions with administrative ethics rules. In addition, the report recommended that the next president appoint a White House staff member to oversee the implementation of the new standard of conduct regulations. Between 1961 and 1963, President John Kennedy and Congress implemented many of the reforms recommended by the Bar Association report.

In 1970 the Association of the Bar of the City of New York issued another report, which was entitled *Congress and the Public Trust*. The report called for a significant tightening of congressional ethics rules and for more effective ways for resolving allegations of unethical conduct by members of Congress. Unlike the experience with its 1960 report dealing with executive branch ethics, Congress did not greet the recommendations of the Bar Association with open arms. Through the 1970s Congress slowly tightened ethics rules governing the conduct of its members.

After the issuance of its 1970 report, the Association of the Bar of the City of New York ceased playing a leadership role in federal ethics reform. During the 1970s, **Common Cause**, a new citizen's lobby, and Ralph Nader's **Public Citizen** assumed leadership roles in the government reform movement. Besides supporting the tightening of federal ethics rules, Common Cause and Public Citizen would take the lead in lobbying Congress for the passage of comprehensive campaign finance reform legislation and tighter ethics rules.

Related Entries: Common Cause; Kennedy Administration Ethics Reform Program; Public Citizen

SUGGESTED READINGS: Association of the Bar of the City of New York, *Conflict of Interest and Federal Service*, Cambridge, MA: Harvard University Press, 1960; James C. Kirby, *Congress and the Public Trust*, New York: Atheneum, 1970; Robert Roberts, *White House Ethics: The History of the Politics of Conflict of Interest Regulation*, Westport, CT: Greenwood Press, 1988.

B

BABBITT, BRUCE (June 27, 1938–). Secretary of the Interior, 1993–2000.

During December 1992, President-elect Bill Clinton nominated Bruce Babbitt for the position of secretary of the interior. Prior to joining the Clinton administration, Babbitt held a number of high-level positions in his native state of Arizona, including attorney general and governor. While serving as governor of Arizona during the 1980s, Babbitt became a close friend of Arkansas Governor Bill Clinton. In 1988 Babbitt made an unsuccessful run for the Democratic presidential nomination. As a lifelong environmentalist, Babbitt also served as president of the nonprofit League of Conservation Voters.

In 1997 Babbitt found himself the subject of a congressional investigation involving Democratic Party fund-raising for the 1996 presidential election campaign. Representatives of Wisconsin's Chippewa tribes alleged that the Department of Interior turned down its request for permit to construct and operate a casino, on the site of an unprofitable dog track, for political reasons. The Chippewa tribe alleged that another Wisconsin tribe made large campaign contributions to the Democratic Party in an effort to get the Interior Department to turn down the Chippewa tribe's casino application. The allegation became public as the result of a suit filed by the Chippewa against the Interior Department in an effort to force the Department to grant the license application. In October 1997 testimony before a Senate committee, Secretary Babbitt denied that politics had played any role in the Interior Department's decision not to approve the tribe's casino license application.

In February 1998 Attorney General **Janet Reno** requested that a three-judge federal appeals panel appoint an independent counsel to probe an allegation that Secretary Babbitt lied to Congress regarding contacts with White House officials regarding the casino license. On March 19, 1998, the federal appellate judicial panel appointed Washington lawyer Carol Elder Bruce to determine whether Babbitt perjured himself in Senate testimony or violated the **False Statements**

Accountability Act of 1996 in interviews with federal investigators regarding his involvement in the rejection of the license request. On October 13, 1999, independent counsel Bruce announced that insufficient evidence existed to seek a criminal indictment against Secretary Babbitt.

Related Entries: Clinton Administration Ethics Controversies; Independent Counsel Investigations

SUGGESTED READINGS: Stephen Barr, "Reenergized Babbitt Refuses to Be Sidelined by Probe: Conservationists Hope for a New Initiative," *Washington Post*, July 20, 1999, A03; George Lardner Jr., "Independent Counsel Is Chosen to Probe Babbitt Casino Dispute," *Washington Post*, March 20, 1998, A23.

BABCOCK, GENERAL ORVILLE E. (December 25, 1835–June 2, 1884). Civil War general; Personal Secretary to President Ulysses S. Grant, 1869–1876.

During the Civil War, Orville E. Babcock became one of Union General Ulysses S. Grant's closest friends. By the end of the Civil War, Babcock had risen to the rank of general. Babcock delivered Grant's surrender summons to General Robert E. Lee at Appomattox Courthouse. When Republican presidential candidate Ulysses S. Grant won the 1868 presidential election, he made General Orville Babcock his personal secretary. Besides serving as President Grant's secretary, Babcock also served as commissioner of public buildings for the District of Columbia.

In 1874 President Grant nominated **Benjamin Bristow** as secretary of the treasury. In 1875 rumors of the tax fraud scheme reached Treasury Secretary Bristow. He immediately launched a major investigation of the allegations. The investigation led to the federal prosecution of hundreds of individuals involved in the conspiracy to avoid paying federal excise taxes on distilled spirits. By mid-1875 the **Whiskey Ring** investigation had implicated Orville Babcock in the conspiracy. In February 1876 Babcock went on trial in a St. Louis, Missouri U.S. District Court. To assist his friend, President Grant agreed to serve as a character witness for Babcock. Although Grant declined to appear in the St. Louis, Missouri, Federal District Court, he agreed to undergo questioning in Washington, D.C. In his testimony Grant expressed his utmost confidence in the integrity of Babcock. Historians generally agree that Grant's testimony proved crucial in persuading the jury to acquit Babcock on all charges.

Related Entries: Bristow, Benjamin Helm; Grant Administration Ethics Controversies; Whiskey Ring

SUGGESTED READINGS: Thomas Bailey, *Presidential Saints and Sinners*, New York: Free Press, 1981; C. Vann Woodward, ed., *Responses of the Presidents to Charges of Misconduct*, New York: Delacorte, 1974.

BAIRD, ZOE (June 20, 1952–). Corporate lawyer; attorney general nominee, 1993.

In early January 1993, Clinton nominated corporate lawyer Zoe Baird as at-

torney general. Clinton's choice for attorney general initially received rave reviews. Baird had served in the White House during President Jimmy Carter's
term and had risen to become a senior vice president and general counsel at
Aetna Life and Casualty Co.

By the middle of January 1993, Baird found herself embroiled in a major
ethics controversy. A number of newspapers reported that Baird and her husband
had "employed two Peruvians living in the United States illegally as her baby
sitter and part-time driver for nearly two years." The reports also alleged that
the Bairds also had not paid Social Security taxes for the couple. Critics of the
Baird nomination argued that the Senate should not confirm as attorney general
someone who had violated a federal law. On January 22, 1993, President Clinton
withdrew Zoe Baird's nomination as attorney general. A short time later, President Clinton nominated New York Judge **Kimba Wood** for attorney general.
Reports that Judge Wood and her husband had also failed to pay social security
taxes for an undocumented worker that they had employed as a nanny forced
Judge Wood to withdraw her name from consideration for attorney general.
During February 1993 the Senate easily confirmed President Clinton's third
nominee, Miami prosecutor **Janet Reno**, as attorney general.

In the aftermath of the Zoe Baird and Kimba Wood nominations, President
Bill Clinton faced considerable criticism for not fighting for the confirmation of
either Baird or Wood. On July 20, 1993, Deputy White House Counsel **Vincent
Foster** committed suicide. Subsequent investigations by Justice Department special counsel **Robert Fiske Jr.** and Whitewater **independent counsel Kenneth
Starr** claimed that Foster's depression over the failed Baird or Wood nominations may have played a role in his decision to commit suicide.

Related Entries: Clinton Administration Ethics Controversies; Foster, Vincent;
Reno, Janet; Wood, Kimba

SUGGESTED READINGS: David Johnston, "Clinton's Choice for Justice Department
Hired Illegal Aliens for Household," *New York Times*, January 14, 1993, A1; Michael
Kelly, "Settling In: The President's Day; Clinton Cancels Baird Nomination for Justice
Department," *New York Times*, January 22, 1993, A1.

BAKER, BOBBY (1928–   ). Secretary to the Senate Majority, 1955–1963.

In 1943 at age fourteen, Bobby Baker became a congressional page. In 1955
he became secretary to Senate Majority Leader Lyndon Johnson. His proximity
to Johnson brought Baker power and prestige. When Lyndon Johnson became
vice president in 1961, Baker continued to serve as secretary to Senate Majority
Leader Mike Mansfield.

In September 1963 a vending machine company filed a civil suit against
Baker, alleging that they had failed to win a vending contract at a defense plant
because Baker intervened to obtain the contract for another vending company
in which he held a substantial financial interest. The **conflict of interest** allegation ultimately led to congressional and criminal investigations of Baker's

financial affairs. When President Johnson assumed the presidency after the November 22, 1963 assassination of President Kennedy, official Washington anxiously waited to see whether Baker would implicate President Johnson in wrongdoing. Baker never did. Efforts by the Republican Party to turn the Baker affair into a campaign issue during the 1964 presidential election failed. President Lyndon Johnson easily won the 1964 presidential election against Republican candidate Arizona Senator Barry Goldwater.

On January 5, 1966, a Federal **grand jury** indicted Baker on "nine counts of fraud, conspiracy to defraud the government, and evasion of income taxes in 1962–1964." The charges had nothing to do with the allegations regarding the vending contract. The indictment alleged that Baker had solicited close to $100,000 in campaign contributions from a group of California savings and loan executives and that Baker kept most of the money instead of forwarding the contributions to individual senators or the senatorial campaign committee. During the trial Baker testified he had turned the money over to Senator Robert S. Kerr, D-Okla., for Kerr's reelection campaign. Kerr died before the beginning of the Baker trial.

In January 1967 a U.S. District Court jury convicted Baker on several tax evasion counts. Efforts by Baker to have his conviction overturned failed. In late 1970 he began serving his sentence. After serving sixteen months at a federal penitentiary, in 1972 Baker received a parole. After his 1972 release, Baker continued to maintain his innocence. Through the 1980s he sought to have his case reopened in an effort to clear his name. Yet he never showed any bitterness toward Lyndon Johnson who had quickly distanced himself from Baker after the initial 1963 conflict of interest allegation.

Related Entry: Johnson Administration Ethics Controversies

SUGGESTED READINGS: Bobby Baker and Larry L. King, *Wheeling and Dealing: Confessions of a Capitol Hill Operator*, New York: Norton, 1978; Congressional Quarterly, *Congressional Ethics: History, Facts, and Controversy*, Washington, DC: Congressional Quarterly, 1992, 102; C. Vann Woodward, ed., *Responses of the Presidents to Charges of Misconduct*, New York, Delacorte Press, 1974.

BALLINGER, RICHARD A. (July 9, 1858–June 6, 1922). Secretary of the Interior, 1909–1911. *See* Ballinger-Pinchot Affair

BALLINGER-PINCHOT AFFAIR. In 1901 Vice President Theodore Roosevelt became president after the September assassination of President William McKinley in Buffalo, New York. From 1901 through the end of his presidency in 1909, Roosevelt made preserving the natural resources of the country a top priority. Roosevelt supported an expansion of the national park system and much tighter restrictions on private mining and lumbering operations on land owned by the federal government. For instance the Roosevelt administration placed a moratorium on mining on huge tracts of public lands located in Alaska.

In 1907 Clarence Cunningham filed a petition with the Interior Department's

Secretary of the Interior R. A. Ballinger. Reproduced from the Collections of the LIBRARY OF CONGRESS

General Land Office seeking an exemption from the mining moratorium. Cunningham headed a group that claimed to own the rights to develop thousands of acres of coal land along the Alaskan Bering River. However, a number of other mining interests disputed whether the Cunningham group held the development rights to the land in question. Federal law gave the General Land Office responsibility for resolving disputed claims. At the time of the filing of the Cunningham claim, twenty-four-year-old Louis Glavis headed the Portland, Oregon, field office of the Land Office. Glavis subsequently found the Cunningham group did not have a valid mining claim to the Alaskan land. Richard A. Ballinger, the commissioner of the Land Office, overruled Glavis and approved the claim. The Ballinger decision outraged the conservationists who viewed the action as a betrayal of President Roosevelt's pledge to protect federal land from development. To the dismay of Ballinger, the secretary of interior revoked the approval of the Cunningham claim and ordered Glavis to conduct a new investigation of the claim's validity. A short time after the interior secretary's decision, Ballinger resigned his position and returned to private law practice.

In 1908 Republican William Howard Taft won the presidential election. Early

Gifford Pinchot, December 22, 1921. Reproduced from the Collections of the LIBRARY OF CON-GRESS

in 1909, President Taft nominated Richard A. Ballinger as secretary of the interior. Not surprisingly Taft's action greatly disturbed conservationists. The appointment also disturbed Chief Forester Gifford Pinchot. President Theodore Roosevelt had appointed Pinchot to his position as chief forester and had relied heavily on Pinchot for advice on how best to preserve vast tracts of western lands owned by the government. Conservationists regarded Pinchot as the father of the conservation movement. Louis Glavis had continued to express his strong opposition to the Cunningham claim. During the summer of 1909, Secretary of the Interior Ballinger took the highly controversial step of stripping responsibility for the Cunningham claim from Louisa Glavis. The conservationist movement saw the action as the first step in a plan by Secretary Ballinger to increase the amount of federal land available for development for private mining and logging interests.

With the full support of Chief Forester Gifford Pinchot, Louis Glavis obtained a highly unusual meeting with President Taft. At the August 18, 1909, meeting, Glavis accused Ballinger of gross misconduct in his handling of the Cunningham claim matter. Glavis alleged that after Ballinger resigned as commissioner of the Land Office, the Cunningham claimants hired Ballinger to represent their claims before the Land Office. After providing Ballinger with the opportunity to respond to the allegations, President Taft fired Glavis for gross insubordination. Through 1908 and 1909, Pinchot openly worked to discredit Ballinger and President Taft. On January 7, 1910, Taft fired Pinchot after he openly attacked the conservation policies of Ballinger and President Taft in a letter to an influential senator. Although a subsequent congressional investigation found that Ballinger had not violated any laws after he resigned as commissioner of the Land Office, the Pinchot-Ballinger controversy contributed to a major fissure in the Republican Party.

Conservationists and members of the progressive wing of the Republican Party saw President Taft's handling of the Ballinger affair as strong evidence that Taft planned to dismantle Theodore Roosevelt's conservation program. In 1911, Ballinger resigned as secretary of interior as the direct result of the continuing controversy. In 1912 Theodore Roosevelt ran as the presidential candidate of Roosevelt's Bull Moose Party. President Howard Taft ran for reelection as the presidential candidate of the Republican Party. Woodrow Wilson received the presidential nomination of the Democratic Party. Supporters of Theodore Roosevelt attacked Taft on a wide range of issues, including his alleged abandonment of Roosevelt's conservation policies. Woodrow Wilson subsequently won the 1912 presidential election.

SUGGESTED READINGS: James Penick, *Progressive Politics and Conservation: The Ballinger-Pinchot Affair*, Chicago: University of Chicago Press, 1968; C. Vann Woodward, ed., *Responses of the Presidents to Charges of Misconduct*, New York: Delacorte, 1974.

BARRETT, DAVID. *See* Cisneros, Henry G.; Independent Counsel Investigations

BELKNAP, WILLIAM W. (September 22, 1829–October 13, 1890). Secretary of War, 1869–1876.

From 1869 through 1876, William W. Belknap served as President Ulysses S. Grant's secretary of war. Belknap had become a close friend of Grant during the Civil War when he rose to the rank of general in the Union Army. Between 1860 and 1876, the number of western military posts multiplied as the Army expanded its ability to protect settlers. On many of the military outposts, the War Department established traderships to provide goods to settlers, Native Americans, and soldiers assigned to the remote outposts. Instead of having government personnel operate the traderships, the War Department granted private individuals the right to operate them. By the early 1870s, the vast majority of these traderships had become quite profitable.

Early in 1870, Caleb P. Marsh allegedly asked Secretary Belknap's wife for assistance in obtaining a post tradership. According to the story, Secretary Belknap then contacted a holder of one of the post traderships and brokered a deal where the holder of the tradership made Marsh a partner. Early in 1876 Marsh turned over to a congressional committee a contract that required Marsh's tradership

Major General William W. Belknap, Officer of
the Federal Army. Reproduced from the
Collections of the LIBRARY OF CONGRESS

partner to pay him $12,000 annually. Marsh also told the committee he had a sep-
arate arrangement with Mrs. Belknap which required him to pay her $6,000 a year.
According to Marsh, when Mrs. Belknap died one year after the payments began,
he continued to make the payments to Mrs. Belknap's oldest child and then to Secretary Belknap's second wife who was the sister of Secretary Belknap's first wife.
Most damaging Marsh told the committee that Secretary Belknap had provided
the instructions on how to deliver the money.

The documents and testimony provided by Caleb Marsh established that Secretary Belknap knew about and directed the payments of the kickbacks from the
trader ship deal. On March 2, 1876, Secretary Belknap learned that the committee investigating the matter planned to request that the House Judiciary Committee begin **impeachment proceedings** against him. Before the committee
could act, Belknap submitted his resignation to President Grant who immediately
accepted it, infuriating a number of members of Congress. The full House subsequently voted to impeach Belknap and forwarded the case to the Senate for
trial. After an impeachment trial, the Senate voted 37 to 24 not to convict
Belknap. Many of the Republican senators who voted to acquit Belknap did

so on the grounds that the Senate lacked authority to impeach Belknap because President Grant had earlier accepted his resignation.

Related Entries: Grant Administration Ethics Controversies, Impeachment Proceedings

SUGGESTED READINGS: Allan Nevins, *Hamilton Fish: The Inner History of the Grant Administration*, Rev. ed., New York: Ungar, 1967; C. Vann Woodward, ed., *Responses of the Presidents to Charges of Misconduct*, New York, Delacorte Press, 1974.

BENNETT, ROBERT S. (1939–   ). Federal prosecutor; Keating Five Counsel; private attorney.

Born in 1939 Robert S. Bennett grew up in Brooklyn, New York. While attending Georgetown law school during the 1960s, Bennett became the part-time aide to Washington lawyer and lobbyist Thomas Corcoran who had served as a close advisor to President Franklin Roosevelt. After working a number of years as a **federal prosecutor**, Bennett entered private law practice in Washington, D.C. In 1989 the **Senate Select Committee on Ethics** appointed Bennett as a special counsel for the so-called **Keating Five** investigation. In 1990 five senators became the subject of an investigation for contacting federal bank regulators on behalf of Charles Keating, the owner of California-based Lincoln Savings and Loan. The failure of the savings and loan cost the U.S. government some $2 billion.

In 1994 President Bill Clinton hired Robert Bennett to represent him in the lawsuit by Arkansas state employee **Paula Jones**. Jones alleged that in 1991 Arkansas Governor Bill Clinton made an improper sexual advance to her in a Little Rock, Arkansas, hotel room. From 1994 until the September 1998 settlement of the Paula Jones lawsuit, Bennett mounted a vigorous defense of President Clinton. Throughout the time Robert Bennett represented President Clinton, reporters frequently commented on the fact that **William J. Bennett**, Robert Bennett's brother, was one of the most vocal critics of President Clinton's character.

Related Entries: Bennett, William J.; Jones, Paula; Keating Five Affair.

SUGGESTED READINGS: Francis X. Clines, "For the Defense of a President, a Street Fighter," *New York Times*, March 22, 1998, Section One, 28; Lloyd Grove and David Segal, "A Jury of His Peers; There's No Shortage of Verdicts on Bob Bennett's Handling of the President's Case," *Washington Post*, January 28, 1998, D1; Sharon Walsh, "Requisites for a Heavyweight; Bob Bennett Has the Moves and the Moxie to Be the Top Lawyer in Town," *Washington Post*, March 29, 1993, D1.

BENNETT, WILLIAM J. (July 31, 1943–   ). Chairman, National Endowment for the Humanities, 1981–1985; Secretary of Education, 1985–1987; Director, Office of National Drug Control Policy, 1989–1990.

Brother of Washington lawyer **Robert S. Bennett**, William Bennett served in a series of high-level positions in the Reagan and Bush administrations between 1981 and 1990. As chairman of the National Endowment for the Humanities, secretary of education, and director of the Office of National Drug Control Policy, Bennett strongly supported the conservative policies of Presidents Reagan and Bush. After leaving government service, Bennett became the codirector of the conservative think tank Empower America and authored the best selling book *The Book of Virtues: A Treasury of Great Moral Stories*. From 1992 until the end of Bill Clinton's second term Bennett served as one of President Clinton's most vocal critics. Bennett focused much of his criticism on the personal behavior of President Clinton, including his alleged sexual relationship with **Monica Lewinsky**. In his 1998 book *The Death of Outrage: Bill Clinton and the Assault on American Ideals*, he argued that President Clinton's conduct prior to and after becoming president helped to lower public expectations regarding the conduct of public officials. He did not allow the fact that his brother, Robert S. Bennett, represented President Bill Clinton in the **Paula Jones** sexual harassment lawsuit to damage their relationship.

Related Entries: Bennett, Robert S.; Clinton Administration Ethics Controversies; Lewinsky, Monica

SUGGESTED READINGS: William Bennett, *The Book of Virtues: A Treasury of Great Moral Stories*, New York: Simon & Schuster, 1993; William Bennett, *The Death of Outrage; Bill Clinton and the Assault on American Ideals*, New York: Simon & Schuster, 1998; Melinda Henneberger, "Between Adversaries, the Ties That Bind," *New York Times*, June 21, 1998, Section One, 1.

BERNSTEIN, CARL (February 14, 1944–   ). Journalist; Watergate figure; political commentator.

During the early 1970s, *Washington Post* reporters Carl Bernstein and **Bob Woodward** became key figures in the **Watergate scandal**. After many reporters lost interest in the June 17, 1972, break-in at the office of the Democratic National Committee located in the Washington, D.C., Watergate complex, Bernstein and Woodward tirelessly continued to work the story. With the help of an unidentified source, Woodward and Bernstein succeeded in uncovering a relationship between the burglars arrested in the Watergate and Nixon's 1972 Committee to Re-Elect the President (CREEP) by tracing the money used to pay the burglars back to the Committee. Woodward and Bernstein also discovered that **G. Gordon Liddy, E. Howard Hunt**, and James McCord had worked in the Nixon White House prior to joining CREEP. Police arrested all three for their involvement in the Watergate burglary.

With coauthor Bob Woodward, Bernstein wrote the best-selling books *All the President's Men* and *The Final Days*, which chronicled the Watergate break-in and the effort by President Nixon and other members of his administration to cover it up, as well as other illegal acts by members of the Nixon administration. The authors credited "Deep Throat" as the source of many of their Watergate stories. In 1977 Carl Bernstein left the *Washington Post* to become the Washington bureau chief and senior correspondent for ABC-News. In 1992 *Time* magazine hired Bernstein as a senior foreign correspondent. During the mid-1990s, Bernstein worked as a contributing editor for *Vanity Fair* magazine and as a *CBS News* consultant. In the years following Watergate, Bernstein became a frequent critic of the increased coverage of the media of the private lives of public officials and other public figures. Early in January 1999, Knopf Publishing Company announced that it had signed Carl Bernstein to write a book on First Lady **Hillary Rodham Clinton**.

Related Entries: Watergate Scandal; Woodward, Bob

SUGGESTED READINGS: Carl Bernstein and Bob Woodward, *All the President's Men*, New York: Simon & Schuster, 1974; Carl Bernstein and Bob Woodward, *The Final Days*, New York: Simon & Schuster, 1976; Patrick M. Reilly, "Publishers Swarm to Get Inside Scoop on Hillary Clinton—Knopf Signs Carl Bernstein to Produce 'Major Book,' Gail Sheehy Is Courted," *Wall Street Journal*, January 6, 1999, B7.

"BILLYGATE." *See* Carter Administration Ethics Controversies

BLAINE, JAMES G. (January 31, 1830–January 27, 1893). Member of U.S. House of Representatives 1863–1876; Speaker of the U.S. House of Representatives 1869–1875; U.S. Senator 1876–1881; Secretary of State, 1889–1892.

From the early 1860s through the 1880s, James G. Blaine became one of the most influential and powerful political figures in the United States. Through much of his political career, he faced allegations of illegal conduct; the most serious involved Blaine's alleged involvement in the **Credit Mobilier scandal** and the so-called Mulligan's letters affair.

Blaine's involvement with the Credit Mobilier scandal began with a story published in the *New York Sun* a short time before the 1872 presidential and congressional elections. According to the story, Congressman Oakes Ames, a director of the Credit Mobilier Company, provided a number of Congressmen with the opportunity to purchase discounted stock in an effort to keep Congress from investigating the company. The Union Pacific Railroad had established the Credit Mobilier to construct its part of the transcontinental railroad. Through much of the 1860s, the Credit Mobilier made large profits as the result of being paid excessive amounts for the construction of the rail line. A letter written by Congressman Oakes indicated that Speaker of the House James Blaine had taken advantage of the opportunity to purchase the discounted stock. A subsequent congressional investigation cleared Speaker Blaine of any wrongdoing but did recommend the expulsion of Congressman Oakes Ames and James Brooks. The House subsequently voted to censure both Oakes and Brooks. Historians continue to debate the involvement of Blaine in the Credit Mobilier scandal.

Early in 1876, a number of Republicans positioned themselves to succeed President Ulysses S. Grant. Political observers of the time regarded former Speaker of the House Blaine as the leading contender. By May 1876 Blaine

Hon. James G. Blaine, representative from Maine, engraved by Geo. E. Perine. Reproduced from the Collections of the LIBRARY OF CONGRESS

found himself at the center of another influence-peddling scandal. Reports surfaced that in April 1869, while Blaine served as Speaker of the House, he blocked congressional efforts to make the Little Rock and Fort Smith Railroad ineligible for federal land grants. Congress had provided railroads land grants as a way to subsidize the construction of rail lines. After the bill died, the railroad gave Blaine the opportunity to sell mortgage bonds issued by the railroad. After Blaine sold the bonds to friends, their value collapsed. Blaine then bought the bonds back at their original value. The Union Pacific and two other railroads then bought the bonds from Blaine, effectively covering his loss.

On May 31, 1876, James Mulligan, the former bookkeeper for one of the promoters of the Little Rock and Fort Smith Railroad, appeared before a House committee investigating Blaine's conduct. Mulligan testified that the Union Pacific bought the bonds from Blaine as a favor to the Speaker of the House and not as a legitimate business expense. Mulligan also claimed to have letters from Blaine to the Little Rock and Fort Smith Railroad which indicated that Blaine knew that the Union Pacific and other railroads bought back Blaine's bonds to curry favor with him as Speaker of the House. According to historians, after learning of Mulligan's testimony Blaine went to Mulligan's Washington, D.C., boardinghouse to plead with Mulligan for the letters. When Mulligan refused to return the letters, Blaine allegedly took the letters and ran. On June 5, 1876, Blaine marched onto the House floor and read from parts of the letters that indicated Blaine had no knowledge of an effort by the railroads to curry favor. Blaine then proclaimed his innocence. Even though Blaine would refuse to hand over the letters to the congressional committee, his theatrics carried the day.

Yet James Blaine paid a heavy price for his alleged indiscretion. Instead of nominating Blaine as the 1876 Republican presidential candidate, after a number of ballots the convention nominated Ohio's reform governor **Rutherford B. Hayes**. Despite the fact that Hayes would lose the popular vote in the 1876 presidential election to New York Democrat Samuel Tilden, the House would elect Hayes as president after both Tilden and Hayes failed to win the majority of electoral votes.

In the years following the 1876 presidential election, James G. Blaine held a series of high-level government positions. He served in the Senate from 1876 through 1881. After failing to obtain the 1880 Republican nomination, Blaine served as President James Garfield's secretary of state. In 1884 Blaine received the Republican presidential nomination. The **election of 1884** turned out to be one of the nastiest in American history. The Democratic Party nominated Grover Cleveland. Throughout the campaign both parties engaged in nonstop mudslinging. Democrat supporters of Cleveland dredged up Blaine's alleged participation in Credit Mobilier and the Mulligan letters. Blaine's Republican supporters attacked Cleveland for having an illegitimate child. After his 1884 presidential election defeat, Blaine declined the 1888 Republican nomination. He ended his lifetime of public service by serving as secretary of state in the administration of President Benjamin Harrison from 1889 to 1892.

Related Entries: Credit Mobilier Scandal; Election of 1876; Election of 1884

SUGGESTED READINGS: Stephen Gettinger, "Hard Lesson in Ethics from Last Century," *Congressional Quarterly Weekly Report*, January 25, 1997, 262; Nathan Miller, *Stealing from America: A History of Corruption from Jamestown to Reagan*, New York: Paragon, 1992, 228–229; C. Vann Woodward, ed., *Responses of the Presidents to Charges of Misconduct*, New York, Delacorte Press, 1974.

BLIND TRUSTS. After the Second World War, there was heightened popular sentiment over financial conflicts of interests involving public officials and employees. Beginning with Dwight Eisenhower, who took office in 1953, presidents and other high-level federal officials began to place their financial holdings in blind trusts as a defensive tactic to prevent allegations that they took particular actions to benefit their financial affairs. Up until the passage of the **Ethics in Government Act of 1978**, the presidential nominees worked with Department of Justice and Senate confirmation committees on the details of blind trust agreements, which were on a case by case basis. The typical blind trust agreement provided for the appointment of an independent trustee to oversee the financial holdings of the president or other high-level public officials. This included authorizing the trustee to buy and sell financial assets for the trust without notifying the public official of the details of the transaction.

Concern over the informal nature of blind trust agreements led Congress to include statutory blind trust requirements in the Ethics in Government Act of 1978. The Ethics Act established two types of blind trusts: the "Qualified Diversified Trust" and the "Qualified Blind Trust." And the Ethics Act gave the **U.S. Office of Government Ethics** (USOGE) responsibility for administering the new blind trust requirements. As a result the number of blind trusts established by high-level federal officials declined through the 1980s. Recognizing the problems associated with blind trusts, Congress included a provision for the issuance of **certificates of divestiture** in the **Ethics Reform Act of 1989**. Under the law federal employees who were required to sell a financial interest to comply with federal ethics rules were now eligible for a certificate of divestiture permitting them to roll over any capital gains from a forced sale of a financial interest into a diversified financial instrument.

Related Entries: Certificate of Divestiture; Ethics in Government Act of 1978; Ethics Reform Act of 1989; Financial Conflict of Interest Prohibition; U.S. Office of Government Ethics

SUGGESTED READINGS: Robert Roberts, *White House Ethics: The History of the Politics of Conflict of Interest Regulation*, Westport, CT: Greenwood Press, 1988; Robert Roberts and Marion T. Doss, *Watergate to Whitewater: The Public Integrity War*, Westport, CT: Praeger, 1997.

BLUMENTHAL, SIDNEY (November 6, 1948–   ). Washington journalist, Clinton White House aide, 1994–2000.

Sidney Blumenthal joined the White House staff of President Bill Clinton in 1997 after working as a journalist for the *Washington Post*, the *New Yorker*, and the *New Republic*. From 1992 until accepting his White House post, Blumenthal had faced criticism for being too close to President Bill Clinton and **Hillary Rodham Clinton**. After the **Monica Lewinsky** story broke during January 1998, Blumenthal became a key figure in independent counsel **Kenneth Starr**'s 1998 Monica Lewinsky investigation.

Through the winter and spring of 1998, President Clinton and Kenneth Starr engaged in a legal battle over whether Starr could require members of the White House staff and Secret Service agents to testify before the Monica Lewinsky **grand jury**. President Clinton invoked **executive privilege** in an effort to prevent Kenneth Starr from calling key White House aides and Secret Service agents before the grand jury. Late in May 1998, President Clinton dropped the executive privilege claim for a number of his aides, including Sidney Blumenthal. Early in June, Blumenthal testified before the Monica Lewinsky grand jury.

In his September 1998 impeachment referral to the House Judiciary Committee, independent counsel Kenneth Starr used Blumenthal's grand jury testimony to support his argument that President Bill Clinton knowingly lied to his aides regarding his relationship with Monica Lewinsky in an effort to obstruct Kenneth Starr's investigation. Starr argued that Clinton knew a strong likelihood existed that Clinton aides would be subpoenaed to testify before the Monica Lewinsky grand jury. The aides would then tell the grand jury the explanation President Clinton provided his aides. According to the September 1998 **Starr Report**, Blumenthal told the grand jury that President Clinton told Blumenthal, "I haven't done anything wrong." The president then told Blumenthal "Monica Lewinsky came on to me and made a sexual demand on me." After the House Judiciary Committee and the full House voted to impeach President Bill Clinton, the House impeachment managers selected Blumenthal as one of three witnesses to videotape as part of their case for President Clinton's impeachment. The House impeachment managers also took videotaped depositions of Monica Lewinsky and longtime Clinton friend **Vernon Jordan**. In the end Blumenthal's testimony did little to change the minds of senators regarding whether to vote to remove President Clinton from office.

Related Entries: Impeachment Proceedings; Lewinsky, Monica; Starr, Kenneth; Starr Report

SUGGESTED READINGS: Geraldine Baum, "Trial of the President: A Clinton Warrior Relishes the Fight," *Los Angeles Times*, February 3, 1999, A13; James Bennet, "Aide Says He Backed Clinton on His Denials on Lewinsky," *New York Times*, June 26, 1998, A20; Michael Powell, "Blumenthal, Giving as Good as He Gets," *Washington Post*, September 25, 1998, B01.

BORK, ROBERT (March 1, 1927–   ). Solicitor General of the United States, 1973–1975; Acting Attorney General, 1973–1974; U.S. Court of Appeals Judge; U.S. Supreme Court nominee 1987; law professor.

Late in June 1987, Associate Supreme Court Justice Lewis Powell announced his intention to leave the Supreme Court. President Reagan then nominated U.S. Court of Appeals Judge Robert Bork to replace Justice Powell. As a Yale Law School professor and as a Court of Appeals judge, Robert Bork had a national reputation as a conservative judicial scholar. Largely because of his conservative judicial philosophy, opposition to the Bork nomination quickly developed. During confirmation proceedings Bork also faced renewed criticism over his October 21, 1973, dismissal of **Watergate** special prosecutor **Archibald Cox**. In the so-called **Saturday Night Massacre**, President Richard Nixon ordered Attorney General **Elliot Richardson** to fire Archibald Cox. Subsequently both Attorney General Archibald Cox and Deputy Attorney General William Ruckleshaus resigned rather than carry out Nixon's order. After appointing Solicitor General Robert Bork as acting attorney general, Bork fired Archibald Cox. Late in October of 1987, the Senate voted 58 to 42 to reject the Bork nomination to the Supreme Court.

Related Entries: Cox, Archibald; "Saturday Night Massacre"; Watergate Scandal

SUGGESTED READINGS: Peter B. Levy, *Encyclopedia of the Reagan-Bush Years*, Westport, CT: Greenwood Press, 1996; Steven V. Roberts, "Reagan Vows New Appointment as Upsetting to Foes as Bork's," *New York Times*, October 14, 1987, 1.

BRANTI V FINKEL, 445 U.S. 507 (1980). The passage of the **Pendleton Act of 1883** represented the first major law enacted by Congress to protect federal employees from being forced to engage in partisan political activity or from being required to make campaign contributions as part of a **political assessment** system. From 1883 through the 1970s, Congress passed a number of measures designed to prohibit federal employees from engaging in partisan political activities. For instance in 1939 Congress passed the **Hatch Act** which barred merit system federal employees and officials from engaging in such partisan political activities as campaign fund-raising. During the same time period, many states and local governments passed their own civil service laws designed to limit the power of political parties over government employees. Yet, a significant number of local and state government employees remained outside the protection of civil service systems.

In 1976 the Supreme Court held in *Elrod v Burns* (427 U.S. 347) that the First and Fourteenth Amendments of the Constitution prohibited local governments from dismissing government employees solely because of their political beliefs or affiliations unless the employee occupied a policy-making position. In 1980 the Supreme Court issued the *Branti v Finkel* decision which further limited the dismissal of government employees solely on the basis of political affiliation. The *Branti* decision prohibited state and local government employers from dismissing any government employees solely because of their political affiliation or political views unless the public employer first demonstrated "that party affiliation [was] appropriate requirement for the effective performance of the office." The high court subsequently extended the *Branti* rule to public employees hired by state and local government agencies.

Related Entries: Hatch Act Reform Amendments of 1993; Patronage Crimes; Pendleton Act of 1883; Spoils System

SUGGESTED READINGS: *Branti v Finkel*, URL: *http://laws.findlaw.com/US/445/507. html*; Stephen L. Hayford, "First Amendment Rights of Government Employees: A Primer for Public Officials," *Public Administration Review* 45 (January–February 1985): 241–248.

BRIBERY AND CONFLICT OF INTEREST ACT OF 1962. Between 1950 and 1960, several conflict of interest controversies involving high-level Truman and Eisenhower appointees focused national attention on the regulation of financial conflicts of interest involving government employees and officials employed by federal executive branch departments and agencies. In 1960 the **Association of**

the Bar of the City of New York issued a report that argued that the combination of antiquated criminal ethics statutes and the lack of clear ethics guidelines had led to many of the ethics controversies. The report recommended that Congress and the next president overhaul the executive branch ethics system by updating the key criminal ethics prohibitions and issuing new ethics guidelines to cover issues such as acceptance of gifts and outside employment.

Early in 1961 newly elected President John F. Kennedy announced a series of steps to improve the effectiveness of the executive branch ethics program, including updating criminal ethics restrictions. In October 1962 Congress passed and President Kennedy signed into law the most significant revision of the major federal bribery and conflict-of-interest statutes during the twentieth century. Popularly known as the Bribery and Conflict of Interest Act of 1962, the legislation included many of the recommendations found in the 1960 New York Bar Association report.

First the law placed all the main federal criminal bribery statutes and all of the major federal criminal conflict of interest statutes at one place in the United States Code, between sections 201 and 209 of title 18. This made it easier for federal employees and officials to become familiar with the most important federal ethics laws.

Second the law modified a number of the statutes to close loopholes and to reduce their impact on part-time federal employees and consultants. For instance the new conflicting financial interest statute, section 208, prohibited all executive branch employees and officials from taking any action that might affect a financial interest held by a federal employee or official. The new statute treated the financial interests of an employee's spouse, minor children, or business partner as a financial interest of the federal employee or official. Significantly the new provision did not require federal employees or officials to sell. It only required federal employees and officials to disqualify themselves from particular matters which might impact a financial interest of the employee or official.

Third ethics rules had deterred badly needed experts from accepting part-time consulting or advisory positions with the federal government. So the new law exempted tens of thousands of paid and unpaid part-time federal employees from the ban on federal employees and officials representing someone other than the United States in a wide variety of federal proceedings. First enacted in 1852, Congress had enacted the in-service representation ban in an effort to prevent federal employees from helping private parties prosecute claims against the federal government. Through the 1950s federal agencies complained that many individuals would not accept paid or unpaid federal positions because they feared the law would prohibit them from contacting federal agencies on behalf of their full-time employers.

Fourth the law enacted a number of new restrictions on lobbying by former federal employees and officials. The new section 207 put in place a lifetime ban on all former federal employees representing anyone before a federal agency or in a federal proceeding with respect to specific matters they had responsibility for while serving in the government. The new section 207 also placed a two-year switching sides prohibition which applied to matters in which the former employee had official responsibility while serving in government.

Through the 1960s the new federal ethics law succeeded in eliminating much of the confusion surrounding the key executive branch criminal ethics restrictions. The new lobbying or so-called **"revolving door" restrictions** did not cause a mass exodus of federal employees in an effort to avoid being covered by the new restrictions. The new conflicting financial interest prohibition was to have the greatest impact on federal ethics management. Federal ethics officials learned that federal employees and officials could easily violate the provision unless they paid close attention to their financial holdings. Consequently the new law forced federal agencies to devote more time and attention to educating federal employees and officials with respect to the new prohibitions. The **Ethics in Government Act of 1978** and the **Ethics Reform Act of 1989** made significant changes to a number of the statutes enacted as part of the 1962 ethics package.

Related Entries: Ethics in Government Act of 1978; Ethics Reform Act of 1989; Financial Conflict of Interest Prohibition; Kennedy Administration Ethics Reform Program; "Revolving Door" Restrictions

SUGGESTED READINGS: "Congress Amends Conflict-of-Interest Laws," *CQ Almanac*, 1962, 385–388; Robert Roberts, *White House Ethics: The History of the Politics of Conflict of Interest Regulation*, Westport, CT: Greenwood Press, 1988; U.S. Office of Government Ethics. Ethics Resource Library. Statutes. URL: *http://www.usoge.gov/usoge006.html#statutes*.

BRISTOW, BENJAMIN HELM (June 20, 1832–June 22, 1896). U.S. attorney, Kentucky, 1866–1870; U.S. Solicitor General, 1870–1872; Secretary of the Treasury, 1874–1876.

Born in 1832 Benjamin Bristow grew up in Kentucky; he subsequently became a well-respected lawyer. In 1860 a sharp split developed in Kentucky between residents supporting a break with the Union and those wishing to remain as part of the United States. When the Civil War broke out after the presidential election victory of Republican Abraham Lincoln, Bristow joined the Union cause and rose to become a general in the Union Army. From 1866 to 1870, after the end of the Civil War, Bristow served as a Kentucky U.S. attorney. During this time Bristow vigorously fought the Ku Klux Klan and openly supported the ratification of the Thirteenth, Fourteenth, and Fifteenth Amendments, which abolished slavery and gave African Americans the right to vote. From 1870 to 1872, Bristow then served as the first U.S. solicitor general.

In 1874 President Ulysses S. Grant nominated Benjamin Bristow as secretary of the treasury in an effort to calm congressional anger over the so-called Sandborn Contract scandal which implicated Secretary of the Treasury William A. Richardson in an alleged scheme to help John D. Sandborn, a private tax collector hired by the Treasury Department, make some $213,000 from the collec-

Benjamin H. Bristow. Reproduced from
the Collections of the LIBRARY OF CON-
GRESS

tion of past due federal taxes between 1872 and 1873. Although a subsequent
congressional investigation cleared Richardson, the investigation indicated that
Sandborn had done little to collect the past due taxes. In fact government tax
collectors had done most of the work.

From 1874 through the spring of 1876, Bristow and a small, hand-picked
group of investigators uncovered one of the greatest tax frauds in American
history. Popularly known as the **Whiskey Ring** scandal, Bristow determined
that a conspiracy between major whiskey distillers, federal revenue agents, private citizens, and government officials had cost the treasury millions of dollars
in unpaid federal excise taxes on distilled spirits. The investigation ultimately
led to a February 1876 trial of **General Orville Babcock**, President Ulysses S.
Grant's personal secretary, on public corruption charges. After President Grant
provided testimony vouching for Babcock's character, a St. Louis, Missouri,
U.S. District Court jury found Babcock not guilty.

When it became clear that President Grant no longer wanted Bristow in his
administration, on June 20, 1876, Bristow resigned and shortly thereafter announced his intention to seek the 1876 Republican presidential nomination. Bristow soon found that his aggressive pursuit of the Whiskey Ring had enraged

Grant loyalists. In addition to Bristow, former Republican Speaker of the House **James G. Blaine** and New York Republican Senator Roscoe Conkling sought the Republican nomination. Blaine and Conkling failed to win a majority of Republican delegates after a number of ballots, and the 1876 Republican convention selected Ohio reform governor **Rutherford B. Hayes** as their presidential candidate. In one of the most controversial presidential elections in American history, Democratic Party candidate Samuel Tilden won the popular vote but failed to win a majority of electoral votes. The House subsequently elected Hayes as president.

After the 1876 presidential election, Bristow moved to New York City and became a successful attorney.

Related Entries: Babcock, General Orville E.; Election of 1876; Grant Administration Ethics Controversies; Whiskey Ring

SUGGESTED READINGS: Thomas Bailey, *Presidential Saints and Sinners*, New York: Free Press, 1981; Ross A. Webb, *Benjamin Helm Bristow, Border State Politician*, Lexington: University Press of Kentucky, 1969; Ross A. Webb, "The Bristol Presidential Boom of 1876," *Hayes Historical Journal* 1 & 2 (1976): 78–87.

BRITTON, NAN (1896–?). Mother of alleged illegitimate child fathered by President Harding.

On August 2, 1923, President Warren Harding died in San Francisco, California, after returning from a trip to Alaska. A short time after his death, Nan Britton published *The President's Daughter*, naming Warren Harding as the father of her daughter. Britton had grown up in Harding's hometown of Marion, Ohio. The book became a nationwide best-seller, coinciding with a number of congressional and criminal investigations of alleged illegal conduct by a number of Harding administration and former Harding administration officials. In contrast to the widespread acceptance of the accuracy of the book at the time of publication, many historians now doubt the truthfulness of Britton's account.

In sharp contrast to continuing debate over the Britton book, in 1963 a Harding historian discovered love letters between Warren Harding and Mrs. Carrie Phillips, the wife of a close Harding friend. The letters confirmed rumors that Harding had a fifteen-year affair with Mrs. Phillips before and during the period Harding served as president.

Related Entry: Harding Administration Scandals

SUGGESTED READING: Robert H. Farrell, *The Strange Death of President Harding*. Columbia: University of Missouri Press, 1996.

BROWN, RONALD (August 1, 1941–April 3, 1996). Secretary of Commerce, 1993–1996.

Ronald Brown served as President Bill Clinton's secretary of commerce from January 1993 to his death in a crash of a military transport plane on a Bosnian mountainside on April 3, 1996. Brown died on a trade mission directed at helping the economic recovery of the war-torn area. Prior to being nominated as secretary of commerce, Brown worked as an influential Washington, D.C., lobbyist and held key positions with the national Democratic Party.

Secretary Brown's ethics problems began less than a year after being confirmed as secretary of commerce. In September 1993 reports appeared in the press that a Vietnamese businessman alleged that he paid Brown $700,000 to lobby for the lifting of the U.S. trade embargo of Vietnam. The **independent counsel act** required that the attorney general—**Janet Reno** in this instance—conduct a preliminary investigation to determine whether "credible evidence" existed to support the allegation as part of the process of deciding whether to request the appointment of an independent counsel to investigate the matter. In February 1994 Attorney General Reno ended the investigation after finding insufficient credible evidence of a possible criminal violation.

Less than a year after Reno cleared Brown, new allegations surfaced regarding Brown's financial affairs. Congressional investigators determined that when Brown became secretary of commerce a business associate paid Brown $500,000 for his interest in a company they jointly owned. The buyout raised eyebrows because Brown allegedly had not put any of his money into the company when he became a partner. Equally troubling to congressional investigators, Brown's partner had also defaulted on a $24 million government guaranteed loan she used to purchase a broadcasting company. After conducting a preliminary investigation, Attorney General Janet Reno requested that a three-judge appellate panel appoint an independent counsel to investigate Secretary Brown's financial affairs. Early in July 1995, the panel appointed Miami attorney Daniel Pearson to conduct the investigation. Pearson ended his investigation after the April 3, 1996, death of Secretary Brown.

Related Entries: Clinton Administration Ethics Controversies; Independent Counsel Investigations

SUGGESTED READINGS: Todd S. Purdum, "Crash in the Balkans: In Washington; Jet Crash Casts a Sudden Shadow over Official Washington," *New York Times*, April 4, 1996, A1; Robert Roberts and Marion T. Doss, *From Watergate to Whitewater: The Public Integrity War*, Westport, CT: Praeger, 1997.

BRUCE, CAROL ELDER. *See* Cisneros, Henry G.; Independent Counsel Investigations

BUCHANAN, JAMES (April 23, 1791–June 1, 1868). President of the United States, 1857–1861. *See* Buchanan Administration Political Corruption Scandals

BUCHANAN ADMINISTRATION POLITICAL CORRUPTION SCANDALS.
By the 1850s the growing national debate over slavery and the right of states to withdraw from the Union led to the birth of the Republican Party. To keep control of the White House, not unexpectedly, the Democratic Party pulled out

all the stops to assure the election of James Buchanan in the 1856 presidential election. Despite the promise of presidential candidate Buchanan to clean up politics, the Buchanan administration had few reservations about using the White House and federal agencies and departments for partisan political purposes. The Buchanan administration illegally naturalized a large number of immigrants to make them eligible to vote for Democratic candidates. Government contracts went to companies and individuals who then made large political contributions to the Democratic Party. Many government agencies, for instance, routinely relied on private printers to print government forms and other government material. At the time, Congress had not established an independent Government Printing Office.

From the beginning of the nineteenth century, the vast majority of large city newspapers had openly supported political parties and candidates. By the 1850s major political parties relied heavily on support from major newspapers to get their message to the voters. So the practice of the Buchanan administration's funneling printing contracts to friendly newspapers made strong political sense. Up through the 1858 congressional midterm election, the Democratic Party and the Buchanan administration felt free to use whatever means necessary to assure political victory. Control of Congress effectively prevented any serious congressional investigation of the questionable political activities by the Buchanan administration. The situation changed dramatically when Republicans took control of the House of Representatives after the 1958 election. The House Republican majority took full advantage of their power to launch an investigation of the political activities of the Buchanan administration.

Led by Congressman John Covode of Pennsylvania, the investigation turned up evidence of widespread political corruption within the Buchanan administration. Covode's investigation uncovered the common practice of the recipients of government printing contracts making large political contributions to the Democratic Party. In addition the investigation developed persuasive evidence that Buchanan's secretary of war, John W. B. Floyd, steered procurement contracts to individuals and companies friendly to the Buchanan administration.

Not unexpectedly President Buchanan and Democratic members of Congress responded with anger to the allegations, refusing to cooperate with the Covode investigation. During the 1860 presidential election campaign, Republican presidential candidate Abraham Lincoln and the Republican Party make effective use of the political corruption issue. Supporters of Lincoln contrasted Lincoln's reputation for honesty with Buchanan's alleged tolerance for massive political corruption by touting Lincoln as "Honest Abe." In the end Republican opposition to the expansion of slavery and the right of states to secede from the Union proved to be the key issues in Abraham Lincoln's 1860 presidential election victory. Still Abraham Lincoln's reputation for honesty and President Buchanan's reputation for political corruption helped to give the young Republican Party its first presidential election victory.

Related Entry: "Honest Abe"

SUGGESTED READINGS: C. Vann Woodward, ed., *Responses of the Presidents to Charges of Misconduct*, New York: Delacorte, 1974; David Meerse, "Buchanan, Corruption and the Election of 1860," *Civil War History* 12 (1996): 116–131.

***BUCKLEY V VALEO*, 424 U.S. 1 (1976).** In 1925 Congress passed the Federal Corrupt Practices Act (FCPA) which established campaign contribution limits for candidates for the House and Senate, and required House and Senate candidates to disclose campaign contributions over $100 and the names of those contributors. In addition FCPA established campaign expenditure limitations for House and Senate candidates. Finally FCPA continued the prohibition on corporate campaign contributions. Between 1925 and 1970, however, House and Senate candidates found numerous ways to legally get around the law.

In 1971 Congress passed the **Federal Election Campaign Act of 1971 (FECA)** in an effort to control the escalating cost of running for Congress and the presidency of the United States. The law placed a spending ceiling of "10 cents per eligible voter for all forms of media advertising—radio and television time, newspapers, magazines, billboards and automatic telephone equipment." In 1974, Congress passed major amendments to FECA after the **Watergate scandal** revealed serious gaps in the 1971 campaign finance reform law.

Within a short time of the passage of the **FECA amendments of 1974**, New York Republican Senator James L. Buckley, former Minnesota Democratic Senator Eugene J. McCarthy, the New York City Civil Liberties Union, and *Human Events*, a conservative magazine, brought suit arguing that key provisions of FECA violated their First Amendment rights to freedom of speech and association. The U.S. Court of Appeals for the District of Columbia subsequently upheld all the provisions of the law. On August 14, 1976, the Supreme Court in *Buckley v Valeo* issued a decision upholding and striking down key provisions of FECA.

First the Supreme Court upheld the FECA provision limiting individual contributions to federal candidates to $1,000 and total individual campaign contributions to $25,000 a year. The high court also upheld the FECA provision limiting contributions by political action committees to $5,000 to any single candidate. Second the Supreme Court upheld the FECA provision that required candidates for federal office to keep detailed contribution and expenditure records and to publicly disclose the identity of campaign contributors. Third the high court upheld the FECA provision providing for partial public financing of presidential primary and general election campaigns. Fourth the Supreme Court found unconstitutional the FECA provision that limited independent political expenditures on behalf of a candidate for federal office to $1,000 per election. Fifth the high court found unconstitutional the FECA provision placing a ceiling on overall campaign expenditures by federal candidates. Sixth the Supreme Court struck down the FECA provision on how much a candidate could spend of her or his own money on their own election campaign. Seventh the high court found unconstitutional the method established by FECA to select the members of the **Federal Election Commission (FEC)**. In 1976 Congress passed a number of amendments to FECA in order to bring the law into compliance with the *Buckley v Valeo* decision.

Related Entries: Campaign Finance Reform (Federal); Federal Election Campaign Act Amendments of 1974; Federal Election Campaign Act Amendments of 1976; Federal Election Campaign Act of 1971; Federal Election Commission (FEC); Hard Money; Soft Money

SUGGESTED READINGS: *Buckley v Valeo* (1976): URL: *http://laws.findlaw.com/US/ 424/1.html*; Robert E. Mutch, *Campaigns, Congress and the Courts: The Making of Campaign Finance Laws*, Westport, CT. Praeger, 1988.

BUDDHIST TEMPLE CONTROVERSY. *See* Election of 1996

BUNDLING. The term bundling describes a legal campaign funding practice under FECA. Under the practice, a campaign fund-raiser solicits legal $1,000 campaign contributions from a number of individuals. The campaign fund-raiser then forwards the individual $1,000 contributions in a so-called "bundle" to a presidential, Senate, or House election campaign. Because federal law prohibits corporations or unions from making so-called **hard money** contributions, critics of bundling argue that it permits corporations and unions to get around the prohibition. Federal law does not prohibit a corporate executive or union official from asking employees or union members whether they would like to make a campaign contribution. Federal law does make it a crime for anyone to coerce someone to make a federal campaign contribution. In addition critics of bundling argue that some individuals may make campaign contributions because of concern that they may face some type of retaliation if they don't.

On the other hand, supporters of "bundled" contributions argue that they have a much greater impact on a political candidate than single contributions. Consequently a group of individuals with a common interest in a particular matter may have an easier time getting the attention of a candidate for federal office through bundled contributions rather than through scattered individual contributions.

Related Entries: Campaign Finance Reform (Federal); Federal Election Campaign Act Amendments of 1974; Federal Election Campaign Act Amendments of 1976; Federal Election Campaign Act of 1971 (FECA)

SUGGESTED READINGS: Ruth Marcus and Charles Babcock, "The Business of 'Bundling'; After Dole Fund-Raiser's Solicitation of Firm, 44 Linked to Company Contributed $1,000 Each," *Washington Post*, April 25, 1996, A01.

BUREAU OF INTERNAL REVENUE SCANDAL. During the late 1940s and early 1950s, the administration of President Harry Truman faced a number of serious ethics controversies, with the Bureau of Internal Revenue scandal creating the greatest congressional and public uproar.

Beginning in the early part of the twentieth century, presidents appointed the sixty-four regional collectors of the Bureau of Internal Revenue. Not surprisingly a large number of individuals sought these well-paying **patronage** positions. In 1950 rumors began to circulate that a number of taxpayers had resolved serious tax problems by paying Bureau of Internal Revenue employees and officials to look the other way. Delaware Republican Senator John J. Williams then demanded a full congressional investigation of the allegations. Between 1951 and 1952, Treasury Department and congressional investigations uncovered a pattern of regional Bureau of Internal Revenue collectors accepting favors and payments for helping individuals with their tax problems. The scandal also led to the dismissal or prosecutions of a number of other Bureau of Internal Revenue employees, including close Truman friend James P. Finnegan, collector for the St. Louis, Missouri, district.

Early in 1952 Attorney General Howard McGrath appointed New York lawyer **Newbold Morris** to serve as a Justice Department special assistant responsible for uncovering public corruption in federal agencies and departments. In early April 1952, Attorney General McGrath fired Morris as the result of sharp differences over the scope of the Morris investigation. McGrath then resigned as attorney general. The failure of the Morris investigation helped to speed the passage of legislation to reorganize the Bureau of Internal Revenue. The reform legislation eliminated almost all patronage positions within the Bureau. The president only kept the authority to nominate the commissioner of the Bureau.

The legacy of the Bureau of Internal Revenue Scandal extended beyond the end of the Truman administration in early 1953. In 1955 a federal **grand jury** indicted former Truman White House aide **Matthew J. Connelly** for illegally accepting oil royalties in exchange for agreeing to help a St. Louis, Missouri, distributer of shoes with an income tax evasion case. In 1956 a U.S. District Court jury subsequently convicted Connelly and T. Lamar Caudle, who had headed the Justice Department's tax division during the Truman administration, of illegal influence peddling. Both Connelly and Caudle received six-month federal prison sentences. In 1960 Connelly and Caudle served their six-month sentences after their appeals failed. In 1962 President Kennedy granted Connelly a full pardon. In 1965 President Johnson granted Lamar Caudle a full pardon.

Related Entries: Connelly, Matthew J.; Morris, Newbold; Truman Administration Ethics Controversies

SUGGESTED READINGS: Andrew J. Dunar, *The Truman Scandals and the Politics of Morality*, Columbia: University of Missouri Press, 1984; Robert Roberts, *White House Ethics: The History of the Politics of Conflict of Interest Regulation*, Westport, CT: Greenwood Press, 1988; C. Vann Woodward, ed., *Responses of the Presidents to Charges of Misconduct*, New York: Delacorte Press, 1974.

BUSH, GEORGE. (June 12, 1924–). Vice President of the United States, 1981–1989; President of the United States, 1989–1993. *See* Bush Administration

Ethics Controversies; Bush Administration Ethics Reform Program; Iran-contra Scandal.

BUSH, GEORGE W. *See* Election of 2000

BUSH, NEIL. *See* Bush Administration Ethics Controversies

BUSH ADMINISTRATION ETHICS CONTROVERSIES. From January 1981 through the end of President Ronald Reagan's second term in January 1989, many Reagan administration officials and former Reagan administration officials became the subject of congressional and criminal ethics investigations. In contrast, from January 1989 through January 1993, the administration of President George Bush experienced relatively few ethics problems.

Early in 1989 after a brief controversy, White House Counsel C. Boydon Gray gave up his $50,000 a year salary as chairman of his family's communication firm and placed his financial holding in a **blind trust**. A much more serious controversy developed over the nomination of former Texas Senator **John Tower** as secretary of defense. Although Tower initially received strong Senate support, rumors regarding Tower's drinking habits led a number of senators to withdraw their support. On March 10, 1989, the Senate voted 53 to 47 to reject the Tower nomination with all Republican senators voting for Tower and all Democratic senators voting against.

In late April 1991, the *Washington Post* reported that White House Chief of Staff **John Sununu** had used military aircraft to make some sixty trips during the preceding two years. The article also claimed that Sununu used military aircraft for personal business and to attend political events. Sununu maintained that each of the trips involved official business and that he used military aircraft for security reasons. Sununu also faced criticism for allegedly using a government car to drive from Washington to New York to attend a stamp auction and for soliciting free rides on corporate jets without obtaining prior White House approval. On December 3, 1991, Sununu resigned his position as White House chief of staff in an effort to avoid having the controversy over his travel become a campaign issue in the 1996 presidential campaign.

While not involving a member of the Bush administration, the legal troubles of Neil Bush, one of President Bush's sons, created public relations problems for the Bush White House. On April 19, 1991, Timothy Ryan, the director of the Office of Thrift Supervision (OTS), reprimanded Neil Bush for conflicts of interests while he had served as one of the directors of Silverado Banking, Savings and Loan Association. By the time of the reprimand, the savings and loan had gone out of business. Savings and loan industry experts regarded the reprimand as the mildest sanction available to the OTS. The Bush reprimand did not end the controversy over Neil Bush's involvement with Silverado. In July 1996, in the midst of the 1992 presidential election campaign, the National Democratic Committee admitted that it had hired private investigators to look into whether the Bush administration had given favorable treatment to Silverado Banking, Savings and Loan Association because Neil Bush had served as a Silverado director. Subsequently Democratic National Party chairman **Ronald Brown** denied allegations that the investigation had crossed the line as being a legitimate part of a presidential campaign.

Related Entries: Sununu, John Henry; Tower, John

SUGGESTED READINGS: Sharon LaFraniere, "Neil Bush Reprimanded for Conflicts of Interest; S & L Regulator Issues Mildest Sanction," *Washington Post*, April 19, 1991, A4; Frank J. Murray, "Sununu Leaves the Line of Fire; 'Political Negatives' for Campaign Feared," *Washington Times*, December 4, 1991, A1; Robert Roberts and Marion T. Doss, *Watergate to Whitewater: The Public Integrity War*, Westport, CT: Praeger, 1997; Sununu Resignation Letter: Historical Documents. Resignation.com. URL: *http:// www.resignation.com/historicaldocs/speech.phtml?id-71.*

BUSH ADMINISTRATION ETHICS REFORM PROGRAM. On January 25, 1989, President George Bush issued an executive order that established the **President's Commission on Federal Ethics Law Reform**. President Bush appointed U.S. Court of Appeals Judge Malcolm Wilkey to chair the commission and former Carter administration Attorney General Griffin B. Bell as commission vice chairman. Bush directed the commission to "take a fresh look at the ethical standards" for the three branches of the federal government. From January 1981 through January 1989, a number of Reagan administration officials and former Reagan administration officials had become the subject of congressional and criminal misconduct investigations. During the same period, a number of members of Congress faced congressional and criminal ethics investigations.

In March 1989 the Bush Ethics Commission issued its report, which included twenty-seven recommendations. Besides recommending that the Bush White House rewrite President Johnson's **Executive Order 11222**, "Prescribing Standards of Ethical Conduct for Government Officers and Employees," issued May 1965, the Commission recommended a governmentwide ban on federal employees accepting **honorariums**, the establishment of a congressional ethics office, the extension of a number of criminal ethics statutes to members of Congress, and allowing federal employees required to sell assets to comply with ethics rules to roll over any capital gains to defer unanticipated capital gains taxes. In early April 1989, President Bush issued **Executive Order 12674**, "Principles of Ethical Conduct for Government Officers and Employees" which replaced Executive Order 11222. The Bush order included a provision prohibiting all high-level presidential appointees from accepting any honorariums and a new **appearance of impropriety rule**.

From April through October 1989, the Bush White House struggled with Congress to reach a compromise on new ethics legislation. The White House insisted that the new legislation include a ban on members of Congress accepting honorariums. Late in November 1989, President Bush signed into law the **Ethics Reform Act of 1989**. The law included many of the proposals recommended

Stephen Potts, director of the United States Office of Government Ethics, presents Standards of Ethical Conduct to President George Bush, September 5, 1991. George Bush Presidential Library

by the Bush Ethics Commission. In return for President Bush agreeing to sign a pay increase for House members, the act prohibited House members from accepting honorariums. The Ethics Reform Act also tightened restrictions on lobbying by former federal employees and officials, including former members of Congress. Finally the law granted the Director of the **U.S. Office of Government Ethics** the authority to issue **certificates of divestiture** permitting executive branch officials and employees required to divest themselves of assets to avoid conflicts of interest to defer paying capital gains resulting from the sale of the financial assets.

In 1991 the Senate passed legislation prohibiting senators from accepting honorariums. In return President Bush signed legislation raising the pay of senators to the same level as members of the House.

Related Entries: Certificate of Divestiture; Ethics Reform Act of 1989; Executive Order 12674; Honorarium Restrictions; President's Commission on Ethics Law Reform; "Revolving Door" Restrictions

SUGGESTED READINGS: David Hoffman, "Bush Selects Panel to Study Ethics; President Instructs Members to 'Take a Fresh Look' at Standards," *Washington Post*, January 26, 1989, A5; Robert Roberts and Marion T. Doss, *Watergate to Whitewater: The Public Integrity War*, Westport, CT: Praeger, 1997.

BUTTERFIELD, ALEXANDER (April 6, 1926–   ). White House aide to President Richard Nixon, 1969–1973; Federal Aviation Agency administrator, 1973–1975.

During the spring and summer of 1973, the **Senate Watergate Committee** held hearings into the conduct of President Richard Nixon's 1972 presidential reelection campaign. The hearings focused on the possible involvement of the Nixon White House and President Nixon's reelection campaign in the June 1972 break-in at the Democratic National Committee headquarters located in the Washington, D.C., Watergate complex.

Early in July 1973, White House Counsel **John Dean** laid out the story of direct White House involvement in the cover-up of the Watergate break-in. On July 13, 1973, former White House aide official Alexander Butterfield appeared before the Senate Watergate Committee. To the surprise of millions of Americans, Butterfield revealed to the nation the existence of a White House taping system. According to Butterfield, Nixon had ordered the installation of the taping system "to record things for posterity."

The Senate Watergate Committee and Watergate special prosecutor **Archibald Cox** immediately recognized that the White House tapes might permit the committee to confirm or discount the testimony of John Dean. Both the Watergate Committee and Cox issued subpoenas for the tapes. On July 24, 1973, President Nixon invoked the doctrine of **executive privilege** as grounds for refusing to comply with subpoenas. On July 24, 1974, the Supreme Court ruled in *United States v Nixon* that the doctrine of executive privilege did prevent Watergate special prosecutor **Leon Jaworski** from issuing a subpoena for the White House tapes. Jaworski had replaced Cox as the Watergate special prosecutor after Nixon dismissed Cox during October of 1973. On August 8, 1973, President Nixon announced his decision to resign the presidency.

Historians generally agree that disclosure of the White House taping system constituted a crucial turning point in the Watergate investigation.

Related Entries: Senate Watergate Committee; *United States v Nixon*; Watergate Scandal

SUGGESTED READING: Lawrence Meyer, "President Taped Talks, Phone Calls; Lawyer Ties Ehrlichman to Payments: Principal Offices Secretly Bugged Since Spring of 1971," *Washington Post*, July 17, 1973, A01.

C

CAMERON, SIMON (March 8, 1799–June 26, 1889). Secretary of War, 1861–1862.

In 1861 Lincoln appointed Simon Cameron as secretary of war. A wealthy Pennsylvania businessman, Cameron controlled the Pennsylvania Republican Party. Prior to being nominated as secretary of war, Cameron had acquired a fortune in various Pennsylvania business ventures. After switching from the Democratic to the Republican Party, Cameron was elected to the U.S. Senate in 1856. He had earlier served as a Democratic senator from Pennsylvania from 1845 to 1849. Cameron had also played a major role in the growth of the Republican Party during the 1850s, as well as having a major role in helping Abraham Lincoln win the 1860 presidential election.

A year into the war, it became increasingly clear that Secretary of War Cameron lacked the ability to manage a War Department forced to oversee a mobilization unprecedented in American history. The first year of the Civil War saw a number of disastrous defeats for the Union. Many supporters of the Union cause had expected the war to be over in weeks. President Lincoln soon realized that the war might go on for years and that the Union would need to recruit and equip the largest army in American history. During the first year of the war, the Union's desperate need for equipment and supplies made the Department of War an easy target for war profiteers and individuals seeking to use their political contacts to obtain lucrative War Department procurement contracts. Because of the almost entire absence of reliable procurement procedures, the War Department found itself paying far too much for inferior supplies and equipment.

Understandably Congress looked for someone to blame for the Union defeats and the massive amounts of procurement fraud. Despite any evidence that Cameron personally profited from the placement of procurement contracts, it became clear that politics played a role in awarding a number of procurement contracts. Incident after incident of Cameron's War Department paying vast sums for spoiled food and defective equipment threatened public confidence in the Union

Secretary of War Simon Cameron. Reproduced from the Collections of the LIBRARY
OF CONGRESS

war effort. In January 1862 Lincoln removed Cameron as secretary of war and
appointed him minister to Russia. This action failed to satisfy some members
of Congress. On April 30, 1862, the House censured Cameron for approving a
number of fraudulent contracts. After the censure Lincoln vigorously defended
Cameron and took full responsibility for all contract abuses. President Lincoln's
willingness to take full responsibility for procurement related abuses helped to
calm the rebellion in Congress.

Secretary of War Edwin Stanton, Lincoln's replacement for Cameron, instituted a number of major reforms in the War Department's procurement of provisions and equipment through the remainder of the Civil War. These reforms
played a major role in permitting the Union to take full advantage of its industrial advantage over the states of the confederacy.

SUGGESTED READINGS: Erwin S. Bradley, *Simon Cameron, Lincoln's Secretary of
War; A Political Biography*, Philadelphia: University of Pennsylvania Press, 1966; Fred
A. Shannon, *The Organization and Administration of the Union Army, 1861–1865*,
Gloucester, MA: P. Smith, 1965; C. Vann Woodward, ed., *Responses of the Presidents
to Charges of Misconduct*, New York: Delacorte Press, 1974.

CAMPAIGN CONTRIBUTION LIMITS. *See* Federal Election Campaign Act Amendments of 1974; Federal Election Campaign Act Amendments of 1976; Federal Election Campaign Act of 1971

CAMPAIGN DISCLOSURE AGENCIES. At the federal, state, and local level, the responsibility for the enforcement of federal and state campaign finance disclosure laws rests with a number of federal, state, and local agencies. The 1974 amendments to the **Federal Election Campaign Act (FECA)** established the **Federal Election Commission (FEC)** to oversee the enforcement of FECA's campaign contribution limits and disclosure requirements. In addition Congress gave the FEC responsibility for administering the program for partial public funding of presidential primary and general election campaigns. Candidates for federal office must file required campaign disclosure reports with the Washington office of the FEC and designated state disclosure agencies. By the end of the 1990s, the FEC and a number of states had established programs permitting the public to access federal and state campaign finance disclosure statements by the Internet. The FEC established the system of dual filing to make it easier for citizens and members of the media to inspect campaign disclosure statements. In the late 1990s, the FEC began providing access to campaign finance disclosure reports available through the internet.

In contrast states make use of a number of different types of agencies to enforce state campaign finance laws. These include Secretary of State offices, State Boards of Election, state Ethics Commissions, and State Registry of Election Finance. Candidates for statewide offices must file campaign finance disclosure statements with the Secretary of State or Commonwealth offices of the states of Alabama, Arizona, Arkansas, California, Colorado, Connecticut, Florida, Georgia, Idaho, Kansas, Michigan, Mississippi, Nevada, New Hampshire, New Mexico, North Dakota, Ohio, Oregon, South Dakota, Vermont, West Virginia, and Wyoming. The states of Alaska, Georgia, Hawaii, Iowa, Kansas, Maine, Missouri, Nebraska, New Jersey, Ohio, Oklahoma, South Carolina, Texas, and Washington require candidates of state offices to submit campaign finance information to various types of commissions. Election boards oversee campaign disclosure laws in the states of Illinois, Indiana, Maryland, Minnesota, New York, North Carolina, Rhode Island, and Wisconsin. The states of Kentucky and Tennessee use state Registry of Election Finance to enforce their state's campaign finance disclosure laws. State election commissioners oversee the enforcement of campaign disclosure laws in the states of Delaware and Montana.

Related Entries: Federal Election Campaign Act Amendments of 1974; Federal Election Campaign Act of 1971 (FECA)

SUGGESTED READINGS: CQ Researcher, "Campaign Finance Reform: Are Laws Needed to Police the System?" February 9, 1996, 121–144; Federal Election Commission: Citizen Guide. URL: *http://www.fec.gov*.

CAMPAIGN FINANCE REFORM (FEDERAL). Starting in the late 1820s and early 1830s, the country saw the growth of political parties capable of running candidates for local, state, and federal offices. As political parties grew, they faced the problem of finding money to run the parties and to conduct political campaigns. Prior to the **Andrew Jackson** 1828 presidential election, political affiliation did not play a role in the appointment of the vast majority of federal employees. From 1829 through 1836, under the banner of Jacksonian Democracy, President Jackson significantly increased the number of patronage appointments to federal positions. Equally important, Jackson expanded the use of **political assessments** as a means of raising funds for the Democratic Party. As a condition of keeping their federal jobs, the system required federal employees to return a percentage of their salary to the Democratic Party in the form of a campaign contribution. Political assessments would remain a fixture of the federal personnel system through the 1870s.

Through the 1830s, 1840s, and 1850s, few members of Congress found it in their interest to challenge the **spoils system**. In 1860 the Covode Committee, headed by Pennsylvania Republican Representative John Covode, uncovered massive use of the federal agencies and their employees by the **administration of President James Buchanan** for partisan political activities. Yet, after the Civil War, the Republican congressional majority demonstrated little interest in dealing with massive amounts of public corruption. Historians generally regard the administration of President Ulysses S. Grant (1869–1877) as the most corrupt in American history.

In 1883 Congress passed the **Pendleton Act**. From the end of the Civil War, members of the civil service reform movement argued that unless Congress enacted legislation ending the spoils system, efforts to end corruption in federal agencies and departments would fail. After a disgruntled office seeker assassinated President James Garfield in 1881, President **Chester A. Arthur** threw his support behind the Pendleton Act. Besides providing for the establishment of a new merit system, the act created a number of so-called **patronage crimes** directed at prohibiting political campaigns from forcing federal employees to participate in partisan political activities.

First the act prohibited any federal employee or official from soliciting a campaign contribution from another federal employee. Second any federal employee or official was prohibited from retaliating against a federal employee for refusing to make a campaign contribution. Third the Pendleton Act prohibited any federal employee or official from soliciting a campaign contribution from inside a federal building.

By the end of the 1890s, reform efforts shifted from civil service reform to the regulation of campaign contributions. The period from 1880 through 1900 saw large industrial corporations gradually increase campaign contributions to state and federal candidates. For instance 1896 Democratic presidential candidate William Jennings Bryan blamed his loss on large corporate campaign contributions to the campaign of Republican presidential candidate William Mc-

Kinley. Controlled by the Republican Party, Congress rejected calls for restrictions on corporate campaign contributions to federal election campaigns. Both the 1900 and 1904 presidential election campaign again saw the Republican Party depend heavily on corporate campaign contributions.

However, in the aftermath of President Theodore Roosevelt's 1904 presidential election victory, allegations surfaced that the Republican Party had agreed to oppose any new antitrust legislation in return for the corporate contributions. Roosevelt had assumed the presidency after the September 6, 1901, assassination of William McKinley. Despite the fact that a subsequent congressional investigation failed to find any evidence to confirm the alleged deal, the allegations deeply disturbed President Roosevelt. On December 5, 1905, in his annual message to Congress, President Theodore Roosevelt proposed prohibiting corporations from making any campaign contributions to federal campaigns. Equally important the 1904 election led to the establishment of the National Publicity Law Association to lobby for a ban on corporate campaign contributions and the disclosure of campaign contributions and expenditures.

In 1907 Congress passed the **Tillman Act** which prohibited corporations from making campaign contributions to federal elections. In 1910 Congress passed the Publicity Act which established the first requirement that candidates for federal office disclose campaign contributions. In 1911 Congress amended the Publicity Act to prohibit candidates for the House to spend more than $5,000 and candidates for the Senate from spending more than $10,000. In 1924, the **Teapot Dome scandal** rocked Washington. In 1925 Congress passed the Federal Corrupt Practices Act (FCPA) which continued the prohibition on corporate campaign contributions, established a campaign expenditure ceiling for House campaigns and Senate campaigns, and expanded campaign finance disclosure requirements.

Between 1925 and 1970, Congress made only minor changes to federal campaign finance laws despite the fact that federal candidates quickly found ways to legally avoid complying with the campaign finance disclosure and expenditure requirements of the law. However, in 1939 Congress passed the Hatch Act which prohibited all federal civil service employees and officials from engaging in most types of partisan political activities, including running for public office, and in 1947 Congress passed the Taft-Hartley Act which prohibited unions from making direct campaign contributions to candidates for federal office.

Because of a major loophole in the **Corrupt Practices Act**, the 1940s saw the birth of the **political action committee** as a way to funnel corporate and union money to candidates for federal office. The Corrupt Practices Act and the Taft-Hartley only prohibited directed campaign contributions by corporations and unions. Nothing prevented corporations and unions from making contributions to independent political committees, which, under federal law, could make direct contributions to federal candidates.

Through the 1950s and 1960s, the demands for more and more money to pay for escalating campaign costs brought about by the advent of television led to a revival of interest in campaign finance reform. In 1971, Congress passed the **Federal Election Campaign Act (FECA)**. Key provisions of the act included (1) new contribution limits for individuals and the families of candidates, (2) requirements for comprehensive disclosure of campaign contributions and expenditures, and (3) limits for how much campaigns could spend on campaign commercials. In addition the 1971 act put in place a system to provide for the public funding of presidential primary and general election campaigns. However, critics of FECA argued it did not go far enough. Established in 1971, **Common Cause**, the new citizens' lobby, argued that Congress needed to establish an independent commission to collect campaign finance reports and to enforce the other requirements of the law.

In the aftermath of the **Watergate scandal**, in 1974 Congress amended FECA. The amended law established a new **Federal Election Commission (FEC)**, which put in place much lower individual and political action committee contribution limits, placed caps on how much individuals could spend of their own money on their own political campaign, and established lower total campaign expenditure limits for federal campaigns. In 1976 came the landmark *Buckley v Valeo* decision in which the high court upheld and struck down key provisions of FECA. *Buckley v Valeo* upheld FECA's individual and political action committee contribution limits and held that Congress had the authority to require federal campaigns to file campaign finance disclosure reports. And the high court upheld the provision of the law providing for partial public funding of presidential primary and general election campaigns. However, the Supreme Court struck down FECA's ceilings on campaign expenditures, limits on the size of political contributions by a candidate to his or her own campaign, and limits on independent political expenditures.

Then in 1979 the FEC issued regulations permitting political parties to accept unlimited amounts of so-called **soft money** to pay for such traditional party building activities as voter registration and get-out-the-vote campaigns. The FEC acted in response to criticism that FECA's provisions made it impossible for political parties to adequately fund such activities and consequently weakened the role of political parties in American politics. Not unexpectedly both the Republican and Democratic Parties quickly learned to take full advantage of the FEC's soft money ruling. From 1980 to 1996, soft money contributions grew from a trickle to a flood. More important, both the Republican and Democratic Parties began to pay for **issue ads** with soft money. In 1996, for example, the Democratic National Committee raised close to $40 million in soft money to pay for a blitz of issue ads touting the successes of the Clinton administration months before the beginning of the 1996 presidential campaign.

In the aftermath of the 1996 election campaign fund-raising controversy, support for banning soft money increased in Congress and on the part of the American people. Through September 2000, Congress failed to enact new restrictions on soft money contributions to political parties. However, the summer of 2000 saw Congress turn its attention to closing the so-called Section 527 group loophole.

Section 527 of the Internal Revenue Code provides for the establishment of tax-exempt organizations permitted to use contributions to pay for **issue ads**. During the late 1990s, so-called Section 527 groups began to use contributions to pay for ads attacking candidates for federal office. However, federal law did not require Section 527 groups to disclose the sources of contributions. The loophole received national attention during the March 2000 South Carolina Republican presidential primary. A Section 527 group ran attack ads against Arizona Senator John McCain. Yet the summer of 2000 saw Congress enact and President Clinton sign into law legislation requiring Section 527 tax-exempt groups or organizations to disclose the sources of soft money contributions to such organizations.

Related Entries: Federal Election Campaign Act of 1971 (FECA); Federal Election Commission (FEC); Hard Money; Issue Ads; Soft Money

SUGGESTED READINGS: "Campaign Finance Reform: Are Tighter Laws Needed to Police the System?" CQ Researcher, February 9, 1996, 122–144; Center for Response Politics, Money in Politics: Reform Principles, Problems, and Proposals, URL: *http:// www.opensecrets.org/pubs/reform/reformindex.htm*; Robert E. Mutch, *Campaigns, Congress and the Courts: The Making of Federal Campaign Finance Law*, Westport, CT: Praeger, 1988.

CAMPAIGN FINANCE REFORM (STATE). From 1830 through the 1870s, a number of northeastern and midwestern states experienced the growth of powerful urban political machines. During the late nineteenth and early twentieth centuries, the populist and **progressive movements** lobbied state legislatures, as well as the Congress, to adopt reforms designed to break the power of well-entrenched political machines. The period saw many states adopt election reforms which included voter registration systems, the secret ballot, and placing election administration in the hands of state and local elections boards. In contrast only a small number of states enacted limited campaign disclosure laws: New York in 1890, Massachusetts in 1892, and California in 1893. On the other hand, a much larger number of states made it illegal for corporations to make direct campaign contributions to candidates for state offices.

Much like the federal experience, from the early 1920s through the late 1960s, few states enacted new campaign finance reform legislation. The rising cost of running for elections and the flood of special interest money into political campaigns led many states during the early 1970s to pass campaign finance disclosure laws. Supporters of comprehensive disclosure laws argued that the "sunlight" of disclosure would deter campaign contributions by special interest groups. As a result of aggressive lobbying by **Common Cause** and other good government groups, the late 1970s and early 1980s saw many states pass laws limiting the size of campaign contributions and requiring campaign finance disclosure. Equally important, a number of states established independent commissions with responsibility for the enforcement of state campaign finance disclosure laws.

During the second half of the 1990s, the states of Arizona, Maine, Vermont, and Massachusetts passed so-called "Clean Money Campaign Reform (CMCR)" laws which provided for limited public funding of state races.

SUGGESTED READINGS: Campaign Finance Law 98: A Summary of State Campaign Finance Laws With Quick Reference Charts. Washington, DC: Federal Election Commission. URL: *http://www.fec.gov/pages/citnlist.htm*; Center for Responsive Politics, *A Brief History of Money in Politics: The States: "Laboratories of Reform,"* 1996. URL: *http://www.opensecrets.org/pubs/history/history4.htm*; Center for Responsive Politics, *Reform, Principles, Problems and Prospects*, Appendix B. State Contribution Limits, 1996: URL: *http://www.opensecrets.org/pubs/reform/reform9.htm*.

CAMPAIGN FUND-RAISING. *See* Campaign Finance Reform (Federal)

CARTER, BILLY (BILLYGATE). *See* Carter Administration Ethics Controversies

CARTER, JIMMY (October 1, 1924–   ). President of the United States, 1977–1981 *See* Carter Administration Ethics Controversies; Carter Administration Ethics Reform Program

CARTER ADMINISTRATION ETHICS CONTROVERSIES. In the 1976 presidential election, former Georgia governor and Democratic Party presidential candidate Jimmy Carter defeated President Gerald Ford. Carter made integrity in government the central theme of his presidential campaign. Even before being sworn in as president, the Carter transition announced its intention to require nominees and appointees to comply with strict new ethics regulations. President Carter signed into law the **Ethics in Government Act of 1978** which required high-level federal officials in all three branches to file annual **public financial disclosure** statements, established procedures for the appointment of special prosecutors to investigate possible criminal wrongdoing by high-level executive branch officials, and expanded restrictions on lobbying by former federal officials. Yet the Carter White House would find itself confronted with a number of serious ethics controversies.

On September 27, 1977, **Bert Lance** resigned as director of the Office of Management and Budget (OMB) in order to fight allegations of improprieties related to his management of a Georgia bank prior to being confirmed as director of OMB. On May 23, 1979, an Atlanta, Georgia, federal **grand jury** indicted Bert Lance and three of his business associates for allegedly illegally obtaining bank loans for themselves, their families, and business associates. On April 30, 1980, a U.S. District Court jury acquitted Bert Lance on nine counts of bank fraud and failed to reach a verdict on three other counts. Federal prosecutors subsequently declined to retry Lance on the three remaining counts.

Jimmy Carter greets his brother Billy at the Georgia Institute of Technology commencement ceremonies, February 20, 1979. Jimmy Carter Library

The second major ethics controversy of the Carter administration involved Billy Carter, the president's brother. During 1978 and 1979, Billy Carter made several trips to Libya as the guest of Libyan dictator Muammar Qaddafi. Carter traveled to Libya on behalf of a Georgia business partner interested in purchasing oil from Libya. Early in December 1979, a number of news sources reported an ongoing Department of Justice investigation of whether federal law required Billy Carter to register as a foreign agent. While in Libya, the Libyan government had asked Billy Carter to help obtain permission from the U.S. government for the Libyan government to purchase a number of large American-built transport planes. Billy Carter subsequently disclosed that the Libyan government had given him a $220,000 loan.

The Billy Carter controversy could not have come at a worse time for the Carter White House. The Iranian hostage crisis, double-digit inflation, and an approaching presidential election had seriously eroded public confidence in President Carter. The appearance of the president's brother entering into a business dealing with a dictator who provided financial support to terrorist organizations only added to his woes. Early in August 1980, the Senate held open hearings into Billy Carter's financial dealings with the Libyan government. Billy Carter denied ever having asked anyone in the Carter administration for preferential treatment.

On August 4, 1980, the Carter White House issued a lengthy report denying that Billy Carter had played any role in the formulation and implementation of U.S. foreign policy or that anyone in the Carter administration helped Billy Carter obtain preferential treatment for the Libyan government. In a nationally televised news conference on the same day, President Carter declared, "Neither I nor any member of my administration violated any law or committed any impropriety." The White House report and Carter press conference helped to defuse the growing media **"feeding frenzy"** over Billy Carter's financial dealings with Libya.

In November 1980 former California Governor Ronald Reagan defeated President Jimmy Carter in the 1980 presidential election. On April 22, 1981, after the beginning of the Reagan administration, the Justice Department announced that it had no evidence of illegal conduct by any federal government employees or official as the result of their involvement in the Billy Carter case. President Jimmy Carter's 1980 presidential election defeat did not end Billy Carter's legal troubles. The Internal Revenue Service ruled that Billy Carter had failed to pay required taxes on income he made from giving talks and making appearances. In addition Billy Carter had failed to repay loans to a Plains, Georgia, bank. In June 1981 Billy Carter auctioned off his Plains, Georgia, house, gas station, and softball field to pay the IRS and the bank. On September 25, 1988, Billy Carter died of pancreatic cancer. A year after his death, the clinic that had helped Billy Carter deal with his alcoholism published Carter's autobiography entitled *Billy*. Coauthored by Billy Carter's wife, Sybil, and Ken Esters, Carter's book maintained that the Libyan investigation had forced him to spend tens of thousands of dollars to hire lawyers to defend himself against the allegations of improper or illegal conduct.

In addition to the Bert Lance and Billy Carter affairs, during 1979 and 1980, the Carter White House saw two special prosecutors appointed to investigate allegations of illegal drug use by Carter White House Chief of Staff **Hamilton Jordan** and Carter presidential campaign manager Timothy Kraft. In a 1980 report, special prosecutor Arthur Christy found insufficient evidence to seek an indictment of Hamilton Jordan for alleged illegal drug use at a New York City night club and at a California party. In 1981 special prosecutor Gerald Gallinghouse found insufficient evidence of possible illegal drug use by Timothy Kraft.

Related Entries: Ethics in Government Act of 1978; Independent Counsel Investigations; Jordan, Hamilton.

SUGGESTED READINGS: John F. Berry, "Lance Acquitted on Nine Counts; Mistrial on Three; Bert Lance Is Acquitted on 9 Counts," *Washington Post*, May 1, 1980, A1; Billy Carter, Sybil Carter, and Ken Estes, *Billy: Billy Carter's Reflections on His Struggle with Fame, Alcoholism & Cancer*, Newport, RI: Edgehill Publications, 1989; Resignation Letter of Director of the Office of Management and Budget Bert Lance, September 27, 1977. URL: *http://www.resignation.com/historicaldocs/speech.phtml?id=40*; Edward Walsh, "No 'Impropriety' in Billy Affair, Carter Says," *Washington Post*, August 5, 1980, A1.

CARTER ADMINISTRATION ETHICS REFORM PROGRAM. On January 4, 1977, President-elect Jimmy Carter announced new ethical guidelines for all high-level presidential nominees and appointees. The guidelines required appointees to file detailed financial disclosure statements and to divest themselves of any financial interests that might create the appearance of a financial conflict of interest. To prevent former officials from cashing in on their high-level experience, President-elect Carter required his nominees and appointees to agree not to lobby their former federal agencies, on any matter, for one year after leaving government. During the 1976 presidential campaign, presidential candidate Carter promised to take steps to deal with the so-called **"revolving door"** problem. Finally the new Carter White House ethics guidelines imposed much tighter requirements for the establishment of **blind trusts**. Although **Common Cause**, the Washington-based citizen's lobby, strongly endorsed the Carter ethics initiatives, critics argued that the new rules might make it more difficult to retain and recruit badly needed talent to help the country deal with pressing domestic and international problems.

Despite concern over tightening federal ethic regulations, between January 1977 and October 1978, the Carter White House worked with Congress to enact a new law designed to rebuild public trust in government. The efforts culminated with the passage of the **Ethics in Government Act of 1978**. The new ethics law went far beyond the Clinton ethics guidelines, requiring thousands of executive, legislative, and judicial branch officials to file annual public financial disclosure statements. It included provisions for the appointment of special prosecutors to investigate allegations of criminal conduct by high-level executive branch officials by a special three-judge federal appellate panel. Equally important the act included new criminal restrictions on former executive branch employees and officials lobbying their former government agencies and statutory requirements for the establishment of blind trusts. Finally the Ethics Act established a new **U.S. Office of Government Ethics** to oversee the executive branch ethics program.

The full impact of the Carter administration ethics reform program did not become apparent until after the 1980 presidential election of former California governor Ronald Reagan. During late December 1980 and January 1981, President-elect Reagan's transition team experienced considerable difficulty complying with the complex provisions of the Ethics Act, particularly the **public financial disclosure** provisions of the law. Several Reagan administration and former Reagan administration officials would become the subject of independent counsel investigations between 1981 and 1989.

The long-term impact of the Carter administration ethics reform program remains a subject of considerable debate. In the decades following the Ethics Act, support remained strong for the public financial disclosure provisions. On the other hand, through the 1980s and 1990s, opposition to the special prosecutor (independent counsel) provisions of the act grew. First in 1991 and then in 1999, Congress allowed the provisions of the **Independent Counsel Act** to expire.

Related Entries: Common Cause; Ethics in Government Act of 1978; Independent Counsel Act; Public Financial Disclosure; "Revolving Door" Restrictions

SUGGESTED READINGS: Robert Roberts, *White House Ethics: The History of the Politics of Conflict of Interest Reform*, Westport, CT: Greenwood Press, 1988; Robert Roberts and Marion T. Doss, *From Watergate to Whitewater: The Public Integrity War*, Westport, CT: Praeger, 1997.

CARVILLE, JAMES (October 25, 1944–   ). Political Consultant.

During the 1980s and 1990s, James Carville, the colorful "Ragin' Cajuin," served as a political campaign consultant to a number of Democratic candidates. In December 1991, Carville joined the Arkansas governor Bill Clinton's campaign for the 1992 Democratic presidential nomination. Throughout the 1991 presidential primary and general election campaign, Carville played a major role in defending Bill Clinton against a number of allegations related to Clinton's character. For instance Carville helped prepare Bill Clinton and **Hillary Rodham Clinton** for their January 1992 *60 Minutes* interview regarding Bill Clinton's alleged affair with former Arkansas state employee **Gennifer Flowers**. Prior to the interview, Flowers had alleged a twelve-year affair with Arkansas governor Bill Clinton in an article that appeared in a national tabloid.

After the 1992 election victory of Bill Clinton, James Carville became one of his most vocal defenders. Between 1993 and the end of Bill Clinton's second term, Carville appeared hundreds of times on network and cable news shows to defend Clinton from allegations associated with the **Whitewater investigation** and to attack the independent counsel investigation of **Kenneth Starr**. Throughout the Clinton presidency, Carville blamed President Clinton's legal problems on a vast right-wing conspiracy intent on overturning the popular will of the American people by forcing Clinton from office. Between 1993 and the end of 1999, James Carville published two books defending President Clinton's record and denouncing his critics: *We're Right, They're Wrong* (1995) and *And the Horse He Rode in On: The People against Kenneth Starr* (1998).

Through much of 1998 and early 1999, Carville conducted a one-person campaign to defend President Clinton against impeachment as the result of his alleged sexual relationship with former White House intern and White House employee **Monica Lewinsky**. Carville viewed the Monica Lewinsky affair as simply another effort by Clinton critics to destroy his presidency.

Related Entries: Clinton Administration Ethics Controversies; Impeachment Proceedings; Starr, Kenneth; Whitewater Investigation.

SUGGESTED READINGS: Carville, James, *And the Horse He Rode in On: The People Against Kenneth Starr*, New York: Simon & Schuster, 1998; Carville, James, *We're Right, They're Wrong*, New York: Random House, 1995; *Current Biography Yearbook*, James Carville, 1993, 105–108; Howard Kurtz, "In the Pit Bully Pulpit; James Carville, Barking Up the Right's Tree," *Washington Post*, January 14, 1999, C01.

CASEY, WILLIAM (March 13, 1913–May 6, 1987). Director, Central Intelligence Agency (CIA), 1981–1987.

Between 1981 and his death in 1987, William Casey became one of the most controversial figures of the Reagan administration. Ronald Reagan's 1980 presidential campaign manager, Casey played a major role in fashioning Ronald Reagan's landslide victory over incumbent Democratic President Jimmy Carter. Having previously served as chairman of the Securities and Exchange Commission (SEC) and undersecretary of state for economic affairs and chairman of the Export-Import Bank during the Nixon and Ford administrations, Casey was seen by Reagan as an individual who could provide his new administration with badly needed experience. Although Ronald Reagan's selection of William Casey as director of the Central Intelligence Agency (CIA) raised a few eyebrows, Casey quickly made it clear that he intended to be a hands-on CIA director.

Early in 1983 Casey faced a minor ethics problem. As a partner in an influential New York City law firm, Casey had acquired substantial financial holdings before becoming CIA director. Instead of establishing a **blind trust** to shield himself from possible conflict of interest problems, Casey decided to disqualify himself from any decisions that might have an impact on the value of his financial holdings. Although federal ethics laws and rules did not require Casey to place his financial holdings in a blind trust, a number of senators argued that Casey's plan to disqualify himself from matters that might impact upon his financial interests simply would not work. As a result of the criticism, in July 1983 Casey announced that he would establish a blind trust.

Almost immediately upon being sworn in as director of the CIA, Casey moved to significantly increase U.S. support for anticommunist insurgencies around the world. President Reagan had made clear that he did not intend to allow any further spread of communism. Between 1981 and Casey's death in 1987, the CIA funneled billions of dollars into insurgent operations around the world, including countries such as Angola and Afghanistan. CIA support for the Nicaraguan contras proved the most controversial of Casey's anticommunist initiatives and ultimately led to the 1980s **Iran-contra scandal**.

In December 1982, the House passed the so-called Boland amendment which prohibited any direct U.S. financial support for any effort to overthrow the Nicaraguan government. However, the Reagan administration saw the Nicaraguan government as a threat to Central America because Cuba and the Soviet Union provided financial and military support to Nicaragua. The Boland amendment led Casey to look for other ways to maintain support for the contras. In 1985, with the strong backing of William Casey, President Reagan approved a plan developed by National Security Council staffer Oliver North to sell arms to Iran in an effort to gain the release of American hostages being held by pro-Iranian terrorists in Lebanon. In November 1986 the secret plan became publicly known. Besides the arms for hostage deal, the White House disclosed the diversion of profits from the arms sales to support the contras. From December 1986 through much of 1994, independent counsel **Lawrence Walsh** would conduct an investigation into the controversial Iran-contra affair. On May 6, 1987 William Casey died, making it impossible for Lawrence Walsh to determine his role in the diversion plan.

Related Entries: Iran-Contra Scandal; Reagan Administration Ethics Controversies; Walsh, Lawrence E.

SUGGESTED READINGS: Charles Fenyvesi, "A Spy and His Secrets Are Buried: Death of Central Intelligence Agency Chief, William Casey," *U.S. News & World Report*, May 18, 1987, 29; Peter B. Levy, *Encyclopedia of the Reagan-Bush Years*, Westport, CT: Greenwood Press, 1996.

CENSURE. The U.S. Constitution gives the House and Senate authority to discipline their members for misconduct. Expulsion, censure, reprimand, condemnation, and denouncement have constituted the most common methods used for disciplining members. It requires a vote of two-thirds of the House to expel a representative and a vote of two-thirds of the Senate to expel a senator. In contrast for the House or Senate to censure, reprimand, or condemn one of its members only requires a vote of a simple majority of the House or Senate. Historically members of Congress have regarded censure as the second most serious punishment that the House or Senate may impose. The House and Senate have considered reprimand, condemnation, and denouncement as less serious forms of punishment.

Although the Constitution clearly gives the House and Senate the authority to censure their members, constitutional scholars generally agree that the Constitution does not give the House and Senate the authority to censure a member of the executive or judicial branches of the federal government. The Constitution only grants the House the authority to impeach and the Senate the authority to remove an employee or official of the executive or judicial branch. Only once in American history has Congress censured the president of the United States.

In 1832 Senator Henry Clay introduced a resolution to censure President Andrew Jackson for removing federal funds from the National Bank and then directing that those funds be deposited in state banks. They were bitter political enemies: Jackson had defeated Clay in the 1832 presidential election. Between 1829 and 1832, Andrew Jackson had made abolishing the National Bank his top priority. Strong opposition from Whig members of Congress had blocked Jackson's efforts. After Jackson's 1832 reelection, Whig members of Congress continued to oppose legislation closing down the National Bank. President Jackson then ordered Treasury Department officials to stop depositing federal receipts with the National Bank. Instead he directed that treasury officials place federal deposits in state banks. On March 28, 1834, by a vote of 26 to 20, the Senate voted to censure President Jackson. Jackson supporters regarded the Senate action as partisan politics at its worst. As a result Jackson supporters in Congress worked for years to have the censure expunged from the record. During January 1837 the Senate voted to expunge Jackson's censure from the Senate journal.

Early in September 1998, independent counsel **Kenneth Starr** filed a report with the House Judiciary Committee supporting the **impeachment** of President Bill Clinton for allegedly lying about his relationship with former White House intern **Monica Lewinsky** and for allegedly taking certain actions to obstruct and delay Kenneth Starr's investigation of the Clinton/Lewinsky affair. In response to the start of impeachment proceedings by the House Judiciary Committee, a number of members of the House and Senate suggested that the House censure President Clinton instead of proceeding with impeachment. Not surprisingly a large number of constitutional scholars sharply criticized the proposed censure remedy as not provided for by the Constitution. Subsequently the House voted to impeach President Clinton, and the Senate voted to acquit him on all articles of impeachment.

Related Entries: Dodd, Thomas J.; Jackson, Andrew

SUGGESTED READINGS: Congressional Quarterly, *Congressional Ethics: History, Facts, and Controversy*, Washington, DC: Congressional Quarterly, 1992; Juliet Eilperin, "New Calls on Hill to Censure Clinton; Impeachment Ruling Would Be Avoided," *Washington Post*, August 23, 1998, A10.

CENTER FOR PUBLIC INTEGRITY. The Center for Public Integrity, a Washington, D.C., nonprofit, nonpartisan research organization, was established in 1989 to conduct investigations of abuses of the public trust by political campaigns, government agencies, and public officials. It was founded by former network news producer Charles Lewis. From 1989 through the 1990s, the Center issued some thirty investigative reports examining the role of money in politics. For instance in 1996 the Center released the *Buying of the President* which detailed special interest political contributions to presidential campaigns of Republican Bob Dole and Democratic President Bill Clinton. During August 1996, the Center issued a report entitled *Fat Cat Hotel* which provided a comprehensive list of campaign donors given the opportunity by President Clinton to spend a night in the White House, including spending the night in the Lincoln bedroom, and in 1998, the Center published *The Buying of Congress* which argued that special interest campaign contributions to members of Congress had a direct impact on the outcome of the legislative process.

During June 1998, the John D. and Catherine T. MacArthur Foundation selected Charles Lewis as one of twenty-nine MacArthur fellows for 1998. Lewis received a $275,000 award with his selection. In making the award, the MacArthur Foundation cited the Center for Public Integrity for producing "high quality, high impact, public service journalism, releasing more than 30 influential investigative reports on issues related . . . to government accountability and public and private service ethics."

Related Entry: Campaign Finance Reform (Federal)

SUGGESTED READINGS: Kevin Merida, "Watchdog Group Founder Rewarded for His Bark; Charles Lewis Among 29 MacArthur Fellows," *Washington Post*, June 2, 1998,

D01; Web Link: Center for Public Integrity: URL: *http://www.publicintegrity.org/main. html.*

CENTER FOR RESPONSIVE POLITICS. The Center for Responsive Politics is a Washington, D.C.–based nonprofit organization established to promote campaign finance reform, open government, and the enforcement of whistle-blower protection laws. Print and broadcast news operations make frequent use of information provided by the center to supplement their coverage of the role of money in politics. The Center serves as a clearinghouse for federal and state campaign finance reform information and publishes an annual report on the Washington lobbying industry entitled *Influence, Inc.: The Bottom Line of Washington Lobbying.* The Center for Responsive Politics pioneered the use of the Internet to provide the media and public access to financial disclosure reports filed by lobbyists and political campaigns. It maintains an online version of the report which permits anyone with access to the Internet to access an industry-by-industry breakdown of lobbying expenditures. In addition the Center maintains a presidential election contribution and expenditure database which permits individuals to track fund-raising and expenditures by presidential primary and general election campaigns. Finally the Center provides a number of links to state sites.

Related Entry: Campaign Finance Reform (State)

SUGGESTED READINGS: Center for Responsive Politics: URL: *www.opensecrets.org*; Peter H. Stone, "Tracker on the Political Money Trail," *National Journal* 25 (November 13, 1993): 2734.

CERTIFICATE OF DIVESTITURE. The **Ethics Reform Act of 1989** included a provision granting the director of the **U.S. Office of Government Ethics** (USOGE) the authority to issue executive branch employees and officials certificates of divestiture to individuals required to sell financial assets to comply with federal conflict-of-interest laws and regulations. Congress enacted the certificate of divestiture after President Bush's Commission on Federal Ethics Law Reform strongly endorsed the proposal and after President Bush included a certificate of divestiture measure in ethics legislation sent to Congress during the spring of 1989.

As enacted the certificate of divestiture measure permitted federal employees, who are required to sell financial interests in order to comply with ethics rules, to apply to the director of the USOGE for a certificate of divestiture. Once granted a certificate of divestiture, federal employees may roll over the proceeds of the sale of a financial asset into a widely held financial instrument such as a mutual fund and defer paying any capital gain taxes resulting from the sale of the asset.

For example, a newly confirmed secretary of defense owns 100,000 shares of stock in a major defense contractor. The director of the Office of Government Ethics orders the defense secretary to sell his stock in the defense contractor.

The secretary's accountant informs him that he will owe $100,000 in capital gains taxes. The secretary receives a certificate of divestiture from the director of the USOGE. The secretary then directs his financial advisor to place the proceeds from his stock sale into a widely held mutual fund.

Related Entries: Ethics Reform Act of 1989; Financial Conflict of Interest Prohibition.

SUGGESTED READINGS: Robert Roberts and Marion T. Doss, *From Watergate to Whitewater: The Public Integrity War*, Westport, CT: Praeger, 1997; Robert N. Roberts, Marion T. Doss Jr., and Scott J. Hammond, "Lobbyists Beware: The Rise of the Illegal-Gratuity Statute," *Journal of Social, Political and Economic Studies* 21 (Winter 1996): 383–430.

CHAPPAQUIDDICK SCANDAL. On the night of July 16, 1969, while returning from a party, U.S. Senator Edward M. Kennedy (D-Mass.) drove his car off a bridge located on Chappaquiddick Island. Senator Kennedy succeeded in getting out of his car, but his passenger, twenty-eight-year-old Mary Jo Kopechne, drowned. Shortly after the accident, the public learned that Kennedy did not notify the police until the morning after the accident. Police divers found Kopechne's body in the submerged car. Although law enforcement officials did not file criminal charges against Kennedy for the accident, the circumstances surrounding the accident ended speculation that Kennedy might challenge Richard Nixon for the presidency in 1972. The scandal did not end Kennedy's political career: through the 1970s, 1980s, and 1990s, Massachusetts voters continued to return Kennedy to the U.S. Senate. Today, decades later, controversy still continues over the facts surrounding the accident.

SUGGESTED READINGS: Michael Beschloss, "Chappaquiddick's Echoes; The 'Character Issue' Has Never Stopped," *New Yorker*, July 25, 1994, 4–6; Leo Damore, *Senatorial Privilege: The Chappaquiddick Cover-up*, Washington, DC: Regnery Gateway, 1988.

"CHECKERS" SPEECH. On September 18, 1952, the *New York Post* reported that a group of wealthy California businessmen had given Senator Richard M. Nixon, the Republican vice presidential nominee, some $16,000 in gifts and favors since Nixon had become senator. The headline of the *New York Post* read "Secret Rich Men's Trust Fund Keeps Nixon in Style Far Beyond His Salary." The disclosure set off a firestorm. Prior to the disclosure, the Republican Party attempted to make the ethics record of the Truman administration a major campaign issue. From 1949 through the end of 1952, the so-called Truman scandals created untold problems for the Truman White House.

Not surprisingly major newspapers across the country published editorials calling for Nixon to withdraw from the Republican ticket. Within the Republican Party, growing calls for Nixon to withdraw from the ticket threatened Nixon's future in American politics. To the surprise of many political observers who had already written Nixon's political obituary, Nixon decided to go on nationwide television to plead for his political survival. Up until 1952 few politicians had made use of television to make a case to the voters.

In his September 23, 1952, television address Nixon portrayed himself as an honest public servant with few financial resources. Nixon argued that the California businessmen had made legal campaign contributions to his Senate campaign fund and that he had not used any of the money to cover personal expenses. Equally significant Nixon succeeded in painting a picture of a family who had made major sacrifices to enable Nixon to serve the nation. "I should say this, that Pat doesn't have a mink coat. . . . But she does have a respectable Republican cloth coat, and I always tell her she would look good in anything." The most effective part of the speech involved Nixon's explanation of his acceptance of a dog for his family. Nixon explained, "A man down in Texas heard Pat on the radio mention that our two youngsters would like to have a dog, and, believe it or not, the day before this campaign trip we got a message from Union Station in Baltimore, saying they had a package for us. We went down to get it. You know what it was? It was a little cocker spaniel dog, in a crate that he had sent all the way from Texas, black and white, spotted, and our little girl Tricia, the six-year-old, named it Checkers. And you know, the kids, loved the dog, and I just want to say this, right now, that regardless of what they say about it, we are going to keep it."

Although serious questions remained whether Nixon improperly used the contributions to pay personal expenses, the speech produced an entirely unexpected positive response from viewers. The speech persuaded Republican presidential candidate Dwight Eisenhower to keep Nixon on the 1952 presidential ticket.

Related Entry: Eisenhower Administration Ethics Controversies

SUGGESTED READINGS: David Frier, *Conflict of Interest in the Eisenhower Administration*. Ames: Iowa State University Press, 1969; Web Link: The History Place: Great Speeches: Richard M. Nixon. "Checkers Speech," URL: *http://www.historyplace.com/speeches/nixon-checkers.htm*.

CHRISTY, ARTHUR. *See* Independent Counsel Investigations; Jordan, Hamilton.

CISNEROS, HENRY G. (June 11, 1947–   ). Secretary of housing and urban development, 1993–1996.

Early in 1993 President Bill Clinton nominated Henry Cisneros as secretary of the Department of Housing and Urban Development (HUD). Prior to being nominated, Cisneros served as mayor of San Antonio, Texas. During March 1987 Cisneros began an extramarital affair with Linda Medlar (now Linda Jones), a political fund-raiser. The affair ended in 1989, and Cisneros subsequently reconciled with his wife.

At the time the Clinton White House nominated Cisneros as secretary of HUD, the affair had become widely known in San Antonio, Texas. As part of the routine FBI background check for presidential nominees, the FBI asked Cisneros about his relationship with Jones. Cisneros told investigators that he had paid Jones no more than $10,000 a year and that he had ended the payments. During late 1994 reports surfaced that Cisneros paid Jones much more than the amount revealed to the FBI. After a request by Attorney General **Janet Reno**, on May 25, 1995, a special three-judge federal appellate court appointed David Barrett as an independent counsel to investigate the allegation that Cisneros had made false statements to the FBI about payments he had made to his former mistress. On November 20, 1996, Cisneros resigned from the Clinton cabinet to become the president of Univision, a large Spanish-language television network.

In December 1997 a federal **grand jury** indicted Cisneros on eighteen felony counts of conspiracy, false statements, and obstruction of justice. The grand jury also indicted Jones and two former employees of a Texas communications company that Cisneros ran prior to becoming HUD secretary. The indictment was for lying to federal investigators during his background investigation. In late March 1998, a federal judge sentenced Linda Jones to three and one-half years in prison for conspiracy and bank fraud. Although not directly related to the Cisneros indictment, the prison sentence persuaded Jones to cooperate with Barrett's independent counsel investigation of Cisneros. On September 7, 1999, Cisneros pleaded guilty to a single misdemeanor charge of lying to the FBI regarding payments he made to his former mistress. As part of the plea agreement, Cisneros agreed to pay a $10,000 fine. Equally significant the agreement did not require that Cisneros serve any time in prison or be put on probation.

Not surprisingly the media saw the agreement as a victory for former HUD secretary Henry Cisneros and a major defeat for independent counsel David M. Barrett. The Cisneros investigation lasted four years and cost taxpayers more than $9 million. On January 20, 2001, shortly before leaving office, President Clinton pardoned Cisneros

Related Entries: Clinton Administration Ethics Controversies; False Statements Accountability Act of 1996; Independent Counsel Investigations

SUGGESTED READINGS: Toni Locy, "Court Appoints D.C. Lawyer as Special Counsel in Cisneros Case," *Washington Post*, May 25, 1995, A8; Bill Miller, "Cisneros Pleads Guilty to Lying to FBI Agents: $9 Million Probe Yields Fine, No Jail," *Washington Post*, September 8, 1999, A01.

CIVIL SERVICE REFORM. *See* Pendleton Act of 1883

CIVIL SERVICE REFORM ACT OF 1883. *See* Pendleton Act of 1883

CLEVELAND, GROVER. (March 18, 1837–June 24, 1908). President of the United States, 1885–1889; Second Term, 1893–1897. *See* Election of 1884

CLINTON, HILLARY RODHAM (October 26, 1947–). First Lady of the United States, 1993–2001; U.S. Senator, 2001– .

Born in Chicago, Illinois, on October 26, 1947, Hillary Rodham Clinton entered Wellesley College in 1965. After graduation she attended Yale Law School from 1969 through 1973. While attending Yale Law School, she met Bill Clinton, another Yale Law School student. In 1974 she served on the staff of the House Judiciary Committee while the committee considered the **impeachment** of President Richard Nixon. That same year she moved to Arkansas and married Bill Clinton in 1975. A short time after arriving in Arkansas, she joined the Rose law firm and later became a partner. In 1978 Bill and Hillary Rodham established the Whitewater Development Corporation with Little Rock, Arkansas, friends **Susan McDougal** and **Jim McDougal** to develop a tract of land for vacation and retirement homes.

In 1985, **James McDougal** hired the Rose Law Firm to represent Madison Guaranty Savings and Loan with respect to various legal problems related to the worsening financial condition of the savings and loan. Hillary Rodham Clinton billed Madison Guaranty for some 60 hours of work. In 1989, Madison Guaranty failed, costing federal taxpayers tens of millions of dollars. Early in 1991, Arkansas Governor Bill Clinton announced his intention to run for the Democratic presidential nomination. During late March of 1992, a report appeared in the *New York Times* raising questions of a possible relationship between the failure of Madison Guaranty and the **Whitewater** Development Corporation. After the article, the Clinton campaign reported that the Clintons lost some $60,000 as the result of the failure of the development. Bill Clinton went on to win the 1996 presidential election. In May 1993, the White House announced the firing of seven employees of the White House **travel office** due to suspicions of financial improprieties in the operation of the office. Following the firings, a major controversy erupted over whether Hillary Rodham Clinton and other White House officials might have orchestrated the firing.

Early in January 1994, Attorney General **Janet Reno** appointed **Robert Fiske Jr.** to serve as the Justice Department's Whitewater special counsel. Fiske immediately began an investigation into whether the failure of the Whitewater Development Corporation played a role in the 1989 failure of Madison Guaranty Savings and Loan. After Congress voted to renew the independent counsel law, a special federal appeals panel appointed **Kenneth Starr** as the Whitewater **independent counsel**. As part of his investigation, Starr subpoenaed Hillary Clinton's Rose Law Firm billing records. However, Clinton was unable to locate the records. On January 4, 1996, White House officials found her billing records on a table in the White House residence. On January 26, 1996, Clinton testified before a federal **grand jury** that she did not know how the records appeared. Then, in April 1998, she again testified before the Whitewater grand jury. Early in 2000, Hillary Rodham Clinton announced her intention to run for the U.S. Senate from New York State.

On June 22, 2000, independent counsel Robert Ray announced his decision not to seek an indictment of Hillary Rodham Clinton for making false statements regarding her involvement in the 1993 firings of White House travel office employees. In announcing his decision, Ray concluded that insufficient evidence existed to prove beyond a reasonable doubt that Mrs. Clinton made false statements regarding her role in the travel office firings. On September 20, 2000, Ray concluded the six-year Whitewater investigation by announcing that the investigation had failed to develop sufficient evidence to prove that the Clintons engaged in any unlawful conduct related to the Whitewater development and other business dealings in the 1970s and 1980s. In November 2000, the voters of New York elected Hillary Rodham Clinton to the U.S. Senate.

Related Entries: Whitewater Investigation; Travel Office Firings

SUGGESTED READINGS: Kathy Kiely, "Ray criticizes, won't prosecute Independent counsel says he doesn't have evidence to persuade a jury Clinton perjured herself in travel firings," *USA Today*, June 23, 2000, A4; Bill Miller, "Probe of Clintons' Land Deal Is Closed," *Washington Post*, September 21, 2000, A1.

CLINTON, WILLIAM JEFFERSON (BILL). (August 19, 1946–). President of the United States, 1993–2001. *See* Clinton Administration Ethics Controversies; Election of 1996; Whitewater Investigation

CLINTON ADMINISTRATION ETHICS CONTROVERSIES. From almost the time former Arkansas governor Bill Clinton announced his intention to run for the 1992 Democratic presidential nomination through the end of his second term in January 2001, President Bill Clinton, **Hillary Rodham Clinton**, and members of the Clinton administration faced a number of congressional, Justice Department, and independent counsel investigations of alleged improper or illegal acts. The series of ethics controversies culminated in Clinton's Senate **impeachment** trial during January and February of 1999 for perjury and obstruction related to President Clinton's efforts to conceal his relationship with former White House intern and White House employee **Monica Lewinsky**.

Late in January 1992, former Little Rock, Arkansas, television reporter and Arkansas state employee **Gennifer Flowers** alleged in a national tabloid that she had had a twelve-year extramarital affair with Arkansas Governor Bill Clinton. In March 1992 the first articles appeared in the press raising questions about Bill and Hillary Rodham Clinton's failed **Whitewater** land development investment. The same period also saw questions raised about how Bill Clinton obtained permission to enter the Arkansas national guard after receiving a draft notice. Despite questions raised by these stories, Bill Clinton easily won the Democratic presidential nomination and defeated Republican incumbent President George Bush and Reform Party candidate H. Ross Perot in the general election.

Then in the early months of 1993, the Clinton White House found itself forced to withdraw the nominations of attorney general nominees **Zoe Baird** and **Kimba Wood** after both nominees revealed they had failed to pay Social Se-

President Bill Clinton delivers the State of the Union address, January 19, 1999. The White House

curity withholding taxes for undocumented immigrant household employees. President Clinton's third attorney general nominee, Miami prosecutor **Janet Reno**, easily won Senate confirmation.

In early May 1993, the White House announced the firing of the seven employees of the White House travel office on the grounds of gross financial mismanagement. Within days of the **travel office firings**, media reports raised serious questions regarding the reasons for the dismissals. In early July 1993, the White House issued a report sharply criticizing a number of White House staff members involved in the firings. Late in December 1995, a U.S. District Court jury found the former director of the travel office not guilty of embezzlement. In March 1996 testimony before a House committee investigating the travel office firing, a former White House aide testified that Hillary Rodham Clinton and former deputy White House Counsel **Vincent Foster** pressured him to fire the travel office staff. Prior to the testimony, Hillary Rodham Clinton denied that she ever directed the firing of the travel office staff. Faced with the conflicting testimony of Hillary Rodham Clinton and former White House aide David Watkins, Attorney General Janet Reno asked a special federal three-judge appeals panel to give Whitewater independent counsel the authority to determine whether David Watkins had lied in his congressional testimony regarding Hillary Clinton's involvement in the travel office firings.

Besides the Zoe Baird and Kimba Wood confirmation problems and the travel office controversy, by January 1994 President Clinton found himself under intense pressure to request the appointment of a special counsel to conduct a full investigation of the Whitewater Development Corporation. At President Clinton's request, Attorney General Janet Reno appointed New York lawyer **Robert Fiske Jr.** as the Justice Department Whitewater special counsel. Attorney General Reno also requested that Fiske investigate the circumstances of the July 1993 apparent suicide of deputy White House Counsel Vincent Foster.

In March 1994 **Webster Hubbell** resigned as associate attorney general. A short time after Hubbell's resignation, it became known that Hubbell faced a criminal investigation for allegedly overbilling clients of the Little Rock, Arkansas, Rose Law Firm. Like Hillary Clinton, Webster Hubbell had served as a partner in the Rose law firm prior to joining the Justice Department. In December 1994, Hubbell pled guilty to one count each of mail fraud and tax evasion related to the alleged overbilling of Rose Law Firm clients. On June 28, 1995, a federal judge sentenced Hubbell to 21 months in federal prison for his actions.

Early in August 1994, a special three-judge federal appeals panel appointed **Kenneth Starr** as the Whitewater independent counsel. Prior to the appointment, President Clinton had signed into law a new **independent counsel act**. Congress had allowed the independent counsel law to expire in 1991 in the midst of the **Iran-contra** investigation. From August 1994 through the end of President Bill Clinton's second term in January 2001, Whitewater independent counsels Kenneth Starr and Robert W. Ray pursued issues related to the Whitewater Development, the failure of **James McDougal**'s Madison Guaranty savings and loan, and the Monica Lewinsky affair.

On May 6, 1994, former Arkansas state employee **Paula Jones** filed suit against President Clinton alleging that on May 6, 1991, then–Arkansas governor Bill Clinton engaged in "willful, outrageous and malicious conduct" at the Little Rock, Arkansas Excelsior Hotel by "sexually harassing and assaulting" her. Earlier, President Clinton had hired Washington lawyer **Robert Bennett** to defend him from the expected lawsuit.

On September 9, 1994, a three-judge federal appeals panel named Los Angeles Attorney Donald Smaltz to determine whether Secretary of Agriculture **Mike Espy** had violated any federal laws by allegedly accepting gifts from companies regulated by the Department of Agriculture. On December 2, 1998, a U.S. District Court jury found former Agriculture Secretary Espy not guilty of accepting $35,000 in illegal gifts. Espy had resigned as agriculture secretary in October 1994 to spend full time fighting the allegations. In the course of the investigation, independent counsel Smaltz obtained guilty pleas from a number of companies for providing Espy with **illegal gratuities**.

In March 1995 a special three-judge federal appeals panel appointed David Barrett to investigate whether Secretary of Housing and Urban Development **Henry Cisneros** made false statements to FBI agents regarding the amount of payments Cisneros made to a woman he had an extramarital relationship with while he served as major of San Antonio, Texas. Cisneros had acknowledged the affair a number of years prior to being nominated as secretary of housing and urban development. In September 1999 Cisneros pled guilty to a single count, and agreed to pay a $10,000 fine. On January 20, 2001, shortly before leaving office, President Bill Clinton pardoned Henry Cisneros.

On July 6, 1995, a special three-judge panel appointed Miami lawyer Daniel Pearson to investigate whether **Ronald Brown** violated federal law when a business partner paid Brown some $400,000 for Brown's share of a business venture. In April 1996 independent counsel Daniel Pearson ended his investigation after Brown died in a crash of a military transport on a mountainside near the Croatian city of Dubrovnik while on a trade mission directed at helping the war-torn area recover from years of armed strife.

In late spring 1996, a controversy erupted over White House requests for FBI background files. Reports surfaced that the White House security office had obtained hundreds of **FBI files** for former members of the Reagan and Bush administrations. The White House security office had responsibility for approving security passes for frequent White House visitors. The White House subsequently claimed that a bureaucratic mistake led to director of personnel security Craig Livingstone and Livingstone's aide Anthony Marcceca to improperly obtain hundreds of FBI background files on former Republican appointees to the Bush and Reagan administrations. Late in June 1996, a three-judge federal appeals panel gave independent counsel Kenneth Starr authority to investigate whether former White House officials made false statements to the FBI regarding the reasons they needed access to FBI files on former members of the Reagan and Bush administrations.

In late October 1996, **Common Cause** filed a complaint with the **Federal Election Commission** alleging that the Republican National Committee and Democratic National Committee had violated provisions of the **Federal Election Campaign Act** by using millions of dollars in **soft money** to pay for **issue ads** used to support the election of Democratic President Bill Clinton and Republican presidential candidate Bob Dole. In the aftermath of the presidential **election of 1996**, allegations flew over alleged illegal fund-raising by President Clinton and Vice President Albert Gore. In 1997 Attorney General Janet Reno ruled that Vice President Gore and President Clinton had not violated provisions of the 1883 **Pendleton Act** by making campaign fund-raising calls from the White House. Reno also ruled that President Clinton had not violated any law by hosting White House coffees for potential campaign contributors and by providing potential campaign contributors with the opportunity to spend a night in the White House Lincoln bedroom. Throughout 1997 and 1998, Attorney General Reno rejected calls to appoint independent counsels to investigate possible wrongdoing by President Clinton and Vice President Gore.

In November 1996 a three-judge appeals panel appointed Curtis Von Kann to investigate an allegation that Eli Segal had violated federal law by helping a private group raise funds while Segal headed AmeriCorps, the National Service Organization. Segal helped to establish a private group, Partnership for National Service, to help raise private funds to support the goals of AmeriCorps. In

August 1997 independent counsel Von Kann ruled that Segal had not violated any federal laws and that he had not profited personally from the establishment of the group.

In early January 1998, President Clinton appeared at a deposition related to the Paula Jones sexual harassment lawsuit. At the deposition lawyers representing Paula Jones asked President Clinton whether he ever had sexual relations with former White House intern and White House employee Monica Lewinsky. Clinton denied ever having sex with Lewinsky. Within days of the deposition, *Newsweek* broke the story of the alleged relationship between President Clinton and Lewinsky. *Newsweek* had gained access to tapes made by Department of Defense employee **Linda Tripp** in which Lewinsky had provided Tripp with details of her ongoing, intimate relationship with President Clinton. A three-judge federal appeals panel subsequently granted Whitewater independent counsel Kenneth Starr the authority to determine whether President Clinton or other individuals had violated any law in their efforts to conceal President Clinton's relationship with Lewinsky.

On March 19, 1998, a three-judge appeals panel appointed Carol Bruce Elder to investigate whether Secretary of Interior **Bruce Babbitt** provided false testimony to a congressional committee regarding the reasons why the Department of Interior, in 1995, turned down a license for a proposed Indian gambling casino in Hudson, Wisconsin. Prior to the naming of independent counsel Elder, a Wisconsin tribe had alleged in a civil suit challenging the Interior Department's decision that political pressure by another Indian tribe had played a role in the 1995 Interior Department decision. Specifically, the suit alleged that a tribe that already operated a gambling casino pressured the Interior Department to turn down the license request. Campaign finance records indicated that in 1996 the tribe opposed to the license gave $360,000 to the Democratic Party after the Interior Department's decision to turn down the license. On October 13, 1999, independent counsel Elder announced that she did not intend to seek any criminal indictments arising out of her investigation.

On May 26, 1998, a three-judge appeals panel appointed Maine lawyer Ralph I. Lancaster Jr. to investigate whether Secretary of Labor Alexis Herman, while serving as a White House aide in 1994, solicited illegal campaign contributions for the Democratic Party and demanded a kickback before she would help a friend obtain an FCC license for a satellite phone system. On April 5, 2000, independent counsel Lancaster announced that he would not seek an indictment of Labor Secretary Herman.

Early in September 1998, independent counsel Starr forwarded his Lewinsky report to the House. The report argued that President Clinton had committed a number of impeachable offenses related to his efforts to conceal his relationship with Monica Lewinsky. On December 19, 1998, the House of Representatives voted two articles of impeachment related to President Clinton's alleged efforts to conceal his relationship with Lewinsky. The first impeachment article charged

President Clinton with perjury before the Lewinsky **grand jury**. The second article charged President Clinton with obstruction of justice. On February 12, 1999, the Senate found the President not guilty of both impeachment articles.

The Senate acquittal of President Clinton on perjury and obstruction of justice charges did not end independent counsel Kenneth Starr's various investigations or the Justice Department investigation of alleged campaign fund-raising abuses during the 1996 presidential campaign. On March 13, 2000, independent counsel Robert W. Ray announced that his office did not intend to seek any indictments related to the FBI files matter. A special federal judicial panel had appointed Ray as the Whitewater independent counsel after Starr resigned as independent counsel late in August 2000. On June 22, 2000, Ray announced that his office did not intend to seek the indictment of Hillary Rodham Clinton for making false statements regarding her involvement with the White House Travel Office firings. Then on June 30, 2000, the Arkansas Supreme Court Committee on Professional Conduct filed a complaint requesting the disbarment of Bill Clinton. The complaint alleged that President Clinton had lied about his relationship with Monica Lewinsky in his January 1998 deposition in the Paula Jones sexual harassment lawsuit. In late-August 2000, Attorney General Janet Reno declined to appoint a Justice Department special counsel to investigate allegations that Vice President Albert Gore had not told the truth about his fund-raising activities.

On Wednesday, September 20, 2000, Ray ended the six-year Whitewater investigation. In a six-page statement, he announced that the investigation uncovered insufficient evidence "to prove to a jury beyond a reasonable doubt that either President or Mrs. Clinton knowingly participated in any criminal conduct." Then, on January 20, 2001, Independent Counsel Robert Ray ended his Monica Lewinsky investigation after President Clinton admitted to unintentionally making false statements during proceedings related to Lewinsky.

Related Entries: Babbitt, Bruce; Baird, Zoe; Brown, Ronald; Cisneros, Henry G.; Election of 1996; Espy, Mike; FBI Files Flap; Flowers, Gennifer; Foster, Vincent; Hubbell, Webster; Jones, Paula; Lewinsky, Monica; Lincoln Bedroom Fund-raising Controversy; Ray, Robert; Starr, Kenneth; Travel Office Firings; Wood, Kimba; Whitewater Investigation

SUGGESTED READINGS: Peter Baker, *The Breach: Inside the Impeachment and Trial of William Jefferson Clinton*, New York: Scribner, 2000; Bill Miller, "Probe of Clintons' Land Deal Is Closed," *Washington Post*, September 21, 2000, A1; Susan Schmidt and Michael Weisskopf, *Truth at Any Cost: Ken Starr and the Unmaking of Bill Clinton*, New York: HarperCollins, 2000; Bob Woodward, *Shadow: Five Presidents and the Legacy of Watergate*, New York: Simon & Schuster, 1999.

CLINTON V JONES, **520 U.S. 681 (1997).** On February 11, 1994, **Paula Jones** held a news conference alleging that on May 8, 1991, Arkansas Governor Bill Clinton made a sexual advance to her in a Little Rock, Arkansas, hotel room. At the time, the Arkansas Industrial Development Commission employed Paula Jones as an office assistant. In early May 1994, the White House announced that Clinton had hired prominent Washington attorney **Robert S. Bennett** to defend President Clinton from a possible sexual harassment lawsuit initiated by Jones. On May 6, 1994, Jones brought suit in Federal District Court in Little Rock, Arkansas, alleging that Clinton had violated her civil rights.

Through the remainder of 1994, the Clinton defense team sought to have the Jones suit dismissed or delayed until Clinton left office. In December 1994 U.S. District Judge **Susan Webber Wright** ruled that the Jones lawsuit could not go forward until Clinton left office. However, Judge Wright ruled that the Jones lawyers had the right to proceed with the process of taking depositions from witnesses. In January 1996 the U.S. Court of Appeals for the Fifth Circuit held that the Constitution did not prohibit the Jones lawsuit from proceeding while Bill Clinton served as president because the alleged "unofficial acts" took place before Clinton became president of the United States.

On May 27, 1997, the Supreme Court ruled by a vote of 9 to 0 that the Constitution did not grant President Clinton immunity from private civil damage lawsuits arising out of matters that involved personal conduct. Equally important the high court held that the separation of powers doctrine did not require that the Federal District Court delay the trial until after President Clinton left office. In the 1982 decision of *Nixon v Fitzgerald*, the Supreme Court had granted President Richard Nixon absolute immunity from a civil suit resulting from the performance of his official duties. However, the high court gave Judge Wright the authority to delay the trial if President Clinton made a sufficient showing that a trial would make it difficult to perform his official duties. Subsequently Judge Wright ordered President Clinton to submit to questioning by lawyers representing Jones. In January 1998 lawyers representing Jones questioned President Clinton in the Washington offices of Robert Bennett, Clinton's lawyer. Jones's lawyer spent most of the deposition questioning President Clinton about an alleged relationship with former White House intern **Monica Lewinsky**. Within days of the deposition, the story of the alleged relationship between Lewinsky and President Clinton became a topic of worldwide attention. A short time later, a special three-judge panel granted the Whitewater independent counsel authority to investigate whether President Clinton violated any laws in his effort to conceal his relationship with Lewinsky.

On April 1, 1998, U.S. District Judge Webber Wright dismissed the Paula Jones civil suit. In her ruling Judge Wright found that Jones failed to provide any evidence that President Clinton or anyone in Arkansas state government punished Jones for her rejection of the alleged sexual advances by Bill Clinton. Paula Jones then appealed the decision to the U.S. Court of Appeals for the Fifth Circuit. On November 14, 1998, lawyers representing Paula Jones announced a settlement of the Jones civil suit. President Clinton agreed to pay Jones $850,000 to settle the suit. The settlement did not require President Clinton to apologize or admit to any wrongdoing. On April 12, 1999, Judge Webber Wright issued an order finding President Bill Clinton in contempt of court for answering questions in a manner "designed to obstruct" the lawsuit.

Related Entries: Impeachment Proceedings; Jones, Paula; Lewinsky, Monica

SUGGESTED READINGS: Peter Baker, "Jones v. Clinton Suit Dismissed; Judge Finds 'No Genuine Issues for Trial,' " *Washington Post*, April 2, 1998, A1; Joan Biskupic, "From Nixon to Clinton: The Jones Decision Has a Watergate Precedent," *Washington Post*, June 1, 1997, C01; *Clinton v Jones* (1997) *http://laws.findlaw.com/US/000/95–1853.html*; Frank J. Murray, "Clinton Will Pay Jones $850,000 to Settle Suit; Deal Doesn't Force Him to Apologize," *Washington Times*, November 14, 1998, A1; Roberto Suro and Joan Biskupic, "Judge Finds Clinton in Contempt of Court, Wright Says Answers in Jones Civil Suit Were 'Designed to Obstruct,' " *Washington Post*, April 13, 1999, A1.

CODE OF ETHICS FOR FEDERAL EMPLOYEES AND OFFICIALS. Codes of ethics for government employees and officials have a long history in the United States. **Amos Kendall**, postmaster general of the United States from 1829 to 1840, issued a strict code of conduct for postal employees. Kendall's ethics code established a long list of rules governing the work habits, office conduct, use of government property, and personal conduct of postal service employees. Between 1840 and the passage of the **Pendleton Act of 1883**, the presidents and Congress generally left it up to federal agencies and departments to establish standards of conduct for federal employees and officials. However, between 1883 and 1940, Congress enacted a number of measures designed to limit the political activities of federal employees and officials. In addition to establishing a new federal merit system and creating the Civil Service Commission, the Pendleton Act prohibited the practice of requiring federal employees to pay **political assessments** to political candidates or parties. In 1939 Congress enacted the Hatch Act which prohibited most federal employees from engaging in partisan political activities, including running for public office.

Between 1949 and 1960, a series of **Truman administration ethics controversies** and **Eisenhower administration ethics controversies** highlighted serious gaps in federal ethics laws and regulations. In 1958 by a concurrent resolution, Congress adopted a Code of Ethics for Government Service for all federal employees and officials. Although the 1958 ethics code did not include any penalties for violations, the new code directed all federal employees and officials from engaging in any conduct that might raise questions regarding the objectivity or impartiality of the employee or official. For instance the Code directed federal employees and officials never to "discriminate unfairly by dispensing of special favors or privileges to anyone, whether for remuneration or not, and never accept, for self or family favors or benefits under circumstances which might be construed by reasonable persons as influencing the performance of governmental duties."

Shortly after taking office, President John Kennedy instituted a government-wide rule of the federal ethics program. On May 5, 1961, President Kennedy issued **Executive Order 10939**, To Provide a Guide on Ethical Standards to Government Officials. The order established a new code of ethics for high-level presidential appointees. President Kennedy later extended the new ethics code to all federal employees and officials. The new code dealt with a number of conflict-of-interest issues, including the acceptance of gifts and misuse of non-public information. On May 9, 1965, President Lyndon Johnson issued **Executive Order 11222**, Prescribing Standards of Ethical Conduct for Government Officers and Employees. Besides keeping in place the key restrictions of the Kennedy ethics directive, the Johnson order required thousands of executive branch employees and officials to file annual confidential financial disclosure statements.

Between 1965 and 1989, Presidents Nixon, Ford, Carter, and Reagan did not modify the provisions of Executive Order 11222. On April 12, 1989, President George Bush issued **Executive Order 12674**, Principles of Ethical Conduct for Government Officers and Employees. Although the Bush ethics directive replaced the 1965 Johnson ethics directive, it generally left in place rules governing financial conflicts of interest, acceptance of gifts, outside employment, and misuse of nonpublic information for personal financial gain. In 1992 the **U.S. Office of Government Ethics** issued detailed regulations implementing the Bush ethics directive. For the first time, the comprehensive ethics regulations gave detailed guidance regarding a host of common ethics problems commonly faced by federal employees and officials.

Related Entries: Bush Administration Ethics Reform Program; Executive Order 10939; Executive Order 11222; Executive Order 12674; Kennedy Administration Ethics Reform Program

SUGGESTED READINGS: Robert Roberts, *White House Ethics: The History of the Politics of Conflict of Interest Regulation*, Westport, CT: Greenwood Press, 1988; Robert Roberts and Marion T. Doss, *From Watergate to Whitewater: The Public Integrity War*, Westport, CT: Greenwood Press, 1997; United States Office of Government Ethics, *www.usoge.gov*.

COLFAX, SCHUYLER. *See* Credit Mobilier Scandal

COLSON, CHARLES W. (1932–). Special counsel to President Richard Nixon, 1969–1973.

Charles Colson served as special counsel to President Richard Nixon from 1969 to 1973. He became one of the key figures in the **Watergate scandal**. During Colson's four years in the White House, he became known as one of the toughest members of Nixon's White House staff. In 1976 Colson served seven months in prison for conspiracy and obstruction of justice. After being released from prison, Charles Colson established the Prison Foundation to bring Christian ministries into prisons in the United States. Later Colson's foundation established volunteer prison ministries in some fifty-four other countries. In 1993 Charles Colson received the Templeton Prize for Progress in Religion worth some $939,575. Colson donated the prize to the Prison Foundation. Besides establishing the Prison Foundation, Charles Colson has authored a number of books on religion in American society.

Related Entry: Watergate Scandal

SUGGESTED READING: Charles Colson, *Born Again*, Old Tappan, NJ: Chosen Books, 1976.

COMMITTEE ON STANDARDS OF OFFICIAL CONDUCT. The Constitution grants to the House and Senate responsibility for disciplining members for misconduct. Prior to the 1960s, the House and Senate lacked specific procedures for investigating allegations of misconduct by members. In 1967, in the aftermath of the 1966 expulsion of **Adam Clayton Powell**, the House of Representatives established a new twelve-member, bipartisan standing Committee on Standards of Official Conduct. Today the committee consists of ten members equally divided between Republicans and Democrats.

Besides conducting investigations of alleged violations of House rules, the committee provides House members with expert assistance with respect to House ethics rules and public financial disclosure requirements. This includes publishing and maintaining the House Ethics Manual.

Related Entries: Gingrich, Newt; Mills, Wilbur; Wright, Jim

SUGGESTED READINGS: Committee on Standards of Official Conduct. United States House of Representatives. URL. *http://www.house.gov/ethics/*; Dennis F. Thompson, *Ethics in Congress: From Individual to Institutional Corruption*, Washington, DC: Brookings Institution, 1995.

COMMON CAUSE. In 1970 a group of concerned citizens established Common Cause after growing increasingly concerned over the direction of the nation's political system. In particular it focused its energy on lobbying Congress to enact **campaign finance reform** in an effort to try to control the role of money in politics. Common Cause played a major role in persuading Congress to pass the **Federal Election Campaign Act of 1971** which established new campaign contribution limits and placed limits on campaign expenditure limits on candidates for the House and Senate. After the August 1973 resignation of President Richard M. Nixon, Common Cause lobbied heavily for the passage of **Federal Election Campaign Act Amendments of 1974** which established the **Federal Election Commission**.

In 1975, Common Cause turned its lobbying efforts to federal ethics reform. Through the first half of the 1970s, it had joined with other public interest groups to sharply criticize the so-called **"revolving door"** problem. In a series of studies, Common Cause sharply criticized a number of federal regulatory agencies and commissions for hiring officials from companies regulated by these regulatory agencies. The reports also criticized former employees and officials of these regulatory agencies and commissions for going to work for companies regulated by their former government agencies. Common Cause argued federal regulatory agencies that employed large numbers of individuals who worked previously for regulated companies tended to favor regulatory policies favorable to the companies and industries they regulated. In addition to pushing for new laws prohibiting lobbying by former federal employees and officials, it strongly supported public financial disclosure for high-level federal employees and officials, including all members of Congress and federal judges and provisions for the appointment of special prosecutors to investigate allegations of possible criminal wrongdoing by high-level executive branch officials. In 1978 Congress passed the **Ethics in Government Act of 1978** which included provisions for the appointment of independent counsels to investigate allegations of criminal conduct by high-level executive branch officials, public financial disclosure by high-level officials in the three branches of the federal government, and new restrictions on the postemployment activities of former federal officials and employees.

From 1982 through the end of the second term of President Reagan, Common Cause called for **independent counsel investigations** of a number of high-level Reagan administration officials. Independent counsels subsequently conducted lengthy investigations of White House counselor and Attorney General **Edwin Meese III**, former Reagan White House aides **Michael Deaver** and **Lyn Nofziger** and a number of Reagan administration officials as part of independent counsel's **Lawrence Walsh**'s **Iran-contra** investigation.

In the late 1980s, Common Cause turned its attention to lobbying Congress to prohibit representatives and senators from the widespread practice of accepting **honorariums** for giving speeches or for attending conferences. In late 1989 President George Bush signed into law the **Ethics Reform Act** which prohibited House members from accepting honorariums. In return for agreeing to ban honorariums, President George Bush signed into law a large pay increase for House members. In 1991 the Senate voted to prohibit senators from accepting honorariums. A short time after the decision, President Bush signed into law legislation raising the salary of senators to the same level as House members.

In 1988 Common Cause joined with House Republicans to demand an investigation of Democratic Speaker of the House **Jim Wright** for alleged financial improprieties. Despite denying that he had intentionally violated House ethics rules, on May 31, 1989, Speaker Wright announced his decision to resign from Congress. In October 1989 Common Cause requested that the Senate Ethics Committee and Justice Department investigate five U.S. senators for contacting federal savings and loan regulators on behalf of Charles Keating, the owner of a financially troubled California savings and loan. Each senator had received campaign contributions from Keating. The 1990 **Keating Five** investigation raised serious questions about the role of senators in helping constituents resolve problems with federal regulatory agencies.

In 1994 Republican Speaker of the House **Newt Gingrich** found himself the subject of ethics complaints filed by House Democrats and Common Cause. Both alleged that Gingrich had improperly used funds raised by a nonprofit organization to pay for a college lecture course that advocated the election of Republicans to the House prior to the 1994 congressional midterm elections. Despite denying that he had intentionally violated House ethics rules, on January 21, 1997, Speaker Gingrich accepted a House reprimand and agreed to pay a $300,000 fine to cover the cost of the Committee on Standards of Official Conduct's investigation.

In October 1996 Common Cause called upon Attorney General **Janet Reno** to appoint an independent counsel to investigate Democratic and Republican National Committee fund-raising practices during the **election of 1996**. It argued that both the DNC and RNC had violated the Federal Election Campaign Act by raising tens of millions of dollars in so-called **soft money** and then using the money to pay for **issue ads** designed to support the reelection effort of Democratic President Bill Clinton and Republican challenger Bob Dole. Both Clinton and Dole had accepted over $60 million in federal funds to pay the cost of their general elections campaigns. In return federal law prohibited both campaigns from spending any more money on their respective political campaigns. After the 1996 presidential election victory by President Clinton, Attorney General Reno found insufficient evidence to possible criminal wrongdoing by President Clinton or Vice President Albert Gore to support a request for the appointment of an independent counsel under the **Ethics in Government Act of 1978**.

From the early 1970s through the end of the 1990s, Common Cause took the lead in lobbying Congress and presidents to enact and support various good government reforms, ranging from restrictions on the size of campaign contributions to the enactment of new restrictions on members of Congress accepting honorariums. On the other hand, by the end of the 1990s, Common Cause had failed to persuade Congress to pass legislation limiting soft money contributions to political parties.

Related Entries: Campaign Finance Reform (Federal); Election of 1996; Ethics in Government Act of 1978; Ethics Reform Act of 1989; Federal Election Campaign Act of 1971 (FECA); Gingrich, Newt; Keating Five Affair; Wright, Jim

SUGGESTED READINGS: "Common Cause 1970–1990," *Common Cause Magazine* (Fall 1992): 1–40; Common Cause: *www.commoncause.org*; Ann McBride, "Fighting for the Health of Democracy: Reform Battle Heats Up," *Common Cause Magazine* 22 (Spring/Summer 1996): 38; *Serving Two Masters: A Common Cause Study of Conflicts of Interest in the Executive Branch*, Washington, DC: Common Cause, 1976.

CONFLICT OF INTEREST PROHIBITIONS. Federal executive branch employees and officials must comply with both criminal and administrative conflict of interest restrictions designed to protect public officials in the impartiality and objectivity of federal employees and officials. These restrictions regulate (1) gifts from outside sources, (2) gifts between employees, (3) conflicting financial interests, (4) outside employment and activities, (5) misuse of position, and (6) restrictions on former employees.

The **Bribery and Conflict of Interest Act of 1962** brought together under Title 18 of the United States Code the most important federal criminal conflict-of-interest prohibitions. Section 202 prohibits federal employees and officials from accepting bribes and **illegal gratuities**. Section 203 prohibits members of Congress and all other federal employees and officials from accepting payment for representing private parties with respect to any federal proceeding. Section 205 prohibits executive branch employees and officials from representing anyone with respect to a federal proceeding with or without compensation. Section 207 prohibits former executive branch employees and members of Congress from representing private parties before federal agencies and departments with respect to certain matters. Section 208, the federal financial conflict-of-interest prohibition, prohibits executive branch employees and officials from participating in any matter in which they have a financial interest. Section 209 prohibits anyone from supplementing the salaries of executive branch employees and officials. In addition to the criminal conflict of interest prohibitions, executive branch employees must comply with the standard of conduct regulations issued by the **U.S. Office of Government Ethics** under the provisions of **Executive Order 12731**.

Like federal executive branch employees, members of Congress face criminal prosecution for violating certain criminal conflict of interest prohibitions such as the prohibition on accepting illegal gratuities. In addition representatives must comply with the provisions of the House Ethics Manual which impose noncriminal restrictions on the conduct of representatives and senators. The House **Committee on Standards of Official Conduct** and the **Senate Select Committee on Ethics** have responsibility for investigating allegations of wrongdoing by members of the House and Senate. And like executive branch officials and members of Congress, federal judges must comply with a number of criminal conflict of interest statutes, as well as the Code of Judicial Conduct issued by the Judicial Conference of the United States.

The **Public Integrity Section of the Department of Justice** and U.S. attorney offices across the country have responsibility for investigating and prosecuting criminal violations of conflict-of-interest statutes by all federal employees and officials, including members of Congress and federal judges.

Related Entries: Bribery and Conflict of Interest Act of 1962; Ethics in Government Act of 1978; Ethics Reform Act of 1989; Executive Order 12731; U.S. Office of Government Ethics

SUGGESTED READINGS: Robert Roberts, *White House Ethics: The History of the Politics of Conflict of Interest Regulation*, Westport, CT: Greenwood Press, 1988; Robert Roberts and Marion T. Doss, *From Watergate to Whitewater: The Public Integrity War*, Westport, CT: Praeger, 1997; United States Office of Government Ethics: *http://www.usoge/*.

CONGRESSIONAL ETHICS REGULATION. From 1789 until 1958, the U.S. House of Representatives and the U.S. Senate did not require representatives and senators to comply with the provisions of a specific ethics code. Despite the absence of an ethics code, the period saw both the House and Senate discipline a relatively small number of members for various types of official misconduct. From the late 1940s through the late 1950s, a series of well-publicized ethics controversies involving members of the Truman and Eisenhower administration focused national attention on serious gaps in federal ethics regulations. In 1958 Congress adopted the Code of Government Service by concurrent resolution. The new code directed "highest moral principles." Yet the new code did not include any mechanisms for executive branch agencies or Congress to enforce the vague provisions of the new code.

During the 1960s a series of highly publicized congressional ethics controversies placed tremendous pressure on the House and Senate to tighten their ethics rules and to establish effective ways to resolve allegations of unethical conduct by House and Senate members. The most serious involved **Bobby Baker** and Representative **Adam Clayton Powell**. Prior to his 1963 resignation, Bobby Baker had served as secretary to Senate Majority Leader Lyndon Johnson until Johnson's 1960 election as vice president and then as secretary to Senate Majority Leader Mike Mansfield. New York City Representative Adam Clayton Powell had risen to the position of the chairman of the powerful House Education Committee. Both Baker and Powell faced accusations of financial improprieties. By the end of the 1960s, the House and Senate had established new ethics committees and had adopted new ethics codes governing the conduct of members.

In the aftermath of the August 1974 resignation of President Richard Nixon, in 1977, the House and Senate adopted new ethics codes. The new codes prohibited members from raising private funds to help defer the cost of running their congressional offices. In addition the new codes placed restrictions on representatives and senators using the franking privilege to mail material to constituents. Reflecting growing concern over the outside activities of members, the new codes established a 15 percent earned income limit. In other words members were prohibited from earning more than 15 percent of their congressional salaries by holding a part-time job. Continuing controversies led the House and Senate to prohibit members from accepting gifts of more than $100 from lobbyists or foreign nationals. And the new codes required both House and Senate members to file annual public financial disclosure statements. Finally the Senate voted to replace the **Senate Committee on Standards and Conduct** with the **Senate Select Committee on Ethics**. In 1967 the House had established the **Committee on Standards of Official Conduct**. In 1978 Congress passed the **Ethics in Government Act** which included a number of measures requiring members of Congress, federal judges, and high-level executive branch officials to file annual public financial disclosure statements.

The adoption of new House and Senate ethics codes and the passage of the 1978 Ethics Act did not end pressure on Congress to further tighten congressional ethics rules. For instance the 1980 **Abscam investigation** saw an FBI **sting** result in the criminal prosecution and conviction of a number of representatives and one senator for accepting bribes from FBI agents playing the role of individuals seeking preferential treatment for foreign nationals. Through the 1980s critics of congressional ethics pounded away at the fact that Congress still permitted members to accept thousands of dollars in **honorariums** for giving speeches and attending events. Yet Congress refused to ban the practice.

Late in May 1989, Democratic Speaker of the House **Jim Wright** announced his decision to resign from the House. Wright's decision to resign came after a yearlong Committee on Standards of Official Conduct investigation of alleged financial improprieties involving Speaker Wright. Although Wright denied intentionally violating House ethics rules, his resignation placed strong pressure on the House to tighten ethics rules. Late in 1989 President George Bush signed into law the **Ethics Reform Act** which included a ban on House members accepting honorariums. To obtain this concession from House members, President Bush had agreed to a provision in the law providing House members with a substantial pay increase. In addition the Ethics Reform Act prohibited former members of Congress from appearing before either the House or Senate or any legislative branch office with the "intent to influence official action on behalf of any third party."

From 1990 to November 1994, the **Keating Five, House Bank**, and **House Post Office** did further damage to public trust in the Democratic leadership of the House. Congressional Republicans made effective use of these scandals to take back control of the House for the first time in decades. The new Republican majority did not end criticism of House ethics rules and the conduct of members of Congress. In 1994 a number of House Democrats filled ethics complaints against new Republican Speaker of the House **Newt Gingrich**. The most serious allegation alleged that during the 1994 congressional midterm election campaign, Georgia representative Gingrich used money raised by a nonprofit organization to finance a college course which advocated the election of Republican members of Congress.

Then in late 1995, Congress passed and President Clinton signed into law the **Lobbying Disclosure Act** which significantly increased the number of individuals required to register with Congress as lobbyists and to disclose their income and their lobbying expenditures. In late December 1996, Speaker of the House Gingrich agreed to accept a House reprimand and agreed to pay a $300,000 fine for allegedly violating House rules by using funds raised by a nonprofit organization to fund partisan activities. Although Gingrich denied having intentionally violated House ethics rules, the subsequent January 21, 1997, House reprimand constituted the first time the House had voted to reprimand a House speaker for ethical wrongdoing.

Related Entries: Committee on Standards of Official Conduct; Senate Select Committee on Ethics

SUGGESTED READINGS: Congressional Quarterly, *Congressional Ethics: History, Facts, and Controversy*, Washington, DC: Congressional Quarterly, 1992; House Ethics Highlights, *http://www.house.gov/ethics/Highlightshtmlversion.htm*; Dennis Thompson,

Ethics in Congress: From Individual to Institutional Corruption, Washington, DC: Brookings Institution, 1995. Senate Ethics Rules: *http://www.senate.gov/learning/learn _rules.html#37.*

CONKLING, ROSCOE (October 30, 1829–April 18, 1888). U.S. Senator, 1867–1881. *See* Arthur, Chester A.; Customs Collectors Scandals; Hayes, Rutherford B.

CONNALLY, JOHN BOWDEN (February 27, 1917–June 15, 1993). Former Texas governor and secretary of the treasury, 1971–1972.

On November 22, 1963, President John F. Kennedy was assassinated as he rode in a Dallas, Texas motorcade. Texas Governor John B. Connally was seriously wounded as he rode with President Kennedy in the open convertible. After recovering Connally completed a second term as Texas governor and returned to private life. In 1971 Connally joined the administration of President Richard Nixon as secretary of the treasury. In 1972 he led the "Democrats for Nixon" organization that supported President Nixon's 1972 reelection campaign.

In 1973 Vice-President **Spiro Agnew** resigned after being confronted with allegations that during the 1960s he had accepted kickbacks and bribes from individuals and companies doing business with the State of Maryland when Agnew had served as governor. Agnew's resignation led to speculation that Connally might be named by Nixon to serve as vice president until the 1976 presidential election. However, in 1974, a federal **grand jury** indicted John Connally for allegedly accepting a $10,000 bribe from an organization representing milk producers. A federal jury subsequently acquitted Connally on all charges.

Cleared of criminal charges, between 1977 and 1980 John Connally set his sights on winning the 1980 Republican presidential nomination. Despite raising millions of dollars, by early 1980 it became clear that Connally had very little Republican support for his candidacy. The Republican Party went on to nominate former California governor Ronald Reagan as their presidential candidate. After his failed presidential candidacy, Connally again returned to private business where he acquired a fortune and lost it as the result of a significant downturn in the national economy during the early 1990s. On June 15, 1993, John B. Connally died of pulmonary fibrosis at age seventy-six.

SUGGESTED READING: Richard Pearson, "Freewheeling Texas Governor John Connally Dies," *Washington Post*, June 16, 1993, C7.

CONNELLY, MATTHEW J. (1907–1976). Aide to President Harry S. Truman, 1948–1952.

From 1948 through 1952, Matthew J. Connelly served as President Harry Truman's presidential appointments secretary. In 1951 a major scandal erupted over allegations that Bureau of Internal Revenue officials and employees had accepted gifts and favors from taxpayers seeking help with their tax problems.

President Truman's appointments secretary Matthew J. Connelly (far right), March 1, 1948. U.S. Navy/Harry S. Truman Library

The ensuing investigation forced President Truman and Congress to implement a major overhaul of the Bureau of Internal Revenue. The scandal also resulted in the dismissal of a number of Bureau of Internal Revenue employees and officials.

After the end of the Truman administration, the Justice Department continued its investigation of alleged influence peddling in the Bureau of Internal Revenue. In 1956 a U.S. District Court jury convicted Matthew Connelly and Lamar Caudle, former head of the Justice Department's tax division, for conspiring to help a St. Louis, Missouri, shoe wholesaler with a tax evasion problem. Interestingly a U.S. District Court subsequently convicted and fined the businessman for tax evasion. The government alleged that Connelly had accepted clothing and an oil royalty worth $7,000 from a lawyer representing the businessman for unspecified assistance. The alleged illegal conduct occurred when Connelly served as President Truman's personal secretary. Connelly claimed that he purchased the oil royalty for $750 and that he had not attempted to illegally help the St. Louis shoe distributer with his tax problems. Despite Connelly's denials a federal jury convicted him of illegal influence peddling and sentenced him to six months in jail. After appeals failed Connelly served six months in federal prison during 1960. In 1962 President John Kennedy granted Connelly a full pardon.

Related Entries: Bureau of Internal Revenue Scandal; Truman Administration Ethics Controversies

SUGGESTED READINGS: Robert Hanley, "Matthew J. Connelly Dies; Served as Aide to Truman," *New York Times*, July 12, 1976, B2; C. Vann Woodward, ed., *Responses of the Presidents to Charges of Misconduct*, New York: Delacorte Press, 1974.

CONSTITUTIONAL TORT. From the early 1950s through the 1960s, the Supreme Court held that the Constitution provided the vast majority of local, state, and federal officials absolute immunity from federal civil rights suits alleging that government officials violated the constitutional rights of citizens. In these decisions the Supreme Court argued that permitting civil rights suits against government officials would have a chilling effect on the performance of official duties. However, in the early 1970s the Supreme Court began to issue a number of decisions holding that the Constitution only provides the majority of public employees and officials **qualified immunity** from so-called constitutional tort suits. The abandonment of the **absolute official immunity doctrine** led to an explosion in federal civil rights suits filed against local, state, and federal government officials.

Yet in the 1982 *Nixon v Fitzgerald* decision, the Supreme Court held that the Constitution provides the president of the United States with absolute immunity from civil suits for money damages for actions taken in the course of the performance of presidential duties. On the other hand, in the high court's 1994 *Clinton v Jones* decision, the Supreme Court held that the Constitution did not prohibit a U.S. District Court from hearing a civil rights lawsuit by former Arkansas state employee **Paula Jones** which alleged that in 1991 Arkansas Governor Bill Clinton had engaged in improper sexual advances toward Jones in a Little Rock, Arkansas, hotel room. The high court distinguished the Jones case from that of former Department of Defense employee Ernest Fitzgerald on the grounds that the alleged unlawful acts by President Clinton took place before he became president in January 1993. In November 1998 President Clinton settled the Paula Jones civil suit for some $850,000 even though he denied all of the allegations.

From the 1970s through the end of the 1990s, constitutional tort suits became a major way to hold local, state, and federal officials accountable for actions that violated established constitutional or statutory rights of citizens.

Related Entries: Absolute Official Immunity Doctrine; *Clinton v Jones*; Qualified Official Immunity Doctrine

SUGGESTED READING: Harvey Berkman and Marcia Coyle, "Jones' Victory May Be Short-Lived; Now She Faces the Tough Part, Proving a Violation under 28 U.S.C. 1983," *National Law Journal*, June 9, 1997, A7.

CONTRIBUTION LIMITS. *See* Federal Election Campaign Act of 1971 (FECA); Hard Money

CONTRIBUTIONS, POLITICAL. *See Buckley v Valeo*; Campaign Finance Reform (Federal); Campaign Finance Reform (State); Federal Election Campaign Act of 1971; Hard Money; Soft Money

CORRUPT BARGAIN OF 1824. *See* Election of 1824

CORRUPT PRACTICES ACT OF 1910 (PUBLICITY ACT). After the 1904 presidential election victory of Theodore Roosevelt, allegations surfaced that the Roosevelt campaign had received large campaign contributions from powerful business interests who saw the contributions as a way to stop federal efforts to regulate or break up a number of large trusts. Vice President Theodore Roosevelt had assumed the presidency after the 1891 assassination of President William McKinley. Democratic members of Congress demanded a full investigation into the fund-raising practices of the Republican Party and into whether the Roosevelt campaign had promised to pursue certain policies in return for corporate campaign contributions. A subsequent congressional investigation failed to find any evidence to support the allegation that Roosevelt had promised anything to campaign contributors.

Despite being cleared by the investigation, the allegation deeply disturbed Theodore Roosevelt. Throughout his political career, Roosevelt had fought for political reform and against corruption in government. In his 1905 and 1906 annual messages to Congress, President Roosevelt proposed legislation to prohibit corporations from making political contributions to candidates for federal office. The same period also saw the establishment of the National Publicity Law Organization to lobby for the passage of campaign finance reform legislation. On January 26, 1907, Congress passed the **Tillman Act** which prohibited corporations and national banks from making a political contribution to any federal election. With the support of Theodore Roosevelt, progressive members of Congress pushed for the enactment of stronger campaign finance reform legislation. In 1910 Congress passed the Corrupt Practices Act. In addition to keeping in place the prohibition on corporate campaign contributions, the new so-called Publicity Act required national party committees and their congressional campaign committees to file postelection campaign finance reports of campaign receipts and expenditures for House races with the House clerk. The act did not cover Senate races or presidential election campaigns.

The provisions of the 1910 Corrupt Practices Act failed to satisfy progressive critics of the system for financing federal elections. In 1911 Congress voted to strengthen the act by requiring both House and Senate campaign committees to report receipts and expenditures for primary and general election campaigns before and after primary and general elections. Even more significant the amendments prohibited House candidates from spending more than $5,000, and Senate candidates from spending more than $10,000 in a political campaign unless state law imposed lower campaign expenditure requirements.

Although the Corrupt Practices Act of 1910 and the 1911 amendments significantly expanded the scope of federal campaign finance regulation, in the long run they had little impact on the system for financing federal elections. The Republican and Democratic Parties quickly found legal ways to avoid the reporting and campaign expenditure limitations. Not until the passage of the **Federal Election Campaign Act of 1971** did Congress enact somewhat effective campaign finance reform legislation.

Related Entries: Campaign Finance Reform (Federal); Campaign Finance Reform (State); Tillman Act

SUGGESTED READINGS: Congressional Quarterly, *Congressional Ethics, 2nd ed.*, Washington, DC: Congressional Quarterly, 1980; Anthony Corrado, Thomas E. Mann, Daniel R. Ortiz, Trevor Potter, and Frank J. Sorauf, *Campaign Finance Reform: A Sourcebook*, Washington, DC: Brookings Institution, 1997.

CORRUPT PRACTICES ACT OF 1925. In the aftermath of the disclosure of the **Teapot Dome scandal**, Congress faced renewed pressure to enact legislation to demonstrate congressional concern with corruption in government. Although the Teapot Dome scandal had little to do with campaign fund-raising and expenditures, Congress passed the Corrupt Practices Act in an effort to require greater disclosure of campaign contributions and expenditures and to place caps on campaign expenditures for House and Senate races. First the act established a $25,000 expenditure limit for Senate campaigns and a $5,000 expenditure limit for House campaigns unless a state adopted lower limits. Second the act required House candidates, Senate candidates, and multistate political committees to file quarterly reports of all campaign contributions over $100. Third the act continued the provisions of the Tillman Act by prohibiting campaign contributions by corporations and federally chartered banks. Fourth the act expanded the scope of so-called **patronage crimes** by prohibiting the solicitation of federal employees for campaign contributions by candidates or other federal employees. Because of an earlier Supreme Court decision holding that Congress did not have the authority to regulate campaign contributions to candidates in primary races for federal offices, Congress limited the provisions of the law to House and Senate general election campaigns.

Much like the Corrupt Practices Act of 1910, the new law lacked any mechanism for the effective enforcement of the campaign disclosure and expenditure requirements of the law. Again like prior experience, the Republican and National Democratic Parties, as well as House and Senate candidates, soon found ways to avoid compliance with the provisions of the law. Equally important, the law did not apply to presidential campaigns.

Related Entry: Campaign Finance Reform (Federal)

SUGGESTED READING: Congressional Quarterly, *Congressional Ethics, 2nd ed.*, Washington, DC: Congressional Quarterly, 1980.

COVODE PUBLIC CORRUPTION INVESTIGATION. *See* Buchanan Administration Political Corruption Scandals

COX, ARCHIBALD (May 17, 1912–   ). Lawyer, educator, author, labor arbitrator, Watergate special prosecutor, 1973.

On May 18, 1973, Attorney General–designate **Elliot L. Richardson** appointed Harvard Law School Professor Archibald Cox as the **Watergate special prosecutor**. Cox had served as solicitor general during the Kennedy and Johnson administrations.

From the day of his appointment, Cox made clear that he planned to pursue his investigation wherever it might lead. On July 16, 1973, **Alexander Butterfield**, administrator of the Federal Aviation Administration and former aide to White House Chief of Staff H. R. Haldeman, testified before the **Senate Watergate Committee** that Nixon had ordered the installation of devices to tape conversations in the president's White House and Executive Office Building offices. President Nixon subsequently invoked **executive privilege** as grounds for refusing to comply with subpoenas issued for the tapes by special prosecutor Archibald Cox and the Senate Watergate Committee. On October 20, 1973, in the so-called **Saturday Night Massacre**, President Nixon ordered Attorney General Richardson to dismiss special prosecutor Cox. Both Attorney General Richardson and Deputy Attorney General William D. Ruckelshaus resigned after they refused to fire Cox. President Nixon then appointed Solicitor General **Robert Bork** as acting attorney general. Bork then fired Archibald Cox.

Congressional, media, and public reaction to the dismissal created a tidal wave of support for an even more aggressive investigation of the Nixon White House. On November 1, 1973, President Nixon appointed Houston lawyer **Leon Jaworski** to replace Watergate special prosecutor Cox and Senator William B. Saxbe to replace Richardson as attorney general. In July 1974 the Supreme Court ruled that Nixon had to turn over the White House tapes to Watergate special prosecutor Jaworski.

After being dismissed as Watergate special prosecutor, Cox returned to Harvard University to resume teaching. From 1980 through 1992, Cox served as chairperson of **Common Cause**, a citizen's advocacy group. During this time, Common Cause lobbied heavily for a range of good government reforms.

Related Entry: Watergate Scandal

SUGGESTED READING: Ken Gormley, *Archibald Cox: Conscience of a Nation*, Reading, MA: Addison-Wesley, 1997

CRANDON V UNITED STATES, **494 U.S. 152 (1990).** In 1917 Congress passed a law prohibiting executive branch employees from accepting salary supplements from private sources. Congress enacted the law to prevent large private foundations or companies from trying to influence the actions taken by federal employees and officials by supplementing their government salaries with additional private payments. When Congress passed the **Bribery and Conflict of Interest Act of 1962**, it continued the salary supplementation ban. From the 1960s through the early 1980s, the Department of Justice held that the salary supplementation ban prohibited private corporations from making large lump-sum payments to employees and officials who accept positions with federal agencies and departments.

After the November 1980 presidential election victory of California governor Ronald Reagan, the Reagan transition team aggressively recruited private sector experts and executives. To help with a planned military buildup in 1981, the Reagan Department of Defense recruited a number of Boeing Corporation employees to help implement the planned defense. To compensate these employees for their loss in pay due to lower paying government positions, Boeing made large severance payments to each. Early in 1986 the Department of Justice brought suit in *United States v Boeing Co.*, 653 F. Supp. 1381 (1987) against Boeing and the Boeing employees in an effort to recover the payments they received in 1981. Because the statute of limitations on the criminal salary supplementation ban had passed, the Justice Department could only proceed against Boeing and the former Boeing employees through a civil suit. A U.S. District Court judge subsequently ruled that Boeing and the former Boeing employees had violated the salary supplementation ban. Then the U.S. Court of Appeals reversed the finding of the District Court judge by holding that Boeing and the former Boeing employees had violated the supplementation of salary ban.

In the 1990 case of *Crandon v United States*, the Supreme Court ruled that Harold Crandon, a former Boeing computer scientist, had not violated section 208 of title 18 of the United States Code, the salary supplementation ban. Crandon had accepted a large severance payment from Boeing prior to accepting a position as a defense department representative to the North Atlantic Treaty Organization. The high court found that the language of the salary supplementation ban did not prohibit severance payments received by individuals prior to becoming a federal employee. Interestingly Congress declined to amend the language of the salary supplementation ban to include severance payments made to individuals prior to entering the federal government.

Related Entry: Bribery and Conflict of Interest Act of 1962

SUGGESTED READINGS: Ruth Marcus, "Court Sees No Conflict in Boeing Severance Payments," *Washington Post*, February 28, 1990, A6; Robert Roberts and Marion T. Doss, *From Watergate to Whitewater: The Public Integrity War*, Westport, CT: Praeger, 1997.

CREDIT MOBILIER SCANDAL. In 1862 Congress passed legislation authorizing federal support for the construction of a railroad across the United States. The law granted the Union Pacific and Central Pacific Railroads the right to construct different parts of the line. As an incentive for the two railroads to undertake the risky venture, Congress voted to provide each railroad with large tracts of public land for every mile of track put down. After the passage of the law, the Union

"Every Public Question with an Eye Only to the Public Good." Credit Mobilier cartoon by Thomas Nast, *Harper's Weekly*, March 15, 1873. Reproduced from the Collections of the LIBRARY OF CONGRESS

Pacific established the Credit Mobilier Company, an independent company, to construct the Union Pacific's part of the line from Omaha, Nebraska, westward to meet up with the Central Pacific Railroad working its way from the West Coast. Subsequently the Union Pacific entered into a series of contracts with Credit Mobilier that permitted the company to make large profits and nearly led to the bankruptcy of the Union Pacific. The Central Pacific Railroads and Union Pacific Railroads completed the construction of the line in 1869.

As Credit Mobilier profits grew, the directors grew concerned that Congress might begin an investigation of its massive profits as Congress grew more and more concerned over the financial stability of the Union Pacific Railroad. Interestingly, Massachusetts Congressman Oakes Ames served as one of the directors of the Credit Mobilier Company. Congressional ethics rules did not prohibit members from holding such positions. Between 1867 and 1868, Congressman Ames gave a number of members of Congress the opportunity to purchase Credit Mobilier stock at prices far below market price. In the end the congressmen who purchased the stock made very little money. On September 4, 1872, the *New York Sun* claimed that the Union Pacific and Credit Mobilier company had

Hon. Schuyler Colfax. Reproduced from the Collections of the LIBRARY OF CONGRESS

used Credit Mobilier stock to bribe a number of members of Congress not to
investigate the relationship between Credit Mobilier and the Union Pacific. The
article named former Speaker of the House and Vice President Schuyler Colfax
and Speaker of the House **James G. Blaine** as two members of Congress who
had purchased Credit Mobilier stock.

Coming two months before the 1872 presidential and congressional elections,
the Credit Mobilier seemed to present a serious problem for the Republican
Party. Yet the allegations had little impact upon the remaining days of the 1872
presidential and congressional election campaigns. The Republican Party re-
tained control of Congress and President Ulysses S. Grant easily won a second
term as president of the United States.

Early in 1873 the House established a select committee to investigate the
Credit Mobilier allegations. In February 1873 the Senate appointed its own committee to determine whether any members of the Senate had illegally received
Credit Mobilier stock. Although the House and Senate committees determined
that Credit Mobilier had made exorbitant profits during the construction of the
Union Pacific rail line, the House ended up only censuring two members for
their purchase of Credit Mobilier stock. On February 27, 1873, the House voted
to censure Representatives Oakes Ames, R-Mass., and James Brooks, D-N.Y.,

for their part in the Credit Mobilier stock scandal. The Senate decided not to take any action against Senator James Paterson for purchasing Credit Mobilier stock because his term expired on March 3, 1873. The House investigation also cleared Speaker Blaine of any wrongdoing.

The congressional investigation of the involvement of the alleged involvement of Vice President Colfax became the most controversial aspect of the Credit Mobilier scandal. In 1872 the Republican Party decided not to renominate Colfax for a second term as vice president. After the decision the Credit Mobilier scandal broke into the headlines. Reports appeared that Colfax had purchased Credit Mobilier stock during the time in which he served as Speaker of the House (1863–1869). Despite the fact that Colfax's term as vice president ended on March 3, 1873, the House Judiciary Committee considered starting impeachment proceedings against Colfax. Throughout the controversy, Colfax denied ever having been influenced by the Credit Mobilier Corporation.

Although twentieth-century historians regarded Credit Mobilier as one of the most significant public corruption scandals in American history, the Republican congressional majority Congress did not rush to enact legislation designed to prevent special interests from buying the loyalty of members of Congress.

Related Entries: Blaine, James G.; Congressional Ethics Regulation

SUGGESTED READINGS: Jay Boyd Crawford, *The Credit Mobilier of America*, Westport, CT: Greenwood, 1969; C. Vann Woodward, ed., *Responses of the Presidents to Charges of Misconduct*, New York: Delacorte Press, 1974.

CREEP (COMMITTEE TO RE-ELECT THE PRESIDENT). *See* Watergate Scandal

CURRIE, BETTY (1939–   ). Personal secretary to President Clinton, 1993–2001.

From January 1993 to the end of the Clinton administration in January 2001, Betty Currie served as President Clinton's personal secretary. In mid-January 1998, the **Monica Lewinsky** scandal erupted. After a request by Attorney General **Janet Reno**, a three-judge federal appeals panel gave Whitewater independent counsel **Kenneth Starr** the authority to investigate whether President Clinton might have violated federal law in his effort to prevent the disclosure of his relationship with former White House intern and employee Lewinsky. Between January and September 1998, Betty Currie appeared five times before the Monica Lewinsky federal **grand jury**.

In her grand jury testimony, Currie provided the grand jury with detailed information on the number of times Lewinsky visited President Clinton in the White House. However, Currie testified that she did not have any knowledge of a physical relationship between President Clinton and Lewinsky. Currie also testified that she had retrieved a number of gifts President Clinton had given Monica Lewinsky. On Sunday, January 18, 1998, a day after President Clinton answered questions about his alleged relationship with Lewinsky, asked by lawyers representing **Paula Jones** in her sexual harassment lawsuit, Currie testified that President Clinton asked her to come to the White House. President Clinton, according to Currie, then asked Currie to confirm his recollection that he had never been alone with Lewinsky. In his September 1998 impeachment referral to the House of Representatives, independent counsel Kenneth Starr pointed to Currie's January 18, 1998, conversation as evidence that President Clinton had attempted to obstruct any future investigation of his alleged relationship with Lewinsky. In the end Currie confirmed that President Clinton had met alone with Lewinsky on a number of occasions. On the other hand, Currie's testimony did little to support the argument that President Clinton had engaged in an illegal conspiracy to conceal his relationship with Lewinsky.

Related Entries: Lewinsky, Monica; Starr, Kenneth

SUGGESTED READINGS: Amy Goldstein and Michael Grunwald, "Secretary's Loyalty Didn't Waiver," *Washington Post*, October 3, 1998, A28; Stephen Labaton, "The Testing of the President; The Secretary: Accounts Went from Possibly Hurtful to Hazy," *New York Times*, October, 3, 1998, A8.

CUSTOMS COLLECTORS SCANDALS. From the late nineteenth century through the adoption of the federal income tax, made possible by the 1913 ratification of the Sixteenth Amendment, the federal government received the majority of its revenue from import duties, severance, and excise taxes and the sale of public lands. Through the nineteenth century, the amount of import duties collected by the customs houses operated by the Treasury Department exploded. Beginning in the late eighteenth century, the Treasury Department operated the federal customs houses. Not unexpectedly, through much of the nineteenth century, the New York, Boston, and Philadelphia customs houses collected the largest amount of customs duties. Headed by presidential appointees, by the 1830s the position of chief customs collector became one of the most sought after **patronage** positions.

Through much of the nineteenth century, a series of customs house scandals provided strong evidence of the relationship between the **spoils system** and high levels of public corruption. For instance for much of the 1830s, Samuel Swartwout held the position as chief customs collector for the Port of New York. Appointed to the position by President **Andrew Jackson** in 1829, Swartwout fled to England with over $1 million in customs duties in 1838—a staggering sum for the time. However, the Swartwout scandal did not persuade Congress to end the practice of giving presidents the authority to appoint chief customs house collectors and of allowing chief customs house collectors to fill lower level positions with political appointees. Through the 1840s, 1850s, and 1860s, chief customs house collectors and customs house employees showed few reservations about supplementing their public salaries through theft and by demanding payments from importers.

In 1871, President Ulysses S. Grant appointed New York Republican **Chester A. Arthur** as customs collector of the Port of New York. Prior to his appointment, Arthur had worked his way up through U.S. Senator Roscoe Conkling's

ANOTHER PRESIDENT WHO HAD A RISE IN THE WORLD.

"From the Toe-Path to the White House." President Rutherford B. Hayes dismissing New York Custom House Collector Chester A. Arthur. Reproduced from the Collections of the LIBRARY OF CONGRESS

New York Republican political machine. As expected Arthur used his position to fill the customshouse with loyal supporters of the New York Republican Party. Although historians agree that Arthur did not use his position to line his pockets, he did little to stop the rampant corruption within the New York customshouse.

In 1876 the electoral college elected Ohio Governor **Rutherford B. Hayes** as president of the United States even though Hayes lost the popular vote to New York Democrat Samuel Tilden. Prior to being elected as president, Hayes had established a reputation for honesty as the Republican governor of Ohio. In 1877 President Hayes appointed New York businessman John Jay to head a commission to investigate the mismanagement of the Treasury Department's customs houses. To the surprise of no one, the Jay Commission found that customshouse employees routinely expected importers to provide them with gifts and the majority of customs employees rarely did a day's work for a day's pay. The 1878 report blamed the situation on the **spoils system**. In the aftermath of the report, President Hayes demanded Arthur's resignation as chief customs

collector for the Port of New York. The action infuriated New York Senator
Conkling. Despite a nearly yearlong battle with Conkling over Arthur's replacement, President Hayes prevailed.

Ironically, in 1880 the Republican Party nominated James Garfield as president and Chester Arthur as vice president. In 1881 Arthur became president
after the 1881 assassination of James Garfield by an individual who was angered
by his inability to obtain an appointment to a federal job. In 1883 President
Arthur signed into law the **Pendleton Act** which established a new federal merit
system. In 1890 Congress passed the Customs Administrative Act which instituted a number of reforms designed to professionalize the day-to-day operation
of the customs service and significantly reduce the number of patronage positions in federal customs houses. Between 1890 and 1900, these reforms stopped
much of the corruption associated with the administration of customs houses
during the nineteenth century.

Related Entries: Arthur, Chester A.; Hayes, Rutherford B.

SUGGESTED READING: C. Vann Woodward, ed., *Responses of the Presidents to
Charges of Misconduct*, New York: Delacorte Press, 1974.

D

DAUGHERTY, HARRY M. (January 26, 1860–October 12, 1911). Attorney general of the United States, 1921–1924.

Between 1921 and 1924, Harry Daugherty served as attorney general during the administration of Warren G. Harding. Daugherty became one of the most controversial attorney generals in American history. He was one of the members of President Harding's so-called **Ohio Gang**. Historians place much of the blame on Attorney General Daugherty for helping to create a climate where high level Harding administration officials felt free to use their government positions for personal financial gain. However, the alien property scandal ultimately resulted in the 1927 criminal public corruption prosecution of Daugherty.

In 1921 representatives of a German family filed a claim for the proceeds of the sale of the stock in American Metal Company. At the beginning of World War I, the Alien Property Bureau had seized the stock of the company on the grounds that German nationals held a controlling interest in American Metal Company. Congress had passed the law to prevent German nationals from controlling companies vital to the nation's war effort. The family argued that Swiss, not German, nationals held a controlling interest in American Metal at the time of its seizure by the Alien Property Bureau.

To help pursue their claim in Washington, D.C., the family hired John King, a member of the Republican National Committee. King then contacted Jess Smith who served as a personal aide to Attorney General Daugherty. According to a subsequent criminal investigation, King and Smith persuaded Colonel Thomas Miller, custodian of the Alien Property Bureau, to release $7 million to the representative of the German family. Also according to the investigation, the representative then paid King approximately $425,000, Jess Smith some $224,000, and Colonial Miller $50,000 for services rendered. Jess Smith subsequently deposited $50,000 in a joint bank account he maintained with Attorney General Daugherty in an Ohio bank owned by Daugherty's brother.

Attorney General Harry Daugherty. Still Picture Branch, National Archives and Records Administration

In 1922, a Senate committee learned of the payment of the claim and began a full-scale investigation. Through 1922 and 1923, a war of words raged between angry senators and Attorney General Daugherty over the payment of the claim. On May 30, 1923, Jess Smith committed suicide in his Washington, D.C., apartment. The Smith suicide added further mystery to the claims controversy and the alleged involvement of Attorney General Daugherty. On August 2, 1923, President Warren G. Harding died of a heart attack in San Francisco, California, after a trip to Alaska.

Unlike President Harding, President Calvin Coolidge demonstrated little tolerance for political scandals. He moved quickly to distance himself from President Harding and the members of the Ohio Gang. In addition to the alien property controversy, by the beginning of 1924, tremendous pressure had developed in Congress to get to the bottom of the **Teapot Dome** controversy. Early in 1924 President Coolidge nominated former Democratic Senator Atlee Pomerene and Republican lawyer Owen J. Roberts to serve as the Justice Department's Teapot Dome special prosecutors. In March 1924 President Coolidge requested the resignation of Attorney General Daugherty.

In 1926 a federal **grand jury** indicted former Attorney General Daugherty, former and alien property custodian Thomas W. Miller, and John King for conspiracy to defraud the government. King died before trial. The first trial of Colonel Miller and Daugherty resulted in a hung jury. In 1927, after a second trial a U.S. District Court jury convicted Colonel Thomas Miller on conspiracy charges and sentenced him to eighteen months in prison and a $5,000 fine. However, the jury again failed to convict Daugherty on conspiracy charges. Through the remainder of his life, former Attorney General Daugherty worked relentlessly to clear his name. In 1932 Daugherty authored a book entitled *The Inside Story of the Harding Administration* in which he denied any wrongdoing.

Related Entries: Harding Administration Scandals; Teapot Dome Scandal

SUGGESTED READINGS: Harry M. Daugherty, *The Inside Story of the Harding Tragedy*, New York: Churchill Co., 1932; James N. Giglio, *H. M. Daugherty and the Politics of Expediency*, Kent: Kent State University Press, 1978; Nathan Miller, *Stealing from America: A History of Corruption from Jamestown to Reagan*, New York: Paragon House, 1992.

DEAN, JOHN (October 14, 1938–). White House Counsel to President Nixon, 1970–1973.

In 1970 John Dean became White House counsel to President Richard Nixon after serving as associate deputy attorney general. Between the June 1972 break-in of the Watergate office of the Democratic National Committee and the August 1974 resignation of President Richard Nixon, Dean became a key figure in the White House efforts to coverup the involvement of the Committee to Re-elect the President (CREEP) and the White House in the Watergate break-in. As revealed by President Nixon's White House tapes, from June 1972 until spring 1973, President Nixon, Dean, and other White House aides participated in a number of conversations on how to contain the damage from the Watergate break-in and other arguably illegal acts by the Nixon White House. On April 30, 1973, President Nixon fired White House counsel John Dean. On the same day, Nixon accepted the resignations of White House Chief of Staff **H. R. Haldeman**, domestic policy advisor **John Ehrlichman**, Attorney General Richard Kleindienst, and FBI Director L. Patrick Gray.

In June 1973 Dean became the star witness before the **Senate Watergate Committee**, speaking of a "cancer growing on the Presidency." Before nationally televised hearings, John Dean provided a detailed account of President Nixon's personal involvement in efforts to conceal the relationship between the Watergate burglars and the President's reelection campaign and the White House. However, White House aides Haldeman and Ehrlichman as well as the former chairman of President Nixon's 1972 reelection campaign, **John Mitchell**, provided the Watergate committee with a very different picture of President Nixon's involvement in damage control efforts.

In the end the White House Watergate tapes confirmed much of Dean's testimony before the Senate Watergate Committee, which led to the prosecution

John Dean at the Watergate hearing. © Bettmann/CORBIS

of Haldeman, Ehrlichman, and Mitchell for various criminal offenses related to the Watergate cover-up. Dean served a four-month term for obstruction of justice. In 1975 Dean authored the book *Blind Ambition*, which provides his account of the efforts by President Nixon and the White House staff to conceal the Nixon administration involvement in the break-in at the Democratic National Committee headquarters. After completing his sentence, Dean moved to California to become an investment banker.

Through much of the 1980s, Dean and his wife Maureen kept a low profile. Then, in 1991, Len Colodny and Robert Gettlin wrote a book entitled *Silent Coup: The Removal of a President*, which accused Dean of initiating the Watergate break-in to recover documents related to his future wife, Maureen Biner. According to the book, when the break-in failed Dean shifted the blame to Nixon and his aides in order to save himself. In 1992 John Dean filed a multimillion dollar libel and slander suit against the authors of the book and St. Martin's Press. In July 1997, Dean reached an out-of-court settlement with St. Martin's Press.

Interestingly Dean again returned to the public spotlight during the 1998 and early 1999 investigation of President Bill Clinton and his relationship with **Monica Lewinsky**. Numerous print and broadcast journalists asked Dean to compare Watergate with the Lewinsky investigation. In January 2000 excerpts of the Watergate tapes went on sale, including a number of conversations between President Richard Nixon and John Dean.

Related Entries: Senate Watergate Committee; Watergate Scandal

SUGGESTED READINGS: Carl Bernstein and Bob Woodward, "Dean Alleges Nixon Knew of Cover-Up Plan," *Washington Post*, June 3, 1973, A1; Len Colodny and Robert Gettlin, *Silent Coup: The Removal of a President*, New York: St. Martin's Press, 1991; John W. Dean, *Blind Ambition*, New York: Simon & Schuster, 1975.

DEAVER, MICHAEL (April 11, 1938–   ). Deputy Chief of Staff to President Reagan, 1981–1985.

From 1981 until 1985, Michael Deaver served as President Ronald Reagan's deputy chief of staff. Prior to joining the Reagan White House, Deaver played a key role in Reagan's 1980 presidential campaign. In 1985 Deaver resigned his position in the White House to open a high profile Washington, D.C., public relations and lobbying firm. In April 1986 reports surfaced that Deaver might have violated the **"revolving door"** lobbying restrictions enacted as part of the **Ethics in Government Act of 1978**. The so-called one year no contract provision prohibited former high-level executive branch officials from lobbying officials in their former government agencies for one year after leaving the government. Deaver had allegedly contacted members of the White House staff on behalf of his clients without waiting for the one-year period to elapse. Based on these reports, a number of Democratic members of Congress demanded that Attorney General **Edwin Meese III** appoint an **independent counsel** to determine whether Deaver had violated the "revolving door" prohibition.

On May 29, 1986, after a request by Attorney General Meese, a three-judge federal appeals panel appointed former U.S. Attorney Whitney North Seymour Jr. to investigate the allegations of illegal lobbying by former White House staffer Deaver. In late March 1987, a federal **grand jury** indicted Michael Deaver for lying to Congress and a federal grand jury regarding his lobbying activities after leaving the Reagan White House. Interestingly independent counsel Seymour did not seek to indict Deaver for violating the Ethics Act. On September 16, 1987, a U.S. District Court convicted Deaver of lying about his lobbying activities. U.S. District Judge Penfield Jackson sentenced Deaver to three years' probation, 1,500 hours of community service, and a $100,000 fine. However, Judge Penfield Jackson rejected independent counsel Seymour's request that Michael Deaver receive a prison sentence as a penalty for his conviction.

Reaction to the Deaver conviction followed partisan lines. Democrats used the conviction to call for tighter restrictions on the lobbying activities of former government employees and officials. Critics of the independent counsel law used the Deaver prosecution to support their argument that the law gave independent counsels too much discretion on whether to bring criminal charges against the subjects of independent counsel investigations.

Related Entries: Independent Counsel Investigations; Reagan Administration Ethics Controversies; "Revolving Door" Restrictions

SUGGESTED READINGS: Michael Deaver, *Behind the Scenes*, New York: Morrow, 1987; Peter B. Levy, *Encyclopedia of the Reagan-Bush Years*, Westport, CT: Greenwood

Secretary of the Navy Edwin Denby. Still Picture
Branch, National Archives and Records Administration

Press, 1996; Bill McAllister, "Deaver Is Found Guilty of Lying about Lobbying; Former
Reagan Aide Acquitted on 2 Counts," *Washington Post*, December 17, 1987, A1.

DENBY, EDWIN L. (February 18, 1870–February 8, 1929). Secretary of the
Navy, 1921–1924.

Edwin L. Denby served as President Warren Harding's secretary of the navy
from 1921 through 1924. In 1921 Secretary of the Interior **Albert Fall** urged
Denby to transfer the management of naval oil reserves (oil fields) at Elk Hills,
California, and Teapot Dome, Wyoming, to the control of the Interior Department. Fall had convinced President Harding that the Interior Department, not
the Navy Department, had the expertise to manage these important natural resources. Denby agreed to support Fall's oil field management plan. Both President Harding and Fall strongly believed that the U.S. government should help
private enterprise develop the natural resources of the country. In sharp contrast
the conservationist movement sought to protect land owned by the government
from private exploitation.

In late 1921 Secretary Fall quietly granted the drilling rights to the Elk Hills reserve to California reserve oil baron Edward Doheny. In 1922 the Interior Department leased oil drilling rights to the Teapot Dome to Harry F. Sinclair's Mammoth Oil Company. By April 1922 rumors of the leases reached Congress. From spring 1922 through summer 1923, Fall vigorously defended the Harding administration's decision to lease the two naval oil reserves. On August 2, 1923, President Warren Harding died in San Francisco, California. In late February 1923, at the request of President Calvin Coolidge, the Senate confirmed the nominations of Owen J. Roberts and Atlee Pomerene as **Teapot Dome special prosecutors**. Secretary of the Navy Denby resigned his position in March 1924.

The Teapot Dome investigation continued through 1929. U.S. District Court juries would only convict former Secretary of Interior Fall on public corruption charges. The investigation found no evidence that former Navy Secretary Denby participated in the Teapot Dome conspiracy.

Related Entries: Harding Administration Scandals; Fall, Albert; Teapot Dome Scandal

SUGGESTED READINGS: Burl Noggle, *Oil and Politics in the 1920s*, Westport, CT: Greenwood Press, 1980; C. Vann Woodward, ed., *Responses of the Presidents to Charges of Misconduct*, New York: Delacorte Press, 1974.

DI GENOVA, JOSEPH. *See* Independent Counsel Investigations

"DIRTY TRICKS." From January 1969 until March 1973, Dwight Chapin served as President Richard Nixon's appointments secretary. Besides performing his administration duties, Chapin developed a plan to hire someone to play "political pranks" on contenders for the 1972 Democratic presidential nomination, hoping to create dissension within the ranks of the Democratic Party. With the approval of White House Chief of Staff **H. R. Haldeman**, Chapin hired Donald Segretti to conduct an extensive dirty tricks campaign. During the last half of 1971 and the first half of 1972, Segretti engaged in a number of activities directed at disrupting the campaigns of Edwin Muskie, Washington Senator Henry Jackson and former Vice President Hubert Humphrey. For instance Segretti allegedly distributed a letter on Muskie stationery accusing Senator Jackson of being a homosexual and Senator Humphrey of cavorting with prostitutes provided by lobbyists. In 1974 a U.S. District Court jury convicted Chapin on two counts of making "false material declarations," before a federal **grand jury** established to investigate Republican "dirty tricks" during the 1972 presidential campaign. Also in 1974 Segretti pled guilty to a misdemeanor charge of distributing political material without identifying its source.

Related Entry: Watergate Scandal

SUGGESTED READING: Bob Woodward and Carl Bernstein, *All the President's Men*, New York: Simon & Schuster, 1974.

DISPUTED ELECTION OF 1876. *See* Election of 1876

Dwight Chapin, deputy assistant to the president.
Nixon Presidential Materials Staff

DISPUTED ELECTION OF 2000. *See* Election of 2000

DISQUALIFICATION RULE. As part of the provisions of the **Bribery and Conflict of Interest Act of 1962,** Congress passed a new financial conflict of interest prohibition for all federal executive branch employees and officials. Section 208 of title 18 of the United States Code prohibits all federal employees and officials from taking action with respect to any particular matter in which they hold a financial interest. Congress adopted the so-called disqualification rule in an effort to protect public confidence in actions taken by federal employees and officials without requiring them to sell financial assets.

From the early 1960s through the end of the 1990s, the disqualification rule created serious compliance problems for federal employees and officials. Many federal employees found it difficult to determine when the performance of their official duties might impact on the value of their financial holdings so Congress included in the **Ethics in Government Act of 1978** a requirement that high-level federal officials file annual **public financial disclosure** statements.

Related Entries: Bribery and Conflict of Interest Act of 1962; Financial Conflict of Interest Prohibition

SUGGESTED READING: Robert Roberts, *White House Ethics: The History of the Politics of Conflict of Interest Regulation*, Westport, CT: Greenwood Press, 1988.

DIVESTITURE RULE. As part of the provisions of the **Bribery and Conflict of Interest Act of 1962**, Congress passed a new financial conflict of interest prohibition for all federal executive branch employees and officials. Section 208 of title 18 of the United States Code prohibits all federal employees and officials from taking action with respect to any particular matter in which they held a financial interest. In other words the new conflict-of-interest measure did not require federal employees and officials to sell any financial interests in order to revolve potential conflict-of-interest problems. In addition to the criminal **disqualification rule**, separate federal criminal statutes prohibit federal employees and officials working for specific federal agencies and departments from owning certain types of financial interests. For instance employees and officials working for the Nuclear Regulatory Commission may not own stock in public utilities that operate nuclear power plants.

In 1989 Congress passed the **Ethics Reform Act of 1989** which included a new **certificate of divestiture** in an effort to reduce the tax liability of government employees required to sell financial assets to comply with federal ethics laws. The provision authorized the director of the **U.S. Office of Government Ethics** to issue certificates of divestiture to federal employees and officials required to sell financial holdings in order to comply with federal ethics regulations. The provision authorized any federal employee or official who received a certificate of divestiture to roll over any capital gains from the sale of a financial asset into a widely held financial instrument such as a mutual fund.

Related Entries: Blind Trusts; Certificate of Divestiture; Ethics Reform Act of 1989; Financial Conflict of Interest Prohibition.

SUGGESTED READINGS: John W. Moore, "Hands Off: To Avoid Conflict-of-Interest Questions, Many of President Bush's Appointees Are Holding on to Corporate Stocks but Disqualifying Themselves from Issues Involving Specific Firms," *National Journal*, July 1, 1989, 1678–1683; Robert Roberts and Marion T. Doss, *From Watergate to Whitewater: The Public Integrity War*, Westport, CT: Praeger, 1997.

DIXON-YATES AFFAIR. From 1953 to 1961, the administration of President Dwight David Eisenhower faced a number of serious ethics controversies. Although none of the controversies implicated President Eisenhower in any wrongdoing, they forced the Eisenhower White House to devote considerable time and resources in an effort to contain political damage. Ironically the 1952 Eisenhower presidential campaign had used the ethics record of the Truman administration to support their argument that voters should return a Republican president to the White House for the first time since the 1928 presidential election of Herbert Hoover.

The Dixon-Yates affair grew directly out of the controversy over whether to permit the Tennessee Valley Authority (TVA) to increase its capacity to generate

electric power. From the early 1930s through the early 1950s, the TVA trans-
formed the Tennessee Valley area by the construction of a number of large
dams which permitted the TVA to construct a number of power plants to provide
the region with inexpensive electric power. As strong supporters of the TVA,
Presidents Franklin Roosevelt and Harry Truman had backed efforts of the TVA
to obtain additional congressional funding to permit the construction of new
power plants. Besides serving private customers, the TVA found itself called on
to meet the growing power needs of the Atomic Energy Commission. On the
other hand, many Republicans viewed the expansion of the TVA as a direct
threat to stockholder-owned public utilities.

By the early 1950s, the TVA found itself unable to meet the projected power
needs of the Atomic Energy Commission and the growing city of Memphis,
Tennessee. As a presidential candidate, Dwight Eisenhower had expressed his
opposition to allowing the TVA to expand its production of electric power on
the grounds that the private sector should produce the nation's electric power.
Shortly after Eisenhower took office in January 1953, the Bureau of the Budget
enlisted the help of Adolphe Wenzell, vice president and director of the First
Boston Corporation, to determine whether the private sector could meet the
power needs of the Atomic Energy Commission. Wenzell served as an unpaid
consultant. Among its activities First Boston frequently arranged the financing
for the construction of power plants operated by public utilities. Wenzell subsequently recommended against permitting the TVA to expand its power generating capacity.

During the winter of 1954, the Bureau of the Budget and the Atomic Energy
Commission entered into negotiations with Edgar H. Dixon and Eugene A. Yates
to meet the power needs of Memphis, Tennessee. Dixon and Yates served as
executives with two private power companies that operated in the Memphis,
Tennessee, area. Under the contract the federal government would help finance
the construction of a new private power plant. The new plant would then sell
power to the City of Memphis. Freed of the obligation to sell Memphis power,
the TVA would have the ability to meet the power needs of the Atomic Energy
Commission. To provide technical assistance on the proposed contract, the Bureau of the Budget called upon the services of Adolphe Wenzell of First Boston
Corporation. First Boston Corporation subsequently received the contract from
the new Mississippi Valley Generating Company to arrange the financing for
the new power plant. Not unexpectedly the announcement of the contract produced an outpouring of criticism from supporters of the TVA. Critics saw the
contract as the first step in an effort by the Eisenhower administration to dismantle the TVA.

Through the first half of 1955, critics of the contract looked for ways to bring
public and congressional pressure on the Eisenhower administration to cancel
the contract. In February 1955 critics of the Dixon-Yates contract learned of the
involvement of Adolphe Wenzell in the negotiation of the Dixon-Yates contract
and that the Dixon-Yates power consortium had selected First Boston to arrange

the financing for their new power plant. The disclosure led to demands for a full-scale investigation of whether Wenzell had violated federal law by serving as an unpaid consultant on the Dixon-Yates contract while First Boston competed for the right to arrange the financing for the project.

Throughout the controversy Wenzell denied any wrongdoing. He maintained that he did nothing to help First Boston Corporation obtain the contract to arrange the financing for the new power plant. In July 1955 President Eisenhower announced the cancellation of the contract on the grounds that Memphis had decided to build its own power plant and no longer needed the power that would be generated by the new private power plant. When the government refused to pay the multimillion dollar contract cancellation fee, the Mississippi Valley Generating Company brought suit in the U.S. Court of Claims. The Court of Claims subsequently ruled that the contract required the federal government to pay the cancellation fee. In the 1961 landmark decision of *United States v Mississippi Valley Generating Company*, the Supreme Court overturned the decision of the Court of Claims and found that Wenzell's role in negotiating the contract while he also served as a vice president of First Boston Corporation created the appearance of a conflict of interest that provided grounds for the government to cancel the contract and refuse to pay the cancellation fee. The Supreme Court reached the decision despite the fact that the Department of Justice earlier had found that Wenzell had not violated any federal law by serving as a Bureau of the Budget consultant at the same time the Dixon-Yates Power consortium sought to obtain the contract to arrange the financing for the power plant.

Beyond the immediate facts of the controversy, Dixon-Yates succeeded in raising concern with executive branch agencies and Congress over the need to update federal conflict of interest laws in order to eliminate the growing confusion over the scope of federal conflict of interest restrictions. From the beginning of the administration of President John Kennedy in 1961 to the end of the presidency of Lyndon Johnson in 1969, Congress and the Kennedy and Johnson administrations would make a number of significant changes in executive branch ethics rules and regulations.

Related Entry: Eisenhower Administration Ethics Controversies

SUGGESTED READINGS: David A. Frier, *Conflict of Interest in the Eisenhower Administration*, Ames: Iowa State University Press, 1969; Aaron Wildavsky, *Dixon-Yates: A Study in Power Politics*, Westport, CT: Greenwood Press, 1976.

DODD, THOMAS J. (May 15, 1907–May 24, 1971). U.S. Senator, 1959–1971.

Early in 1966 newspaper columnists Drew Pearson and Jack Anderson alleged that Senator Thomas J. Dodd (D-Conn.) had improperly used campaign contributions for personal purposes, had double billed the government and private organizations the cost of a number of trips, and had gone to Germany to help public relations expert Julius Klein with business matters involving the West German government. In an effort to clear his name, Senator Dodd asked the

Senate Committee on Standards and Conduct to investigate the allegations. On April 27, 1967, after holding hearings on the allegations, the committee recommended the censure of Senator Dodd for using campaign contributions for personal purposes and for billing the Senate and private organizations for seven trips. The Senate subsequently voted to censure Senator Dodd for misusing campaign funds for personal purposes, but a majority of the Senate voted 45 to 51 not to censure Senator Dodd for improper billing of travel expenses. The Dodd investigation raised serious questions regarding the effectiveness of Senate ethics rules and the fairness of procedures used to investigate allegations of misconduct made against senators.

Facing a nomination battle within the Connecticut Democratic Party, Senator Dodd decided to run as an independent in the 1970 general election. Dodd finished third in a three-person race. Republican Lowell P. Weicker won Senator Dodd's Senate seat with 42 percent of the vote. On May 24, 1971, Dodd died.

Related Entries: Censure; Senate Committee on Standards and Conduct

SUGGESTED READING: Congressional Quarterly, *Congressional Ethics: History, Facts, and Controversy*, Washington, DC: Congressional Quarterly, 1992, 30.

DONOVAN, RAYMOND (August 31, 1930–   ). Secretary of Labor, 1981–1985.

Raymond Donovan served as President Ronald Reagan's first secretary of labor from February 1981 until his March 1985 resignation. At the time of his nomination as secretary of labor, Donovan served as a top executive with a major New York–area construction company. For all presidential nominees for cabinet positions, the Federal Bureau of Investigation conducted a background investigation, which was true for Donovan. The background investigation turned up rumors that Donovan's company had underworld connections. After the FBI failed to confirm the rumors, the Senate proceeded to confirm Donovan as secretary of labor.

In late 1981, allegations again surfaced of illegal conduct by Donovan's construction company. Specifically it was alleged that Donovan's company made a payoff to a New York City union leader in order to persuade the union leader to challenge another union leader for jurisdiction over union members at the subway project. At the time Donovan's company held a contract to renovate a New York City subway station under the jurisdiction of another union local. Like the earlier allegations, Donovan vigorously denied having made any payments or knowing about any payments to union officials in an effort to guarantee the labor price. In an effort to clear his name and protect the reputation of his former company, Donovan asked Attorney General William French Smith to request the appointment of a special prosecutor (independent counsel) to conduct a full investigation of the allegation.

On December 29, 1981, a three-judge federal appeals panel appointed Leon Silverman to serve as the independent counsel for the investigation. In June

1982 a federal grand jury found "insufficient credible evidence" to support Donovan's indictment on federal bribery charges, and in September Silverman issued a second report finding insufficient credible evidence to support criminal charges with respect to additional allegations. However, the June and September reports by special prosecutor Silverman did not end Donovan's legal problems.

Late in 1984 a New York State **grand jury** indicted Donovan and other officers of Donovan's construction company for allegedly entering into an agreement with a minority subcontractor to make it possible for Donovan's company to qualify to bid on a New York City subway contract. In March 1984 Donovan resigned as secretary of labor to devote full time to his defense. On May 25, 1987, a Bronx, New York, jury acquitted former Labor Secretary Donovan and his codefendants of all criminal charges.

On October 31, 1987, independent counsel Silverman announced he had completed a secret investigation of new allegations involving Donovan. In June 1985 the federal appeals panel requested that Silverman investigate whether Donovan had lied during Silverman's earlier investigation. Again, Silverman found insufficient evidence to seek Donovan's indictment on federal criminal charges.

In subsequent years critics of the **independent counsel law** would point to Raymond Donovan's legal problems as evidence to support the end of that law.

Related Entries: Independent Counsel Investigations; Reagan Administration Ethics Controversies

SUGGESTED READINGS: George Lardner Jr., " 'Insufficient Credible Evidence'; Prosecutor Ends Inquiry of Donovan," *Washington Post*, September 14, 1982, A1; George Lardner Jr., "No Indictment in Secret Probe of Donovan," *Washington Post*, October 31, 1987, A3.

DOUGLAS, PAUL H. (March 26, 1892–September 24, 1976). U.S. Senator, 1949–1967.

From 1948 to 1967, Paul Douglas served as Democratic senator from Illinois. Prior to being elected, Douglas served as a professor of industrial relations at the University of Chicago and in the U.S. Marine Corps from 1942 to 1945 where he distinguished himself.

In 1950 Senator Douglas found himself thrown into the middle of a raging controversy over alleged corruption in the Truman administration. Investigations of the Reconstruction Finance Corporation and the **Bureau of Internal Revenue** placed strong pressure on the Truman White House and Congress to clean up the so-called "mess in Washington." The so-called Truman scandals sharply divided the Democratic Party. Many Democrats saw the allegations as an effort by Republicans to discredit President Truman after his 1948 upset presidential victory. On the other hand, other Democrats criticized President Truman for not taking seriously the growing problem of special interest groups exerting undue influence on federal employees and officials.

Early in 1951 the Senate voted to direct the Committee on Labor and Public

Senator Paul H. Douglas (left of President Harry Truman). National Park Service Photograph-Rowe/Harry S. Truman Library

Welfare to conduct a study of how to restore public trust in government. Douglas served as chair of the subcommittee. Instead of attempting to conduct an investigation into the various allegations, Douglas used the hearings to solicit the input from ethics scholars on how to rebuild public trust in government and how to prevent the reoccurrence of public ethics scandals. On October 17, 1951, the Douglas subcommittee issued its report, *Proposals for Improvement of Ethical Standards in the Federal Government.*

The Douglas report proposed the enactment of strict new ethics codes for executive branch employees and officials. Besides prohibiting federal employees and officials from accepting most gifts from anyone regulated by or having business with the federal government, the Douglas report recommended the enactment of a new federal law requiring high-level public officials in all three branches of the federal government to file annual public financial disclosure reports. In addition the Douglas report recommended that Congress enact new restrictions on former federal employees and officials lobbying their former government agencies on behalf of private clients. The subcommittee argued that the new **"revolving door"** restrictions would help to prevent former government officials from leaving government and immediately begin lobbying for powerful special interests.

With the 1952 presidential election approaching, Congress did not act on the recommendations of the Douglas subcommittee. Republican members of Congress saw the report as an effort to shift public attention away from the alleged indiscretions of Truman administration officials, and congressional Democrats lacked the power to overcome strong Republican opposition. Following the release of the report, Douglas presented a series of lectures at Harvard University on the subject of ethics in government. Published in 1952, *Ethics in Government* became a blueprint for government ethics reform for decades to come. Paul Douglas retired from the Senate in 1967 and resided in Washington, D.C., until his death on September 24, 1969.

Related Entries: Bureau of Internal Revenue Scandal; Truman Administration Ethics Controversies

SUGGESTED READINGS: Paul H. Douglas, *Ethics in Government*, Cambridge, MA: Harvard University Press, 1952; Robert Roberts, *White House Ethics: The History of the Politics of Conflict of Interest Regulation*, Westport, CT: Greenwood Press, 1988.

EAGLETON, THOMAS FRANCIS (September 4, 1929–   ). U.S. Senator, 1968–1987.

On July 12, 1972, Democratic presidential nominee Senator George McGovern of South Dakota surprised the nation by selecting first-term Missouri Senator Thomas F. Eagleton to run as his vice presidential running mate. Few political observers gave the McGovern/Eagleton ticket any chance of defeating President Richard Nixon and Vice President **Spiro Agnew**. At the time Eagleton received the nomination, the June 17, 1972, arrest of burglars caught planting wire tapes at the Watergate headquarters of the Democratic National Committee had done little to reduce the huge lead held by Nixon and Agnew in the public opinion polls. Nixon's successful trip to mainland China and the gradual withdrawal of U.S. forces from Vietnam had helped to build public support.

Late in July 1972, reports surfaced that Eagleton had been hospitalized three times for depression between 1960 and 1966. Eagleton subsequently confirmed reports that he had received shock treatment for his condition. After Eagleton's admission Senator McGovern announced that he had no intention of asking Senator Eagleton to withdraw from the ticket. However, a week later Eagleton withdrew, and on August 5, 1972, Senator McGovern announced that R. Sargent Shriver, husband of John F. Kennedy's sister Eunice, had agreed to run as vice president. The Democratic ticket ended up receiving the electoral votes of only Massachusetts and the District of Columbia.

After his withdrawal from the 1972 Democratic presidential ticket, Eagleton returned to the U.S. Senate. In 1982 he took to the floor of the U.S. Senate to demand the resignation of Senator Harrison Williams Jr. for his involvement with the **Abscam** scandal. After leaving the Senate in 1987, Eagleton returned to St. Louis, Missouri, and became a successful member of the community. In September 1998 former Senator Eagleton found himself drawn into the controversy over President Bill Clinton and the **Monica Lewinsky** investigation. While attending a Mercantile Library luncheon, the *St. Louis Post-Dispatch* reported that Eagleton told those attending the luncheon that Clinton would probably have to settle for being one of the worst ten presidents in American history, placing Clinton on a list with Presidents Warren G. Harding and Ulysses S. Grant. Yet, in October 1998, in a visit to a St. Louis, Missouri area high school, the *St. Louis Post-Dispatch* reported that Eagleton told students that he expected that the House Judiciary Committee would vote to impeach Clinton but doubted that two-thirds of the Senate would vote to remove him from office. According to the report, Eagleton also called President Clinton a brilliant man "who has done an unfortunate thing."

Related Entry: Watergate Scandal

SUGGESTED READINGS: Carolyn Bower, "Eagleton Visits Kirkwood High School, Is Grilled by Students on Clinton Crisis; He Says He Would Vote against Impeachment," *St. Louis Post-Dispatch*, October 23, 1998, C5; Jo Mannies, "Eagleton Rates Clinton as a 'Worst 10' Candidate," *St. Louis Post-Dispatch*, September 7, 1998, B3.

EHRLICHMAN, JOHN D. (March 20, 1925–February 14, 1999). White House aide and Domestic Affairs Advisor for President Nixon, 1969–1973.

From January 1969 until his April 30, 1973, resignation, John Ehrlichman served as President Richard Nixon's chief White House counsel and domestic policy advisor. Along with White House chief of staff **H. R. Haldeman**, John Ehrlichman became one of the two most powerful individuals in the Nixon White House. As Nixon's domestic policy advisor, Ehrlichman became an expert in environmental regulation and played a major role in the 1970 establishment of the Environmental Protection Agency (EPA).

On June 13, 1971, the *New York Times* published parts of a top secret Defense Department study of the involvement of the United States in the Vietnam war. Daniel Ellsberg, a Rand Corporation analyst assigned to work on the project, had leaked the so-called **Pentagon Papers** to the *New York Times*. The report painted a highly critical history of U.S. involvement in Vietnam. Ellsberg's action infuriated President Nixon who then directed John Ehrlichman to find a way to stop leaks of highly sensitive government information to the press. He then ordered White House aides to establish a secret White House unit to plug government leaks. White House aides subsequently hired former CIA operative **E. Howard Hunt** and former FBI special agent **G. Gordon Liddy** for the new unit which came to be known as the plumbers unit.

On September 3, 1971, the plumbers unit burglarized the Los Angeles, California, offices of Daniel Ellsberg's psychiatrist in an effort to obtain information with which the White House could discredit Ellsberg prior to his forthcoming criminal trial for giving the *New York Times* the Pentagon Papers. A short time after the Ellsberg burglary, the White House disbanded the unit. In early 1972 President Nixon's Committee to Re-elect the President (CREEP) hired G. Gordon Liddy, E. Howard Hunt, and James McCord to staff a political intelligence

John D. Ehrlichman, assistant to the president for domestic affairs. Nixon Presidential Materials Staff

unit. On June 17, 1972, District of Columbia police arrested McCord and five Cuban exiles inside the **Watergate** offices of the DNC.

Besides the Watergate break-in, the White House sought to conceal the Ellsberg break-in, illegal campaign fund-raising, and a series of **"dirty tricks"** during the 1972 primary and general election campaign. On April 30, 1973, John Ehrlichman and H. R. Haldeman resigned their White House positions. Attorney General Richard G. Kleindienst also resigned. On the same day, President Nixon fired White House counsel John Dean.

Then on June 13, 1973, the *Washington Post* published a story by **Bob Woodward** and **Carl Bernstein** that the Watergate prosecutors had obtained a memo from White House aides David Young and Egil (Bud) Krogh to John Ehrlichman detailing plans for the break-in at the office of Daniel Ellsberg's psychiatrist. On July 12, 1974, a U.S. District Court jury found Ehrlichman guilty of conspiracy and perjury in relation to the Ellsberg break-in. Early in 1975, the jury also convicted G. Gordon Liddy, Bernard L. Barker, and Eugenio R. Martinez of conspiracy, obstruction of justice, and two counts of perjury related to his participation in the cover-up of the Watergate burglary.

In 1976 Ehrlichman began serving a three-year sentence at a federal correctional facility for perjury and obstruction of justice. In 1978, after serving eighteen months of the sentence, Ehrlichman received a parole. After release from prison, Ehrlichman became an executive for a firm that handled the disposal of hazardous waste. Ehrlichman also wrote two books directly and indirectly related to his Watergate experience. His book, *The Company*, presented a fictional story of a White House with many of the same characteristics of the Nixon White House. And Ehrlichman's memoirs, *Witness to Power*, chronicled the mistakes he had made as a member of Nixon's inner circle and painted an unflattering picture of President Nixon. John Ehrlichman died on February 14, 1999, at the age of seventy-three after a prolonged battle with diabetes.

Related Entries: Pentagon Papers; Watergate Scandal

SUGGESTED READINGS: John Ehrlichman, *Witness to Power: The Nixon Years*, New York: Pocket Books, 1972; Bob Woodward and Carl Bernstein, *All the President's Men*, New York: Simon & Schuster, 1974; Bob Woodward and Carl Bernstein, "Break-in Memo Sent to Ehrlichman," *Washington Post*, June 13, 1973, A1.

EISENHOWER, DWIGHT DAVID. (October 14, 1890–March 28, 1969). President of the United States, 1953–1961. *See* Eisenhower Administration Ethics Controversies

EISENHOWER ADMINISTRATION ETHICS CONTROVERSIES. In 1952 the Republican Party nominated Dwight David Eisenhower as their presidential candidate and Senator Richard Nixon as the vice presidential candidate. Through much of the 1952 presidential election campaign, the Republican Party used the campaign slogan, "Crime, Corruption, Communism and Korea," in an effort to tie Democratic candidates to a series of **Truman administration ethics controversies**. By September 1952 the Eisenhower presidential campaign faced their own controversy.

On September 18, 1952, the *New York Post* reported that Republican vice presidential candidate Richard Nixon received between $16,000 and $17,000 in payments from a group of California backers after he entered the U.S. Senate in 1951. In his so-called **"Checkers" speech**, Nixon responded by insisting that he had done nothing wrong, and he told viewers that the Nixon family would not return the family dog, Checkers, which had been a gift. Eisenhower and Nixon went on to win a landslide 1952 victory.

Not since the 1928 election of Herbert Hoover had the American people elected a probusiness Republican to serve as president. The Eisenhower White House moved quickly to recruit individuals from the private sector to serve in key government positions. Some Eisenhower nominees faced intense scrutiny of their financial affairs by the Senate committees responsible for reviewing their qualifications. For instance, after President Eisenhower nominated General Motors executive Charles E. Wilson as secretary of defense, Wilson touched off

Republican presidential nominee General Dwight D. Eisenhower, with vice presidential running mate Senator Richard M. Nixon, September 10, 1952. National Park Service, Abbie Rowe/Courtesy Harry S. Truman Library

a firestorm by initially refusing to sell 39,470 shares of General Motors stock. At the time General Motors was a major defense contractor.

During confirmation hearings held by the Senate Armed Services Committee, one senator asked Wilson whether he could envision a conflict between his duties as secretary of defense and his prior relationship to General Motors. Wilson replied to the question by saying, "I cannot conceive of one because for years I thought what was good for our country was good for General Motors, and vice versa." Wilson agreed to sell his General Motors stock after the Senate Armed Services Committee sent word to the Eisenhower White House that the committee would oppose Wilson's confirmation unless he sold his stock.

Between January 1953 and the end of the Eisenhower administration in January 1961, a number of Eisenhower appointees also faced criticism for alleged financial impropriety. Early in 1955 press reports alleged that Secretary of the Air Force Harold E. Talbot had solicited business for his former management consulting firm Mulligan & Company. An investigation by the Senate Permanent Investigation Subcommittee concluded that during 1953 Talbot made numerous phone calls and wrote a number of letters on behalf of Mulligan & Company. On August 15, 1955, Talbot resigned without admitting any wrongdoing.

From a historical perspective, the **Dixon-Yates** and **Sherman Adams** affairs proved much more damaging for the Eisenhower administration. The Dixon-Yates affair had its origins in a 1953 decision by President Eisenhower not to allow the Tennessee Valley Authority to construct a new power plant in order to supply the power needs of Memphis, Tennessee. President Eisenhower directed the Bureau of the Budget (BOB) to find a way to help the private sector meet the electric power needs of Memphis. Later the Dixon-Yates corporation and the BOB entered into a contract whereby Dixon-Yates agreed to build a new power plant to meet the power needs of Memphis, which freed the TVA to sell more power to the Atomic Energy Commission (AEC). The federal government agreed to help finance the construction of the new private power plant. Dixon and Yates were executives of two Memphis, Tennessee, area power companies.

By 1955 the Dixon-Yates contract had turned into a major embarrassment to the Eisenhower White House after critics of the contract learned that the BOB had used the services of Adolphe Wenzell, a vice president with First Boston Corporation, to negotiate the contract. First Boston then received the contract to arrange the financing for the new power plant. The appearance forced President Eisenhower to cancel the contract. In January 1961 the Supreme Court ruled that President Eisenhower legally ordered the cancellation of the contract because of Adolphe Wenzell's alleged financial conflict of interest.

On September 23, 1958, President Eisenhower's chief of staff Sherman Adams resigned after a controversy over whether Adams had improperly intervened with a number of federal regulatory agencies on behalf of Bernard Goldfine, the owner of a New England fabric mill. Although Adams denied having attempted to obtain preferential treatment for Goldfine, in June 1958 Adams confirmed reports that he had allowed Goldfine to pay his hotel bills at the exclusive Boston Sheraton-Plaza hotel and that Goldfine had given him a number of other expensive gifts. With the November 1958 congressional midterm election approaching, Adams decided to resign rather than having his ethics problems become a major campaign issue.

Although the Eisenhower administration ethics controversies did little to weaken public confidence in President Eisenhower, the controversies helped to persuade government ethics experts of the need for a major overhaul of the federal ethics program. In November 1960, Massachusetts senator John F. Kennedy won the presidential election. Shortly after taking office in January 1961, President Kennedy announced a series of public ethics initiatives.

Related Entries: Adams, Sherman; Dixon-Yates Affair

SUGGESTED READINGS: David A. Frier, *Conflict of Interest in the Eisenhower Administration*, Ames: Iowa State University Press, 1969; Robert Roberts, *Conflict of Interest Regulation and Federal Service*, Westport, CT: Greenwood Press, 1988.

ELECTION FINANCE. *See* Campaign Finance Reform (Federal), Campaign Finance Reform (State)

ELECTION FUND-RAISING. *See* Campaign Finance Reform (Federal); Campaign Finance Reform (State)

ELECTION OF 1824. Historians regard the election of 1824 as one of the watershed presidential elections in American history. By 1824 serious divisions had developed within the Democratic-Republican Party. Candidates for president included General Andrew Jackson (Tenn.), William Crawford (Ga.), John Quincy Adams (Mass.), and Henry Clay (Ky.). All ran as Democratic-Republicans, but each one represented a different faction of the party.

Even though the battle took place after Britain and the United States had agreed to end the War of 1812 by signing the Treaty of Ghent on December 24, 1814, Andrew Jackson had become a national hero after defeating British troops at the Battle of New Orleans on January 8, 1815. In the November 2, 1824, election, Jackson received a plurality of popular votes. John Quincy Adams came in second. However, when the electors cast their ballots, Jackson failed to receive an electoral majority. When such a situation occurred, the Constitution required the House of Representatives to select the next president. After suffering a stroke, William Crawford withdrew from consideration. To block Jackson from becoming president, Henry Clay threw his support behind John Quincy Adams. The House then elected John Quincy Adams as president. In return for his support, President Adams appointed Henry Clay as secretary of state.

The deal struck between John Quincy Adams and Henry Clay outraged Andrew Jackson and his supporters. In 1828 Jackson again ran for president. This time Jackson won both the popular vote and the majority of electoral votes.

Related Entries: Election of 1828; Political Assessments; Spoils System

SUGGESTED READINGS: James T. Havel, *U.S. Presidential Candidates and the Elections: A Biographical and Historical Guide. Volume Two: Elections 1789–1992*, New York: Macmillan Library Reference, 1996; National Archives and Records Administration: Election of 1824/Tally of Electoral Votes, *http://www.nara.gov/exhall/originals/tally.html*.

ELECTION OF 1828. In 1828 Andrew Jackson won the presidential election under the banner of Jacksonian Democracy. Within a short time of taking office, President Jackson announced his intention to sharply increase the number of political appointments to federal agencies and departments. Although Andrew Jackson did not invent the **spoils system**, he provided popular justification for patronage appointments by developing the theory of "rotation-in-office." According to Jackson the use of political appointments provided the common man with the opportunity to serve his nation and then return home. In addition to an increase in the number of patronage appointments, the period of 1829 to the end of Jackson's second term in 1837 saw **political assessments**, the practice of requiring government employees to make campaign contributions or face losing their jobs, become commonplace. Within a short time, political assessments became a key source of money for political parties and played a major role in the future growth of local, state, and national political parties.

Related Entries: Election of 1824; Political Assessments; Spoils System

SUGGESTED READING: Leonard D. White, *The Jacksonians*, New York: Free Press, 1965.

ELECTION OF 1856. *See* Buchanan Administration Political Corruption Scandals

ELECTION OF 1860. *See* "Honest Abe"

ELECTION OF 1876. By 1876 serious economic problems and a long series of public corruption scandals had eroded public support for the Republican Party. President Ulysses S. Grant (1869–1877) declined to seek a third term. The Republican Party had yet to heal the wounds from the 1872 presidential election. Instead of supporting the reelection of Ulysses S. Grant, the so-called Liberal Republican wing of the Republican Party had nominated newspaper editor Horace Greeley as their presidential candidate. Despite the split Grant easily won reelection. After Grant's reelection, the majority of Liberal Republicans returned to the Republican Party. The battle for the 1876 Republican presidential nomination pitted the reform wing of the Republican Party against the conservative wing of the party intent upon continuing President Grant's policies.

Former Secretary of the Treasury **Benjamin H. Bristow**, largely responsible for uncovering the so-called **Whiskey Ring** scandal, sought support of the reform wing of the Republican Party. Former Republican Speaker of the House of Representatives **James Blaine** and New York Senator Roscoe Conkling represented the conservative wing of the Republican Party. A number of other state favorite son candidates, including Ohio Governor **Rutherford B. Hayes**, also sought the Republican nomination. As governor of Ohio, Hayes had established a strong record for honesty in government. On the seventh ballot, Hayes received the Republican presidential nomination. The Democratic Party had nominated Samuel J. Tilden of New York as their presidential candidate.

In a repeat of the **election of 1824**, Samuel Tilden won the majority of the popular votes but fell one vote short of the necessary electoral votes to become president. Nineteen electoral votes remained in dispute from the states of Louisiana, South Carolina, and Florida. Both Republicans and Democrats had engaged in massive voter fraud and intimidation in the disputed states in an effort to make certain that their parties won the electoral votes of these key states. In a confusing series of events, slates of Democratic and Republican electors came to Washington from each of the three states. To resolve the dispute, Congress established an electoral commission in an effort to sort out the mess. Voting strictly along party lines, the Republican majority on the commission voted to seat all nineteen Republican electors. House Democrats threatened to conduct a filibuster to prevent Hayes's election. For a time it seemed that the dispute might ignite armed conflict.

To persuade House Democrats not to block the election of Hayes, House Republicans agreed to vote for the removal of the remaining federal troops from Louisiana and South Carolina and to end federal oversight of elections in the former states of the confederacy. The action had a profound impact on the southern political system. Beginning in 1877 a number of southern states began to enact so-called Jim Crow laws which enforced segregation in southern states from the late 1870s through the 1950s. Between 1890 and 1908, every southern state enacted measures effectively stripping African Americans of the right to vote.

As president from 1877 to early 1881, Rutherford B. Hayes made more enemies than friends within the Republican Party. He attempted to stop corruption in government agencies and programs and control the **spoils system**.

Related Entries: Blaine, James G.; Bristow, Benjamin Helm; Hayes, Rutherford B.

SUGGESTED READING: Ari Hoogenboom, *Rutherford B. Hayes: Warrior and President*, Lawrence: University of Kansas Press, 1995.

ELECTION OF 1884. The 1884 presidential election saw the Democratic Party nominate New York's reform governor Grover Cleveland to challenge Republican nominee **James G. Blaine** of Maine. The election of 1884 campaign quickly turned into one of the nastiest in American history. Democrats attacked Blaine for his earlier alleged involvement in the **Credit Mobilier** scandal and the Mulligan letters affair. Republicans returned the fire by widely publicizing the story that Grover Cleveland had fathered an illegitimate child. Without acknowledging paternity Cleveland then publicly admitted that he financially supported the child. Through much of the campaign, Republicans taunted Democratic supporters of Grover Cleveland by chanting, "Ma, ma, where's my pa." After Cleveland won the 1884 presidential election, Cleveland supporters chanted, "Gone to the White House, ha, ha, ha."

SUGGESTED READINGS: Grover Cleveland, URL; *http://www.whitehouse.gov/WH/glimpse/presidents/html/gc2224.html*; Rexford G. Tugwell, *Grover Cleveland*, New York: Macmillan, 1968.

ELECTION OF 1904. Born into a wealthy and politically well-connected New York City family, Theodore Roosevelt entered public service as a member of the reform wing of the New York Republican Party. Between 1881 and 1884, Theodore Roosevelt served in the New York State Assembly. From 1889 and 1895, Roosevelt served as a member of the Civil Service Commission. As police commissioner of New York from 1895 to 1897, Roosevelt worked to rid the police department of corruption. As assistant secretary of the navy from 1897 to 1898, he worked diligently to modernize the U.S. Navy. With the outbreak of the

Another voice for Cleveland.

"Another voice for Cleveland." The cartoon shows a woman holding a baby that is crying out "I want my Pa!" as "Grover the Good" Cleveland passes. *Judge*, September 27, 1884. Reproduced from the Collections of the LIBRARY OF CONGRESS

Spanish-American War, Roosevelt took the lead in organizing a volunteer military unit that came to be known as the "Rough Riders." Roosevelt returned from Cuba as a national hero. From 1899 to 1900, he served as governor of New York.

In 1900 Theodore Roosevelt received the Republican vice presidential nomination on the ticket with President William McKinley. Republican party leaders placed McKinley on the ticket in an effort to satisfy the reform wing. However, many conservative members regarded Roosevelt as a threat to politics as usual and to close ties with big business. On September 6, 1901, an anarchist shot President McKinley at the Pan-American Exposition in Buffalo, New York; he died nine days later. At age forty-two Roosevelt assumed the presidency.

To the great dismay of Republican Party conservatives, Roosevelt wasted little time in using the presidency to pursue a progressive reform agenda. Roosevelt took on the trusts and pushed forward with civil service reform. Equally important he pushed legislation through Congress expanding the national parks and placing vast tracts of federal land under federal protection. When Roosevelt ran for reelection in 1904, he received an overwhelming mandate from the American people by receiving some 336 electoral votes.

However, the Roosevelt election victory brought to public attention serious problems with the system for funding presidential campaigns. During the campaign a number of corporations made large campaign contributions to the Roosevelt campaign. Democratic presidential candidate Judge Alton B. Parker alleged that the Roosevelt campaign had received the contributions in return for President Roosevelt agreeing to stop pursuing the breakup of large corporations and antitrust legislation in Congress. To Theodore Roosevelt the allegations threatened his legacy as a president committed to political reform. Roosevelt vigorously denied the allegations, and a subsequent congressional investigation found insufficient evidence to give credibility to them. To help counter the allegations and to demonstrate his public concern over campaign fund-raising practices, in 1905 Roosevelt proposed prohibiting corporations from making campaign contributions. The next year Congress passed the **Tillman Act** which prohibited corporations from making direct campaign contributions to candidates for federal office.

Related Entries: Campaign Finance Reform (Federal); Tillman Act

SUGGESTED READING: Edmund Morris, *The Rise of Theodore Roosevelt*, New York: Coward, McCann and Georghegan, 1979.

ELECTION OF 1972. *See* "Dirty Tricks"; Watergate Scandal

ELECTION OF 1996. In November 1996 President Bill Clinton and Vice President Albert Gore defeated Republican presidential nominee Bob Dole and vice presidential nominee Jack Kemp to become the first Democratic presidential ticket to win a second term since Franklin Roosevelt. Even before election day, serious questions had arisen over the fund-raising practices of the Democratic Party during the 1996 presidential campaign. Early in 1995 President Clinton and the Democratic National Committee had embarked on an aggressive campaign to raise hundreds of millions of dollars in so-called **soft money** to support the Clinton/Gore reelection campaign and Democratic congressional candidates.

Late in October 1992, **Common Cause** filed a complaint with the **Federal Election Commission**, alleging that both the Democratic and Republican Parties had violated federal election laws by using soft money to directly support the election of presidential candidates Bill Clinton and Bob Dole. Early in 1993 the Justice Department opened a full investigation into the fund-raising practices during the 1996 presidential campaign. In addition the summer of 1997 saw the Senate conduct lengthy hearings into disclosures that Democratic Party fund-raisers had collected illegal campaign contributions from foreign nationals, including officials of the Chinese government.

Between 1997 and 2000, Attorney General **Janet Reno** faced strong pressure to request the appointment of an **independent counsel** to investigate possible criminal wrongdoing by President Clinton, Vice President Gore, and other Clinton administration officials related to campaign fund-raising during the 1996 presidential election campaign.

Related Entries: Campaign Finance Reform (Federal); Clinton Administration Ethics Controversies; Common Cause; Reno, Janet; Soft Money

SUGGESTED READING: Susan Schmidt, and Roberto Suro, "Troubled from the Start, Basic Conflict Impeded Justice Probe of Fund-Raising," *Washington Post*, October 3, 1997, A01.

ELECTION OF 2000. The 2000 presidential election pitted Democratic nominee Vice President Albert Gore against Texas governor George W. Bush, the son of former U.S. president George Bush. Through fall 2000, Gore and Bush battled for the support of the majority of the American people and for the all important 270 electoral votes. Despite three presidential debates and the expenditure of hundreds of millions of dollars in **hard** and **soft money**, by election day candidates Gore and Bush found themselves in a statistical dead heat in the polls. As the November 7, 2000 election day approached political observers increasingly speculated that one candidate might win the popular vote and the other candidate win the 270 electoral votes necessary to win the presidency. Early in the evening, the major television networks called the State of Florida for Vice President Albert Gore. Throughout the campaign, both the Gore and Bush campaigns regarded a win in Florida as vital to their campaigns. As the evening wore on, it became clear that Bush, not Gore, seemed to hold a substantial lead in the Florida popular vote.

At approximately 3:00 A.M. on November 8, the major television networks awarded Bush Florida and then declared Bush president-elect. The announcement gave Bush 271 electoral votes; one more than the number necessary to win the majority of electoral votes. Shortly thereafter, Vice President Gore phoned George Bush to concede the election. A half-hour later, Vice President Gore make a second call to George Bush, rescinding his earlier concession. As morning broke, George Bush clung to a lead of some 1,700 votes. Despite the fact that Gore had received 48 percent of the popular vote, Bush had the lead in electoral votes. Only three times in American history had a presidential candidate won the popular vote and ultimately failed to receive a majority of electoral votes.

Throughout the day of November 8, allegations flew regarding irregularities in Florida voting. In particular, Democratic supporters of Gore alleged that the ballot used in Palm Beach County had confused thousands of voters by placing ballot punch holes for Gore and presidential candidate Pat Buchanan next to each other. For the next several weeks, turmoil swirled over the Florida vote count. The Bush campaign fought efforts by the Gore campaign to undertake a full hand count of ballots from Palm Beach County. The recount dispute ended when the U.S. Supreme Court ordered an end to the state-wide recount ordered by the Florida Supreme Court. (Final vote tallies: Bush 50,456,141 [47.87%], Gore 50,996,039 [48.38%], Nader 2,882,807 [2.73%].) Subsequently, the electoral college voted to elect Bush as president of the United States. Not unexpectedly, the controversy led to calls of the abolition of the electoral college and for the popular election of U.S. presidents.

Related Entries: Election of 1824; Election of 1876

SUGGESTED READING: Brinkley, Douglas, *36 Days: The Complete Chronicle of the 2000 Presidential Election Crisis*, New York: Times Books, 2001.

ELLSBERG, DANIEL. *See* Pentagon Papers

ERVIN, SAM (September 27, 1896–April 23, 1985). U.S. Senator 1954–1974.

From June 5, 1954, until his retirement on December 31, 1974, Sam Ervin served as the U.S. senator from North Carolina. Despite his long service in the Senate, Sam Ervin received little media attention until the **Watergate scandal**. Between the June 17, 1972, break-in of the Watergate offices of the Democratic National Committee and the spring of 1973, pressure increased for a full congressional investigation of whether President Nixon's Committee to Re-Elect the President and the Nixon White House engaged in illegal activities during the 1972 presidential election campaign. On May 18, 1973, the Senate Select Committee to Investigate Campaign Practices, chaired by Sam Ervin, began nationally televised hearings on possible illegal conduct. The televised hearings made seventy-six-year-old Committee Chairman Sam Ervin a national figure.

Through much of the summer of 1973, the nation stayed glued to their television sets as witness after witness appeared before the **Senate Watergate Committee**. Despite periodic disagreements between Republican and Democratic members of the committee, Chairman Ervin managed to keep partisan infighting to a minimum. The testimony of former White House counsel **John Dean** and the revelation of former White House aide **Alexander Butterfield** of a White House taping system were the highlights of the hearings. Although nearly a year would elapse between the start of the Watergate hearings and President Richard Nixon's August 9, 1974, resignation, the Watergate hearings succeeded in focusing national attention on a wide range of abuses.

On December 31, 1974, Senator Ervin retired from the U.S. Senate and returned to his home town of Morgantown, North Carolina. On April 23, 1985, Sam Ervin (D-N.C.) died of respiratory failure brought on by kidney failure and other serious health conditions.

Related Entries: Butterfield, Alexander; Watergate Scandal

SUGGESTED READINGS: Clancy, Paul, *Just a Country Lawyer: A Biography of Senator Sam Ervin*, Bloomington: Indiana University Press, 1974; Ervin, Sam, *Preserving the Constitution: The Autobiography of Senator Sam J. Ervin, Jr.*, Charlottesville, VA: Michie Co., 1984; James R. Dickenson, "Sen. Sam Ervin, Key Watergate Probe, Dies," *Washington Post*, April 24, 1985, A01.

ESPY, MIKE (November 30, 1953–   ). Secretary of Agriculture, 1993–1994.

From January 1993 to October 1994, Michael Espy served as President Bill Clinton's secretary of agriculture. Prior to becoming secretary of agriculture,

Espy had served as a member of Congress from Mississippi. Before his 1986 election to the House, he served in a number of important positions in Mississippi state government, including assistant secretary of state, chief of Mississippi Legal Services, assistant secretary of Public Lands, and assistant state attorney general.

In June 1994 reports first appeared in the press, alleging that Espy had accepted gifts, free travel, and entertainment from companies and other private interests regulated by the Department of Agriculture. Between June and October 1994, new reports that Espy had accepted gifts from individuals and companies regulated by the Department of Agriculture led to demands by members of Congress that Attorney General **Janet Reno** appoint an independent counsel to investigate whether Secretary Espy might have violated federal law by accepting gifts and other favors from individuals and companies subject to Department of Agriculture regulation. On September 9, 1994, a special three-judge panel of the U.S. Court of Appeals for the District of Columbia appointed Los Angeles Attorney Donald C. Smaltz to serve as the independent counsel for the Espy investigation. Under the provisions of the **Independent Counsel Act,** Smaltz only had the authority to review the record for possible criminal law violations. In other words Smaltz did not have the authority to determine whether Mike Espy had violated Department of Agriculture gift acceptance rules. On October 3, 1994, Espy resigned as secretary of agriculture to devote his full attention to the Smaltz independent counsel investigation.

Over the next four years, Smaltz conducted a wide-ranging investigation of the financial affairs of Mike Espy and the gift-giving practices of a number of companies, including Tyson Foods and Sun Growers Cooperative of California. On August 27, 1997, a federal grand jury indicted Espy on 39 counts of accepting some $33,000 in illegal gifts under the federal **illegal gratuity statute**. Besides obtaining an indictment, Smaltz also obtained indictments against Tyson Foods and Sun Growers Cooperative of California for providing gifts to Espy. On December 29, 1997, Tyson Foods pleaded "guilty to giving former Secretary of Agriculture Mike Espy over $12,000 in gratuities and agreed to pay $6,000,000 in fines and investigative expenses." Espy and a number of other defendants indicted refused to plead guilty.

During the late fall of 1998, the Espy case went to trial in the Washington, D.C. Federal District Court. Smaltz called numerous witnesses who detailed the gifts received by Espy and his girlfriend from Tyson, Inc. and other private sources. Throughout the trial defense counsel for Espy pounded away at the fact that the government failed to produce a single witness to allege that Espy had taken an official action on behalf of any of the companies or individuals who had provided Espy with gifts. On the other hand, Smaltz maintained that the illegal gratuity statute did not require that he proved that Espy either asked for the gifts or took an official action as the result of receiving the gifts. According to Smaltz, the illegal gratuity statute only required that he prove that Espy knew he received the gifts because of his position as secretary of agriculture. On

December 2, 1998, a federal jury acquitted Espy on all counts. In the aftermath of the trial, a number of the members of the Espy jury sharply criticized Smaltz for failing to show that the favors influenced Espy in any way.

Related Entries: Clinton Administration Ethics Controversies; Illegal Gratuity Statute; Independent Counsel Act; Independent Counsel Investigations.

SUGGESTED READING: Bill Miller, "A Harsh Verdict for Espy's Prosecutor, Jurors Say Independent Counsel Wasted Tax Dollars, Didn't Make a Case," *Washington Post*, December 5, 1998, A01.

ESTES, BILLIE SOL. *See* Kennedy Administration Ethics Controversies

ETHICS CODES FOR FEDERAL EMPLOYEES AND OFFICIALS. *See* Code of Ethics for Federal Employees and Officials

ETHICS COMMISSIONS. *See* Public Integrity Bureaucracy

ETHICS IN GOVERNMENT ACT OF 1978. On October 28, 1978, more than four years after the **Watergate scandal** forced President Richard Nixon to resign the presidency on August 9, 1974, President Jimmy Carter signed the Ethics in Government Act of 1978 into law. Supporters of the law argued that it would help to restore public trust in government.

The Ethics Act contained five key provisions. The act required **public financial disclosure** for high-level federal officials in the executive, judicial, and legislative branches of the federal government. Specifically the Ethics Act required high-level executive branch officials, members of Congress, and federal judges to file annual public financial disclosure statements with the appropriate ethics units in each branch of government. Besides requiring covered federal officials to disclose their financial assets and liabilities, the Ethics Act required the reporting of financial assets and liabilities of spouses and minor children. To reduce the burden of complying with disclosure requirements, the Ethics Act permitted covered individuals to report financial assets and liabilities in broad dollar ranges instead of specific dollar amounts. Although not directly related to the new public financial disclosure requirements, the Ethics Act included new statutory requirements for the establishment of **blind trusts**, which reduced the attractiveness of blind trusts as a way to resolve the financial conflict of interest problems of federal employees and officials.

Congress included a provision for the appointment of special prosecutors to investigate allegations of illegal conduct by high-level executive branch officials, including the president and vice president of the United States. In 1982 Congress changed the name of the independent investigator from special counsel to **independent counsel**. To prevent future presidents from exercising control over the appointment or dismissal of a special prosecutor, the Ethics Act required that the attorney general request a three-judge panel of the U.S. Court of Appeals

President Jimmy Carter signing the Ethics in Government Act, October 26, 1978.
Jimmy Carter Library

for the District of Columbia to appoint a special prosecutor if the attorney general found credible evidence of a violation. In an effort to protect the independence of special prosecutors, the Ethics Act did not limit the length of a special prosecutor investigation or restrict how much money a special prosecutor could spend.

When Congress included provisions for the appointment of independent counsels in the Ethics Act, it anticipated a constitutional challenge. Critics argued that the Constitution required that an executive branch official appoint the independent counsel. The Ethics Act delegated that responsibility to a panel of three federal judges. In the 1988 case of *Morrison v Olson* (487 U.S. 654), the Supreme Court upheld the constitutionality of the independent counsel law.

The Ethics in Government Act also established the **U.S. Office of Government Ethics** (USOGE) within the Office of Personnel Management to oversee the federal executive branch ethics program. However, the Ethics Act left the day-to-day responsibility for enforcing federal ethics rules in the hands of designated agency ethics officials (DAEOs) and the responsibility for criminal investigations and prosecutions with the **Public Integrity Section of the Department of Justice** and U.S. attorneys. Additionally the Ethics Act established a new restriction on lobbying by former federal employees and officials. The so-called, one-year "cooling off" provision prohibited former federal employees and officials from attempting to influence anyone in their former government agency for one year after leaving the federal government.

Finally the Ethics Act established a 15 percent earned income limit for high-level presidential appointees. Prior to the passage of the earned income limit, federal ethics regulations permitted federal employees and officials from supplementing their government salaries by holding down another job, consulting, or giving speeches. However, federal ethics rules prohibited presidential appointees from accepting **honorariums** for speaking on matters related to the performance of their official duties. Advocates of the new outside income restriction argued that it would help to prevent special interests from using offers of lucrative outside employment to curry favor with high-level federal officials; critics argued it would make it more difficult for future presidents to recruit individuals who lacked substantial personal wealth.

Related Entries: Blind Trusts; Independent Counsel Act; Public Financial Disclosure; "Revolving Door" Restrictions; U.S. Office of Government Ethics

SUGGESTED READINGS: Robert N. Roberts, *White House Ethics: The History of the Politics of Conflict of Interest Regulations*, Westport, CT: Greenwood Press, 1988; United States Office of Government Ethics, URL: *http://www.usoge.gov/*.

ETHICS REFORM ACT OF 1989. Between 1983 and 1989, a number of high-ranking officials of the administration of President Ronald Reagan found themselves the subject of Justice Department criminal investigations or congressional misconduct inquiries. The **Reagan administration ethics controversies** had led to the appointment of a number of **independent counsels** to investigate possible criminal wrongdoing by current and former administration officials. By the late 1980s, these ethics controversies led to demands for the enactment of new public ethics restrictions. In addition the late 1980s saw increased criticism of the practice of former U.S. trade negotiations leaving government and going to work for foreign companies and governments. At the same time, other critics of federal ethics regulations argued that federal ethics rules constituted a major barrier to the recruitment of badly needed professional and technical personnel. Shortly after being sworn in as president in January 1989, President George Bush appointed the **President's Commission on Federal Ethics Law Reform**. In March 1989 the commission made a series of recommendations designed to make government ethics rules uniform across the three branches of the federal government.

On November 28, 1989, President Bush signed the Ethics Reform Act of 1989 into law after lengthy negotiations with Congress. First the act authorized an increase in the salaries of members of the House from $89,500 to $120,000 by 1991. In return for the pay raise, the act prohibited members of the House from accepting speaking fees and other **honorariums** starting in 1991. Because the Senate had balked at applying the new honorarium ban to senators, the act did not provide for a pay increase for senators; the Bush Ethics Commission had strongly endorsed the honorarium ban. On August 15, 1991, President Bush signed a bill raising the pay of senators after the Senate agreed to prohibit senators from accepting honorariums.

Second the act included a number of new **"revolving door"** restrictions. The Act extended the existing one-year no lobbying ban, to former members of Congress and high-level congressional staff, and the law prohibited former "very senior" executive branch employees and officials from contacting anyone in their former agency on behalf of someone other than the federal government and "very senior" officials in all federal agencies and departments. Congress adopted the complex provision to close a perceived loophole in revolving door restrictions. Although existing restrictions prohibited former high-level officials from lobbying anyone in their former agency for one year after leaving the government, it did not prohibit former officials from lobbying high-level officials in other federal agencies. Equally important the act established a new restriction on former senior and very senior employees representing, aiding, or advising foreign governments of foreign political parties before an agency or department of the United States for one year after leaving the government. Congress adopted the measure to limit the ability of former U.S. trade negotiators to help foreign governments with trade negotiations.

Third the act provided for the issuance of **certificates of divestiture** to permit federal employees and officials directed to sell financial holdings to comply with federal ethics regulations. Since the 1950s federal officials had bitterly complained about being required to pay unanticipated capital gains taxes. The Bush Ethics Commission had strongly endorsed the provision as a way of making it easier for the White House and federal agencies to fill essential government positions.

Fourth the act granted all federal agencies and departments **gift acceptance** authority. Prior to the passage of the Ethics Reform Act, the majority of federal agencies and departments had limited authority to accept free travel and lodging for their employees and officials from nonfederal sources. Faced with strapped travel budgets during the 1980s, federal agencies and departments lobbied heavily for gift acceptance authority. After the passage of the Ethics Act, the General Services Administration (GSA) prohibited federal employees from soliciting travel reimbursements from nonfederal sources but permitted federal agencies to accept unsolicited travel reimbursements from nonfederal sources.

In February 1995 the U.S. Supreme Court ruled in *United States v National Treasury Employees Union* that the Ethics Reform Act's honorarium ban violated the First Amendment rights of millions of career federal employees and officials. Although the high court found that Congress had the authority to prohibit members of Congress and high-level political appointees from accepting honorariums, it lacked the authority to extend the blanket prohibition to rank and file federal employees.

Related Entries: Certificate of Divestiture; Gift Acceptance Prohibitions; Honorariums; "Revolving Door" Restrictions

SUGGESTED READING: Robert Roberts and Marion T. Doss, *From Watergate to Whitewater: The Public Integrity War*, Westport, CT: Praeger, 1997.

EVANS V UNITED STATES, **504 U.S. 225 (1992).** In 1946 Congress passed the **Hobbs Act** to make it a federal crime for anyone to interfere with interstate commerce by either robbery or extortion. Congress passed the act to attempt to stop criminals from threatening to interfere with the operation of private businesses unless the businesses made payments to the criminals. Congress saw the establishment of the extortion prohibition as necessary to prevent the spread of organized crime. In the late 1960s and early 1970s, **federal prosecutors** began to use the Hobbs Act to prosecute state and local government officials for accepting bribes. Federal prosecutors argued that state and local government officials violated the act when they accepted anything of value from private sources for the performance of any official duty.

From the perspective of federal prosecutors, the act did not require the government to prove that a public official demanded a payment in return for taking an official action. In the 1992 case of *Evans v United States* the high court handed federal prosecutors a major victory. The Supreme Court held "that an affirmative act of inducement by a public official, such as a demand, is not an element of the offense of extortion under color of official right" prohibited by the Hobbs Act. In other words the act did not require the government to prove that the public official asked for something of value. Through the 1990s, federal prosecutors continued to view the Hobbs Act as one of the most effective weapons to combat state and local government corruption.

Related Entries: Federal Prosecutor; Hobbs Act

SUGGESTED READINGS: Linda Greenhouse, "Court Upholds Widened Use of U.S. Extortion Law," *New York Times*, May 27, 1992, p. 17; *Evans v United States* (1992) URL: *http://laws.findlaw.com/US/504/255.html.*

EXECUTIVE ORDER 10939, TO PROVIDE A GUIDE ON ETHICAL STANDARDS TO GOVERNMENT OFFICIALS. On May 5, 1961, President John Kennedy issued Executive Order 10939, which established new ethical guidelines for heads and assistant heads of federal agencies and departments, full-time members of federal boards and commissions appointed by the president, and members of the White House staff. The new ethics directive prohibited federal employees from engaging in any "outside employment or other outside activity not compatible with the full and proper discharge of the responsibilities of his office or position." In addition the order prohibited high-level federal officials from accepting "any fee, compensation, gift, payment or expenses, or any other thing of monetary value in circumstances in which acceptance may result in, or create the appearance of, resulting in: (a) Use of public office for private gain; (b) An undertaking to give preferential treatment to any person; (c) Impeding Government efficiency or economy; (d) Any loss of complete independence or impartiality; (e) The making of a Government decision outside official channels; or (f) Any adverse effect on the confidence of the public in the integrity of the Government."

In addition the Kennedy ethics directive prohibited covered presidential appointees from accepting any **honorariums** for giving speeches, writing articles, or attending events substantially related to the performance of official duties. The order did not prohibit presidential appointees from accepting honorariums for giving a speech on a matter unrelated to the duties of the official. President Lyndon Johnson's **Executive Order 11222** extended the honorarium ban to all federal employees and officials. Although the **Ethics Reform Act of 1989** prohibited all executive branch employees from accepting any honorariums, the 1995 U.S. Supreme Court decision in *United States v National Treasury Employees Union* held that Congress did not have the authority to prohibit lower level career federal employees and officials from accepting honorariums for giving speeches or writing articles unrelated to the performance of their official duties.

Related Entries: Appearance of Impropriety Rule; Code of Ethics for Federal Employees and Officials; Ethics Reform Act of 1989; Executive Order 11222; Honorariums

SUGGESTED READINGS: Robert Roberts, *White House Ethics: The History of the Politics of Conflict of Interest Regulation*, Westport, CT: Greenwood Press, 1988; Robert Roberts and Marion T. Doss, *From Watergate to Whitewater: The Public Integrity War*, Westport, CT: Praeger, 1997.

EXECUTIVE ORDER 11222, PRESCRIBING STANDARDS OF ETHICAL CONDUCT FOR GOVERNMENT OFFICERS AND EMPLOYEES.

Early in 1964 the U.S. Civil Service Commission and the administration of President Lyndon Johnson began work on a government ethics executive order. Johnson became president after the November 1963 assassination of President John Kennedy. Prior to being elected as vice president in 1960, Johnson had served as Senate majority leader. During his service in the Senate, he had not shown a strong interest in government ethics reform. In contrast, between 1961 and the end of 1963, Civil Service Commission Chairman **John Macy** had played a major role in the development and implementation of President Kennedy's ethics reform program.

By the beginning of 1964, a number of public ethics controversies persuaded the Johnson White House and Macy to move forward with major ethics reform initiatives. In 1963 former secretary to Senate Majority Leader Lyndon Johnson, **Bobby Baker**, had become the subject of congressional and criminal investigations for alleged financial improprieties. With the 1964 presidential election approaching, the media and Republican critics placed Johnson's financial affairs under a microscope. While serving in Congress, Johnson and his wife Lady Bird Johnson had become millionaires. To defuse the controversy, Johnson placed his financial holdings in a **blind trust** prior to the 1964 presidential election.

Then in 1965 an ongoing General Accounting Office (GAO) investigation found that major defense contractors routinely provided defense department employees with free gifts, lodging, and entertainment. More disturbing the GAO alleged that the contractors then deducted the expense of the hospitality from their corporate income taxes.

On May 10, 1965 President Johnson issued Executive Order 11222. The Johnson ethics directive replaced President Kennedy's May 1961 **Executive Order 10939**. First the order gave the Civil Service Commission overall responsibility for the executive branch ethics program. Second the order required each federal agency and department to appoint a designated agency ethics official (DAEO) to manage their agency's ethics program. Third the Johnson ethics directive established updated guidelines governing the (1) acceptance of gifts, entertainment, and favors; (2) outside employment, teaching, and writing; (3) financial self-dealing; and (4) use of government information for private personal gain. Fourth the new ethics code directed all executive branch employees and officials to avoid any action, whether specifically prohibited by the order "which might result in or create the appearance of (1) using public office for private gain; (2) giving preferential treatment to any organization or person; (3) impeding government efficiency or economy; (4) losing complete independence or impartiality of action; (5) making a government decision outside official channels; or (6) adversely affecting the confidence of the public in the integrity of the government." Fifth and most controversial, the order directed the Civil Service Commission to establish a confidential financial reporting system for thousands of high-level executive branch officials.

From May 10, 1965, to the issuance of President George Bush's **Executive Order 12674** in April 1989, Executive Order 11222 served as the most important executive branch public ethics directive. The **Ethics in Government Act of 1978** placed the United States Office of Government Ethics in charge of the executive branch ethics program, and it established a governmentwide **public financial disclosure** system.

Related Entries: Appearance of Impropriety Rule; Ethics in Government Act of 1978; Executive Order 12674; Public Financial Disclosure.

SUGGESTED READINGS: John W. Macy, *Public Service: The Human Side of Government*, New York: Harper & Row, 1971; Robert Roberts, *White House Ethics: The History of the Politics of Conflict of Interest Regulation*, Westport, CT: Greenwood Press, 1988.

EXECUTIVE ORDER 12674, PRINCIPLES OF ETHICAL CONDUCT FOR GOVERNMENT OFFICERS AND EMPLOYEES. Shortly after taking office in January 1989, President George Bush announced plans for a top to bottom examination of the federal ethics program. From the beginning of the administration of Ronald Reagan in 1981 to its end in January 1989, a number of Reagan administration and former Reagan administration officials had become the subject of public ethics investigations. As a first step, President Bush ap-

President George Bush signing Executive Order 12674, Principles of Ethical Conduct for Government Officers and Employees, April 12, 1989. George Bush Presidential Library

pointed the **President's Commission on Ethics Law Reform**. On March 10, 1989, the Commission issued its report entitled *To Serve with Honor: Report of the President's Commission on Federal Ethics Law Reform*, which recommended a governmentwide ban on federal employees and officials accepting **honorariums** and a governmentwide gift acceptance rule. The commission also recommended that President Bush replace President Johnson's Executive Order 11222 with a new standards of conduct executive order.

On April 12, 1989, President Bush issued Executive Order 12674. The Order replaced President Lyndon Johnson's May 10, 1965, **Executive Order 11222**. The fourteen principles of Executive Order 12674 clarified the ethics rules established by Executive Order 11222 with the (1) acceptance of gifts from nonpublic sources, (2) restrictions on outside employment, (3) financial conflicts of interest, (4) misuse of public office for private gain, (5) meeting their financial obligations, and (6) complying with all equal employment opportunity laws.

The adoption of a new **appearance of impropriety rule** constituted the most important change in ethics rules made by the Bush ethics directive. Executive Order 11222 had directed all employees to avoid even the appearance of impropriety in the performance of their official duties. The new rule directed executive branch employees and officials to "endeavor to avoid any actions creating the appearance that they are violating the law or the ethical standards promulgated pursuant to this order." Critics had argued that its broad language made it too easy to accuse individuals of violating the prohibition. The new policy required critics of the conduct of a federal employee or official to point to a specific regulation or law when filing a complaint alleging that a violation of the rule has taken place. The Bush ethics directive also prohibited any presidential appointee to a full-time position from accepting any outside earned income. The **Ethics in Government Act of 1978** had placed a 15 percent earned income limit on high-level presidential appointees.

Finally **Executive Order 12674** directed the **United States Office of Government Ethics** to issue a "single, comprehensive, and clear set of executive-branch standards of conduct that shall be objective, reasonable, and enforceable." On April 23, 1991, the USOGE issued a proposed set of new standard of conduct regulations. After receiving extensive comments from federal agencies and departments, the new standard went into effect in 1992.

Related Entries: Appearance of Impropriety Rule; Executive Order 11222; President's Commission on Ethics Law Reform; U.S. Office of Government Ethics

SUGGESTED READINGS: Dana Priest, "Suddenly 'Being Taken Seriously' at Office of Government Ethics; For Low-Key Agency, Overseeing Standards Is Field with Growth," *Washington Post*, January 15, 1992, A21; "Principles of Ethical Conduct For Government Officers and Employees," *http://www.usoge.gov/exorders/eo12674.html*; Robert Roberts and Marion T. Doss, *Watergate to Whitewater: The Public Integrity War*, Westport, CT: Praeger, 1997.

EXECUTIVE ORDER 12731, PRINCIPLES OF ETHICAL CONDUCT FOR GOVERNMENT OFFICERS AND EMPLOYEES.

On October 17, 1990, President George Bush issued Executive Order 12731. The order made a number of technical changes in **Executive Order 12674**, Principles of Ethical Conduct for Government Officers and Employees, which President Bush had issued on April 12, 1989, as part of an effort by the Bush White House to update federal ethics rules and regulations.

Related Entries: Executive Order 12674; United States Office of Government Ethics

SUGGESTED READING: "Principles of Ethical Conduct for Government Officers and Employees" URL: *http://www.usoge.gov/exorders/eo12731.html*.

EXECUTIVE ORDER 12834, ETHICAL COMMITMENTS BY EXECUTIVE BRANCH APPOINTEES.

On January 20, 1993, President Bill Clinton issued Executive Order 12834. First the order required every senior Clinton appointee to agree not to lobby any officer or employee in their former government agency for five years after leaving the government. Second the agreement prohibited former senior appointees in the Executive Office of the President, for five years after leaving the government, from lobbying any officer or employee of any other executive agency with respect to a matter in which the former appointee had personal and substantial responsibility. Third the agreement prohibited senior appointees from engaging in any activity on behalf of a foreign government if the activity would require the former senior appointee to register under the Foreign Agent's Registration Act of 1938. Fourth the agreement prohibited former senior appointees who had substantial participation in trade negotiations within five years of leaving the government from "representing, aiding or advising any foreign government, foreign political party or foreign business entity with the intent to influence a decision of any officer or employee of any executive agency, in carrying out his or her official duties."

The Clinton White House issued the ethics directive in response to a number of controversies that had surfaced during the 1992 presidential election. Through much of the 1992 campaign, Reform Party candidate Ross Perot attacked President Bush for not supporting a free trade agreement. In addition Perot blamed the situation in part on former U.S. trade negotiators working for foreign governments. Although the **Ethics Reform Act of 1989** had placed some limits on lobbying by former U.S. trade negotiators, Perot claimed the law did not go far enough. The lobbying restrictions were repealed by Clinton in December 2000.

Related Entries: Ethics Reform Act of 1989; "Revolving Door" Restrictions

SUGGESTED READINGS: Al Kamen and David Von Drehle, "Ethics Policy Toughened; Top Appointees to Face 5-Year Lobbying Curb," *Washington Post*, December 10, 1992, A1; Robert Roberts and Marion T. Doss, *From Watergate to Whitewater: The Public Integrity War*, Westport, CT: Praeger, 1997; Hobart Rowen, "Government's Revolving Door Needs Slowing," *Washington Post*, December 24, 1989, H1; Web Link: "Ethics Commitments by Executive Branch Appointees," *http://www.usoge.gov/exorders/eo12834.html.*

EXECUTIVE PRIVILEGE DOCTRINE. Through much of American history, presidents of the United States have argued that they have a right to refuse to turn over certain information to Congress in order to protect the ability of the president to conduct the business of the nation. Up through the **Watergate scandal**, presidents and Congress usually worked out executive privilege disputes in order to avoid Supreme Court decisions that might either establish a broad presidential right to executive privilege or sharply limit the right of a president to invoke executive privilege.

In July 1973 the **Senate Watergate Committee** learned from former White House aide **Alexander Butterfield** that President Richard Nixon had ordered the installation of a White House taping system. After learning of the taping system, the Senate Watergate Committee and Watergate special prosecutor **Archibald Cox** issued subpoenas for the tapes. Relying on the doctrine of executive privilege, President Nixon refused to comply with either subpoena. On July 24, 1974, in *United States v Nixon*, the Supreme Court voted 8 to 0 to require that President Nixon turn over the White House tapes to special prosecutor Leon Jaworski. Although the high court recognized that a president could invoke executive privilege "for matters dealing with diplomatic or national security secrets," the high court rejected Nixon's argument that executive privilege permitted a president to block access to information needed as part of a legitimate criminal investigation. On August 5, 1974, the Nixon White House turned over the tapes to Watergate special prosecutor **Leon Jaworski**. On August 9, 1974, Nixon resigned from the presidency.

Almost twenty-five years later, President Bill Clinton invoked the doctrine of executive privilege in an effort to prevent **Whitewater** independent counsel **Kenneth Starr** from calling members of the White House staff and members of the Secret Service before a federal **grand jury** responsible for determining whether President Clinton violated any federal laws in an effort to keep secret his relationship with former White House intern and employee **Monica Lewinsky**. From January through September of 1998, federal courts rejected the executive privilege claims of the Clinton White House and ordered a number of Secret Service agents and White House aides to testify.

Related Entries: Cox, Archibald; Jaworski, Leon; Lewinsky, Monica; Starr, Kenneth; Watergate Scandal

SUGGESTED READINGS: John P. MacKenzie, "Court Orders Nixon to Yield Tapes; President Promises to Comply Fully: Justices Reject Privilege Claim in 8-to-0 Ruling," *Washington Post*, July 25, 1974, A01; Susan Schmidt, "Executive Privilege Invoked for 2 Aides," *Washington Post*, March 21, 1998, A01.

FALL, ALBERT (November 26, 1861–November 30, 1944). Secretary of the Interior, 1921–1923.

Between 1921 and 1929, Albert Fall became one of the central figures in the **Teapot Dome scandal**. Early in 1921 Republican President Warren G. Harding nominated New Mexico U.S. Senator Fall to be secretary of the interior. Harding believed that Fall would represent the interests of westerners in the development of federal policies governing the use of western lands owned by the United States. The young conservation movement strongly opposed allowing private interests to pump oil, mine, or cut lumber on federal land.

Early in 1921, Albert Fall proposed to President Harding and Secretary of the Navy **Edwin Denby** the transfer of the Navy's Elk Hills, California, and Teapot Dome, Wyoming, oil fields to the control of the Interior Department. The Navy Department maintained the fields to guarantee an emergency supply of oil to power the nation's growing fleet. Shortly after receiving the proposal, President Harding and Secretary Denby agreed to approve the transfer. In late 1921 Fall quietly leased the Teapot Dome fields to oil developer Harry F. Sinclair; early in 1922 he leased the Elk Hills, California, oil fields to oil producer Edward L. Doheny.

Late in 1922 news of the leases leaked to a number of members of Congress. Through 1922 and the first half of 1923, President Harding, Interior Secretary Fall, and Navy Secretary Denby defended the leases as in the best interest of the United States. The conservation movement and progressive members of Congress attacked the leases as a sellout to powerful private interests intent on exploiting the nation's valuable natural resources. On August 2, 1923, President Warren Harding died in San Francisco, California, and Vice President Calvin Coolidge became president. Within a short time, Albert Fall resigned. Early in 1924 President Coolidge nominated Owen Roberts and Atlee Pomerene as Justice Department special counsel to look into all aspects of the alleged oil fraud.

Secretary of the Interior Albert Fall. Still Picture Branch, National Archives and Records Administration

The investigation by Roberts and Pomerene developed strong evidence that Fall had secretly received some $400,000 from Sinclair and Doheny for the leases. A civil suit also led to the cancellation of the Teapot Dome and Elk Hills oil leases. Late in 1929 a U.S. District Court jury convicted Fall of conspiracy to defraud the government. Fall received a one-year prison sentence and a $100,000 fine. After failing to win a reversal of his conviction on appeal, Albert Fall entered federal prison on July 18, 1931. He was the first cabinet secretary to serve time in jail. Ironically U.S. District Court juries found both Sinclair and Doheny innocent, although Sinclair spent time in jail for contempt of Congress.

Related Entries: Denby, Edwin L.; Harding Administration Scandals; Teapot Dome Scandal

SUGGESTED READING: David Stratton, *Tempest over Teapot Dome: The Story of Albert B. Fall*, Norman: University of Oklahoma Press, 1998.

FALSE STATEMENTS ACCOUNTABILITY ACT OF 1996. Section 1001 of title 18 of the United States Code makes it a federal crime for anyone directly or indirectly to make false statements to the federal government. The False Statements Act applies to a wide range of statements made to federal officials or submitted in writing to federal officials and agencies. For instance the act covers false invoices, false applications to obtain documents, and false Food Stamp, Medicaid, Medicare, and Social Security claims. In other words Section 1001 generally applies to any statements made or documents submitted in an effort to "profit under false pretenses." Equally significant the False Statements Act applies to statements made to federal administrative or law enforcement officials investigating possible violations of administrative or criminal rules or policies. For example, on September 8, 1999, former Secretary of Labor **Henry Cisneros** pleaded guilty to a single count of lying to the FBI regarding the amount of money he had paid to his former mistress. Cisneros made the statements late in 1992 as part of an FBI background investigation required for anyone nominated for a cabinet position.

Congress passed the False Statements Accountability Act of 1996 in response to the 1995 U.S. Supreme Court decision in *Hubbard v United States* which held that Section 1001 did not cover false statements made by members of Congress. The 1996 act made clear that the provisions applied to all members of the executive, legislative, and judicial branches of the federal government, and that Section 1001 applied to oral and written statements of federal employees and officials, as well. The fact that Congress moved so quickly to clarify the scope of the False Statements Act provides strong evidence of its importance.

Related Entry: Cisneros, Henry G.

SUGGESTED READINGS: Bridget Fitzpatrick and John Torraco, "False Statements," *American Criminal Law Review* 36 (Summer 1999): 607; Gabriel Kahn, "Judiciary Panel's 'Assess' Decision Nixing Law to Indict Members," *Roll Call*, May 22, 1995; Bill Miller, "Cisneros Pleads Guilty to Lying to FBI Agents; $9 Million Probe Yields Fine, No Jail," *Washington Post*, September 8, 1999, A01.

FALSE STATEMENTS ACT. *See* False Statements Accountability Act of 1996

FBI FILES FLAP. The "filegate" controversy had its origin during the early months of the Clinton administration. For understandable reasons anyone entering the White House must undergo a prior security check. To reduce the strain on the clearance system, the White House Office of Personal Security historically issued passes to individuals who worked in the White House or the Executive Office Building or who needed to enter the White House on a regular basis. In 1993 the Clinton White House appointed Craig Livingstone to serve as director of the Office of Personal Security. Prior to receiving his White House appointment, Livingstone had served as an advance person for the Clinton 1992 presidential campaign. Livingstone brought in Anthony Marceca, a civilian employee of the Army's criminal-investigation division, as his assistant. Like Livingstone, Marceca had worked previously on a number of Democratic campaigns.

In June 1996, reports appeared in the press that the White House Office of Personal Security had obtained hundreds of FBI background files on individuals who had served in the Reagan and Bush administrations and who no longer needed passes to enter the White House. The disclosure immediately led to speculation that the Clinton White House had obtained the FBI files to obtain negative information on individuals who had served in the Reagan and Bush administrations. The White House immediately denied that it had obtained the files as part of a secret **"dirty tricks"** operation. President Bill Clinton and other members of the White House staff blamed the files flap on a major "bureaucratic snafu."

According to the White House, after Livingstone took over the Office of Personal Security and began the process of updating White House passes, the Secret Service supplied Livingstone and Marceca with an inaccurate list of White House pass holders which included hundreds of individuals held over from prior administrations. Livingstone and Marceca then used the erroneous list to request hundreds of FBI background files, including the files of hundreds of former Reagan and Bush administration officials. When Marceca left to return to the Department of Defense in early 1994, Marceca's replacement recognized the problem and informed Craig Livingstone about the error.

In subsequent congressional testimony, FBI director Louis Freeh placed most of the blame for the mistake on the White House. Freeh explained that the FBI relied on an honor system when responding to White House requests for background files. In an effort to expedite the files investigation, Attorney General **Janet Reno** requested that a special three-judge federal panel give **Whitewater independent counsel Kenneth Starr** the authority to investigate the FBI files matters. Further complicating the controversy, **Judicial Watch**, a Washington, D.C., nonprofit legal organization, brought suit on behalf of former employees of the Reagan and Bush administrations who claimed that the White House and FBI had violated the federal Privacy Act by requesting and turning over the files to Marceca and Livingstone.

On March 16, 2000, Whitewater independent counsel Robert W. Ray announced that his investigation had not found "substantial and credible" evidence that **Hillary Rodham Clinton** or any senior White House official had requested the confidential FBI background files of Bush and Reagan administration officials. Ray also reported that his investigation had not uncovered any "substantial or credible" evidence that former White House counsel Bernard Nussbaum had testified falsely before Congress regarding his involvement in the FBI files controversy.

Related Entries: Clinton Administration Ethics Controversies; Starr, Kenneth

SUGGESTED READINGS: Lorraine Adams, "Report Clears First Lady and Others in FBI Files Case," *Washington Post*, March 17, 2000, A4; Judicial Watch: *http://judicialwatch.org*; Jerry Seper, "White House Got 338 FBI Files after Dale's; Calls It 'Bureaucratic Mistake,' Says Records Not Read," *Washington Times*, June 8, 1996, A1.

FEDERAL ELECTION CAMPAIGN ACT AMENDMENTS OF 1974. The passage of the **Federal Election Campaign Act of 1971** represented the beginning of a new era in federal campaign finance reform. Yet the **Watergate scandal** uncovered major gaps in the 1971 campaign finance law. From early 1973 through the summer of 1974, Watergate investigations by Congress and Watergate special prosecutors **Archibald Cox** and **Leon Jaworski** uncovered massive campaign fund-raising abuses by President Nixon's Committee to Re-Elect the President (CREEP) and Nixon White House officials during the 1972 presidential campaign. On August 9, 1974, President Richard Nixon became the first President to resign the presidency. Then on October 15, 1974, President **Gerald Ford** signed into law the Federal Election Campaign Act Amendments of 1974.

First the 1974 FECA amendments put in place lower campaign contribution limits for individuals and political action committees. The act placed a $1,000 limit on individual contributions to a candidate for federal office or a federal candidate's campaign committee and a $25,000 limit on individual campaign contributions to a national political party or other type of political committee. Equally important the 1974 amendments prohibited individuals from making more than $25,000 in campaign contributions during a calendar year. On the other hand, the act did not place a cap on campaign contributions by **political action committees** (PACs); instead it placed a $5,000 limit on PAC contributions to individual federal candidates.

Second the 1974 FECA Amendments established new campaign expenditure limitations for the presidential, House, and Senate races. The law prohibited presidential campaign committees from spending more than $10 million on the primary campaign and more than $20 million on the general election; The House candidates could spend $70,000 each election; and the amendments authorized Senate campaign committees to spend 8 cents per voter or $100,000 on a primary campaign and 12 cents per voter or up to $150,000 on the general election campaign.

Third the Act created an eight-member **Federal Election Commission** and assigned it responsibility for assuring compliance with the campaign finance disclosure and expenditure requirements of the law. Fourth a mechanism was put in place for funding the Presidential Election Campaign Funds Act of 1971. To provide the millions of dollars necessary to fund a future presidential primary and general election races, the amendments direct taxpayers to put part of their tax payments into a new presidential election campaign fund.

Not everyone applauded the passage of the 1974 FECA amendments. Senator James L. Buckley (Republican Senator from New York) and Eugene McCarthy (former Democratic Senator from Minnesota) brought suit against Francis R. Valeo, the secretary of the Senate, in an effort to overturn key provisions of the new campaign finance reform law. Buckley and McCarthy argued that the provisions of the act violated the First Amendment rights of citizens to engage in protected political speech by placing limits on campaign contributions and expenditures.

On January 30, 1976, the Supreme Court issued the landmark decision of *Buckley v Valeo*, which upheld and struck down key provisions of the 1974 FECA amendments. The high court upheld the constitutionality of the disclosure and campaign contribution limits of the act. On the other hand, the Supreme Court found the FECA provisions that placed a cap on campaign expenditures unconstitutional. The high court also found unconstitutional expenditure limitations on **independent political expenditures**. To bring FECA into compliance with the *Buckley* decision, Congress passed the **Federal Election Campaign Act Amendments of 1976**.

Related Entries: Campaign Finance Reform (Federal); Federal Election Commission (FEC); Political Action Committees; Public Financing of Presidential Elections

SUGGESTED READING: Congressional Quarterly Inc., *Congressional Ethics*, Washington, DC: Congressional Quarterly, Inc., 1997.

FEDERAL ELECTION CAMPAIGN ACT AMENDMENTS OF 1976. On May 11, 1976, President **Gerald Ford** signed into law the Federal Election Campaign Act Amendments of 1976 after the Supreme Court struck down key provisions of the FECA Amendments of 1974 in the 1976 *Buckley v Valeo* decision. First the amendments replaced the eight-member **Federal Election Commission (FEC)** appointed by Congress and the president with a six-member panel nominated by the president and confirmed by the Senate. The Supreme Court had held in *Buckley* that it violated the separation of powers doctrine for Congress to appoint any of the members of the Federal Election Commission. Second, the 1976 amendments required the reporting of **independent political expenditures** of $1,000 or more to the FEC and included provisions clarifying campaign disclosure requirements. Third the Amendments removed limits on total campaign expenditures by candidates for federal office, and fourth they removed expenditure limits on how much candidates for federal office could spend of their own money on their own political campaigns.

Related Entries: *Buckley v Valeo*; Campaign Finance Reform (Federal); Federal Election Commission (FEC)

SUGGESTED READINGS: Congressional Quarterly, Inc., *Congressional Ethics*, Washington, DC: Congressional Quarterly, Inc., 1977; Anthony Corrado, Thomas Mann, Daniel R. Ortiz, Trevor Potter, and Frank J. Sorauf, eds., *Campaign Finance Reform: A Sourcebook*, Washington, DC: Brookings Institution, 1997.

FEDERAL ELECTION CAMPAIGN ACT OF 1971 (FECA). In 1971 Congress passed the Federal Election Campaign Act of 1971 in an effort to deal with the rising cost of running for federal office. The act constituted the first major revision of federal campaign finance laws since the passage of the **Corrupt Practices Act of 1925**. First the law placed limits on how much candidates for federal office could legally spend for campaign advertising. The act limited media expenditures to "10 cents per eligible voter, or $50,000, whichever was greater." Second the act prohibited candidates for federal office to promise anyone employment or any benefit in return for their political support. Third the act placed caps on how much a candidate could contribute to their own campaign: $50,000 for president or vice president; $35,000 for Senate races; and $25,000 for House races. Fourth the act required candidates and committees to file detailed reports of contributions and expenditures four times a year. Fifth the act put in place a system for providing public funds to pay the cost of presidential elections.

Between the June 17, 1972, break-in at the **Watergate** offices of the Democratic National Committee and the August 1974 resignation of President Richard Nixon, the Watergate-related investigations by Congress, the press, and Watergate independent counsels **Archibald Cox** and **Leon Jaworski** uncovered massive violations of FECA by the Nixon White House and President Nixon's Committee to Re-Elect the President which included raising tens of millions of illegal campaign contributions. The campaign finance abuses related to the 1972 presidential campaigns highlighted serious gaps in the 1971 campaign finance reform law. In response to these abuses, Congress passed the **Federal Election Campaign Act Amendments of 1974** which established the **Federal Election Commission** and established much lower campaign contribution and expenditure limits.

Related Entries: Campaign Finance Reform (Federal); Watergate Scandal

SUGGESTED READING: Congressional Quarterly, Inc., *Congressional Ethics*, Washington, DC: Congressional Quarterly, Inc., 1977.

FEDERAL ELECTION COMMISSION (FEC). The Federal Election Campaign Act Amendments of 1974 established the Federal Election Commission. The 1974 Amendments provided for the appointment of an eight-member commission with four members nominated by the president and four members nominated by Congress. The 1976 *Buckley v Valeo* decision struck down the system for selecting FEC commissioners on the ground that it violated the separation of powers doctrine because Congress appointed four members of the eight-member commission. Because the FEC exercised executive responsibilities, the Supreme Court held that Congress must give the president responsibility for nominating all of the FEC commissioners. As a result of the *Buckley* decision, Congress passed the **Federal Election Campaign Act Amendments of 1976** which included a measure that replaced the eight-member commission with a six-member commission all nominated by the president and confirmed by the Senate.

First, the **Federal Election Campaign Act** assigns the FEC responsibility for collecting and making available for public inspection the campaign contribution and campaign expenditure reports required of candidates for federal office. The reporting program provides the media, interest groups, and political opponents with the opportunity to determine the sources of political contributions and where campaigns are spending their resources. More recently the FEC has encouraged political parties and political campaigns to file reports electronically.

Second the Federal Election Campaign Act gives the FEC responsibility for administrating the Presidential Election Funds Act. Under this act, the FEC distributes federal tax dollars to presidential primary and general election candidates who agree to abide by voluntary expenditure limitations. Third the Federal Election Campaign Act delegates to the FEC responsibility for issuing rules that interpret the provisions of the Federal Election Campaign Act and pursuing legal actions against candidates and political parties for violations of FEC regulations.

Almost from the date of its establishment, the FEC has faced strong criticism for not enforcing aggressively. On the other hand, supporters of the FEC argue that Congress and the courts have sharply limited its authority to close numerous loopholes which enable candidates for federal office to get around campaign contribution limits. For instance in the aftermath of the election of 1996, the FEC faced strong criticism for opening the **soft money** loophole.

Related Entries: Buckley v Valeo; Campaign Finance Reform (Federal); Federal Election Campaign Act Amendments of 1974; Federal Election Campaign Act Amendments of 1976; Federal Election Campaign Act of 1971; Hard Money; Public Financing of Presidential Elections; Soft Money

SUGGESTED READING: Federal Election Commission *http://www.fec.gov./*.

FEDERAL PROSECUTION OF PUBLIC CORRUPTION. *See* Federal Prosecutor

FEDERAL PROSECUTOR. Federal law gives the **Public Integrity Section** of the Criminal Divisions of the U.S. Department of Justice and U.S. attorneys the primary responsibility for prosecuting alleged violations of federal criminal law by federal employees and officials and pursuing civil sanctions against federal officials and employees for certain federal law violations. In addition federal law authorizes the president of the United States to nominate U.S. attorneys to serve in ninety-three districts across the country. Federal law also gives each U.S. attorney the authority to hire assistant attorneys and the necessary support staff. Although the Department of Justice does not manage the day-to-day operations of U.S. attorneys' offices, it requires that the attorneys follow the prosecutorial guidelines established by the Department of Justice. From January 1979 to the expiration of the special prosecutor (**independent counsel**) law in December 1992 and from July 1994 to the second expiration of the independent counsel law at the end of June 1999, special prosecutors and independent counsels exercised the same powers as federal prosecutors working for the Department of Justice and the U.S. attorneys.

The role of federal prosecutors in combating public corruption took a dramatic turn in the late 1960s. Across the country U.S. attorneys significantly increased prosecutions of public officials on public corruption charges. In 1975 the Department of Justice established the Public Integrity Section, within the Criminal Division of the Department of Justice, to coordinate efforts to combat public corruption. The late 1970s also saw the Federal Bureau of Investigation (FBI) shift substantial resources to public corruption at the local, state, and federal level.

Related Entry: Independent Counsel Investigations

SUGGESTED READINGS: Robert Roberts and Marion T. Doss, *From Watergate to Whitewater: The Public Integrity War*, Westport, CT: Praeger, 1997; U.S. Department of Justice, *A Federal Prosecutor's Job: The Role of the Assistant United States Attorney in the Criminal Justice System, http://www.usdoj.gov/usao/eousa/kidspage/index.html.*

"FEEDING FRENZY." In his 1991 book *Feeding Frenzy*, Professor Larry Sabato argued that print and broadcast journalists had lost the ability to distinguish between minor personal indiscretions by public figures and serious public ethics scandals involving abuses of the public trust. Professor Sabato referred to this type of media coverage of political scandals as a "feeding frenzy." Published three years after former Democratic Senator **Gary Hart** withdrew from the 1988 presidential primary race as the direct result of media coverage of his alleged extramarital relationship with Donna Rice, the Sabato book touched off a major debate within the media over how the private lives of political figures should be reported.

The 1992 presidential campaign provided the media with the opportunity to apply the recommendations of the Sabato book. In late January 1992, a national tabloid published an allegation by former Little Rock, Arkansas, television reporter **Gennifer Flowers** that she had had a twelve-year affair with Bill Clinton while he served as Arkansas governor. The story threatened Bill Clinton's efforts to win the 1992 Democratic presidential nomination. Yet the Gennifer Flowers story attracted relatively little attention from the mainstream media. To put the matter to rest, Bill and **Hillary Rodham Clinton** appeared on *60 Minutes* after the 1992 Super Bowl. In the interview Bill Clinton admitted to previous problems in his marriage but denied ever having an affair with Gennifer Flowers. After winning the Democratic presidential nomination, Bill Clinton went on to defeat Republican President George Bush and Reform Party candidate Ross Perot in the 1992 presidential election. Early in 1998 the disclosure of President Clinton's alleged sexual relationship with former White House intern **Monica Lewinsky** again raised questions over the scope of media coverage of the private lives of public figures.

Related Entries: Clinton Administration Ethics Controversies; Flowers, Gennifer; Hart, Gary; Lewinsky, Monica

SUGGESTED READING: Larry Sabato, *Feeding Frenzy*, New York: Free Press, 1991.

FERRARO, GERALDINE (August 26, 1935–). Member of the House of Representatives, 1979–1985.

From January 3, 1979, through January 3, 1985, Geraldine Ferraro served as Democratic Representative from New York in the U.S. House of Representatives. In 1984 Democratic Party presidential nominee Walter H. Mondale selected her as his vice presidential running mate. Ferraro became the first woman nominated by the Democratic or Republican parties to receive a major party nomination. The Mondale decision helped to breathe new life into a Democratic campaign that appeared to have little hope of denying President Ronald Reagan a second term.

However, within a month of securing the nomination, Ferraro found herself in the middle of a controversy over the financial affairs of her husband, New York City real estate developer John Zaccaro. The initial controversy involved Ferraro's failure to report the financial holdings of her husband on her congressional **public financial disclosure** statement as required by the **Ethics in Government Act of 1978**. Ferraro defended her actions on the grounds that House ethics rules did not require her to disclose the financial holdings of her husband if she had no knowledge of her husband's financial affairs. Because Ferraro served as the secretary-treasurer of her husband's company, this was difficult for many observers to accept.

The controversy did little to help the struggling Mondale/Ferraro ticket. In the 1984 presidential election, voters gave President Ronald Reagan a landslide victory. After the election the House **Committee on Standards of Official Conduct** ruled that Ferraro had improperly claimed the public disclosure exemption with respect to her husband's business holdings. However, the committee found that she had acted without "deceptive intent."

The findings of the House Ethics Committee did not end the legal scrutiny of Zaccaro. On January 7, 1985, he pleaded guilty in a Manhattan, New York, court to a misdemeanor fraud charge "that accused him of inflating his net worth by more than $17 million and overstating the value of five apartment buildings in order to secure a loan for a client." As a result of the guilty plea, New York temporarily suspended his real estate license. A year later Zaccaro found himself under investigation for allegedly being part of a municipal corruption scheme. On October 1, 1986, a New York City **grand jury** indicted Zaccaro for allegedly requesting a fee from a cable television company in return for using his influence with city officials to obtain a city franchise for the company. Then on October 14, 1987, a New York jury acquitted Zaccaro of all charges. The decision opened the door for Ferraro's political comeback.

In 1992 Ferraro entered the contest for the 1992 New York Democratic Party Senate nomination. Although at the beginning of the primary campaign, Ferraro held a large lead, her lead evaporated after allegations surfaced that she and her husband had received favors from organized crime figures. Despite vigorously denying the allegations, Ferraro lost the nomination to New York Attorney General Robert Abrams. Many political observers blamed Ferraro's 1992 primary defeat on the allegations which turned out to be totally false. Republican Senator Alfonse D'Amato subsequently defeated Robert Abrams for the New York Senate seat. In 1998 Ferraro again sought the Democratic Senate nomination. But again she lost the primary. On September 15, 1998, Democratic voters selected Brooklyn congressman Charles Schumer to take on Republican Senator D'Amato. After a hard-fought race, Schumer succeeded in unseating D'Amato.

SUGGESTED READINGS: Richard Cohen, "The Sins of the Husband," *Washington Post*, January 9, 1985, A21; Geraldine Ferraro with Linda Bird Francke, *Ferraro: My Story*, New York: Bantam Books, 1985.

FINANCIAL CONFLICT OF INTEREST PROHIBITIONS. In 1962 Congress passed the **Bribery and Conflict of Interest Act**. The comprehensive revision of federal criminal conflict of interest statutes included a new financial conflict of interest prohibition. Section 208 of title 18 of the United States Code prohibits federal executive branch employees from participating personally and substantially in specific matters that might impact the value of their financial interests. Like other conflict of interest prohibitions, Congress enacted the new financial conflict of interest measure to protect public confidence in the objectivity and impartiality of actions taken by federal employees and officials. The passage of the so-called **disqualification rule** helped to build support for the adoption of financial reporting requirements for federal employees. In May 1965 President Johnson issued **Executive Order 11222** which included a requirement that thousands of federal employees file confidential financial disclosure statements with their agencies and departments. Then in 1978 Congress passed the **Ethics in Government Act** which required high-level federal officials in all three branches of the federal government to issue annual public financial disclosure statements.

From 1962 passage of new federal financial conflict of interest rules through the passage of the **Ethics Reform Act of 1989**, many public ethics experts argued that federal conflict of interest rules worked an undue financial hardship on federal employees and officials required to sell financial assets in order to comply with federal ethics rules. Federal officials often found themselves forced to pay unanticipated capital gains taxes. To reduce the burden, the Ethics Reform Act authorized the issuance of **certificates of divestiture** to federal employees and officials required to sell financial assets to comply with federal ethics rules.

Related Entries: Certificate of Divestiture; Disqualification Rule; Divestiture Rule; Ethics in Government Act of 1978; Ethics Reform Act of 1989; Public Financial Disclosure

SUGGESTED READINGS: Robert Roberts, *White House Ethics: The History of the Politics of Conflict of Interest Regulation*, Westport, CT: Greenwood Press, 1988; U.S. Office of Government Ethics, Ethics Program Topics, URL: *http://www.usoge.gov/*.

FINANCIAL DISCLOSURE STATEMENT. *See* Ethics in Government Act of 1978; Public Financial Disclosure

FINANCING OF PRESIDENTIAL ELECTIONS. *See* Public Financing of Presidential Elections

FISK, JAMES. *See* Gold Ring Scandal of 1869

FISKE, ROBERT, JR. (1931–   ). Whitewater special counsel, 1992.

In December 1992 Congress failed to renew the **independent counsel** law as the result of growing concern over the cost and length of **independent counsel investigations**, particularly the **Iran-contra** investigation of independent counsel **Lawrence Walsh**. With the expiration of the independent counsel law, the Justice Department assumed responsibility for appointing special counsels to investigate allegations of criminal conduct by high-level federal officials.

On January 20, 1994, Attorney General **Janet Reno** appointed Robert Fiske Jr. as the Justice Department's **Whitewater** special counsel. Between March 1992 and January 1994, a controversy had developed over Bill Clinton and his 1980s Arkansas Whitewater land development. Attorney General Reno also gave Fiske the authority to investigate the circumstances surrounding the July 1993 death of deputy White House counsel **Vincent Foster**.

Upon receiving the appointment, Fiske immediately set up operations in Little Rock, Arkansas, and Washington, D.C. In early spring 1994, Fiske issued a report confirming that deputy White House counsel Vincent Foster committed suicide in July 1993. Then on June 30, 1994, President Clinton signed into law the reauthorization of the independent counsel law. On August 5, 1994, a special three-judge federal judicial panel appointed **Kenneth Starr** to serve as the Whitewater independent counsel. Besides serving as a Court of Appeals judge, Starr had served as solicitor general during the Reagan administration. As a result of Starr's background, critics wondered whether Starr could conduct an impartial investigation of possible criminal conduct related to the Whitewater land development. In addition, the decision not to appoint Robert Fiske Jr. caused a major controversy.

Related Entries: Foster, Vincent; Independent Counsel Investigations; Starr, Kenneth; Whitewater Investigation

SUGGESTED READINGS: Kim Masters, "Poised over Whitewater; Special Counsel Robert Fiske Jr., Calmly Plumbing the Depths," *Washington Post*, April 4, 1994, B1; Susan Schmidt, "Judges Replace Fiske as Whitewater Counsel: Ex-Solicitor General Starr to Take over Probe," *Washington Post*, August 6, 1994, A1; Andrew Taylor, "First Phase of Whitewater Probe Yields No Criminal Charges," *Congressional Quarterly Weekly Report*, July 2, 1994, 1771–1772.

FLOWERS, GENNIFER (1950–   ).

During the week of January 24, 1992, the *Star*, a national tabloid, published a story alleging a twelve-year affair between then Arkansas governor Bill Clinton and Gennifer Flowers. At the time Clinton was in the middle of a battle for the 1992 Democratic presidential nomination. In the article Flowers alleged that the affair lasted from 1977 through 1989 and that it began during a time when

Flowers worked as a Little Rock, Arkansas, television reporter. According to her, the affair continued through the 1980s. Flowers had left her television job to become a cabaret singer and an Arkansas state employee. Upon publication of the story, the Clinton campaign moved rapidly to discredit the allegation. On Sunday, January 26, 1992, Bill and **Hillary Rodham Clinton** appeared on the CBS news magazine *60 Minutes* after the Super Bowl. Millions of Americans watched the interview, which aired a few weeks before the crucial New Hampshire primary.

After Clinton admitted that he knew Gennifer Flowers, CBS reporter Steve Kroft asked him whether he "ever had an affair with Gennifer Flowers." Clinton responded, "I've said that before and so has she." However, Clinton acknowledged "causing pain" in his marriage during the course of the interview. Bill and Hillary Rodham Clinton's *60 Minutes* appearance succeeded in defusing the marital infidelity issue. Instead of the mainstream media pressing Bill Clinton on the details of the relationship, the vast majority of political commentators turned their attention to the issue of whether the media should be covering the private lives of candidates for public office.

Almost six years after the *Star* article and the *60 Minutes* interview, Gennifer Flowers returned to the public spotlight as part of the **Paula Jones** sexual harassment suit against President Bill Clinton and the **Monica Lewinsky** investigation. In a March 13, 1998, declaration completed by Flowers for the Jones lawsuit, Flowers repeated her earlier claim that she had had a long-term sexual relationship with Clinton and that he had helped her find an Arkansas state job, and she repeated her allegation of a twelve-year affair in a number of 1998 appearances on such television shows as CNN's *Larry King Live*.

Related Entries: Clinton Administration Ethics Controversies; Jones, Paula

SUGGESTED READINGS: Dan Balz, "Clinton Concedes Marital 'Wrongdoing'; In TV Interview, Presidential Hopeful Asks Public to Drop Questions," *Washington Post*, January 27, 1992, A1; Declaration of Gennifer G. Flowers: March 13, 1998: *http://www.washingtonpost.com/wp-srv/politics/special/pjones/docs/flowers03198.htm*.

FORBES, CHARLES. *See* Harding Administration Scandals

FORD, GERALD R. (July 14, 1913–   ). President of the United States, 1974–1977.

In 1972 the Department of Justice developed strong evidence that Vice President **Spiro Agnew** had accepted bribes and kickbacks while he served as governor of Maryland during the 1960s. The investigation led to his October 1973 resignation, which triggered the Twenty-fifth Amendment. The amendment required that President Nixon nominate an individual to serve as vice president. In the midst of the **Watergate scandal**, President Nixon nominated Representative Gerald Ford.

With the August 9, 1974, resignation of Nixon, Ford became the first person to serve as president of the United States without first being elected.

Related Entries: Agnew, Spiro T.; Ford Administration Ethics Controversies

SUGGESTED READINGS: Thomas Baily, *Presidential Saints and Sinners*, New York: Free Press, 1981; Bob Woodward, *Shadow: Five Presidents and the Legacy of Watergate*, New York: Simon & Schuster, 1999.

FORD ADMINISTRATION ETHICS CONTROVERSIES. On August 9, 1994, Richard Nixon became the first president in U.S. history to resign the presidency, and Vice President **Gerald Ford** became president of the United States. On September 8, 1974, President Ford granted Nixon a "full, free, and absolute pardon" for "all offenses against the United States or taken part in" while Nixon served as president. President Ford justified the pardon on the grounds that the nation and Nixon had already gone through enough as the result of the **Watergate scandal**.

The pardon rocked the young Ford administration. Speculation raged over whether Ford and Nixon had entered into a secret deal in which Nixon agreed to resign the presidency in return for receiving a pardon. In subsequent congressional testimony, President Ford vigorously denied the existence of a secret pardon agreement. Despite Ford's denial, political historians continue to debate the existence of some type of understanding between Ford and Nixon over a pardon.

Besides the pardon controversy, the Ford administration experienced relatively few public ethics controversies between August 1974 and January 1977. The most serious of these controversies involved a 1976 probe by the Joint Committee on Defense Production which revealed that a number of civilian Defense Department officials had accepted free gifts and lodging from major defense contractors in violation of Defense Department ethics rules. A number of employees and officials were subsequently reprimanded for violating **gift acceptance** policies. Another gift acceptance controversy involved Secretary of Agriculture Earl Butz. In 1976, Secretary Butz admitted that the Southern Railway Company had provided free lodging at a company-owned hunting lodge; Butz subsequently reimbursed the company for the cost of the trip and lodging.

Besides a number of gift acceptance controversies, between 1974 and 1976 the General Accounting Office issued a number of reports highly critical of the agency ethics program. The reports alleged that a number of independent federal regulatory agencies had failed to collect and review confidential financial disclosure statements required by President Johnson's May 1965 **Executive Order 11222**. Then in October of 1976, **Common Cause**, the Washington-based good government lobby, issued a report entitled *Serving Two Masters: A Common Cause Study of Conflicts of Interest in the Executive Branch*. The report sharply criticized federal agencies and departments for allowing federal officials "to have stock holdings that conflicted with their duties."

Equally important the Common Cause report also focused on the so-called

President Gerald R. Ford pardons Richard M. Nixon, September 8, 1974. Courtesy Gerald R. Ford Library

"revolving door" problem. The report found that a significant number of individuals working in key positions in federal regulatory agencies had previously worked for companies regulated by their government employers. According to Common Cause, the movement of individuals between regulatory agencies and regulated companies led to a situation where government regulators all too often protected the interests of regulated industries rather than the public interest. To deal with this perceived problem, Common Cause urged Congress to enact new restrictions on the lobbying activities of former federal employees and officials.

In the 1976 presidential election, former Georgia governor Jimmy Carter defeated Ford. The pardon of Richard Nixon probably cost Gerald Ford the 1976 presidential election.

Related Entries: Executive Order 11222; Gift Acceptance Prohibitions

SUGGESTED READINGS: Thomas Bailey, *Presidential Saints and Sinners*, New York: Free Press, 1981; Robert Roberts, *White House Ethics: The History of the Politics of Conflict of Interest Regulation*, Westport, CT: Greenwood Press, 1988; Bob Woodward, *Shadow: Five Presidents and the Legacy of Watergate*, New York: Simon & Schuster, 1999.

FORTAS, ABE (June 19, 1910–April 5, 1982). Associate Justice of the U.S. Supreme Court, 1965–1969.

In May 1966 President Lyndon Johnson nominated close friend and presidential advisor Abe Fortas as an associate justice of the U.S. Supreme Court. Fortas had played a key role in helping to develop and gain congressional approval of President Johnson's Great Society program, which led to the creation

Supreme Court nominee Abe Fortas and President Lyndon Johnson, July 29, 1965.
LBJ Library Photo by Yoichi Okamoto

of hundreds of new federal programs directed at combating urban and rural poverty in the United States. Equally important Fortas had a strong record for supporting the enactment and enforcement of civil rights legislation. The Senate quickly confirmed Fortas as an associate justice.

Then, during the summer of 1968, Chief Justice Earl Warren announced his intention to resign, and President Johnson nominated Fortas for the position. Through the summer and early fall of 1968, President Johnson worked to build sufficient support in the Senate to confirm Fortas. Despite strong lobbying by Johnson, Senate Republicans refused to back Fortas. Republican senators argued that the next president of the United States should be be given the opportunity to nominate the chief justice. The November 1998 election of Richard Nixon as President ended Johnson's efforts.

Then in the spring of 1969, *Life* magazine published a story that alleged that Justice Fortas had received a $20,000 payment from a charitable foundation managed by the family of wealthy businessman Louis Wolfson. After being convicted of stock manipulation, Wolfson was serving a one-year prison term. According to the story, Wolfson agreed to pay Fortas $20,000 a year from the foundation for the remainder of his life. In return for the payment, Fortas agreed to provide the foundation with expert advice regarding foundation matters. The announcement of a decision by Justice Fortas to end his relationship with the foundation did little to end the controversy.

Facing the possibility of a lengthy congressional investigation and congressional calls for his impeachment, Justice Fortas resigned from the Supreme Court on May 14, 1969, and returned to private law practice. The Fortas resignation provided President Nixon with a second opportunity to make a Supreme Court nomination. In May 1970 the Senate confirmed Harry A. Blackmun as an associate member of the Supreme Court. Prior to Blackmun's nomination and confirmation, the Senate had rejected Nixon's first two nominees, judges Clement Haynsworth Jr. and Harold Carswell.

SUGGESTED READING: Bruce Allen Murphy, *Fortas: The Rise and Ruin of a Supreme Court Justice*, New York: W. Morrow, 1988.

FOSTER, VINCENT (1945–July 20, 1993). Deputy White House Counsel, 1993.

Vincent Foster served as deputy White House counsel from January 1993 until his July 20, 1993, suicide in Fort Marcy Park. The park is located in Virginia along the Potomac River near Washington, D.C. Prior to taking the position with the White House counsel's office, Foster served as a partner with the Little Rock, Arkansas, Rose law firm; the same law firm where **Hillary Rodham Clinton** worked prior to Bill Clinton's 1992 presidential election victory.

As a deputy White House counsel, Foster reviewed the backgrounds of presidential nominees for problems that might interfere with the nominee's confirmation. From January through June 1993, the Clinton White House experienced a number of serious confirmation problems. The most serious involved attorney general nominees **Zoe Baird** and **Kimba Wood**. Disclosures that both Baird and Wood had failed to pay Social Security withholding taxes for undocumented household employees forced them to withdraw their names from consideration. After the failed Baird and Wood nominations, President Clinton nominated Miami prosecutor **Janet Reno** as attorney general; she was easily confirmed by the Senate.

Then in May 1993, the White House announced the firing of the entire staff of the White House Travel Office. The seven employees of the travel office served at the pleasure of the president. Years earlier the White House had established the travel office to make arrangements for members of the media who needed to cover the president and other administration officials on trips. After making the arrangements, media organizations would pay the travel office for the cost of the travel. Within days of the firings, it became clear that the White House lacked hard evidence that all of the employees of the travel office had engaged in improper or illegal conduct. Early in July 1993, the White House issued an internal report sharply critical of the handling of the matter by a number of White House officials. Despite the fact that the report did not criticize Vincent Foster for his participation in the firings, Foster apparently blamed himself for the White House travel office controversy.

On July 20, 1993, U.S. Park Police received a report of a body in Marcy Park, which is located along the Potomac River near Washington, D.C. The

Park Police quickly identified the body as Deputy White House Counsel Vincent Foster. Because the death occurred on federal park property, the Park Police took responsibility for investigating the circumstances surrounding Vincent Foster's death. Soon after the discovery of the body, a major controversy erupted over the fact that White House officials removed boxes of files from Foster's office after being informed of Foster's death. The White House had not waited for the arrival of Park Police detectives before removing the files. Later the Park Police concluded that Foster had committed suicide. This finding did little to end the controversy surrounding Foster's death. To end the controversy, in early March 1994 Attorney General Reno authorized **Whitewater** special counsel **Robert Fiske Jr**. to conduct an independent investigation of the circumstances surrounding Foster's death. In late June 1994, Fiske issued a report concluding that Foster had indeed committed suicide.

The Fiske report did not end the Foster controversy. After President Clinton signed into law a bill reauthorizing the **independent counsel law**, a three-judge federal appeals panel appointed **Kenneth Starr** as the Whitewater independent counsel. A short time after receiving the appointment, Starr announced that he would conduct a third investigation into Foster's death. On October 11, 1997, Kenneth Starr issued a report that concluded Foster committed suicide. However, the finding did not end Starr's investigation. Besides having authority for the Whitewater investigation, Starr also received authority to investigate the White House travel office firings. Starr learned that nine days before his suicide Foster had met with a private lawyer with respect to the travel office firings. In an effort to find out what Foster had told his lawyer, Starr issued a subpoena for the lawyer's handwritten notes. On June 8, 1998, the Supreme Court ruled in *Swidler & Berlin v United States* that the attorney-client privilege continued beyond Foster's death. In other words Starr did not have the authority to require Foster's lawyer to hand over his handwritten notes.

Related Entries: Clinton Administration Ethics Controversies; Fiske, Robert Jr.; Starr, Kenneth

SUGGESTED READINGS: Dan E. Moldea, *A Washington Tragedy: How the Death of Vincent Foster Ignited a Political Firestorm*, Washington, DC: Regnery, 1998; Susan Schmidt, "Starr Probe Reaffirms Foster Killed Himself; Forensic Details Counter Conspiracy Theories," *Washington Post*, October 11, 1997, A4.

FOX, FANNIE. *See* Mills, Wilbur

FRANK, BARNEY (March 31, 1940–). Members of the House of Representatives, 1981– .

In August 1989 a number of newspapers published stories alleging that Representative Barney Frank of Massachusetts "had hired a male prostitute with a criminal record as a personal aide, housekeeper, and driver" and had employed the individual for eighteen months. In mid-1987 Frank fired the individual after learning that the employee had used his Capitol Hill apartment for prostitution. Early in 1987 Frank publicly made known his homosexual orientation.

After publication of the report, Frank took responsibility for his actions and admitted that he made a serious mistake. An investigation by the House **Committee on Standards of Official Conduct** found that Frank had improperly used his position to fix thirty-three parking tickets. On July 26, 1990, the full House voted 408 to 18 to reprimand Frank for his conduct but rejected calls for Frank's censure or expulsion. In the 1990 congressional midterm elections, the voters returned Frank to the House by a large margin.

SUGGESTED READINGS: Janet Hook, "House Reprimands Frank, Refuses to Censure Him," *Congressional Quarterly Weekly Report*, July 28, 1990, 2379; Tom Kenworthy, "House Votes Reprimand for Frank: Effort to Impose More Severe Sanctions in Ethics Case Rejected," *Washington Post*, July 27, 1990, A1.

G

GALLINGHOUSE, GERALD J. *See* Carter Administration Ethics Controversies; Independent Counsel Investigations

GALPHIN CLAIM CONTROVERSY. After the Revolutionary War, Congress established itself as the branch of the federal government responsible for resolving claims against the United States. Under the system Congress had to appropriate funds individually for each claim. The system remained in place until the 1865 establishment of the Court of Claims. By the early nineteenth century, many individuals seeking congressional payment of their claims began to hire so-called claims agents. Federal employees, former federal employees, and even some members of Congress went into business as claims agents. The Galphin claim controversy had its origins in the pre-Revolutionary War period. George Galphin held claim to a tract of land in Georgia, claiming that before the Revolutionary War both Creek and Cherokee Indians illegally seized a large tract of his land. To avoid a confrontation with the two tribes, the British government agreed to pay Galphin $43,500 to resolve the claim. The outbreak of the Revolutionary War made it impossible for Galphin to collect the payment.

For nearly a half century after the end of the Revolutionary War, the Galphin family pursued their claim before Congress with little success. In the late 1840s, the Galphin family hired attorney George W. Crawford to pursue their claim. Largely as the result of Crawford's intervention, in 1948 Congress passed a bill directing the Treasury Department to pay the claim. However, the legislation left unclear whether the law required the Treasury to pay the interest which had accumulated on the $43,500. Under the arrangement with the Galphin family, Crawford received half of any claim paid by the Treasury.

Early in 1849 before the Treasury Department made a ruling whether the law passed by Congress required the government to pay the interest on the claim as well as the principle, President Zachary Taylor named George Crawford secretary of war. After being sworn in, Crawford requested that Secretary of the Treasury William Morris Meredith pay the claim. Meredith ruled that principal and interest on the claim entitled the Galphin family to some $100,000. After the comptroller of the United States ruled that the government did not owe the Galphin family interest on the claim, Attorney General Reverdly Johnson broke the deadlock by siding with Secretary Meredith. The Treasury Department then paid the Galphin heirs some $191,000, which included a $100,000 payment to Crawford.

The involvement of Secretary of War Crawford, Secretary of the Treasury Meredith, and Attorney General Johnson in the disposition of the Galphin claim outraged Democratic critics of Whig President Taylor. Critics of the payment of the claim coined the phrase "Galphinism" to describe the questionable payment. A congressional investigation found that the Treasury Department had improperly paid the claim, yet concluded that Secretary Crawford had not pressured members of the Taylor cabinet to pay the claim. In direct response to the Galphin claim controversy, Congress, in February 1853, passed a new law prohibiting members of Congress and federal government employees from receiving payment for assisting anyone in the prosecution of a claim against the United States. However, the law did not prohibit members of Congress or federal employees from assisting private claimants, as long as they did not receive any compensation for the assistance.

SUGGESTED READING: C. Vann Woodward, ed., *Responses of the Presidents to Charges of Misconduct*, New York: Delacorte Press, 1974.

GIFT ACCEPTANCE PROHIBITIONS. Today the vast majority of local, state, and federal government employees must comply with criminal and administrative gift acceptance prohibitions. Government gift acceptance prohibitions fall into three categories. First the vast majority of governments prohibit employees from accepting most types of private hospitality from nongovernment sources. De minimus gift acceptance prohibitions permit government employees to accept small gifts unlikely to influence the behavior of the employee or official. For instance government ethics rules generally permit their employees to accept a meal at a widely attended event. Second public ethics codes frequently prohibit public employees and officials from accepting any gifts from nongovernment sources regulated by the government employee's agency. Governments enforce so-called "prohibited source" gift acceptance policies in order to protect public confidence in impartiality of actions taken by their employees and officials. For instance government ethics rules generally prohibit employees from accepting gifts from individuals, companies, or organizations regulated by the government employee's agency. Third many government employees must comply with so-called "official acts" or "salary supplementation" bans. These restrictions prohibit nongovernment sources from rewarding public employees and officials for work performed as part of the performance of official duties.

Related Entries: Adams, Sherman; Espy, Mike; Executive Order 10939; Executive Order 11222; Executive Order 12674; Illegal Gratuity Statute; Vaughan, Harry H.; Wright, Jim

SUGGESTED READINGS: Robert Roberts, *White House Ethics: The History of the Politics of Conflict of Interest Regulation*, Westport, CT: Greenwood Press, 1988; Robert Roberts and Marion T. Doss, *From Watergate to Whitewater: The Public Integrity War*, Westport, CT: Praeger, 1997; Shari Rudavaky, "Executive Branch Gets Standardized Ethics Code: Question of Professional Memberships Unresolved," *Washington Post*, August 7, 1992, A19; U.S. Office of Government Ethics, Ethics Program Topics, URL: *http://www.usoge.gov/*.

GINGRICH, NEWT (June 17, 1943–   ). Representative, 1979–1999; Speaker of the House, 1994–1998.

In January 1979 Newt Gingrich entered Congress as a Republican representative from Georgia. Through the 1980s and early 1990s, Gingrich and a group of conservative House Republicans waged a war against the Democratic leadership of the House. In 1988 Newt Gingrich and other House Republicans filed an ethics complaint against Democratic Speaker of the House **Jim Wright** alleging a number of financial improprieties. On May 31, 1989, Speaker Wright announced his decision to leave the House although he denied intentionally violating House rules. Wright's resignation enhanced Gingrich's status within the Republican Party, but many Democrats blamed Gingrich for using the ethics complaint process for partisan political purposes.

The 1994 congressional midterm elections saw the Republican Party gain control of the House of Representatives. Political observers gave Newt Gingrich much of the credit for the historic Republican victory. Shortly after the 1994 election results, it became clear that House Republicans would elect Newt Gingrich to the position as Speaker of the House. However, late in December 1994, incoming House Speaker Gingrich became the center of a controversy over a multimillion dollar book deal with HarperCollins. The contract provided Speaker Gingrich a $4.5 million advance for a two-book deal. Interestingly the contract did not require Gingrich to repay any part of the advance if book sales fell below the $4.5 million figure. Rupert Murdoch's News Corporation owned HarperCollins. Although House ethics rules permitted Gingrich to receive the book advance, critics argued that Murdoch had a strong interest in actions taken by Congress regarding the regulation of media operations in the United States. As a result critics wondered out loud whether Gingrich had received such a lucrative book contract as part of an effort by Murdoch to curry favor with the next House Speaker. To defuse the controversy, Gingrich agreed to give up the advance and accept customary royalties from the book. Gingrich's book, *To Renew America*, became a best-seller.

Besides the book advance controversy, late in the 1994 congressional election campaign Gingrich's congressional opponent filed a complaint with the House **Committee on Standards of Official Conduct** which alleged that Gingrich had violated House ethics rules by using funds raised by a nonprofit organization to finance the production and distribution of a college course that advocated the election of Republican candidates for Congress. From September 1994 through December 1996, the Committee struggled to resolve a number of ethics complaints filed against Speaker Gingrich. On January 21, 1997, the House voted to reprimand Gingrich and ordered him to pay a $300,000 penalty for violating House rules regarding the use of nonprofit funds for partisan political purposes. Although Gingrich accepted the reprimand, he vigorously denied intentionally violating House ethics rules.

To the dismay of the Republican Party and House Republicans, the 1998 midterm congressional elections saw Democrats pick up a number of House seats. Political observers and many House Republicans blamed the losses on Gingrich. On November 6, 1998, Gingrich announced his intention to step down as Speaker. He subsequently resigned his House seat on January 3, 1999. Controversy continued to follow Gingrich after his resignation. In December 1999, he and his estranged wife, Marianne, agreed to a divorce settlement. Prior to the divorce settlement, media reports had disclosed Gingrich's six-year affair with a staff member of the House Agriculture Committee.

Related Entry: Committee on Standards of Official Conduct

SUGGESTED READINGS: Charles Babcock and Ruth Marcus, "Offenses Go to Core of Gingrich Probe; Admissions Are About-Face on Political vs. Nonpartisan Activities," *Washington Post*, December 24, 1996, A01; Ann Gerhart, "Settled . . . But Not Over; The Gingrich Divorce and Its Repercussions on the Right," *Washington Post*, December 18, 1999, C1; Guy Gugliotta, "Gingrich Steps Down as Speaker in Face of House GOP Rebellion," *Washington Post*, November 7, 1998, A01; John E. Yang, "House Reprimands, Penalizes Speaker," *Washington Post*, January 22, 1997, A01.

GINSBURG, DOUGLAS (May 25, 1946–   ). Judge for the U.S. Court of Appeals for the District of Columbia.

Late in October 1987, President Ronald Reagan nominated U.S. Court of Appeals Judge Douglas Ginsburg for the position of Associate Justice of the U.S. Supreme Court. President Reagan nominated Ginsburg after the Senate voted not to confirm **Robert Bork** as an associate justice. After the Senate rejected Robert Bork, President Reagan promised to nominate someone as conservative as Bork to fill the Supreme Court vacancy left by the retirement of Justice Louis Powell. Although Judge Ginsburg had a record as a conservative judge, most political observers believed that he would win Senate confirmation.

A few days after the announcement of the nomination, reports surfaced that Ginsburg had used marijuana during the 1970s. The reports created serious problems for the Reagan White House. Throughout his administration President Reagan had taken a hard line on the use of illegal drugs. First Lady Nancy Reagan became the administration spokesperson for the "Just Say No," antidrug use campaign. During the 1980s the Reagan Defense Department instituted random drug testing for military personnel. Conservative critics of the nomination argued that confirming Ginsburg would send the wrong message to the youth of the nation. Supporters of the Ginsburg nomination argued that a brief period of marijuana use should not disqualify an individual from being confirmed as a Supreme Court justice or from holding any other high-level public position. Within days of the disclosure of Ginsburg's prior drug use, it became clear that he would face an uphill confirmation battle. Reading the writing on the wall, he withdrew his name from consideration.

SUGGESTED READINGS: Jacob V. Lamar Jr., "If At First You Don't Succeed . . . Reagan Picks Another Conservative for the Court—So He Hopes," *Time*, November 9, 1987, 52; Tom Wicker, "Moralism Wins Again," *New York Times*, November 9, 1987, 27.

GOLD RING SCANDAL OF 1869. In November 1868 Republican presidential candidate Ulysses S. Grant won the presidential election. Coming three years after the end of the Civil War, the vast majority of voters living in Union states regarded Grant as a national hero for leading the Union forces to victory as the commanding general. Yet throughout Grant's two presidential terms, a number of his friends and appointees would become the subject of allegations and investigations of illegal or improper conduct. The so-called Gold Ring Scandal of 1869 constituted the first of many scandals involving friends, associates, and appointees of President Grant.

In 1868 New York financial barons Jay Gould and James Fisk hatched a scheme to make a fortune by cornering the gold market. Gould and Fisk began to buy up large amounts of gold in an effort to drive up the price and create a gold-buying frenzy. Once the price of gold reached a certain level, Gould and Fisk planned to gradually sell off their gold holdings and make a tremendous profit. Gould and Fisk understood that any large sale of gold by the Treasury Department would destroy their scheme. Through 1868 and 1869, the price of gold steadily rose as Gould and Fisk carried out their plan.

Shortly after Grant won the 1868 presidential election, Gould and Fisk sought Abel Corbin's help to find out the intentions of the federal government regarding future gold sales. Corbin's wife Virginia was the sister of President Grant's wife Julia. During June 1869 Fisk entertained President Grant on one of his steamers. At the dinner Gould allegedly lobbied President Grant not to intervene in the financial markets by selling federal gold. Later Corbin also allegedly lobbied Grant against interfering in the financial markets. Then in a letter written in early September 1869, Julia Grant urged her sister Virginia Corbin persuade her husband, Abel, to cease his gold speculation. To this day historians debate whether Julia Grant sent the letter to protect her sister from financial ruin that might result from a sharp drop in gold prices or as a signal for Abel Corbin to sell his gold before the federal government dumped a large quantity of gold on the market in an effort to end gold speculation frenzy.

"The Boss of the Ring." A caricature by Currier and Ives of New York financier James Fisk as a bulldog, 1869. Reproduced from the Collections of the LIBRARY OF CONGRESS

In late September 1869, under heavy Treasury Department pressure, Grant authorized the Treasury Department to sell a large quantity of federal gold. The sale burst the gold speculation bubble. Prior to the announcement of the sale, Corbin allegedly told Fisk and Gould about the letter his wife had received from her sister, Julia. After learning of the letter's contents, Gould and Fisk began to sell off their gold holdings. Although Gould and Fisk survived the crash in gold prices, many other investors did not. Besides ruining a number of investors, the gold crash helped to touch off a nationwide recession.

In the aftermath of the gold collapse, Congress conducted extensive hearings into the Gold Panic of 1869. In the end, the investigation uncovered the details of Gould and Fisk's scheme to corner the gold market. During the investigation President Grant declined to answer the questions regarding the circumstances leading up to the collapse of gold prices. After completing its investigation, the Republican-controlled Congress concluded that Grant had not had prior knowledge of Gould and Fisk's efforts to corner the gold market and that neither President Grant nor his wife had attempted to warn Gould, Fisk, or Corbin of his decision to authorize the sale of federal gold. In addition Grant historians have found little evidence that President Grant or his wife Julia profited from the 1869 gold speculation frenzy.

Related Entry: Grant Administration Ethics Controversies

SUGGESTED READINGS: Kenneth D. Ackerman, *The Gold Ring: Jim Fisk, Jay Gould, and Black Friday, 1869*, New York: Harper Business, 1990; C. Vann Woodward, ed., *Responses of the Presidents to Charges of Misconduct*, New York: Delacorte, 1974.

GOLDFINE, BERNARD. *See* Adams, Sherman

GRAND JURY. In the federal system, federal prosecutors must seek an indictment from a grand jury before charging an individual with a crime. About half of the states have similar grand jury requirements. A grand jury is typically composed of between twelve and twenty-three people. Supporters of the grand jury system saw it as a way to protect citizens from unwarranted prosecution by the government; however, many critics argue that the vast majority of grand juries rarely question the recommendations of public prosecutors.

Besides indicting individuals suspected of violating federal law, federal grand juries frequently review evidence of corruption by local, state, and federal officials. Federal prosecutors have the authority to subpoena individuals to appear before federal grand juries. In sharp contrast to regular trial procedures, individuals called before a grand jury have limited rights. They do not have the right to have their counsel present during questioning. Equally important, if a federal prosecutor grants an individual immunity, a grand jury witness must testify or face going to jail for contempt.

From 1979 through the end of the independent counsel law in June 1999, special prosecutors and independent counsels made extensive use of grand juries to investigate allegations of possible criminal conduct by high-level federal executive branch officials. From January to August 1998, independent counsel **Kenneth Starr** called numerous individuals before a Washington, D.C., federal grand jury in an effort to determine whether President Bill Clinton or other individuals might have violated federal law in their effort to keep secret President Clinton's sexual relationship with former White House intern **Monica Lewinsky**.

Related Entries: Independent Counsel Investigations; Lewinsky, Monica; Starr, Kenneth; Whitewater Investigation

SUGGESTED READINGS: Federal Grand Jury: *http://www.udayton.edu/~grandjur/index.htm*, Tony Locy, "Starr's Reliance on Grand Jury Draws Attention to Secretive Process," *Washington Post*, January 29, 1998, A12; Bill Miller, "Starr Leaks Not Illegal, Appeals Court Rules; No Contempt Sanctions for Prosecutors," *Washington Post*, September 14, 1999, A08.

GRANT, ULYSSES S. *See* Gold Ring Scandal of 1869; Grant Administration Ethics Controversies

President Ulysses S. Grant. Still Picture Branch, National
Archives and Records Administration

GRANT ADMINISTRATION ETHICS CONTROVERSIES. From 1869 through
the end of President Ulysses S. Grant's second term in early 1877, a number of
Grant's friends, appointees, and associates became the subject of public corruption investigations. The period also saw President Grant and the Republican
Party make full use of the **spoils system** to reward supporters and maintain
political power. Today historians regard the Grant administration as one of the
most corrupt in American history.

Between 1869 and 1872, the increased level of public corruption, national
economic problems, and the refusal of the Grant administration to deal with
increased criticism of the spoils system led to a serious split within the Republican Party. (For example the **Gold Ring Scandal of 1869** had implicated President Grant and his wife Julia in a scheme by financial speculators Jay Gould
and James Fisk to corner the gold market.) The so-called Liberal Republican
wing of the Republican Party joined with the Democratic Party to support newspaper publisher Horace Greeley for president during the 1872 presidential election campaign. Despite the split within the Republican Party, President Grant
easily won reelection.

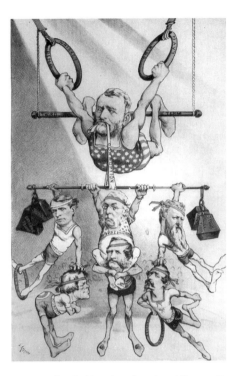

Cartoon by J. Keppler showing Ulysses S. Grant with "corruption" strap in his mouth, February 1880. Reproduced from the Collections of the LIBRARY OF CONGRESS

Between 1873 and 1876, a series of new public ethics controversies provided Grant's critics with even stronger evidence of the level of public corruption in federal agencies and departments. In 1874 President Grant nominated **Benjamin H. Bristow** as secretary of the treasury following a major controversy over the Treasury Department use of private revenue agents to collect past due taxes. Within a short time of taking office, Bristow learned of a major shortfall in federal excise taxes on distilled spirits. Unconcerned by the possible damage to the reputation of the Grant administration, Bristow oversaw an investigation which uncovered a massive conspiracy by whiskey distillers to avoid paying the Treasury Department millions of dollars in federal excise taxes. The so-called **Whiskey Ring** scandal led to the February 1876 St. Louis, Missouri, trial of President Grant's personal secretary, **Orville Babcock**, for participating in the conspiracy. Although a U.S. District Court jury acquitted Babcock of the charges, federal prosecutors obtained convictions of numerous other conspiracy members.

On March 3, 1876, Secretary of War **William W. Belknap** abruptly resigned after a congressional investigation uncovered strong evidence that for a number of years Belknap and his wife had received thousands of dollars in annual payments from an individual Belknap had helped obtain a trader ship on a western military post. During the 1860s and 1870s, trading posts on miliary outposts had grown into extremely profitable businesses. Belknap resigned before the House Judiciary Committee had an opportunity to vote out articles of impeachment. Angered by Belknap's action and President Grant's decision to accept Belknap's resignation, the House voted to impeach Belknap. By a vote of 37 to 24, the Senate voted to acquit Belknap in large measure because a number of senators believed they no longer had the authority to convict Belknap because he had left the government.

By 1876 nearly eight years of scandal had taken their toll. The Democratic Party appeared ready to take back the presidency for the first time since the 1856 election of James Buchanan. A unified Democratic Party nominated Samuel J. Tilden of New York as reform governor of New York State. In sharp contrast a badly split Republican Party nominated Ohio reform governor **Rutherford B. Hayes** in an effort to convince voters of the willingness of the Republican Party to turn over a new leaf. Despite the fact that Samuel Tilden won the popular vote, the House of Representatives elected Rutherford B. Hayes president after Tilden failed to obtain a majority of electoral votes. Between 1877 and 1881, to the pleasant surprise of Tilden supporters and the reform wing of the Republican Party, President Hayes took the first steps in decades to dismantle the spoils system in an effort to restore public trust in government.

Related Entries: Babcock, General Orville E.; Bristow, Benjamin Helm; Gold Ring Scandal of 1869; Whiskey Ring

SUGGESTED READINGS: Mark Summers, *The Era of Good Stealing*, New York: Oxford University Press, 1993; C. Vann Woodward, ed., *Responses of the Presidents to Charges of Misconduct*, New York: Delacorte, 1974.

H

HALDEMAN, H. R. (October 27, 1926–November 12, 1993). Chief of Staff for President Richard Nixon, 1969–1973.

H. R. Haldeman served as President Richard Nixon's chief of staff from January 1969 until the **Watergate scandal** forced Haldeman to submit his resignation on April 30, 1973. Although he exercised great power within the White House through April 1973, Haldeman had kept a very low public profile. In an effort to prevent a full FBI investigation of the Watergate break-in, illegal campaign fund-raising by President Nixon's Committee to Re-Elect the President, and other illegal conduct by the Nixon White House, Nixon directed Haldeman and Ehrlichman to try to persuade the Central Intelligence Agency (CIA) to invoke national security concerns to provide the Federal Bureau of Investigation (FBI) with a reason for not tracing money laundered by President Nixon's Re-Election Committee to pay the Watergate burglars. CIA Director Richard Helms refused to go along with the proposal.

On July 30, 1973, H. R. Haldeman testified before the **Senate Watergate Committee**; he denied any prior White House involvement in the Watergate break-in or that President Nixon or members of the White House staff had attempted to impede the Watergate investigation. However, Haldeman admitted to having knowledge of a **"dirty tricks"** operation designed to disrupt the 1972 primary campaigns of a number of candidates competing for the presidential nomination of the Democratic Party. Later a U.S. District Court jury convicted Haldeman of perjury, conspiracy, and obstruction of justice. He served sixteen months in a federal correctional facility.

Following his release from prison, Haldeman returned to private business in southern California. He authored two Watergate-related books, *The Ends of Power* (1978) and *The Haldeman Diaries: Inside the Nixon White House* (1994), published posthumously. On November 12, 1993, at age sixty-seven, H. R. Haldeman died after a battle with cancer. In the *Haldeman Diaries*, Haldeman

H. R. Haldeman, assistant to the president. Nixon Presidential
Materials Staff

presented a picture of a president and a White House staff that viewed the world
in terms of friends and enemies. According to Haldeman the wartime mentality
within the White House gave birth to an environment that led to the Watergate
break-in and cover-up, along with other illegal activities by Nixon administration
officials and the Committee to Re-Elect the President.

Related Entries: Senate Watergate Committee; Watergate Scandal

SUGGESTED READINGS: Nathan Miller, *Stealing from America: A History of Corrup-
tion from Jamestown to Reagan*, New York: Paragon House, 1992; J. Y. Smith, "H. R.
Haldeman Dies; Was Nixon Chief of Staff; Watergate Role Led to 18 Months in Prison,"
Washington Post, November 13, 1993, A12.

HALE, DAVID. Former Little Rock, Arkansas municipal judge and owner of
Hale's Capital Management.

Between January 1994 and the end of 1999, David Hale became a major
figure in the **Whitewater** investigations of Justice Department special counsel
Robert Fiske Jr. and **independent counsel Kenneth Starr**. During the mid-
1980s, after serving as a Little Rock, Arkansas, Municipal Court Judge, he
established Hale's Capital Management to provide small businesses loans
backed by the Small Business Administration (SBA). On March 22, 1994, David

Hale pleaded guilty to conspiracy and mail fraud related to the fraudulent issuance of loans by Hale Management. In his plea, Hale admitted to having made a number of fraudulent loans. The Whitewater investigation determined that **Susan** and **James McDougal** used a portion of the loan to purchase land for the Whitewater Development Corporation. Hale received a twenty-eight-month prison sentence in return for his guilty plea. Hale also agreed to cooperate with the Whitewater investigation.

In August 1994, a special federal court of appeals panel appointed Kenneth Starr as the Whitewater independent counsel. In 1995, a Little Rock, Arkansas, federal **grand jury** indicted Arkansas governor Jim Guy Tucker and Jim and Susan McDougal for obtaining $3 million in illegal loans from Hale's Capital Management. Tucker and the McDougals went on trial in April 1996. David Hale became the star witness in the trial.

During the trial, Hale testified that then–Arkansas governor Bill Clinton pressured Hale to make a fraudulent $300,000 loan to Susan McDougal. On May 9, 1996, the defense played the videotaped testimony of President Clinton. In his testimony, Clinton denied ever having asked David Hale to make a $300,000 loan to Susan McDougal. Despite Clinton's testimony, the U.S. District Court jury convicted Tucker and the McDougals of fraud. In July 1996, David Hale repeated his testimony before a Senate committee investigating the Whitewater land development. Through the remainder of the Whitewater investigation, prosecutors proved unsuccessful in finding anyone to support Hale's testimony regarding President Clinton.

Related Entries: McDougal, James; McDougal, Susan; Whitewater Investigation

SUGGESTED READING: Susan Schmidt, "Jury Hears Clinton Deny Allegations; Defense Rests in Whitewater Trial," *Washington Post*, May 10, 1996, A01.

HAMILTON, ALEXANDER (January 11, 1755–July 12, 1804). Secretary of the Treasury, 1789–1795.

On April 30, 1789, George Washington was sworn in as the first president of the United States. He faced the immediate problem of finding qualified individuals to fill his cabinet. He especially needed to select a secretary of the treasury with the ability to put the dismal financial affairs of the new nation in order. Washington selected a young New York lawyer named Alexander Hamilton for the daunting task. The Constitution required the federal government to assume the debt issued by the states and Congress prior to and during the Revolutionary War. Early in 1790 Secretary of the Treasury Alexander Hamilton announced a controversial plan for refunding the federal debt. To pay off the outstanding obligations at face value, the Treasury Department would issue new government bonds to be paid off from tariff receipts. Hamilton greatly underestimated congressional opposition to his refunding plans.

Prior to the announcement of the plan, speculators had gambled that the federal government would pay off outstanding debts at face or full value. They had bought up millions of dollars in debt at prices far below the face value of the debt certificates. These speculators stood to make small fortunes if Congress passed Hamilton's debt refinancing plan. Not unexpectedly Jeffersonians attacked Hamilton's debt refinancing plan as an effort by Hamilton to enrich Hamilton's Federalist supporters. Strong backers of state sovereignty, Jeffersonians strongly opposed giving the Treasury Department so much control over the national debt. After a bitter battle, Congress barely approved Hamilton's refunding plan.

In addition to the debt refunding allegations, a number of Hamilton historians have recounted the story of Hamilton's alleged affair with Mrs. Maria Lewis Reynolds. Maria Reynolds and Reynolds's husband subsequently attempted to blackmail Hamilton to keep the affair secret. Also according to the story, when rumors of the affair reached key members of Congress, James Monroe led a secret congressional investigation of whether the affair had compromised Hamilton's position as secretary of the treasury. After Hamilton reassured the special committee that the affair had not compromised his position, the investigation was dropped. Continued rumors of the affair led Hamilton to issue a pamphlet fully disclosing his relationship with Maria Reynolds. Almost two hundred years later, defenders of President Bill Clinton would use the alleged Hamilton/Reynolds affair to argue that President Clinton's sexual relationship with **Monica Lewinsky** did not justify impeachment and the removal of Clinton from office.

SUGGESTED READINGS: Jacob Katz Cogan, "The Reynolds Affairs and the Politics of Character," *Journal of the Early Republic* 16 (1996): 389–417; Henry Cabot Lodge, *Alexander Hamilton*, Boston: Houghton Mifflin, 1898.

HARD MONEY. The **Federal Election Campaign Act of 1971 (FECA)** and subsequent FECA amendments limit how much individuals and groups may contribute to directly support the election of candidates for federal office. Equally important federal law also prohibits direct political contributions to federal candidates by corporations, unions, and foreign nationals. Political experts often refer to contributions made subject to FECA restrictions as hard money. Federal law permits candidates for federal office to use hard money for the purchase of political campaign commercials and other traditional campaign activities directly supporting the election of a particular candidate. In the 1976 ***Buckley v Valeo*** decision, the Supreme Court upheld FECA's hard money contribution limits. Specifically FECA limits individual contributions to candidates for federal office to $1,000 per candidate per election; $20,000 to a national party committee per calendar year; and $5,000 to any other political committee per calendar year. In addition FECA limits total individual hard money contributions to $25,000 per calendar year.

In 1979, as a direct result of growing criticism of the impact of the FECA's hard money limits on the ability of political parties to fund traditional activities such as voter registration and get out the vote campaigns, the **Federal Election**

Commission (FEC) issued new rules permitting national political parties to solicit so-called **soft money** contributions to fund party building activities. Party building activities did not include paying for campaign ads supporting the election of a specific candidate for president or for other federal offices. By the early 1990s, however, both the Republican and Democratic Parties increased the use of soft money to pay for so-called **issue ads**. Although issue ads may not directly advocate the election of a particular candidate for federal office, they may highlight the achievements or perceived failures of a specific candidate. FEC regulations require that political parties use hard money to pay a portion of the cost of running issues ads. Despite the hard money requirement, the presidential **election of 2000** saw both the Republican and Democratic national parties use soft money to pay for tens of millions of dollars in issue ads.

Related Entries: Campaign Finance Reform (Federal); Campaign Finance Reform (State); Election of 1996; Federal Election Campaign Act Amendments of 1974; Federal Election Campaign Act Amendments of 1976; Federal Election Campaign Act of 1971; Federal Election Commission (FEC); Soft Money

SUGGESTED READINGS: Congressional Quarterly Inc., "Campaign Finance Reform: Are Tighter Laws Needed to Police the System?" *CQ Researcher* 6 (February 9, 1996): 121–144; Federal Election Commission: Supporting Federal Candidates: A Guide to Citizens, *http://www.fec.gov/pages/citn0001.htm.*

HARDING, WARREN G. (November 2, 1865–August 2, 1923). President of the United States, 1921–1923. *See* Harding Administration Scandals

HARDING ADMINISTRATION SCANDALS. In November 1920 Republican Warren G. Harding defeated his Democratic opponent, James M. Cox of Ohio, to become president of the United States. Harding received 60 percent of the popular vote. The Republican Party and Warren Harding took full advantage of the fact that the majority of the American people wanted a return to normalcy after the end of the First World War. In sharp contrast to supporters of the **Progressive Movement**, Harding made clear that he welcomed the support of big business for his administration.

To assist him in implementing his election mandate, Harding recruited a number of his Ohio friends and associates. Often referred to as the **Ohio Gang** by historians, Harding's Ohio appointments included Attorney General **Harry M. Daugherty**, Secretary of the Interior **Albert Fall**, Postmaster General Will H. Hays, and Veteran's Bureau head Charles R. Forbes. Congressional investigations of allegations of official misconduct by members of the Ohio Gang began during 1922 and 1923, following Harding's death. By the end of the 1920s, a series of congressional and criminal public corruption investigations uncovered a pattern of Harding appointees using their public position for personal financial gain.

Veteran's Bureau head Charles R. Forbes became the first member of the

President Warren G. Harding. Still Picture Branch,
National Archives and Records Administration

Ohio Gang to face public corruption allegations. At the urging of President
Harding, Congress established a new Veteran's Bureau in an effort to improve
the care of tens of thousands of disabled veterans from the Civil War, Spanish
American War, and World War I. President Harding then appointed Charles
Forbes as the head of the new Veteran's Bureau. In February 1923 Elias A.
Mortimer, a lobbyist for a St. Louis, Missouri, construction company, informed
Attorney General **Harry Daugherty** that Forbes had provided the construction
company he worked for with inside information that permitted the company to
underbid for Veteran's Bureau contracts. Instead of pursuing a criminal inves-
tigation of Forbes, Attorney General Daugherty and President Harding allowed
Forbes to resign on February 23, 1923.

By early summer 1923, Mortimer's allegations reached key members of Congress. Mortimer appeared before a congressional committee and told the members the same story he had earlier told Attorney General Daugherty. He also
told the committee that he personally gave Forbes $5,000 from the owner of
the St. Louis, Missouri, construction company. Mortimer's congressional testimony and the August 1923 death of President Warren Harding dramatically

changed the attitude of the Justice Department toward the Forbes matter. In 1924 a U.S. District Court jury convicted Charles Forbes and John Thompson for conspiracy to defraud the government. Both received two-year jail sentences and a $10,000 fine. According to Mortimer, Thompson, a partner in the St. Louis, Missouri, construction company, gave him the $5,000 to give to Forbes.

The so-called Alien Property scandal constituted the second major scandal that led to the criminal prosecution of a member of Harding's Ohio Gang after Harding's death. In 1917, with the entry of the United States into World War II, Congress passed legislation authorizing the U.S. government to seize the assets of all U.S. companies owned by German nationals. Congress established the Alien Property Bureau to implement the seizure law. In 1921 representatives of a German family hired John T. King, a member of the Republican National Committee, to help persuade the government to return the proceeds of one of the companies seized under the law. The family claimed that at the time of the seizure, a Swiss family held the stock. John King then enlisted the help of Jess Smith, an aide to Attorney General Daugherty, to help with the pursuit of the claim. King and Smith then persuaded the U.S. alien property custodian to release millions of dollars from the sale of the company to a representative of the German family.

In 1926 a federal **grand jury** indicted Attorney General Daugherty, Thomas W. Miller, and King for conspiracy to defraud the government. King received some $391,000 in government bonds and $50,000 in cash for obtaining release of the proceeds from the sale of the company; he then gave Smith $224,000 and Miller $50,000. Smith then deposited $50,000 in bonds in a joint bank account he held with Daugherty. In May 1923 Smith committed suicide. In 1926 a U.S. District Court jury deadlocked on whether Daugherty and Miller had been part of the scheme hatched by King and Smith. King had died before the first 1926 trial. In 1927 a U.S. District Court jury convicted Miller of conspiracy to defraud the government. The jury again deadlocked on Daugherty's guilt or innocence. The government declined to retry Daugherty, and Miller received an eighteen-month sentence and a $5,000 fine.

The **Teapot Dome scandal**, however, remains the best known of the Harding administration public corruption scandals. In 1929 former Secretary of Interior Albert Fall became the first Cabinet secretary convicted of a crime. A U.S. District Court jury found that Fall had accepted hundreds of thousands of dollars from oil barons Harry S. Sinclair and Edward L. Doheny for the right to pump oil from naval oil fields located in Elk Hills, California, and Teapot Dome, Wyoming. Prior to Fall's conviction, the Supreme Court upheld the cancellation of the leases to Sinclair and Doheny. In a twist of fate, U.S. District Court juries failed to convict either Sinclair or Doheny of bribery.

In 1927 **Nan Britton** published her book, *The President's Daughter*. In the book Britton alleged that Warren Harding had fathered her daughter prior to becoming president of the United States. Britton had grown up in Harding's hometown of Marion, Ohio. Despite the popularity of the book, Britton lost a paternity suit seeking part of Harding's estate. Then in 1964 historian Francis Russell found numerous love letters written between Warren Harding and Carrie Phillips between 1910 and 1920. Russell found the letters in the Marion, Ohio, Harding home after the death of Florence Harding, Harding's wife. The letters left little doubt of a long affair.

Related Entries: Daugherty, Harry M.; Fall, Albert; Teapot Dome Scandal

SUGGESTED READINGS: Nathan Miller, *Stealing from America: A History of Corruption from Jamestown to Reagan*, New York: Paragon, 1992; C. Vann Woodward, ed., *Responses of the Presidents to Charges of Misconduct*, New York: Delacorte Press, 1974.

HART, GARY (November 28, 1936–). U.S. Senator, 1975–1987; unsuccessful candidate for the 1988 Democratic presidential nomination.

Early in 1987 many political pundits regarded Colorado Senator Gary Hart as the front-runner for the 1988 Democratic presidential nomination. Because of this status, the media began to closely scrutinize Hart's public and private life. Rumors began to circulate that Senator Hart had extramarital relationships. When pressed by reporters to either confirm or deny the extramarital affair rumor, Senator Hart refused to answer the question on the grounds that the answer had nothing to do with his qualifications for president. His refusal to answer did not satisfy a number of reporters who continued to press for a yes or no answer. Angered by the continuing questions, Hart challenged reporters to provide hard evidence to confirm the rumors.

In May 1987 reporters for the *Miami Herald* spotted aspiring model Donna Rice entering Senator Hart's Washington town house. The reporters confirmed that Rice spent the night. Other stories soon appeared detailing a trip Senator Hart took with Rice on a yacht named *Monkey Business*. A number of newspapers and magazines also published a picture of Rice sitting on Hart's lap on the boat. Despite the best efforts by the Hart campaign to ignore the stories, Hart found himself besieged by questions involving his alleged close personal relationship with Rice. Faced with a media **"feeding frenzy,"** Hart felt he had no choice but to withdraw from the race for the Democratic presidential nomination. In December 1987 Hart reentered the Democratic primary battle after realizing that the revelation had not particularly disturbed Democratic primary voters. Yet he soon found that he lacked the time to jump-start his campaign with the crucial New Hampshire primary less than two months away.

After the 1988 presidential election, the handling of the Hart affair touched off a debate over whether the media should report everything they learn about the private lives of public officials. Critics of the growing practice argued that if the media continued to rip apart the private lives of individuals who ran for public office, the pool of individuals willing to run for public office would continue to shrink. On the other hand, supporters argued that the public had a right to know about the character of individuals who seek public office.

Related Entry: "Feeding Frenzy"

SUGGESTED READINGS: James Grant, "Donna Rice Tells Her Story: How a Small-Town Beauty Got into a Big-Time Mess," *Life*, July 1987, 82; Larry Sabato, *Feeding Frenzy*, New York: Free Press, 1991.

HATCH ACT REFORM AMENDMENTS OF 1993. From the passage of the **Pendleton Act of 1883** through the late 1930s, Congress enacted various laws directed at preventing political parties and candidates from pressuring federal employees to make campaign contributions and to engage in partisan political activities. Through the 1920s the expansion of the federal civil service system helped to protect federal employees from being pressured to engage in partisan political activities. The Great Depression and the 1932 presidential election of Franklin Roosevelt ushered in an era of unprecedented growth in the size of the federal government. Between 1932 and the end of the Second World War, Congress authorized the hiring of hundreds of thousands of new federal employees to staff New Deal agencies. As a result of the economic emergency facing the nation, Congress authorized many New Deal agencies to hire new personnel without following normal civil service selection procedures.

By the end of the 1930s, Congress grew increasingly concerned over the political activities of New Deal agency employees. To deal with the perceived problem, in 1939 and 1940 Congress enacted the so-called Hatch Act to prohibit career federal employees from engaging in most types of partisan political activities. The list of prohibited political activities included running for elective office and raising campaign contributions. Between 1939 and 1993, the key provisions of the Hatch Act remained unchanged despite complaints that the act unfairly prevented federal employees from exercising their First Amendment rights to engage in political activities. On the other hand, defenders of the act argued that relaxing Hatch Act restrictions might subject federal employees to increased pressure to engage in partisan political activities.

On October 6, 1993, President Bill Clinton signed into law the Hatch Act Reform Amendments of 1993. During the 1992 presidential campaign, Clinton had promised to sign legislation relaxing Hatch Act restrictions. Under the 1993 Hatch Act Amendments, federal employees may (1) be candidates for public office in nonpartisan elections; (2) register and vote in all elections; (3) assist in voter registration drives; (4) express opinions about candidates and issues; (5) contribute money to political organizations; (6) attend political fund-raising functions; (7) attend and be active at political rallies and meetings; (8) join and be an active member of a political party or club; (9) sign nominating petitions; (10) campaign for or against referendum questions, constitutional amendments, and municipal ordinances; (11) campaign for or against candidates in partisan elections; (12) distribute campaign literature in partisan elections; and (13) hold office in political clubs or parties.

However, the 1993 Hatch Act Amendments did not eliminate all restrictions on partisan political activities by career federal employees and officials. Federal employees covered by the Hatch Act may not (1) use official authority or influence to interfere with an election; (2) solicit or discharge the political activity of anyone with business before their agency; (3) solicit or receive political contributions; (4) be candidates for public office in partisan elections; (5) engage in political activity while on duty, in a government office, wearing an official uniform or using a government vehicle, and (6) wear partisan political buttons on duty.

Related Entries: Patronage Crimes; Pendleton Act of 1883; Political Assessments; Spoils System

SUGGESTED READINGS: Federal Hatch Act: United States Office of Special Council: URL: *www.osc.gov/hatch_a.htm*; U.S. President Bill Clinton, Statement on Signing the Hatch Act Reform Amendments of 1993, *Weekly Compilation of Presidential Documents* 11, October 11, 1993, 2014.

HAYES, RUTHERFORD B. (October 4, 1822–January 17, 1893). President of the United States, 1877–1881.

Ohio Republican Rutherford B. Hayes received the 1876 Republican nomination for president after serving three terms as governor of Ohio. Hayes emerged as the Republican presidential nominee after a long, drawn-out convention battle between the reform-minded Republicans and the conservative Republicans intent on continuing the policies of President Ulysses S. Grant. Although Democratic candidate Samuel J. Tilden of New York won the popular vote by 4,300,000 votes to 4,036,000, Tilden had failed to win a majority of electoral votes because of a dispute over the electoral votes of Louisiana, South Carolina, and Florida. An electoral commission awarded Hayes the disputed electoral votes, making him president. In return Congress agreed to withdraw the remaining federal troops from southern states.

Having established a strong reform record, President Hayes made clear that he would not tolerate corruption in his administration. From March 1877 through March 1881, Hayes worked diligently to clean up the federal government. However, Hayes greatly underestimated the resistance he would face from members of Congress who had grown accustomed to the use of political patronage to enhance their power.

In an effort to clean up the corruption in the Department of the Interior, Hayes nominated former U.S. senator and civil service reform advocate **Carl Schurz** to serve as secretary of the interior. Between 1877 and the end of his term in 1881, Schurz implemented numerous reforms to improve the management of the Interior Department. First Secretary Schurz put in place a system of competitive exams for the selection of Interior Department employees. Second Schurz instituted a number of measures directed at improving the treatment of Native Americans on Western reservations. Third Schurz started the process of establishing a national park system.

Besides moving to clean up the Interior Department, President Hayes took the bold step of taking steps to clean up the federal customs houses. Since the late 1820s, the New York Customs House had experienced a series of public corruption scandals. Since the Civil War, the Republican political machine had

President Rutherford B. Hayes. Reproduced from
the Collections of the LIBRARY OF CONGRESS

controlled patronage appointments at the New York Customs House, and New
York Senator Roscoe Conkling headed the New York political machine. At the
request of Senator Conkling, President Grant had earlier appointed **Chester A.
Arthur** as collector for the New York Customs House. Although subsequent
investigations did not directly implicate Arthur in illegal activities, as collector
of customs he did little to clean up the New York Customs House. In April
1877 President Hayes directed Treasury Secretary John Sherman to appoint
commissions to investigate the management of all federal customshouses. In
May 1877 the Jay Commission issued a report condemning Arthur for his poor
management of the customshouse. Efforts by President Hayes and Treasury Secretary Sherman to persuade Arthur to resign failed, and the Senate refused to
confirm a replacement for Arthur. During the summer of 1878, Hayes fired
Arthur. Although Senator Conkling attempted to use his power to block the
confirmation of a new customshouse collector, the Senate subsequently relented
and gave President Hayes a major victory.

In 1880 the Republican presidential convention nominated Republican insider
James Garfield as president and Arthur as vice president. In 1876 Rutherford
B. Hayes had promised to serve only one term. Despite the fact that Rutherford

B. Hayes only served one term as president, his reform efforts did have a significant impact on the administration of federal agencies and departments. Through the second half of the 1870s, the civil service reform movements gained considerable support. In the aftermath of the 1881 assassination of President Garfield by a disgruntled individual seeking an appointment to a federal job, demands for the enactment of civil service reform legislation intensified. In 1883 Congress passed An Act to Improve the Civil Service of the United States, commonly known as the **Pendleton Act**.

Related Entry: Arthur, Chester Alan

SUGGESTED READINGS: Rutherford B. Hayes: Nineteenth President. URL: *http://www.whitehouse.gov/WH/glimpse/presidents/html/rh19.html*; C. Vann Woodward, ed., *Responses of the President to Charges of Misconduct*, New York: Delacorte Press, 1974.

HAYS, WAYNE (May 13, 1911–February 10, 1989). Member of the House of Representatives, 1949–1976; chairman of Committee on House Administration.

On May 23, 1976, the *Washington Post* published a story of House of Representatives employee Elizabeth Ray. In the story Ray alleged that Ohio Congressman Wayne Hays had arranged for her to obtain a $14,000-a-year position with a House committee in exchange for sexual favors. At the time of the story, Hays chaired the powerful House Administration Committee. Political observers regarded Hays as one of the most powerful members in Congress. By late May 1976, confirmation of Ray's allegations forced Hays to admit to the House that he had a "personal relationship" with Elizabeth Ray. Despite the admission Hays denied the allegation that Ray received her position with the House Administration Committee because she was his mistress. Early in June 1996, the **Committee on Standards of Official Conduct** began a formal investigation of the relationship between Hays and Ray. On September 1, 1976, Wayne Hays resigned from Congress.

SUGGESTED READING: Congressional Quarterly, Inc., *Congressional Ethics*, Washington, DC: Congressional Quarterly, Inc., 1977.

HEMINGS, SALLY (1773–1835). Slave on Thomas Jefferson's Monticello Plantation.

In 1774 Thomas Jefferson received an inheritance from the estate of John Wayles, his father-in-law. The inheritance included Elizabeth (Betty) Hemings and her young daughter Sally Hemings who had been owned by John Wayles. Historians generally agree that Elizabeth and Sally arrived at Monticello, Thomas Jefferson's Charlottesville, Virginia, home, in 1776. In 1887, fourteen-year-old Sally traveled with eight-year-old Mary Jefferson across the Atlantic to London, England, and then on to Paris to join Thomas Jefferson. In 1889 Sally returned to Monticello with the Jefferson family. According to Jefferson's records, Sally had four surviving children, three sons and one daughter.

In 1802 journalist James Callender wrote an article for the *Richmond Re-*

corder alleging that Thomas Jefferson had fathered a number of illegitimate children with one of his slaves. Of questionable reputation supporters of Jefferson treated that story as a vicious political attack on an outstanding Virginian and American. Throughout the remainder of his life, Thomas Jefferson refused to comment on the accusation despite the fact that critics of Jefferson would raise the issue throughout the remainder of his public life. Jefferson never officially freed Sally Hemings. However historical records indicate that Martha Randolph (Jefferson) freed Sally during the 1820s; historical records also indicate that Sally lived with her son in Charlottesville, Virginia until her death in 1835.

From 1802 through 1998, the controversy over whether Thomas Jefferson fathered Sally Hemings's children has divided Jefferson historians. To resolve the dispute, members of the Hemings and Jefferson families agreed to undergo DNA testing in an effort to determine whether a DNA match existed between the two families. In November 1998 *Nature* published the results. In the article Dr. Eugene Foster reported that the analysis of the DNA samples indicated that Jefferson might have fathered Eston Hemings, Sally Hemings's youngest son; therefore, the report did not end the controversy.

SUGGESTED READINGS: Fawn M. Brodie, *Thomas Jefferson: An Intimate History*, New York: W. W. Norton & Co., 1998; The Hemings-Jefferson Controversy: A Brief Account: URL: *http://www.monticello.org/plantation/hemings-jefferson_contro.html*; Jefferson-Hemings DNA Testing: An On-Line Resource: Thomas Jefferson Memorial Foundation, Inc., May 24, 1999, URL: *http://www.monticello.org/Matters/people/ hemings_resource.html*; Matters of Fact: Sally Hemings (1773–1835) Monticello Foundation: URL: *http://www.monticello.org/Matters/people/Sally_Hemings.html*; Annette Gordon Reed, *Thomas Jefferson and Sally Hemings, an American Controversy*, Charlottesville: University of Virginia Press, 1997.

HILL, ANITA (1956–). Law professor.

Anita Hill grew up in the small town of Morris, Oklahoma. After graduating from high school in 1973, Hill attended Oklahoma State University where she majored in psychology. In 1980 she received a law degree from Yale University. Hill then joined the Washington law firm of Ward, Harkrader & Ross. Late in 1981 she left the law firm to go to accept a position as special counsel to Assistant Secretary of Education Clarence Thomas. The next year President Reagan named Clarence Thomas as the chairman of the Equal Employment Opportunity Commission. Hill then accepted a position at the EEOC. In 1983 she left the EEOC to accept a teaching position at Oral Roberts University; then she accepted a position as a law professor at the University of Oklahoma Law School.

Between 1984 and 1991, Hill established herself as a well-respected law professor. In 1991 Supreme Court Justice Thurgood Marshall announced his intention to resign from the high court. Shortly thereafter President George Bush nominated Clarence Thomas as an associate justice of the U.S. Supreme Court.

In early September 1991, Hill contacted the Senate Judiciary Committee to report alleged acts of sexual harassment by Thomas while she had worked in the Department of Education and the Equal Employment Opportunity Commission between 1981 and 1983. On October 12, 1991, in a nationally televised Senate hearing, Hill testified that while she worked Thomas repeatedly pressured her to go out on dates and spoke to her about scenes from pornographic movies. Following her testimony Thomas appeared before the same Senate committee and forcefully denied the allegations of his former aide.

In the end neither Hill nor Thomas retreated from their positions. Faced with the impossible task of verifying the alleged conversations between Hill and Thomas, on October 15, 1991, the Senate voted to confirm Clarence Thomas as an associate Supreme Court justice. In 1996 Hill resigned her position at the University of Oklahoma and subsequently accepted a position at Brandeis University's Heller Graduate School in Waltham, Massachusetts.

SUGGESTED READINGS: Helen Dewar, "Senate Confirms Thomas by 52 to 48 to Succeed Marshall on Supreme Court," *Washington Post*, October 16, 1991, A1; Ruth Marcus, "Hill Describes Details of Alleged Harassment; Thomas Categorically Denies All Her Charges; Court Nominee Calls Ordeal 'Lynching for Uppity Blacks,'" *Washington Post*, October 12, 1991, A1.

HOBBS ACT. Section 1951 of Title 18 of the United States Code makes it a violation of federal law for anyone to obstruct, delay, or affect commerce "or movement of any article or commodity in commerce, by robbery or extortion." In 1946 Congress enacted the law in an effort to stop criminals from threatening to interfere with private businesses engaged in interstate commerce unless the business owners made payments to the criminals.

Beginning in the late 1960s and early 1970s, U.S. attorneys and **federal prosecutors** significantly increased the use of the Hobbs Act to prosecute state and local public officials and employees on public corruption charges. Federal prosecutors argued that when public officials accepted something of value in return for agreeing to perform an official act they violated the Hobbs Act. Equally important federal prosecutors argued that the Hobbs Act did not require that federal prosecutors prove that the public officials asked for a payment as a condition of performing a specific act. However, the Supreme Court in the 1991 *McCormick v United States* rejected the argument that simply because a public official accepted something of value from a private source the gift was a violation of the Hobbs Act. In other words the Hobbs Act requires proof that the public official has agreed to take some sort of action as a result of the payment.

In the 1992 decision of *Evans v United States*, the Supreme Court rejected the argument that the Hobbs Act required federal prosecutors to prove that public officials solicited payments. Instead the high court broadly defined extortion under the Hobbs Act as "the obtaining of property from another, with his consent, induced by wrongful use of actual or threatened force, violence, or fear,

HONEST ABE TAKING THEM ON THE HALF SHELL..

A cartoon of the 1860 presidential campaign by Currier and Ives. Reproduced from the Collections of the LIBRARY OF CONGRESS

or under color of official right." The *McCormick* and *Evans* decisions helped to clarify the scope of the Hobbs Act by limiting prosecutions to situations where public officials who accepted something of value from a nonpublic source did so with a clear understanding that the payment required some official action by the state or local public official.

Related Entry: Federal Prosecutor

SUGGESTED READINGS: Marion T. Doss and Robert Roberts, "The Federalization of 'Grass Roots' Corruption," *Spectrum* 66 (Winter 1993): 9–12; Robert Roberts and Marion T. Doss, *From Watergate to Whitewater: The Public Integrity War*, Westport, CT: Praeger Press, 1997.

"HONEST ABE." Throughout Abraham Lincoln's 1860 battle for the Republican presidential nomination and against President James Buchanan in the 1860 general election campaign, supporters of Lincoln used the slogan "Honest Abe" to distinguish their candidate from his challengers. In 1858 the Republican Party won control of the House of Representatives. During 1859 and early 1860, House Republicans conducted a controversial investigation of alleged political misconduct by the Buchanan administration. The so-called Covode Committee, named after Republican Representative John Covode of Pennsylvania, uncovered numerous instances where the Buchanan administration allegedly used federal government agencies for partisan political purposes.

Not unexpectedly President Buchanan and his Democratic supporters viewed the Covode investigation as a blatant Republican attempt to dig up dirt to use in the 1860 presidential and congressional elections. Although the 1860 election turned on the issue of whether southern states had a right to secede from the Union and the allowing of slavery in new territories and states, Lincoln's reputation for honesty and integrity clearly helped to distinguish him from Buchanan who had been badly tarnished by the Covode political corruption investigation.

Related Entry: Buchanan Administration Political Corruption Scandals

SUGGESTED READING: David E. Meerse, "Buchanan, Corruption and the Election of 1860," *Civil War History* (1966): 116–131.

HONORARIUM RESTRICTIONS. Members of Congress and other federal officials routinely accepted **honorariums** for giving speeches or attending conferences or special events. However, during the 1950s concern had increased over the appearance of impropriety created by federal officials accepting honorariums from individuals and organizations with a direct interest in matters with which the public officials dealt. Honorarium critics argued that individuals who accepted honorariums from special interests were predisposed to give preferential treatment to the sources of the honorariums. In 1961, President Kennedy issued **Executive Order 10939**, To Provide a Guide on Ethical Standards to Government Officials. The new order included a provision prohibiting high-level presidential appointees from accepting any honorariums for speeches or attending events substantially related to their official duties. In other words the directive prohibited the secretary of the treasury from receiving an honorarium for giving a speech on Wall Street in New York City about federal tax policy. President Johnson's 1965 **Executive Order 11222** expanded the executive branch honorarium ban to include all federal employees and officials.

Through the 1960s, however, Congress showed little willingness to limit the acceptance of honorariums by members. Early in August 1974, President Richard Nixon resigned as the result of the **Watergate scandal**. In October 1974 Congress passed the **Federal Election Campaign Act of 1974** which included a new congressional honorarium restriction. The new provision prohibited Senate and House members from receiving more than $15,000 annually for giving speeches and writing articles or more than $1,000 for a speech or article. The **Federal Election Campaign Act Amendments of 1976** raised the overall honorarium limits for members of Congress from $15,000 to $25,000 and the individual event limit from $1,000 to $2,000. In 1978 Congress passed the **Ethics in Government Act of 1978** which required high-level federal officials to file annual **public financial disclosure** statements. The disclosure law required covered federal officials to report all honorariums they received.

Through much of the 1980s, pressure mounted on Congress to ban members from accepting all honorariums. **Common Cause**, the public interest lobby, mounted an aggressive lobbying campaign. Then, early in 1989 President George Bush appointed the **President's Commission on Ethics Law Reform** to conduct a top to bottom review of federal ethics laws. In March 1989, the Commission issued a report that included a recommendation to prohibit all federal government employees from accepting any honorariums. In April 1989, President Bush issued **Executive Order 12674**, Principles of Ethical Conduct for Government Officers and Employees, which included a provision prohibiting all presidential appointees from accepting any honorariums. After long and difficult negotiations with the Bush White House in November 1989, Congress passed the **Ethics Reform Act of 1989** which included a provision prohibiting House members from accepting any honorariums. In return President Bush agreed to sign into law a significant salary increase for House members. Because the Senate refused to go along with the ban, senators did not receive a salary increase. After the Senate voted to ban senators from accepting honorariums on August 14, 1991, President Bush signed a pay raise for Senators into law.

Within a short time of the passage of the Ethics Reform Act, millions of federal executive branch employees learned that the new honorarium ban prohibited all federal employees from accepting any honorarium for giving any type of speech or writing any type of article. This provision went far beyond the honorarium restriction included in President Bush's Executive Order 12674. In the 1995 case of *United States v National Treasury Employees Union*, the Supreme Court upheld the honorarium ban for members of Congress and high-level executive branch officials; the high court also found that the total ban on honorariums for rank and file federal employees violated their First Amendment rights.

Related Entries: Common Cause; Ethics in Government Act of 1978; Ethics Reform Act of 1989; Executive Order 12674; Federal Election Campaign Act Amendments of 1974; Federal Election Campaign Act Amendments of 1976; President's Commission on Ethics Law Reform, Public Financial Disclosure; *United States v National Treasury Employees Union*

SUGGESTED READINGS: Janet Hook, "Senate's Ban on Honoraria Marks an End of an Era," *Congressional Quarterly Weekly Report*, July 20, 1991, 1955; Jackie Koszczuk and Derek Wills, "Hill's Privately Funded Trips: Well-Traveled Loophole," *Congressional Quarterly Weekly Report*, July 3, 1999, 1594.

HOUSE BANKING SCANDAL. On September 18, 1991, the General Accounting Office released a report disclosing that House members had written over 8,000 bad checks against their House bank accounts during a twelve-month period ending on June 30, 1990. Even though the House leadership assured the American public that the House bank did not use public funds to cover these overdrafts, the assurances did little to calm an outraged public. Millions of Americans understood that they themselves would incur substantial charges for overdrawing a checking account at a bank or savings and loan. During October

1991 the House voted to close the House bank, and shortly thereafter the House leadership directed the **Committee on Standards of Official Conduct** to conduct a full investigation of the affair. The investigation of the House ethics committee determined that 252 sitting and fifty-one former lawmakers had overdrawn their checking accounts. Prior to the report, many House members had publicly revealed that they had bounced checks.

The House Ethics Committee report did not end the House bank controversy. Attorney General William Barr appointed federal Judge Malcolm Richard Wilkey to conduct an independent investigation of possible violations of criminal law associated with the operation of the House bank. In January 1989 President George Bush had appointed Judge Wilkey to serve as chairperson of the **President's Commission on Ethics Law Reform**. Prior to the November 1992 congressional midterm elections, Judge Wilkey sent letters to the vast majority of House members notifying them that the Department of Justice had cleared them of possible criminal wrongdoing. In the long run, the House Banking scandal contributed to a growing perception that Congress had lost touch with the American people.

Related Entry: President's Commission on Ethics Law Reform

SUGGESTED READING: "Wilkey Issues His Final Report on Member's Bank Scandal," *Congressional Quarterly Weekly Report*, December 19, 1992, 3920–3923.

HOUSE ETHICS COMMITTEE. *See* Committee on Standards of Official Conduct

HOUSE ETHICS MANUAL. *See* Committee on Standards of Official Conduct

HOUSE POST OFFICE SCANDAL. Beginning in April 1991, **federal prosecutors** began an investigation into allegations that employees of the House Post Office embezzled public funds and that members of the House used the House Post Office to exchange stamps purchased with public funds for cash. On February 13, 1992, federal prosecutors charged House Postmaster Robert V. Rota and other House Post Office clerks with embezzlement. Within a short time after the indictments, federal prosecutors shifted the focus of their investigation from embezzlement to whether House members might have used the House Post Office to exchange stamps purchased with public funds for cash. In 1992 federal prosecutors issued subpoenas for the expense records of House Ways and Means Committee Chairman **Dan Rostenkowski** (D-Ill.) and Representative Joe Kolter (D-Pa.).

On April 6, 1996, former Illinois Congressman Rostenkowski pleaded guilty to two counts of mail fraud. In return federal prosecutors dropped eleven other criminal charges. Rostenkowski received a sixteen-month federal prison sentence. After entering his guilty plea, he denied that he had misappropriated any money from the House Post Office. On May 7, 1996, former Representative Joe

Kolter (D-Pa.) pleaded guilty to one count of conspiring to illegally convert government purchased stamps into cash. On February 19, 1997, U.S. District Judge Norma Holloway Johnson sentenced former House Post Office Chief of Staff Joanna G. O'Rourke to one year of probation and a $200 fine for her participation in the scandal. Through much of the investigation O'Rourke had cooperated with federal prosecutors. On February 20, 1997, Judge Johnson sentenced former House Postmaster Robert V. Rota to four months in a federal correctional facility for permitting Rostenkowski and Kolter to exchange stamps for cash.

Related Entry: Rostenkowski, Dan

SUGGESTED READINGS: "Chronology of Probe of House Post Office," *Congressional Quarterly Weekly Report*, May 28, 1994, 1363; Melissa Weinstein Kaye, "Ethics: Ex-Rep. Kolter Pleads Guilty in House Post Office Case," *Congressional Quarterly Weekly Report*, May 11, 1996, 1280; Toni Locy, "Probation in Post Office Probe; Cooperating Witness in House Scandal Rewarded In Court," *Washington Post*, February 20, 1997, A21.

HUBBARD V UNITED STATES, 115 S.Ct. 1754 (1995). *See* False Statements Accountability Act of 1996

HUBBELL, WEBSTER (January 18, 1948–   ). Associate Attorney General U.S. Department of Justice, 1993–1994.

After the 1992 presidential election victory by former Arkansas governor Bill Clinton, the Clinton presidential transition team recruited a number of former Arkansas associates of Bill and **Hillary Rodham Clinton** for important White House and Clinton administration positions. Early in April 1993, President Clinton nominated former Arkansas Supreme Court Justice and Rose law firm managing partner Webster Hubbell as associate attorney general of the United States. Mrs. Clinton and Deputy White House Counsel **Vincent Foster** had also served as Rose Law Firm partners.

Despite some Senate concern that President Clinton should have permitted Attorney General **Janet Reno** to select her own associate attorney general, the Senate quickly confirmed Hubbell. In January 1994, Reno appointed **Robert Fiske Jr**. as a Justice Department special counsel to investigate the Clintons' failed **Whitewater** land development. Early in March 1994, Hubbell resigned his position. Reports soon surfaced that he was under investigation for allegedly overbilling clients of the law firm. Then in August 1994, a three-judge federal appeals panel appointed **Kenneth Starr** as the Whitewater **independent counsel**.

Hubbell soon became a central figure in Starr's Whitewater investigation. Because Hillary Rodham Clinton and Webster Hubbell had both served as Rose Law Firm partners, Starr believed that Hubbell might shed some light on the Whitewater matter and the late 1980s failure of **James McDougal**'s Madison Guaranty Savings and Loan. James and **Susan McDougal** had joined in a partnership with the Clintons to form the Whitewater land development corporation. In December 1994 Hubbell pled guilty to fraud related to the overbilling of Rose law firm clients. As part of the guilty agreement, Hubbell agreed to cooperate with Starr. On June 28, 1995, Hubbell received a twenty-one-month sentence in a federal correctional facility for wire fraud and tax evasion.

In spring 1997 reports surfaced that between the time Hubbell left the Justice Department and the time he began serving his prison sentence, he earned over $400,000 in consulting contracts. A number of close Clinton friends had helped Hubbell obtain the consulting contracts. When the story broke, the White House vigorously denied having anything to do with organizing an effort to help Hubbell find employment. The disclosure of the Hubbell consulting contracts led to immediate media speculation that the White House might have orchestrated the payments as a way to persuade Hubbell not to cooperate with Starr's Whitewater investigation.

Then on April 30, 1998, a federal **grand jury** indicted Hubbell and his wife for tax evasion. The indictment alleged that Hubbell unlawfully failed to pay back taxes from the income he earned after pleading guilty to overbilling the Rose Law Firm clients. Hubbell's attorneys immediately attacked the indictments on the grounds that the government had learned of the payments as the result of records that Hubbell provided Starr as part of his earlier overbilling plea agreement. According to Hubbell's lawyers, the plea agreement prevented Starr from seeking additional indictments. On July 1, 1998, a U.S. District Court judge dismissed the tax evasion charge against Hubbell on the grounds that Starr had improperly used the records. Then on January 26, 1999, the U.S. Court of Appeals for the District of Columbia reinstated the tax evasion charge against Hubbell and his wife.

On June 30, 1999, Webster Hubbell pleaded guilty to a single felony of failing to disclose that his father-in-law was one of the partners in the Arkansas Castle Grande real estate development project. During the mid-1980s, the failure of the Castle Grande real estate development had contributed to the failure of Jim McDougal's Madison Guaranty Savings and Loan. Madison Guaranty had loaned the development some $3.8 million. In addition, Hubbell pleaded guilty to a misdemeanor tax evasion violation for failing to declare as income $74,000 of more than $450,000 in fees received after he left the Department of Justice. As part of the plea agreement, prosecutors sought no jail time, restitution, or fine.

Throughout the Starr investigation, Webster Hubbell maintained that he did not have any information that might implicate President Clinton or Mrs. Clinton in wrongdoing. Hubbell maintained that Starr and his deputy independent counsels pressured him to provide damaging information regarding the Clintons. In sharp contrast to Hubbell's allegations, Starr maintained that his office never pressured Hubbell to provide such damaging information.

Related Entries: McDougal, James; McDougal, Susan; Starr, Kenneth; Whitewater Investigation

SUGGESTED READINGS: Neil A. Lewis, "For Starr and Hubbell, an Accord of Sorts," *New York Times*, July 1, 1999, A14; Evan Thomas and Michael Isikoff, "Starr's Longest Siege," *Newsweek*, May 11, 1998, 28–31; Bob Woodward, *Shadow: Five Presidents and the Legacy of Watergate*, New York: Simon & Schuster, 1999.

HUD SCANDAL. In late 1989, after Republican Vice President George Bush won the 1988 presidential election, a series of media reports alleged that during the 1980s well-connected developers received preferential treatment from high-level HUD (Housing and Urban Development) officials which permitted the developers to obtain millions of dollars in low-income HUD housing funds. The reports alleged that the conduct took place while Samuel Pierce served as President Ronald Reagan's secretary of housing and urban development. On March 1, 1990, a three-judge federal appeals panel appointed Arlin Adams as **independent counsel** to investigate allegations that Pierce unlawfully gave certain developers preferential treatment in obtaining HUD low-income housing development funds. In 1995, Larry D. Thompson replaced Adams as the HUD independent counsel. The HUD probe became the longest running independent counsel investigation in history and continued through the end of 1998, lasting close to nine years.

In an October 1998 report to the special three-judge federal appeals panel, Adams and Thompson stated that their investigation had uncovered numerous instances of HUD officials distributing HUD funds to "well-connected individuals" rather than on the basis of merit. The HUD investigation led to "17 criminal convictions, . . . payment of $2 million in criminal fines and resulted in the return of almost $10 million in misapplied housing funds." Despite strongly criticizing the conduct of former Housing Secretary Pierce, Adams decided not to seek an indictment. However, Pierce provided Adams with a statement that as HUD secretary he helped to create an environment where corruption took place.

During the course of the HUD investigation, Adams and Thompson obtained criminal convictions of former U.S. Treasurer Catalina Vasquez Villalpando, and Deborah Gore Dean, executive assistant to Samuel Pierce and Thomas T. Demery, a former HUD assistant secretary. Former Reagan administration Secretary of the Interior **James Watt** became the most well-known figure caught up in the HUD investigation. Watt had served as interior secretary between 1981 and 1983. After returning to the private sector, Watt went into business as a Washington lobbyist. In February 1995 a federal **grand jury** issued a twenty-five-count indictment against Watt, accusing Watt of lying to Congress and a federal grand jury about his lobbying efforts at HUD on behalf of private developers. A three-judge federal panel then appointed Larry D. Thompson as the HUD independent counsel. On March 12, 1996, Watt pleaded guilty to a single misdemeanor for withholding documents from the grand jury investigating the HUD scandal. He received a $5,000 fine, five years' probation, and 500 years of community service.

Related Entries: Independent Counsel Investigations; Watt, James Gaius

SUGGESTED READINGS: Guy Gugliotta, "Pattern of Mismanagement Called 'Ruinous' at HUD," *Washington Post*, March 10, 1993, A1; Toni Locy, "Watt Gets Probation in HUD Scandal: Judge Gives Ex-Interior Secretary 'a Break,' after Plea to Misdemeanor," *Washington Post*, March 13, 1996, A08; Bill Miller, "Report on HUD Details 1980s Pattern of Abuse; Probe Nears Completion After 8 1/2 Years," *Washington Post*, October 28, 1998, A17.

HUNT, E. HOWARD (1918–   ). Watergate figure; mystery writer.

In 1971 Daniel Ellsberg leaked the so-called **Pentagon Papers** to the *New York Times*. The leaking of the highly critical top secret Department of Defense study of how the United States became involved in Vietnam badly embarrassed President Richard Nixon who sought to maintain public support for a gradual reduction in U.S. support for South Vietnam. Angered by the leaking of the Pentagon Papers, President Nixon directed presidential assistant **John Ehrlichman** to find the way to stop future leaks. Ehrlichman subsequently placed White House aides Egil Krogh and David Young in charge of the project. Krogh and Young then hired former FBI special agent **G. Gordon Liddy** and former CIA operative E. Howard Hunt to become part of the so-called White House "plumbers unit."

On September 3, 1971, Hunt and Liddy directed the break-in of the Los Angeles, California, office of Daniel Ellsberg's psychiatrist. White House officials authorized the burglary in an effort to gather information that might be used to discredit Ellsburg, who faced a criminal trial for leaking classified information to the *New York Times*. Shortly after the break-in, the White House disbanded the plumbers unit. In late December 1971, Liddy went to work for CREEP. Early in 1972, Hunt joined him. In the early months of 1972, **John Mitchell**, chairman of the president's reelection campaign, allegedly approved an intelligence gathering plan developed by Liddy.

On May 28, 1972, a team of burglars led by Hunt broke into the DNC offices located at the Watergate. The team planted a number of bugs and took photographs of material found in the office. On June 17, 1972, Gordon Liddy and Howard Hunt supervised a second break-in of the office. At 2:30 A.M. District of Columbia police arrested five members of the team inside DNC offices, including RNC security official James McCord. After making the arrests, police found Hunt's name in one of the burglars' address books. Police then arrested Hunt and Liddy for their alleged involvement in the Watergate burglary and bugging. On September 15, 1972, a federal **grand jury** indicted Hunt and Liddy along with the five burglars, James McCord, Eugenio Rolando Martinez, Frank Sturgis, Virgilio Gonzalez and Bernard Barker. On January 30, 1973, a U.S. District Court jury found McCord and Liddy guilty of breaking into the Democratic headquarters at the Watergate. In March 1973 U.S. District Judge John Sirica handed out stiff sentences to the burglars in an effort to obtain their cooperation in the Watergate break-in. Sirica gave Hunt a provisional thirty-five-year sentence. He also sentenced Liddy, McCord, and the other burglars to similarly long provisional sentences.

House Judiciary Committee Chairman Representative Henry Hyde, September 22, 1998. AP/ WIDE WORLD PHOTO

Hunt spent thirty-three months in federal prison. After completing his prison term, he resumed his career as an author of spy novels. Hunt authored some seventy novels, including *Murder in State* (1990), *Mazatlan* (1993), *Ixtapa* (1994), *Izmir* (1996), *Dragon Teeth* (1997), and *Guilty Knowledge* (1998).

Related Entries: Pentagon Papers; Watergate Scandal

SUGGESTED READING: Nathan Miller, *Stealing from America: A History of Corruption from Jamestown to Reagan*, New York: Paragon House, 1992.

HYDE, HENRY (April 18, 1924–). Representative U.S. Congress, 1975– .

On September 9, 1998, **independent counsel Kenneth Starr** delivered to Congress a report identifying possible impeachment offenses by President Bill Clinton related to his effort to conceal his relationship with former White House intern **Monica Lewinsky**. The House then voted to refer the report to the House Judiciary Committee chaired by Illinois Representative Henry Hyde. Through September and October 1998, the House Judiciary Committee wrangled over impeachment procedures. Instead of following the Watergate precedent of conducting impeachment hearings in secret, the House Judiciary Committee voted to conduct the hearings in public. It soon became apparent that Democratic members of the Judiciary Committee had no intention of cooperating with the Judiciary Committee's Republican majority.

During November and December 1998, Chairman Hyde pressed forward with Judiciary Committee consideration of a number of impeachment counts against President Clinton. On December 16, 1998, the House Judiciary Committee voted along party lines to report to the full House a resolution for the impeachment. Then on December 19, 1998, the full House approved two Articles of Impeachment: Article I (perjury before the grand jury) and Article III (obstruction of justice). Following the House impeachment vote, on January 6, 1999, Chairman Hyde announced the appointment of thirteen House impeachment managers.

Even before the beginning of the Senate impeachment trial in January 1999, the House impeachment managers knew they did not have the Senate votes necessary to remove Clinton as president. Despite this fact the House impeachment managers went forward in presenting their case. In early February the full Senate found Clinton not guilty.

Related Entries: Clinton Administration Ethics Controversies; Impeachment Proceedings

SUGGESTED READING: "Hyde's Summation. 'We Must Never Tolerate One Law for the Ruler and Another for the Ruled.' " *Congressional Quarterly Weekly Report*, January 23, 1999, 211.

ILLEGAL GRATUITY STATUTE. The **Bribery and Conflict of Interest Act of 1962** established two bribery offenses. The first (18 USC § 201 [b][1]) provided for criminal penalties for anyone "who corruptly gives, offers or promises anything of value to a public official with the intent to influence any official act." Section 201(b)(2) "provided the same penalties for any public official who corruptly demands or receives anything of value in return for being influenced in an official act." The so-called quid pro quo prohibition continued the long-standing federal policy of prohibiting federal employees and officials from accepting anything of value in return for the federal employee or official agreeing to take a specific action.

In addition to the traditional quid pro quo bribery prohibition, the 1962 ethics act added a new bribery offense. Found at 18 USC § 201 (c)(1), the new section prohibited federal employees and officials from accepting anything of value "for or because of any official act performed or to be performed." In addition the new prohibition prohibited a nonfederal source giving any federal employee or official something of value because of an official act performed by the federal employee or official.

Up through the passage of the 1962 bribery statute, federal prosecutors had experienced considerable difficulty proving that federal employees and officials took some official action after receiving something of value from a nonfederal source. Beginning in the early 1970s, **federal prosecutors** began to use the new prohibition, commonly known as the illegal gratuity statute, to prosecute federal employees and officials for accepting things of value from nonfederal sources in situations where prosecutors lacked proof that the employees and officials took some official action as the result of receiving something of value. By the end of the 1970s, federal court decisions had firmly established that federal employees and officials could violate the illegal gratuity statute by accepting something of value from a nonfederal source because the employee or official had taken some official act.

In June 1994 President Bill Clinton's Secretary of Agriculture **Mike Espy** found himself the subject of **independent counsel investigation** resulting from allegations that he had accepted illegal gifts from companies regulated by the Department of Agriculture. Independent counsel Donald Smaltz obtained indictments against a number of companies and individuals for allegedly providing Espy with illegal gratuities and Espy for accepting them. Like other federal prosecutors, Smaltz broadly interpreted the scope of the illegal gratuity prohibition, arguing that the illegal statute prohibited federal employees and officials from accepting anything of value from a nonfederal source if the official or employee understood that he or she received the gift because they occupied a government position.

On March 2, 1999, the U.S. Supreme Court in *United States v Sun-Diamond Growers of California* rejected Smaltz's broad interpretation of the illegal gratuity statute. The Supreme Court ruled that "in order to establish a violation of 18 USC & 201(c)(1)(A), the Government must prove a link between a thing of value conferred upon a public official and a specific 'official act' for or because of which it was given." Despite the *Sun-Diamond Growers* decision, the illegal gratuity statute continues to constitute one of the most significant provisions restricting acceptance of gifts by federal employees and officials.

Related Entries: Espy, Mike; *United States v Sun-Diamond Growers of California*.

SUGGESTED READING: John Biskupic, "High Court Narrows Law on Gratuities in Espy Case; Prosecutors Must Tie Gifts to Official Acts," *Washington Post*, April 28, 1999, A01.

ILL-WIND INVESTIGATION. In 1986 the Navy Department received information from a defense industry consultant that a number of major defense contractors had received nonpublic procurement information. The consultant alleged that this information gave these defense contractors an unfair advantage when they bid for defense contracts. The informant alleged that the consultants obtained the information about defense contracts from Defense Department employees. The tip led to the start of the undercover "ill-wind" investigation by the Federal Bureau of Investigation, the Department of Defense, and the Department of Justice.

From June 1986 through June 1988, the **federal prosecutors** and FBI agents obtained thirteen wiretaps as part of an investigation into the sale of procurement information to defense contractors and consultants. With information gathered from the wiretaps, the FBI agents and federal prosecutors obtained more than forty search warrants for Defense Department employees, major defense contractors, defense consultants, and former Defense Department officials. Late in June 1988, the first reports of the investigation appeared in the press. Although the stories did not detail the allegations, the stories did reveal that federal prosecutors had subpoenaed some 275 individuals to appear before an Alexandria, Virginia, federal **grand jury**.

Between June 1988 and January 1994, federal prosecutors obtained sixty-four convictions or guilty pleas from individuals implicated in the procurement fraud scandal. Equally important a number of major defense contractors pleaded guilty to unlawfully obtaining confidential Defense Department procurement information. These defense contractors paid some $250 million in fines. In response to the disclosure of the ill-wind investigation, in late 1988 Congress passed the Office of Federal Procurement Policy Act Amendments of 1988. Popularly known as the **Procurement Integrity Act**, the law put in place new ethics restrictions for current and former federal procurement officials. Specifically the act prohibited defense contractors from providing government procurement officials with gratuities and jobs and from buying or obtaining inside information on government procurement contracts. The act provided for five-years' imprisonment and a fine of up to $100,000 for individuals and up to $1 million for companies convicted of Procurement Act violations.

Interestingly the passage of the new procurement amendments led to complaints that the new restrictions might cause a brain drain in government procurement experts. Critics of the procurement reforms argued that many procurement experts would leave the government because of the fear that if they stayed they might not be able to take future well-paying jobs as private defense consultants or with defense contractors. In 1996 Congress passed the Procurement Integrity Act Amendments of 1996 which relaxed a number of the restrictions enacted as part of the 1988 procurement integrity legislation.

Related Entry: Reagan Administration Ethics Controversies

SUGGESTED READINGS: Charles W. Hall, "Litton Industries Pleads Guilty, Closing the Book on 'Ill Wind' Scandal," *Washington Post*, January 15, 1994, A11; Ruth Marcus, "Details of Defense Probe Remain Shrouded; Disclosures So Far Suggest a Complex Web of Information-Dealing Conspiracies," *Washington Post*, June 26, 1988, A6; Michael Mecham, "Contractors Charge That Proposed Rules Threaten Procurement System," *Aviation Week & Space Technology*, April 24, 1989, 33.

IMPEACHMENT PROCEEDINGS. The U.S. Constitution establishes procedures for the impeachment of executive branch officials, including the president and vice president of the United States and federal judges. Impeachment proceedings begin in the House of Representatives. House rules require that the House Judiciary Committee conduct proceedings to determine whether an executive branch official or federal judge has committed high crimes or misdemeanors. If the House Judiciary Committee finds that an executive branch official or federal judge has committed a high crime or misdemeanor, the House Judiciary Committee votes out an article or articles of impeachment. The full House of Representatives then votes whether to impeach the executive branch official or federal judge by a majority vote of members. If a majority of the House votes to impeach, the Constitution requires that the Senate consider

The Senate as court of impeachment for the trial of President Andrew Johnson.
Reproduced from the Collections of the LIBRARY OF CONGRESS

whether to remove the official from office. Two-thirds of the Senate must vote
to remove an official impeached by the House.

From 1789 to the year 2000, the House of Representatives impeached sixteen
legislative, executive, and judicial branch officials (judges). On January 29,
1798, the House impeached U.S. Senator William Blount of Tennessee for conspiracy to aid a foreign power despite official U.S. neutrality. The House found
that Senator William Blount conspired to conduct a hostile military expedition
against Spanish territory in Florida and Louisiana in an effort to help Great
Britain gain control. On January 11, 1799, Senator Blount was acquitted on the
grounds that a U.S. senator is not a civil officer of the United States for purposes
of the impeachment clause. The Senate then voted to expel Senator Blount. After
the Senate decision not to act on the House impeachment of a U.S. Senator, the
House did not again move to impeach a member of the House or Senate.

On December 30, 1803, the House impeached Federal District Judge John
Pickering after Judge Pickering allegedly refused to condemn a ship and its
cargo for violations of federal customs law and for appearing on the bench in
a state of intoxication. On March 12, 1804, the Senate convicted Judge Pickering
on all counts and then voted to remove him from the bench.

On December 4, 1804, the House voted to impeach Associate Supreme Court
Justice Samuel Chase on the grounds that he committed high crimes and misdemeanors while presiding over the treason trial of John Fries and the libel trial

of James Callendar. On March 1, 1805, the Senate fell far short of reaching the two-thirds majority required to convict Justice Chase on any of the eight counts.

On May 1, 1830, the House voted to impeach Federal District Judge James H. Peck for holding in contempt and having arrested a lawyer who had criticized a decision by Judge Peck in a letter to a newspaper. The case had involved a dispute over territorial lands. Besides having the lawyer imprisoned for twenty-four hours, Judge Peck barred the lawyer from practicing before his court for eighteen months. On January 31, 1831, the Senate acquitted Peck.

On May 19, 1862, the House voted to impeach Federal District Judge West H. Humphreys for making public statements supporting the secession of Tennessee from the Union. On June 26, 1862, the Senate voted to remove Judge Humphreys from office and to disqualify him from holding any public office in the future.

On March 2, 1868, the House voted to impeach President **Andrew Johnson** for unlawfully issuing an order for the removal of Secretary of War Edwin Stanton and appointing Major General Lorenzo Thomas as interim secretary. On May 16, 1868 Johnson was acquitted by a vote of 35 to 19. The Senate fell one vote short of the two-thirds majority needed to convict. The Johnson case represented the first time the House had impeached a president of the United States.

On April 3, 1876, the House voted to impeach Secretary of War **William W. Belknap** for unlawfully taking payments from Caleb P. March as part of an arrangement that permitted March to obtain a trading post on a western military post. Belknap's first and second wives had each received the payments from March for a number of years. Prior to the House vote, Secretary Belknap had submitted his letter of resignation to President Ulysses S. Grant, and Grant had accepted Belknap's resignation. Grant's decision to accept the resignation so angered the House that they voted to impeach Belknap even though he had resigned his position. On August 1, 1876, the Senate acquitted Belknap largely as a result of his resignation. The majority of senators concluded that the Constitution did not permit the Senate to convict an individual who had already resigned his government position.

On January 18, 1905, the House voted to impeach Federal District Judge Charles H. Swayne for falsifying expense account vouchers and for unlawfully using property held in receivership by his court. On February 27, 1905, the Senate voted to acquit.

On July 11, 1912, the House voted to impeach Judge Robert W. Archibald of the U.S. Court of Appeals for the Third Circuit for accepting a bribe and hearing cases in which he held a personal financial interest. On January 13, 1913, the Senate voted to remove Judge Archibald and also disqualified him from holding future public office.

On April 1, 1926, the House convicted Federal District Judge George English for habitual malperformance of duties. On December 13, 1926, the Senate voted

The Senate as court of impeachment for the trial of President William Jefferson Clinton, February 12, 1999. AP/WIDE WORLD PHOTO

not to take any action on the impeachment referral because Judge English resigned from office.

On February 24, 1933, the House voted to impeach Federal District Judge Harold Louderback for using favoritism in appointing receivers. On May 24, 1933, the Senate acquitted.

On March 30, 1936, the House voted to impeach Federal District Judge Halstead L. Ritter for kickbacks, tax evasion, and bringing his court into scandal and dispute. On April 17, 1936, the Senate convicted Judge Ritter for bringing his court into scandal and disrepute.

On July 22, 1986, the House voted to impeach Judge Harry Claiborne for tax evasion. On October 9, 1986, the Senate convicted Judge Claiborne and removed him from office.

On August 3, 1988, the House voted to impeach Judge Alcee L. Hastings for conspiring to accept a $150,000 bribe from a defendant. In 1983 a U.S. District Court jury found Judge Hastings not guilty of accepting a bribe. The U.S. Judicial Conference subsequently referred the alleged conduct of Judge Hastings to the House. On October 20, 1989, Hastings was convicted by the Senate and removed from office.

On May 10, 1989, the House voted to impeach Federal District Judge Walter L. Nixon for making false statements to a federal grand jury. On November 3, 1989, Judge Nixon was convicted and removed from office.

On December 19, 1998, the House voted to impeach President Bill Clinton for perjury before the **Monica Lewinsky grand jury** and for obstruction of justice regarding the efforts by President Clinton to conceal his relationship with Lewinsky.

On February 12, 1999, the Senate voted to acquit the president on both impeachment referrals.

Related Entries: Clinton Administration Ethics Controversies; Johnson, Andrew.

SUGGESTED READINGS: Raoul Berger, *Impeachment: The Constitutional Problem*, Cambridge, MA: Harvard University Press, 1999; United States Impeachments 1789 to Present, National Association of Criminal Defense Lawyers, Testimony before the House Judiciary Committee, 1998, URL: *http:209.70.38.3/Testify/test0023.htm*.

INDEPENDENT COUNSEL ACT. On October 26, 1978, President Jimmy Carter signed into law the **Ethics in Government Act of 1978** which included a provision for the appointment of **special prosecutors** to investigate allegations of possible criminal conduct by high-level executive branch officials. With the strong support of President Carter, Congress included the provision in an effort to prevent the reoccurrence of the October 20, 1973, firing of **Watergate** special prosecutor **Archibald Cox** by President Richard Nixon. In the so-called **Saturday Night Massacre**, President Nixon ordered Attorney General **Elliot Richardson** to dismiss Cox. Attorney General Richardson and Deputy Attorney General William D. Ruckelshaus resigned after refusing to carry out Nixon's order. Nixon then appointed **Robert Bork** as acting attorney general, and he fired Cox.

To guarantee the future independence of criminal investigations of high-level executive branch officials, the Ethics Act put in place a new system for appointing special prosecutors. First the Ethics Act required the attorney general to conduct the preliminary investigation of criminal allegations involving the president, vice president, Cabinet officers, top White House aides, top officials of the Department of Justice, Central Intelligence Agency and Federal Bureau of Investigation (FBI) officials and certain campaign officials. Second the law required the attorney general to request that a special three-judge panel be selected from the U.S. Court of Appeals for the District of Columbia. A special prosecutor was to investigate possible criminal conduct by individuals covered by the Ethics Act if the attorney general found "credible evidence" of a possible criminal law violation. Besides stripping the attorney general of the authority to appoint special prosecutors, the Ethics Act did not establish time limits on **independent counsel investigations** or limit how much money an independent counsel could spend on an investigation. Third the Ethics Act required that Congress reauthorize the special prosecutor provision of the Ethics Act every five years. In 1982 Congress changed the name of special prosecutor to independent counsel.

Between 1983 and 1987, a series of high-profile special prosecutor and independent counsel investigations led to increased criticism of the provision. In addition to criticism of the fairness of the investigations, in 1987 Theodore Olson, a Department of Justice official, challenged the constitutionality of the independent counsel law. Olson had become the subject of an independent counsel investigation due to his congressional testimony related to the 1983 Environmental Protection Agency's Superfund Program. In the lawsuit Olson argued that the provision giving a special three-judge appeals panel responsibility for appointing independent counsels violated the separation of powers doctrine of the Constitution. Despite the lawsuit, on December 15, 1987, President Ronald Reagan signed a five-year extension of the independent counsel law. In January 1988 a three-judge panel of the U.S. Court of Appeals for the District of Columbia found that the provision for the appointment of independent counsels violated the Constitution's separation of powers doctrine. On June 29, 1988, in **Morrison v Olson** the Supreme Court reversed the finding of the D.C. Court of Appeals and upheld the constitutionality of the independent counsel provisions of the 1978 Ethics Act.

By the end of 1992, growing concern over the effectiveness of the independent counsel law made it impossible for supporters to gather enough votes to overturn strong opposition to renew the law. In particular, the five-year **Iran-contra** investigation of independent counsel **Lawrence Walsh** angered many Republican members of Congress who believed Walsh unfairly targeted President Reagan and Vice President George Bush. With the expiration of the law, the **Public Integrity Section of the Department of Justice** assumed responsibility for conducting investigate of alleged criminal violations by high-level executive branch officials, including the president and vice president of the United States.

In January 1994 Attorney General **Janet Reno** appointed **Robert Fiske Jr.** as a Department of Justice special counsel to investigate President Bill Clinton and **Hillary Rodham Clinton**'s involvement in the **Whitewater** development. The Clintons had entered into a partnership with Arkansas friends **James McDougal** and **Susan McDougal** to develop land in the Arkansas Ozark region for vacation and retirement homes during the late 1970s and 1980s. By early summer 1994, the Whitewater investigation led to a change of heart on the part of Congress regarding the need for an independent counsel law. On June 30, 1994, President Clinton signed into law legislation putting the law back in place. Early in August 1994, a special three-judge federal panel appointed **Kenneth Starr** as the Whitewater independent counsel.

From August 1994 through 1998, Attorney General Janet Reno appointed a series of independent counsels to investigate alleged criminal conduct by President Clinton, Mrs. Clinton, and a number of other high-level members of the Clinton administration. Of these investigations Starr's 1998 **Monica Lewinsky** investigation ultimately led to the House impeachment of President Clinton. On February 12, 1999, the Senate voted to acquit President Clinton on charges of perjury before a federal **grand jury** and obstruction of justice. At the end of June 1999, Congress again allowed the independent counsel law to expire.

Related Entries: Ethics in Government Act of 1978; Independent Counsel Investigations; *Morrison v. Olson*

SUGGESTED READINGS: Helen Dewar, "GOP Filibuster Treat Kills Independent Counsel Bill," *Washington Post*, September 30, 1992, A11; Katy J. Harriger, *Independent Justice: The Federal Special Prosecutor in American Politics*, Lawrence: University of Kansas Press, 1992; Roberto Suro, "As Special Counsel Law Expires, Power Will Shift to Reno," *Washington Post*, June 30, 1999, A6.

INDEPENDENT COUNSEL INVESTIGATIONS. In a reaction to the **Watergate scandal** and President Richard Nixon's October 1973 dismissal of Watergate special prosecutor **Archibald Cox**, the **Ethics in Government Act of 1978** included provisions for the appointment of special prosecutors by a special three-judge panel. When Congress extended the independent counsel law for another five years in 1982, it changed the name of special prosecutor to that of independent counsel. Between November 1979 and June 30, 1999, a number of attorney generals requested the appointment of special prosecutors and independent counsels to investigate allegations of criminal conduct involving high-level executive branch officials.

The administration of President Jimmy Carter saw the appointment of two special prosecutors. In 1979 the attorney general requested the appointment of a special prosecutor to investigate allegations of illegal drug use by President Carter's chief of staff, **Hamilton Jordan**. On May 28, 1980, special prosecutor Arthur H. Christy announced that a federal **grand jury** found insufficient evidence to support an indictment of Jordan. In 1980 a special three-judge panel appointed Gerald J. Gallinghouse to investigate another allegation of possible illegal drug use by President Carter's national campaign manager, Timothy Kraft. The investigations of Christy and Gallinghouse cleared both Jordan and Kraft.

Between January of 1983 and the close of 1988, a number of current and former Reagan administration officials became the subject of independent counsel investigations. In 1981 Attorney General William French Smith requested the appointment of an independent counsel to investigate whether Secretary of Labor **Raymond Donovan** lied about ties to organized crime figures prior to joining the Reagan administration. On June 28, 1982, independent counsel Leon Silverman found "insufficient credible evidence" to support a criminal indictment. After new allegations surfaced in August 1982, Silverman reopened his investigation and in September 1982 again found insufficient evidence to warrant an indictment.

In 1984 a three-judge federal panel appointed Jacob Stein as independent counsel to investigate an allegation that White House Counselor **Edwin Meese**

III violated federal law by allegedly filing an incomplete personal financial disclosure statement. On September 20, 1984, Stein issued a report finding insufficient evidence of criminal wrongdoing to support a criminal indictment. In May 1986 a special three-judge federal panel appointed Whitney North Seymour Jr. as an independent counsel to investigate whether former Reagan White House Chief of Staff **Michael Deaver** violated federal lobbying restrictions. In December 1987 a federal jury convicted Deaver of three counts of perjury for lying about his lobbying activities after leaving the White House. Deaver became the first individual convicted of a crime under the independent counsel law. In 1986 Attorney General Meese requested the appointment of an independent counsel to investigate whether Assistant Attorney General Theodore Olson lied to Congress regarding a Justice Department probe of alleged wrongdoing in the Environmental Protection Administration in 1983. Alexia Morrison was appointed as independent counsel. Shortly after the start of the investigation, Olson challenged the constitutionality of the independent counsel law; he argued that the provision of the law giving federal court judges the responsibility for appointing independent counsels violated the separation of powers doctrine of the Constitution. In the 1988 *Morrison v Olson* decision, the Supreme Court ruled that it did not violate the separation of powers doctrine.

In December 1986 Attorney General Meese requested the appointment of an independent counsel to investigate the **Iran-contra scandal**. From December 1986 until the end of 1994, independent counsel **Lawrence Walsh** obtained fourteen indictments, seven guilty pleas, and four convictions. Walsh's victory proved short-lived. The U.S. Court of Appeals for the District of Columbia overturned the criminal convictions of **Oliver North** and **John Poindexter**. Late in December 1992, President Bush pardoned former Secretary of Defense **Caspar Weinberger** which prevented Walsh from bringing Weinberger to trial on Iran-contra related charges. Bush also pardoned a number of other individuals convicted of Iran-contra related crimes.

In 1988 a three-judge federal panel appointed James C. McKay as independent counsel to investigate whether former Reagan White House aide **Lyn Nofziger** violated federal lobbying restrictions. On July 16, 1987, a federal grand jury indicted him for illegal lobbying on behalf of the **Wedtech** corporation. On February 11, 1988, a U.S. District Court jury convicted Nofziger of illegal lobbying. A U.S. District judge subsequently sentenced him to ninety days in prison and a $30,000 fine. Yet, on June 28, 1999, the U.S. Court of Appeals for the District of Columbia reversed Nofziger's conviction on the grounds that the government failed to prove that Nofziger knew his actions violated federal law.

In March 1990 a special three-judge panel appointed Arlin Adams to investigate whether Reagan administration Secretary of Housing and Urban Development (HUD) Samuel Pierce conspired to defraud the federal government with respect to various HUD programs by assisting well-connected individuals in obtaining HUD funds. The subsequent investigation by independent counsels Adams and Larry Thompson lasted through 1996. In the end the investigation resulted in twelve guilty pleas and four criminal convictions.

Between January 1989 and January 1993, the Bush administration and former Bush administration officials became the subject of one independent counsel investigation. In December 1992 after Clinton defeated President George Bush in the November 1992 presidential election, Attorney General William Barr requested that a special three-judge panel appoint an independent counsel to investigate whether White House officials covered up knowledge of an alleged preelection search of Clinton's passport files. On December 1, 1994, independent counsel Joseph E. di Genova announced that he would bring criminal charges against anyone involved in the Clinton passport matter.

From January of 1993 to January of 2000, the Clinton administration saw the appointment of one Justice Department special counsel and seven independent counsels to investigate allegations of possible criminal conduct by President Clinton, **Hillary Rodham Clinton**, and a number of high-level Clinton administration officials.

In January 1994 Attorney General **Janet Reno** appointed **Robert Fiske Jr.** to investigate whether the Clintons might have violated any criminal laws in the course of their 1980s Arkansas **Whitewater** land development. Attorney General Reno made an independent counsel appointment because Congress had allowed the independent counsel provision of the Ethics Act to lapse in 1992. In August 1994, a special three-judge panel appointed **Kenneth Starr** as the Whitewater independent counsel after the independent counsel law was reauthorized. Besides investigating the Whitewater land development, the special federal panel subsequently gave Starr responsibility for investigating the death in July 1993 of Deputy White House Counsel **Vincent Foster**, the firing of the staff of the White House **Travel Office**, the so-called **FBI Files Flap**, and the **Monica Lewinsky** investigation. Early in September 1998, Starr forwarded a report to the House Judiciary Committee concluding that Clinton had committed impeachable offenses related to Monica Lewinsky.

In September 1994 a special three-judge panel appointed Donald Smaltz to determine whether Clinton administration Secretary of Agriculture **Mike Espy** accepted illegal gifts from companies regulated by the Department of Agriculture. Between 1994 and the end of 1998, Smaltz obtained a number of guilty pleas from companies for providing Espy with illegal gifts. However, in December 1998 a U.S. District Court jury found former Agriculture Secretary Espy not guilty of violating the **illegal gratuity statute**.

In May 1995 a special three-judge panel appointed David Barrett to investigate whether Clinton Secretary of Housing and Urban Development **Henry Cisneros** made false statements to the FBI agents during questioning prior to his Senate confirmation hearings. The alleged false statements were related to payments made by Cisneros to a former mistress. On September 7, 1999, Cisneros pleaded guilty to a single misdemeanor. On January 20, 2001, President Clinton issued a pardon for Cisneros.

In July 1995 a special three-judge panel appointed Daniel S. Pearson to investigate whether financial arrangements between Secretary of Commerce **Ronald Brown** and a business associate violated federal law. Pearson ended his investigation in April 1996 after Brown died in the crash of a military aircraft while on a trade mission to war-torn Bosnia. In November 1996 a special three-judge panel appointed Curtis Von Kann to investigate a conflict-of-interest allegation involving a Clinton campaign aide and AmeriCorps Chief Eli J. Segal. In December 1998 independent counsel Curtis Von Kann found insufficient evidence to support a criminal prosecution of Segal.

In March 1998 a special three-judge panel appointed Carol Elder Bruce to investigate whether Secretary of the Interior **Bruce Babbitt** made false statements to Congress regarding his knowledge of the reasons why a Native American tribe made a large campaign contribution to the Democratic Party during the 1996 political campaign. Another Native American tribe had claimed that the tribe had made campaign contributions in order to block them from obtaining permission to build and operate a gambling casino. On October 13, 1999, independent counsel Elder announced that insufficient evidence existed to seek an indictment of Secretary Babbitt for making false statements to Congress.

In May 1998 a special three-judge panel appointed Ralph I. Lancaster Jr. to investigate whether Secretary of Labor Alexis Herman agreed to help a Cameroonian businessman obtain an FCC license for a satellite telephone system in return for an illegal $250,000 campaign contribution. On April 5, 2000, Lancaster announced he would not seek to indict Labor Secretary Herman.

Related Entries: Babbitt, Bruce; Brown, Ronald; Cisneros, Henry G.; Deaver, Michael; Espy, Mike; Fiske, Robert Jr.; Illegal Gratuity Statute; Iran-contra scandal; Lewinsky, Monica; *Morrison v Olson*; North, Oliver; Starr, Kenneth; Travel Office Firings; Walsh, Lawrence E.

SUGGESTED READINGS: "Independent Counsels," *CQ Researcher* 7 (February 21, 1997): 145–168; "Independent Counsels Re-examined," *CQ Researcher* 9 (May 7, 1999): 377–400.

INDEPENDENT POLITICAL EXPENDITURES. The **Federal Election Commission (FEC)** defines an independent political expenditure as an "expenditure for a communication which expressly advocates the election or defeat of a clearly identified candidate but which is made independently of any candidate's campaign." When Congress passed the **Federal Election Campaign Act Amendments of 1974**, it included both campaign contribution and campaign expenditure limitations. In the 1976 ***Buckley v Valeo*** decision, the Supreme Court upheld the constitutionality of campaign contribution limitations but struck down limits on campaign expenditures, including those placed on independent political expenditures. The high court found that restrictions on independent political expenditures had a chilling effect on political speech. In an effort to help the public identify the source of independent political expenditures, FEC regulations require that each independent political expenditure include "the name of the person or committee that paid for the expenditure" and states "that the communication is not authorized by the candidate or his or her authorized committee."

Related Entries: *Buckley v Valeo*; Federal Election Campaign Act Amendments of 1974; Federal Election Campaign Act Amendments of 1976; Federal Election Campaign Act of 1971; Federal Election Commission (FEC)

SUGGESTED READINGS: Independent Expenditures. An excerpt from the Campaign Guide for Congressional Candidates and Committees, December 1995, *http:// www.fec.gov/pages/citnlist.htm*; Bill McAllister, "FEC Admits Failures in Plea for Funding: Agency Outlines Wide Probe of 96 Campaign," *Washington Post*, January 31, 1997, A01.

IRAN-CONTRA SCANDAL. Shortly after his 1980 presidential election victory, President Ronald Reagan made clear in a number of public statements that his administration would oppose the spread of communism around the world. To accomplish this task, Congress and the Reagan White House authorized the Central Intelligence Agency (CIA) to expand covert operations. With the full support of President Reagan, CIA Director **William Casey** started a major covert operation against the Nicaraguan Sandinista government. Earlier President Reagan had accused the Nicaraguan government of providing aide to leftist rebels in El Salvador and of providing the Soviet Union with a base of operations in Central America.

Between 1982 and 1984, the CIA provided extensive support for Nicaraguans opposed to the Sandinista regime. Members of this group came to be known as the contras. During this period Reagan administration officials insisted that the CIA funding of the Nicaraguan contras was not directed at building an army to overthrow the Nicaraguan government. In December 1982 the House passed the Boland Amendment which prohibited the expenditure of any public funds to support the overthrow of the Nicaraguan government. Congressional support for the Boland Amendment had grown as the result of strong evidence that the CIA intended to use the contras.

After the passage of the Boland Amendment, President Reagan made clear to members of his administration that he believed the United States had a moral obligation to the contras. Between December 1982 and the end of 1986, officials of the White House National Security Counsel (NSC) set up two covert operations directed at getting around the Boland Amendment to keep funds flowing to the contras. With the approval of National Security Advisor **Robert Mc-Farlane**, NSC staffers Marine Colonel **Oliver North** and Richard Secord developed a plan to raise funds from foreign governments and wealthy Americans to funnel to the contras. In addition McFarlane and North developed a plan to sell arms to Iran in an effort to obtain the release of American hostages being held in Lebanon by pro-Iranian terrorists. President Reagan subsequently approved the plan. During the fall of 1986, both covert operations became public.

On October 5, 1986, Nicaraguan soldiers shot down an American cargo plane flown by a CIA employee which contained military supplies for the contras. On November 3, 1986, a Lebanese publication reported the secret sale of arms to Iran. Then on November 25, 1986, Attorney General **Edwin Meese III** an-

President Ronald Reagan motioning to Attorney General Edwin Meese during the November 25, 1986 Iran-Contra White House press briefing. Courtesy Ronald Reagan Library

nounced the results of an internal investigation which revealed that President Reagan's National Security Council Advisor **John M. Poindexter** and NSC staffer Oliver North had participated in a plan to divert profits made from the Iranian arms sales to support the contras. In his announcement Meese maintained that President Reagan knew nothing about the diversion of arms sale profits to the contras even though Reagan had approved the arms sale to Iran in an effort to obtain the release of American hostages.

On November 26, 1986, President Reagan announced the appointment of a three-member panel to investigate the Iran-contra affair. Former Texas Republican Senator **John Tower** was appointed to chair the panel. The establishment of the panel did not end pressure on Meese to request an appointment of an **independent counsel** to investigate the Iran-contra affair. Then on December 19, 1986, a special three-judge federal appeals panel appointed **Lawrence Walsh** as the Iran-contra independent counsel. On February 27, 1987, the Tower Commission issued a report sharply critical of the Reagan administration for not exercising greater control over its top advisors. However, the Tower Commission report did not find that President Reagan knew about the diversion of the profits from the Iranian arms sales to the contras.

Following the **Watergate** precedent, Congress proceeded with its own investigation even though Walsh urged Congress not to hold hearings until he completed his investigation. He argued that if Congress provided key Iran-contra witnesses with immunity it would greatly complicate possible future criminal prosecutions because his prosecutors would be prohibited from using any information provided by North to Congress during a trial. Despite Walsh's argument Congress granted North and Poindexter immunity in order to obtain their testimony.

In the course of Walsh's Iran-contra investigation, Assistant Secretary of State Elliot Abrams, former National Security Advisor McFarlane, and CIA operative Alan Fiers pleaded guilty to Iran-contra related charges. On May 4, 1989, a U.S. District Court jury found North guilty of destroying documents and accepting an illegal gratuity. He received a two-year suspended sentence along with 1,200 hours of community service and a $150,000 fine. In April 1990 a U.S. District Court jury convicted Admiral Poindexter on five felony counts related to the Iran-contra affair. On July 20, 1990, the U.S. Court of Appeals for the District of Columbia ordered a new trial for North on the grounds that testimony in North's trial may have been tainted by North's immunized testimony before Congress. Walsh decided not to attempt to retry North. Then the D.C. Court of Appeals overturned the criminal conviction of Admiral Poindexter.

On June 16, 1992, a federal **grand jury** indicted former Secretary of Defense **Caspar Weinberger** for concealing notes regarding Iran-contra from Congress and Walsh's independent counsel investigation. Ironically Weinberger had strongly opposed the arms for hostage plan. The Weinberger indictment angered many congressional House and Senate Democrats and Republicans who had worked closely with Weinberger while he was secretary of defense between 1981 and 1987. On December 24, 1992, outgoing President George Bush pardoned Weinberger, McFarlane, Abrams, and former CIA officials Clair E. George, Alan D. Fiers Jr., and Duane R. "Dewey" Clarridge. In granting the pardons, President Bush emphasized that the Iran-contra investigation had shown that none of those pardoned had profited from the two Iran-contra operations. In addition President Bush justified the pardons as a necessary response to "a profoundly troubling development in the political and legal climate of our country: the criminalization of policy differences: the criminalization of policy differences." Bush maintained that "these differences should be addressed in the political arena, without the Damocles sword of criminality hanging over the heads of the combatants." In an angry response to the pardons, Walsh commented that "the Iran-contra coverup, which has continued for more than six years, has now been completed." The pardons did not produce a significant amount of criticism in Congress, in the media, or from the American public.

Related Entries: Casey, William; Independent Counsel Investigations; North, Oliver; Tower, John; Walsh, Lawrence E.; Weinberger, Caspar

SUGGESTED READINGS: Peter B. Levy, *Encyclopedia of the Reagan-Bush Years*, Westport, CT: Greenwood Press, 1996; Walter Pincus, "Bush Pardons Weinberger in Iran-Contra Affair; 5 Others Also Cleared; Angry Walsh Indicates a Focus on President," *Washington Post*, December 25, 1992, A1; Lawrence E. Walsh, *Iran-Contra: The Final Report*, New York: Times Books, 1994.

ISSUE ADS. In 1974 Congress amended the **Federal Election Campaign Act (FECA)** to place strict limits on individual and **political action committee hard money** campaign contributions, and the **Federal Election Commission** issued regulations requiring candidates for federal office to spend hard money to pay for ads that urge voters to "vote for" or "vote against" a particular candidate. By the end of the 1970s, however, independent political groups learned to take full advantage of the issue ads campaign expenditure exception. Under the exception individuals and political groups have the right to raise and spend unlimited amounts of money on ads taking a position on various public policy issues such as abortion rights and gun control. In contrast to political campaign commercials, issue ads do not urge voters to "vote for" or "vote against" a particular candidate.

In 1979 at the urging of both the Democratic and Republican Parties, the Federal Election Commission issued regulations permitting political parties to raise unlimited amounts of so-called **soft money** for party building activities such as voter registration and get out the vote campaigns. Taking full advantage of the new rules, through the 1980s and early 1990s the Republican and Democratic Parties quickly increased the level of soft money contributions. By the 1996 presidential election, both the Republican and Democratic Parties took the position that federal law permitted them to pay for issue ads with soft money. Through the first half of 1996, the Democratic National Committee spent some $44 million to pay for issue ads highlighting the policy successes of the Clinton administration broadcast. Beginning early in 1995, President Bill Clinton helped to raise millions of dollars in soft money to pay for the issue ad campaign by hosting White House coffees for contributors.

However, Federal Election Commission (FEC) rules required political parties to use so-called **hard money** contributions raised under the FECA's contribution limits to pay for a portion of the cost of running issue ads designed to influence voters in a federal campaign including a presidential campaign. In other words, the FEC required political parties to use both hard and soft money to pay for certain types of issue ads.

In late October 1996, **Common Cause**, the public interest lobby, filed a complaint with the Federal Election Commission alleging that both the Clinton and Dole presidential campaigns have violated the FECA and FEC rules by using soft money contributions to pay for ads that supported either Clinton's or Dole's election. Both campaigns denied any wrongdoing and argued that FEC rules permitted political parties to spend soft money to pay for issue ads that showcased the policies of their candidate or criticized the positions of the other candidate. The FEC subsequently ruled that neither the DNC nor RNC had violated FEC rules.

Related Entries: Campaign Finance Reform (Federal); Election of 1996; Federal Election Commission (FEC); Hard Money; Soft Money

SUGGESTED READINGS: John F. Harris, "Clinton: 1996 'Issue Ads' Passed Legal Test; Attorneys Had Reviewed Spots, President Says in Interview with Justice Dept. Staff,"

Washington Post, November 10, 1998, A6; Roberto Suro, "FEC Lets '96 Campaigns Off on 'Issue Ads'; In Split with Auditors, Panel Votes 6–0 Not to Seek Repayments from Clinton, Dole," *Washington Post*, December 11, 1998, A2; Fred Wertheimer, "Clinton's Subterfuge Is No Technicality," *Washington Post*, November 9, 1997, C1.

J

JACKSON, ANDREW (March 15, 1767–June 8, 1845). President of the United States, 1829–1837.

In the presidential election of 1824, Andrew Jackson received the largest popular vote; however, none of the candidates received a majority of the popular vote. Consequently the Constitution required that the House select the next president. To prevent Jackson from becoming president, Henry Clay threw his support behind John Adams which gave Adams the necessary votes to become president. The so-called "corrupt election of 1824" mobilized Jackson supporters which led to Jackson's 1828 presidential election. In 1832 voters gave Jackson a second term.

Prior to the 1832 presidential election, Jackson vetoed legislation rechartering the Second National Bank. Throughout Jackson's political career, he had expressed strong opposition to the National Bank. Jackson took his 1832 landslide victory as a mandate to dismantle the bank. Without congressional approval Jackson ordered the secretary of the treasury to stop depositing federal funds with the bank. Instead Jackson ordered the secretary to place federal deposits in state chartered banks. When Treasury Secretary Duane refused to follow Jackson's order, Jackson dismissed him and appointed Attorney General Roger Brooke Taney as the acting secretary of treasury. Taney proceeded to carry out Jackson's order. Later President Jackson nominated Taney as chief justice of the U.S. Supreme Court. Whig members of Congress saw Jackson's action as a direct challenge to their authority to regulate the financial affairs of the country. On March 28, 1834, the Senate voted to censure President Jackson by a vote of 26 to 20 for Jackson's action. In the aftermath of the passage of the censure motion, Jackson informed the Senate that it lacked the constitutional authority to **censure** the president.

Between March 1834 and January 1837, Jackson supporters worked to expunge the censure motion. On January 16, 1837, Jackson supporters succeeded

Mrs. Andrew Jackson, engraved by J. C. Buttre, 1883. Reproduced from the Collections of the LIBRARY OF CONGRESS

in mustering a sufficient number of votes to expunge his censure from the Senate record. The Jackson censure constitutes the only time in American history where the House or Senate has censured a president of the United States. During 1998 a number of representatives and senators raised the possibility of censuring President Bill Clinton for his relationship with former White House intern **Monica Lewinsky**. The Jackson precedent helped to persuade Congress that it lacked the authority to take such an action.

Related Entry: Censure

SUGGESTED READING: C. Vann Woodward, ed. *Responses of the Presidents to Charges of Misconduct*, New York: Delacorte Press, 1974.

JACKSON, RACHEL (1767–1828). Wife of President-Elect Andrew Jackson.

In March 1829 President-elect Andrew Jackson buried his wife Rachel Donelson Jackson in the garden at the Hermitage, the Jacksons' home near Nashville, Tennessee. Born in Virginia, Rachel Donelson traveled with her parents to the Tennessee wilderness at the age of twelve. At age seventeen she married Lewis Robards of Mercer County, Tennessee. In 1790 Rachel and her husband separated. Later Rachel came to believe that her husband had filed for divorce.

In 1791 Rachel married Andrew Jackson. Two years after their marriage, Rachel and Andrew Jackson learned that Robards had not filed for divorce. Robards then filed suit for divorce against Rachel alleging that she had committed adultery. In 1794 after Rachel received a divorce, she and Jackson married again.

From 1794 to her death in March 1829, Rachel and Andrew Jackson faced persistent whispers of adultery and bigamy. Historians generally believe that the persistent rumors and gossip helped to destroy Rachel's health. In 1824 and 1828, Jackson was forced to deal with the adultery rumors. In 1824 Jackson won the popular vote but did not win the majority of the electoral votes. After Henry Clay placed his support behind John Adams, the House selected Adams as president. In 1828 Jackson won the presidency in a landslide.

Jackson's 1828 presidential election victory did little to restore Rachel Jackson's declining health. She died Christmas Eve 1828. On her epitaph Andrew Jackson wrote, "A being so gentle and so virtuous slander might wound, but could not dishonor."

Related Entries: Jackson, Andrew; Election of 1824; Election of 1828

SUGGESTED READINGS: Rachel Donelson Jackson: 1767–1828: First Ladies of the United States. URL: *http://www.whitehouse.gov/WH/glimpse/firstladies/html/rj7.html*; C. Vann Woodward, ed., *Responses of Presidents to Charges of Misconduct*, New York: Delacorte Press, 1974.

JAWORSKI, LEON (September 19, 1905–December 9, 1982). Watergate special prosecutor, 1973–1974.

Leon Jaworski served as the second **Watergate** special prosecutor from November 1973 through November 1974. He received the appointment as Watergate **special prosecutor** after the so-called **Saturday Night Massacre** in which President Richard Nixon ordered the dismissal of Watergate special prosecutor **Archibald Cox** and abolished the office of special prosecutor after Cox refused to withdraw his subpoena for tapes from Nixon's White House taping system. Prior to receiving his November 1973 appointment, Jaworski had established a prosperous Houston, Texas, law practice.

After receiving his appointment, Jaworski resumed the effort to obtain Nixon's White House tapes, and President Nixon continued to invoke the doctrine of **executive privilege** in an effort to protect the contents of the tapes from disclosure. On July 24, 1974, the Supreme Court ruled 8 to 0 that Nixon could not refuse to turn over the White House tapes to Jaworski. On August 5, 1994, Nixon released the tapes, and on August 9, 1974, he resigned the presidency. Prior to the July 1974 decision, U.S. District Court juries had convicted a number of Watergate figures of crimes associated with the Watergate break-in and the subsequent cover-up. In November 1974 Jaworski resigned as special prosecutor to return to private law practice.

In 1977 Leon Jaworski returned to the public spotlight as part of the investigation by the **Committee on Standards of Official Conduct** of the so-called **Koreagate** scandal. The investigation involved an allegation that South Korean agents provided members of Congress with close to $1 million a year in cash and gifts in an attempt to create the right climate in Washington. According to the allegation, the Korean government feared that the U.S. government might begin pulling out American troops stationed in Korea or reduce other types of economic support for the Korean government. In the end Jaworski's Koreagate investigation did not turn up credible evidence of a massive conspiracy on the part of the Korean government. Leon Jaworski died on December 10, 1982 of an apparent heart attack while working on his 300-acre Texas farm.

Related Entries: Cox, Archibald; Koreagate Investigation; Watergate Scandal

SUGGESTED READINGS: Leon Jaworski, *The Right and the Power: The Prosecution of Watergate*, New York: Reader's Digest Press, 1976; Martin Well, "Leon Jaworski, Key Watergate Prosecutor, Dies of Apparent Heart Attack at Age 77," *Washington Post*, December 10, 1982, B11.

JAY COMMISSION. *See* Customs Collectors Scandals

JOHNSON, ANDREW (December 29, 1808–July 31, 1875). President of the United States, 1865–1869.

Born on December 29, 1808, in Raleigh, N.C., Andrew Johnson moved to Tennessee to work as a tailor. After serving as mayor of Greeneville, Tennessee, and in the Tennessee House of Representatives, Johnson served in Congress from March 1843 through March 1853. Between 1853 and 1857, Johnson served as governor of Tennessee. Tennessee voters sent Johnson to the U.S. Senate during October 1857.

The 1860 election of Republican presidential candidate Abraham Lincoln ultimately led to the establishment of the confederacy. Although Tennessee seceded from the Union, Johnson remained in the Senate. President Lincoln repaid Johnson's loyalty in 1862 by appointing him as the military governor of Tennessee. In 1864, the Republican Party nominated Johnson, a Southerner and a Democrat, for the vice president candidacy. The 1865 assassination of Lincoln thrust Johnson into the presidency.

Almost immediately on assuming the presidency, Johnson ran into serious trouble with the so-called congressional Radical Republicans. He believed strongly that the former Confederate states must be brought back into the Union as soon as possible. The Radical Republicans wanted to make sure that the Confederate states paid for their disloyalty and that Congress should enact immediate legislation protecting the rights of African Americans in the former Confederate states. Between 1865 and 1868, Congress and President Johnson fought over the shape of Reconstruction. During 1866 Congress passed the Civil Rights Act of 1866, to protect former slaves from discrimination. Congress also advised the states of the Fourteenth Amendment which prohibited them from depriving "any person of life, liberty, or property, without due process of law."

The 1866 midterm congressional election saw Radical Republicans gain an overwhelming congressional majority. These legislative gains permitted the Radical Republicans to push through Congress new Reconstruction legislation, including a measure placing the former Confederate states under military rules.

President Andrew Johnson. Still Picture Branch, National Archives and Records Administration

Congress also passed the Tenure of Office Act which prohibited the president from removing civil officials, including Cabinet members, without the consent of the Senate. When President Johnson fired Secretary of War Edwin M. Stanton, Johnson became the first president of the United States impeached by the House. After a spring 1868 Senate trial, the Senate acquitted Johnson by one vote.

Related Entry: Impeachment Proceedings

SUGGESTED READINGS: Michael Les Benedict, *The Impeachment and Trial of Andrew Johnson*, New York: Norton, 1999, 1973; William H. Rehnquist, *Grand Inquests: The Historic Impeachment of Justice Samuel Chase and President Andrew Jackson*, New York: Morrow, 1993; Harp Week: Finding Precedent: The Impeachment of Andrew Johnson. URL: *http://www.impeach-andrewjohnson.com/*; Hans L. Trefousse, *Andrew Johnson: A Biography*, New York: W. W. Norton & Co., 1989.

JOHNSON, LYNDON BAINES (August 27, 1908–January 22, 1973). President of the United States, 1963–1969. *See* Johnson Administration Ethics Controversies

JOHNSON ADMINISTRATION ETHICS CONTROVERSIES. Like the administration of President John Kennedy, the administration of President Lyndon B.

Johnson managed to avoid major ethics controversies. Yet, the **Bobby Baker** affair created questions about Johnson's business dealings, and the gift-giving practices of defense contractors created some difficulty for the Johnson White House.

From the mid-1950s through 1960, Baker served as secretary to Senate Majority Leaders Lyndon Johnson. After voters elected Johnson as vice president in 1960, Baker served as secretary to Senate Majority Leader Mike Mansfield. In 1963 Baker became the subject of a civil lawsuit alleging that Baker had used his influence to obtain vending machine contracts at a defense plant for a company in which Baker held a financial interest. The owner of the vending company that lost the contract brought the suit. Although Baker never faced criminal charges resulting from the vending contract, the allegation led to a Senate and Justice Department investigation of his financial affairs.

On January 5, 1966, a federal **grand jury** indicted Baker for conspiracy to defraud the government and tax evasion. In January 1967 a U.S. District Court jury convicted him for soliciting campaign contributions from California businessmen on behalf of a number of senators and for keeping the contributions for himself. During the trial Baker maintained he had handed the money over to Senator Robert S. Kerr of Kentucky. At the time Baker claimed Kerr received the contributions, Kerr was serving as the chair of a political committee responsible for raising campaign funds for Democratic candidates for the Senate. After a series of appeals failed, Baker served a federal prison sentence.

In addition to the Bobby Baker controversy, the personal finances of Lyndon and Lady Bird Johnson raised some eyebrows from 1961 through 1968. In 1964 *Life* magazine placed the worth of the Johnson family at some $14 million. Elected to the Senate in 1948, the Johnson family acquired a license to own and operate an Austin, Texas, radio and television station (KTBC). Through the 1950s and 1960s, the value of the station increased rapidly. Throughout Johnson's long period of government service, Lady Bird held the stock in the television station in her name. Johnson gave his wife full credit for amassing the family fortune. When Johnson assumed the presidency after the November 1963 assassination of President Kennedy, his advisors recognized that the financial holdings of the Johnson family might raise conflict-of-interest issues. To avoid controversy Johnson and Lady Bird placed their financial holdings in a **blind trust**. However, Lady Bird Johnson did not sell her television stock.

Related Entries: Baker, Bobby; Blind Trust; Executive Order 11222

SUGGESTED READINGS: Thomas Bailey, *Presidential Saints and Sinners*, New York: Free Press, 1981; Robert A. Caro, *The Years of Lyndon Johnson: Means of Ascent*, New York: Alfred A. Knopf, 1982.

JOHNSON ADMINISTRATION ETHICS REFORM PROGRAM. Between 1961 and his November 1963 assassination, President John F. Kennedy put in place a new executive branch ethics program. The **Kennedy administration ethics reform program** sought to prevent the reoccurrence of the types of ethics controversies that had caused so many problems for President Harry S. Truman and President Dwight David Eisenhower. When the November 1963 assassination of President Kennedy made Vice President Lyndon Johnson president, the question remained whether Johnson would continue to place a high priority on ethics reform. Johnson had served in the U.S. Senate from 1949 through 1960, including holding the position of Senate majority leader from 1955 through the end of 1960. Throughout his period of service in the Senate, Johnson had not demonstrated a strong interest in government ethics reform.

Between late November 1963 and May 1965, a number of factors helped to change President Johnson's views toward ethics reform. First **John Macy**, chairman of the U.S. Civil Service Commission, urged President Johnson and the White House staff to continue the Kennedy administration's ethics reform program. Between January 1961 and November 1963, Kennedy had issued a number of important ethics directives. Johnson had come to rely heavily on Macy's advice with respect to government personnel matters. Second the **Bobby Baker** affair hit close to home. Between 1955 and 1961, Baker had served as secretary to Senate Majority Leader Johnson. From the summer of 1963 through the end of the Johnson administration in 1969, Baker became the subject of congressional and Justice Department investigations for alleged financial improprieties which ultimately led to Baker's spending time in a federal correctional facility.

On May 9, 1965, President Johnson issued **Executive Order 11222**, Prescribing Standards of Ethical Conduct for Government Officers and Employees. Although the Johnson ethics directive made few changes in the rules governing the acceptance of gifts, **honorariums**, outside employment, misuse of government information, and financial conflicts of interests issued earlier by President Kennedy, Executive Order 11222 required thousands of presidential appointees and other high-level career federal employees to file confidential financial disclosure statements. Macy had urged President Johnson to include a financial reporting requirement in the May 1965 executive order. In addition to the confidential reporting requirement, the new ethics directive required each federal agency and department to establish their own ethics program directed by a designated agency ethics official (DAEO). Finally Executive Order 11222 gave the U.S. Civil Service Commission overall responsibility for assuring the effectiveness of the executive branch ethics program.

From May 1965 until April 1989, Executive Order 11222 would remain the most important ethics directive governing the conduct of millions of federal executive branch employees and officials. In April 1989 President George Bush issued **Executive Order 12674, Principles of Ethical Conduct for Government Officers and Employees** which replaced Executive Order 11222.

Related Entries: Appearance of Impropriety Rule; Executive Order 11222; Executive Order 12674; Macy, John W., Jr.

SUGGESTED READINGS: John Macy, *Public Service: The Human Side of Government*, New York: Harper & Row, 1971; Robert Roberts, *White House Ethics: The History of the Politics of Conflict of Interest Regulation*, Westport, CT: Greenwood Press, 1988.

JONES, PAULA (September 17, 1966–   ). Former Arkansas state employee.

On May 6, 1994, Paula Jones filed a civil suit in U.S. District Court in Little Rock, Arkansas, alleging that on May 8, 1991, Arkansas governor Bill Clinton engaged in "willful, outrageous and malicious conduct in a hotel room of the Little Rock, Arkansas Excelsior Hotel." The suit also alleged that after Jones rebuffed Clinton, her career in state government suffered. Prior to the filing of the suit, President Clinton hired Washington attorney **Robert Bennett** to defend him. On July 21, 1974, U.S. District Judge **Susan Webber Wright** granted a motion by President Clinton to delay the Paula Jones lawsuit until President Clinton left the presidency. Jones immediately appealed Judge Wright's decision to the Court of Appeals for the Eighth Circuit. In 1996, a divided Eighth Circuit overturned Judge Wright's order postponing the trial until President Clinton left office. President Clinton then appealed the decision of the Eighth Circuit to the Supreme Court. On May 27, 1997, the Supreme Court ruled in the case of **Clinton v Jones** that the doctrine of presidential immunity did not prevent the Jones case from proceeding while Bill Clinton served as president.

The refusal of the Supreme Court to delay the *Jones* sexual harassment lawsuit permitted the lawsuit to move to the deposition stage. By early January 1998, lawyers representing Jones had learned from **Linda Tripp**, a Defense Department public affairs employee, of President Clinton's alleged sexual relationship with former White House intern **Monica Lewinsky**. On January 16, 1998, after a request by Attorney General **Janet Reno**, a special three-judge federal appeals court granted **Whitewater independent counsel Kenneth Starr** the authority to investigate whether President Clinton or other individuals engaged in illegal conduct as part of an effort to conceal Clinton's relationship with Lewinsky. On January 17, 1998, attorneys representing Paula Jones questioned Clinton in the Washington office of Robert Bennett. During the deposition Clinton denied ever having sexual relations with Lewinsky.

On April 1, 1998, U.S. District Judge Susan Webber Wright dismissed Jones's lawsuit by granting President Clinton's request for summary judgment. Judge Wright's decision did not end the *Jones* lawsuit. On April 16, 1998, Paula Jones announced her intention of appealing the dismissal of her suit by Judge Wright to the U.S. Court of Appeals for the Eighth Circuit.

In the interim, Starr pursued the Lewinsky investigation. Early in September 1998, Starr submitted to the House a report on his investigation. The report concluded that Clinton had engaged in conduct that constituted grounds for impeachment. Facing the probability that the House would vote to impeach him, on November 13, 1998, President Clinton agreed to pay Paula Jones $850,000 to end the lawsuit. The settlement did not require President Clinton to acknowledge any wrongdoing.

On July 29, 1999, Judge Wright ordered President Clinton to pay the lawyers who represented Paula Jones $90,000 in compensation for the extra work resulting from his false testimony in his January 17, 1998, deposition regarding his relationship with Lewinsky. In other words Judge Wright concluded that Clinton had lied during his January 1998 Paula Jones deposition.

Related Entries: Clinton Administration Ethics Controversies; Impeachment Proceedings; Lewinsky, Monica; Starr, Kenneth; Tripp, Linda

SUGGESTED READING: Neil A. Lewis, "Judge Orders Clinton to Pay $90,000 to Jones's Lawyers," *New York Times*, July 30, 1999, A13.

JORDAN, HAMILTON (1945–   ). President Jimmy Carter's White House Chief of Staff, 1979–1981.

On November 29, 1979, a special three-judge federal appeals panel appointed Arthur H. Christy as **special prosecutor** to investigate an allegation that President Carter's Chief of Staff Hamilton Jordan had used cocaine on a June 27, 1978, visit to a New York discotheque and a California nightclub. Prior to the appointment of Arthur Christy as special prosecutor, Hamilton Jordan denied the allegation. On May 28, 1980, Special Prosecutor Christy reported that a federal **grand jury** voted unanimously not to indict Jordan for illegal drug use in New York or California.

Related Entries: Carter Administration Ethics Controversies; Independent Counsel Investigations

SUGGESTED READINGS: George Lardner Jr., "Grand Jury Clears Jordan; Top Carter Aide Cleared of Drug Use Allegations; Top Carter Aide Vindicated in Cocaine Case," *Washington Post*, May 29, 1980, A1; George Lardner Jr., "Prosecutor Appointed in Jordan Case; Special Prosecutor Set to Probe Jordan; New York Lawyer Picked to Probe Cocaine Allegations," *Washington Post*, November 30, 1979, A1.

JORDAN, VERNON (1935–   ). Lawyer, civil rights activist.

Born on August 15, 1935, in Atlanta, Georgia, Vernon Jordan worked his way through DePauw University in Greencastle, Indiana. After graduating from DePauw in 1957, Jordan attended Howard University Law School. Following law school Jordan returned to Atlanta to practice. Soon after returning to Atlanta, Jordan became actively involved in efforts to desegregate Georgia's public colleges and universities and with a number of other civil rights issues. In 1964 Jordan moved to Pine Bluff, Arkansas, and became director of the Southern Regional Council's Voter Education Project. Jordan joined with other civil rights activists to lobby for the passage of a new Voting Rights Act. In 1965 Congress passed the act. Jordan then turned his attention to the registration of African American voters. During 1970, Jordan served as director of the United Negro College Fund, and in 1971 Jordan took over as president of the National Urban League. On May 29, 1980, a would-be assassin shot Jordan in the back with a high-powered weapon. He recovered fully from the wound.

On September 9, 1981, Jordan resigned as president of the Urban League to join the Washington, D.C., office of the Dallas law firm of Akin, Gump, Strauss, Hauer and Feld. Former chairman of the Democratic Party Robert Strauss recruited Jordan to become a managing partner with the firm. Through the 1980s Jordan rarely made public appearances or appeared on public affairs television shows. During the early 1990s, however, Jordan threw his full support behind the presidential bid of Arkansas Governor Bill Clinton. After Bill Clinton won the 1992 presidential election, Clinton chose Warren M. Christopher and Vernon Jordan to head his transition team. From January of 1993 until early 1998, Jordan remained one of Clinton's closest friends outside the government.

Then on December 18, 1997, lawyers representing **Paula Jones** in her sexual harassment lawsuit against President Clinton subpoenaed former White House intern **Monica Lewinsky** as a possible witness in the suit. During this period, Clinton enlisted Jordan's help to find Lewinsky a private sector job. Later in **grand jury** testimony, Jordan testified that on December 19, 1997, he had asked both President Clinton and Lewinsky about their relationship. According to Jordan both denied having sexual relations with each other. Because of that response, Jordan did not have any reservations about helping Lewinsky find private employment in New York City. He also helped her to find a lawyer after she received a subpoena from lawyers representing Paula Jones in her sexual harassment lawsuit.

In his September 1998 impeachment referral to the House, **Kenneth Starr** used President Clinton's contacts with Jordan on behalf of Lewinsky as evidence that the president had attempted to use Jordan to conceal his relationship with Lewinsky. Significantly Starr failed to develop any credible evidence to support the contention that Jordan knew about the relationship.

Related Entries: Clinton Administration Ethics Controversies; Lewinsky, Monica; Starr, Kenneth

SUGGESTED READINGS: "Vernon Jordan Jr.," *Current Biography Yearbook 1993*, New York: H. W. Wilson Company, 296–300; Phil Kuntz, *The Starr Report: The Independent Counsel's Report into President Clinton*, New York: Pocket, 1999; Roberto Suro, "Vernon Jordan; Friend's Efforts Are a Key Facet of Case," *Washington Post*, September 13, 1998, A29.

JUDICIAL WATCH. In 1994 Larry Klayman founded Judicial Watch, Inc., a nonpartisan, nonprofit Washington, D.C., based conservative foundation. Between 1994 and 1999, Judicial Watch filed a number of lawsuits against federal agencies and departments, as well as the Clinton administration and former Clinton administration officials in an effort to uncover evidence of illegal conduct. For instance in *Alexander et al. v FBI*, Judicial Watch brought suit on behalf of former Reagan and Bush administration officials who had their FBI background files reviewed by White House officials without their knowledge. The lawsuit asked for $90 million in damages for alleged violations of the

Privacy Act. The so-called "Filegate" or **Files Flap** erupted during the summer of 1994 after reports surfaced that White House security officials improperly requested hundreds of FBI background files as part of the process of issuing White House passes.

In March 2000 **Whitewater independent counsel** Robert W. Ray closed the probe into whether White House officials illegally obtained FBI files on former members of the Bush and Reagan administrations. Ray reported that he had not found any evidence of criminal wrongdoing by **Hillary Rodham Clinton** or senior White House officials covered by the independent counsel law. However, Ray's investigation did not deal with the issue of whether White House officials had violated the federal Privacy Act.

Related Entries: Clinton Administration Ethics Controversies; FBI Files Flap

SUGGESTED READINGS: Jennifer Harper, "Judicial Watch Keeps Stern Eye on Courts, the System, Clinton," *Washington Times*, June 7, 1998, A4; Judicial Watch: *http://www.judicialwatch.org*.

K

KANN, CURTIS VON. *See* Independent Counsel Investigations

KEATING, CHARLES H., JR. *See* Keating Five Affair

KEATING FIVE AFFAIR. On October 13, 1989, **Common Cause** asked the **Senate Select Committee on Ethics** to conduct a full investigation of alleged ethical violations by U.S. Senators Dennis DeConcini (D-Ariz.), Alan Cranston (D-Calif.), John McCain (R-Ariz.), John Glenn (D-Ohio), and Donald W. Riegle Jr. (D-Mich.). Common Cause alleged that in 1987 the five senators improperly contacted federal thrift regulators on behalf of Charles Keating Jr., the owner of Lincoln Savings and Loan located in California. The Common Cause request followed news reports that Charles Keating Jr. had made large campaign contributions to the five senators. Lincoln Savings and Loan subsequently failed, costing taxpayers some $2 billion to bail out. In December 1989 the Senate Select Committee on Ethics hired Washington lawyer **Robert S. Bennett** to determine whether the conduct of the senators warranted a formal inquiry by the Committee. Bennett subsequently recommended the Committee conduct a full inquiry.

On November 15, 1990, the Senate Select Committee on Ethics began public hearings into the conduct of the five senators. Each one argued full compliance with Senate ethics rules, and each of the five senators emphasized that all senators had contacted executive branch officials on behalf of constituents. In addition each denied that the intervention on behalf of Charles Keating had anything to do with Keating's campaign contributions. The Keating five hearings did little to clarify when and under what circumstances senators might intervene on behalf of constituents.

On February 27, 1991, the Senate Select Committee on Ethics found "substantial credible evidence" of ethics violations by California Senator Alan Cranston. The Committee rebuked Senators Riegle, Glenn, McCain, and DeConcini for poor judgment but did not recommend any further action. Despite the finding of the Committee, Senator Cranston maintained that he had done nothing improper when he intervened on behalf of Keating with federal thrift regulators. The February 1991 finding of the Senate Ethics Committee did not end the Keating five controversy. Through much of 1991, the Ethics Committee remained deadlocked over an appropriate penalty for Senator Cranston. In late November 1991, Cranston decided to accept a Senate reprimand in order to end the matter. He also announced that he would not run for reelection in 1992.

Interestingly during late 1999 and the early months of 2000, Arizona Senator John McCain ran an unsuccessful campaign for the Republican presidential nomination. Early in his campaign, Senator McCain acknowledged that he had acted improperly on behalf of Charles Keating.

Related Entry: Senate Select Committee on Ethics

SUGGESTED READINGS: Helen Dewar, "Cranston Accepts Reprimand; 'Keating 5' Senator Angers Colleagues by Denying Misconduct," *Washington Post*, November 21, 1991, A1; Helen Dewar, "Panel Finds 'Credible Evidence' Cranston Violated Ethics Rules; No Further Action Sought Against 4 Other Senators in Keating Case," *Washington Post*, February 28, 1991, A12.

KENDALL, AMOS (August 16, 1789–November 12, 1869). Postmaster General, 1829–1840.

Born in Dunstable, Massachusetts, on August 16, 1789, Amos Kendall's family subsequently moved to Kentucky. In 1811 Kendall graduated from Dartmouth College. After graduating from college, he established himself as a distinguished journalist and an early supporter of Andrew Jackson. Historians credit Kendall with playing a major role in building support for the election of Jackson in 1824 and again in 1828. From 1829 through 1837, Kendall served as one of President Jackson's inner circle of advisers popularly known as the "kitchen cabinet," and from 1835 to 1840, Kendall served as postmaster general.

As postmaster general Kendall successfully reorganized the Post Office Department. For instance he required all Post Office Department employees to comply with a code of ethics. The code included a long list of rules governing the work habits and on-the-job behavior of Post Office Department employees, including prohibiting Post Office Department employees from accepting "any present or gratuity . . . from any person who has business with the office." Throughout his tenure of office as postmaster general, Kendall resisted efforts to increase the number of political appointments within the Post Office Department.

After returning to private life, Kendall became the legal representative for F. B. Morse, the inventor of the telegraph. The subsequent success of the telegraph made both Morse and Kendall wealthy.

Related Entries: Code of Ethics for Federal Employees and Officials; Spoils System

SUGGESTED READINGS: Steven G. O'Brien, *American Political Leaders: From Colonial Times to the Present*, Santa Barbara, CA: ABC-CLIO, 1991; Leonard White, *The Jacksonians*, New York: Free Press, 1965.

KENDALL, DAVID (1945–). Partner, Washington law firm of Williams & Connolly.

David Kendall served as President Bill Clinton's and **Hillary Rodham Clinton**'s attorney from January 1994 through 1999 with respect to the **Whitewater** and **Monica Lewinsky** investigations conducted by **independent counsel Kenneth Starr**. During the 1970s Kendall attended Yale Law School. After graduating he clerked for Supreme Court Justice Byron White and then became a lawyer with the NAACP Legal Defense Fund in New York City. In 1978 Kendall left the Legal Defense Fund to accept a position with the Washington, D.C., law firm of Williams & Connolly.

Up through January 1998, Kendall worked behind the scenes. However between February 1998 and February 1999, Kendall and Starr found themselves in a public battle over the use of a federal **grand jury** to investigate President Clinton's alleged relationship with Lewinsky. Kendall alleged that Starr illegally gave details of grand jury proceedings to the press. After a request by Kendall, U.S. District Judge Norma Holloway Johnson conducted an investigation into whether Starr and his associates had violated the grand jury secrecy rule by providing a *New York Times* reporter with information regarding the investigation. Later the U.S. Court of Appeals for the District of Columbia ruled that Starr's office had not violated grand jury secrecy rules. Besides challenging the conduct of the investigation, Kendall helped to present Clinton's defense before the House Judiciary Committee and before the full Senate during Clinton's January and February 1999 Senate impeachment trial. The Senate voted to acquit President Bill Clinton on both impeachment counts.

Related Entries: Impeachment Proceedings; Lewinsky, Monica; Whitewater Investigation

SUGGESTED READINGS: Lloyd Grove, "The Clintons' Whitewater Guide; As the First Couple's Attorney, David Kendall Is Navigating Some Tricky Currents," *Washington Post*, February 7, 1994, C1; Linton Weeks, "The Quiet Counsel Erupts; Clinton Attorney David Kendall Comes Out from Behind the Scenes," *Washington Post*, February 11, 1998, D01.

KENNEDY, EDWARD M. (February 22, 1932–). United States Senator, 1962–). *See* Chappaquiddick Scandal

KENNEDY, JOHN FITZGERALD (May 29, 1917–November 22, 1963). President of the United States, 1961–1963. *See* Kennedy Administration Ethics Controversies; Kennedy Administration Ethics Reform Program

KENNEDY ADMINISTRATION ETHICS CONTROVERSIES. From January 1961 through the November 22, 1963, assassination of President John F. Kennedy, Kennedy administration officials experienced relatively few ethics problems. This constituted a marked contrast from the **Truman administration ethics controversies** and the **Eisenhower administration ethics controversies**. However, in the decades following President Kennedy's assassination, historians confirmed his marital infidelity. The ethics controversies confronted by the Kennedy White House demonstrated the continuing problem of money in politics and the appearance of conflicts of interest.

Early in May 1961, Secretary of the Interior Stewart Udall became the subject of newspaper reports that he had asked an oil company executive to sell tickets to a Democratic Party fund-raising dinner to the executive's friends in the oil and gas industry. Tickets to the dinner cost $100. The story appeared less than a week after President Kennedy's message to Congress announcing a significant tightening of executive branch conflict-of-interest rules. Immediately after the story broke, Udall denied ever asking the oil executive to solicit campaign contributions for the Democratic Party. Instead of criticizing Secretary Udall for his conduct, at a subsequent press conference President Kennedy blamed the incident on the system for financing elections which required political parties to constantly raise money to fund the next presidential campaign. Interestingly President Kennedy used the controversy to advocate public funding of presidential elections.

The 1962 Billie Sol Estes scandal proved much more serious. In April 1962 a federal **grand jury** indicted Texas native Estes on fraud charges. Estes had borrowed millions of dollars from investors by putting up as collateral nonexistent ammonia tanks and federal grain warehouse contracts. He used the loans to buy fertilizer contracts in an effort to corner the West Texas fertilizer market. He then planned to sell the fertilizer contracts at inflated prices. When a West Texas newspaper published a story detailing the fact that Estes did not own the ammonia tanks that he pledged as collateral, his financial empire collapsed. In 1963 a U.S. District Court jury convicted Estes for selling fertilizer tanks that Estes did not own to West Texas farmers. Estes received a fifteen-year federal prison sentence. He received a parole in 1971. In 1979 a U.S. District Court judge revoked Estes's parole after a federal jury convicted him for fraud and tax evasion. He received a second parole in 1983.

During the course of the Estes scandal, a congressional committee uncovered the fact that Estes had provided a number of Agriculture Department employees with expensive gifts. This disclosure led a number of members of Congress to wonder whether Department of Agriculture officials might have helped Estes with this fraud scheme. The reports also led former President Dwight David Eisenhower to call for an independent investigation of the gift acceptance allegations. President Eisenhower had not forgotten how Democrats had treated **Sherman Adams,** Eisenhower's chief of staff, after the disclosure that Adams had accepted expensive gifts from businessman Bernard Goldfine. In rejecting calls for an independent inquiry, President Kennedy promised to provide the Senate's Permanent Investigations Subcommittee with all the information necessary to complete a full investigation of the involvement of the Department of Agriculture employees and officials with Billie Sol Estes. Equally important Kennedy expressed his full support for Secretary of Agriculture Orville Freeman.

In November 1964 a conflict-of-interest controversy erupted over the awarding of the Department of Defense TFX fighter bomber contract. From the late 1950s through the early 1960s, the Air Force had conducted a high stakes competition for a new fighter bomber. Defense experts projected that the contract might be worth $6 billion. On November 24, 1962, the Department of Defense announced that Dallas, Texas, based General Dynamics Corporation won the contract. Washington Senator Henry Jackson immediately attacked the decision. Headquartered in Seattle, Washington, Boeing Corporation and Senator Jackson alleged that the civilian leadership of the Department of Defense had overruled the Pentagon's selection board in awarding the contract to General Dynamics in an effort to shore up President Kennedy's sagging political support in Texas. President Kennedy had barely carried Texas in 1960 even though he had selected Texas Senator Lyndon Johnson to run as his vice presidential running mate.

Besides alleging political considerations played a role in the TFX contract decision, critics of the decision demanded an investigation of the role of Deputy Secretary of Defense Rowell L. Gilpatric in the award of the contract. Prior to accepting his Defense Department position, Gilpatric had worked as a partner in a New York City law firm which had represented General Dynamics on a number of matters. Yet Gilpatric had not disqualified himself from participation in the TFX matter; he had returned to his New York law firm early in 1964.

Although a subsequent congressional investigation failed to turn up any evidence that politics played a role in the TFX decision, the investigation did reveal a relationship between Gilpatric and General Dynamics Corporation. Gilpatric had taken a leave of absence from his New York City law firm to serve as deputy secretary of defense. He became the subject of strong criticism for not disqualifying himself from the TFX decision because of his numerous contacts with General Dynamics while working for his New York law firm. The fact that General Dynamics named Gilpatric's former law firm as its counsel after winning the TFX contract added even more fuel to the controversy. Prior to returning to his New York law firm, Gilpatric participated in the lengthy deliberations on how to respond to the placement of Soviet nuclear weapons in Cuba during the October 1963 Cuban missile crisis. A number of individuals who participated in the deliberations subsequently reported that Gilpatric played a key role in persuading President Kennedy to blockade Cuba instead of ordering an immediate military strike against the missile sites in Cuba.

In addition to criticism of Roswell Gilpatric, Secretary of the Navy Fred Korth also faced strong criticism for not disqualifying himself from the TFX contract decision. Prior to accepting the position as secretary of the navy, Korth served as a president of a major Fort Worth, Texas, bank. The TFX investigation revealed that as president of the bank, Korth had approved a $400,000 loan to General Dynamics. The investigation also revealed that Korth held onto some $160,000 in General Dynamics stock after he became secretary of the navy, and it determined that during Defense Department TFX contract negotiations with Boeing and General Dynamics Korth had contacted General Dynamics officials some sixteen times but only contacted Boeing officials twice. Despite denying any wrongdoing, the controversy forced Korth to resign his Defense Department position in August 1963.

Related Entry: Kennedy Administration Ethics Reform Program

SUGGESTED READINGS: Thomas Bailey, *Presidential Saints and Sinners*, New York: Free Press, 1981; C. Vann Woodward, ed., *Responses of the Presidents to Charges of Misconduct*, New York: Delacorte Press, 1974.

KENNEDY ADMINISTRATION ETHICS REFORM PROGRAM. Between 1950 and 1961, President Harry Truman and President Dwight Eisenhower found themselves forced to deal with a number of ethics controversies involving high-level administration officials. These highly publicized controversies raised serious doubts about the fairness and effectiveness of the executive branch ethics program. In January 1961 shortly after being sworn in as president of the United States, John F. Kennedy established an advisory panel on conflict of interest matters. He appointed Dean Jefferson B. Fordham of the University of Pennsylvania Law School, Bayless Manning, and Judge Calvert Magruder to the panel. On March 22, 1961, the panel submitted to President Kennedy a series of recommendations designed to improve the effectiveness of the executive branch ethics program. Although the panel "found no indication of widespread lack of probity or serious departure from basic moral standards in the federal establishment," it endorsed the proposal of the **Association of the Bar of the City of New York** for the appointment of a presidential special assistant to take responsibility for coordinating the executive branch ethics program. Equally significant the panel recommended that President Kennedy issue a series of ethics directives providing federal employees and officials with better guidance regarding how to avoid conflict of interest situations that might reduce public trust in government. Finally the panel endorsed the updating of a number of criminal conflict of interest statutes.

Through 1961 and 1962, President Kennedy, White House officials, and the U.S. Civil Service Commission took a number of actions directed at implementing the recommendations of the president's ethics advisory panel. First on April 27, 1961, President Kennedy sent to Congress a message titled "Ethical Conduct in the Government." The message directed federal employees and officials to turn down any gift motivated by the fact that a federal employee or official held a particular government position. The ethics message also directed all federal employees and officials not to use nonpublic information for personal gain and not to engage in outside employment incompatible with their government employment. Finally the message directed all federal agencies and de-

President John F. Kennedy conferring with former president Harry S. Truman on Kennedy's first day in the White House, January 21, 1961. National Park Service Photograph/Courtesy Harry S. Truman Library

partments to draft new ethics rules for career federal employees and officials to help avoid conflict of interest situations that might raise questions regarding the objectivity or impartiality of federal employees and officials.

Second on May 5, 1961, President Kennedy issued **Executive Order 10939**, To Provide a Guide on Ethical Standards to Government Officials, which covered heads and assistants of departments and agencies, full-time members of federal boards and commissions appointed by the president, and members of the White House staff. The order established new rules governing the acceptance of gifts, outside employment, and financial conflicts of interests. In addition to the general ethics restrictions, the order prohibited high-level presidential appointees from accepting any **honorariums** for giving speeches or writing articles related to the responsibilities, programs, or operations of the official's department or agency.

Third on July 20, 1961, the White House issued a memorandum entitled "Minimum Standards of Conduct for Civilian Employees." Popularly known as the Dutton memorandum after presidential assistant Frederick Dutton who prepared the memorandum, it directed all federal agencies and departments to update their ethics guidelines for millions of career federal employees and officials. Much like the earlier Executive Order 10939, the memorandum prohibited all executive branch employees and officials from accepting honorariums for giving speeches related to the performance of their official duties, and it required all federal employees and officials to comply with much stricter **gift acceptance** rules. Finally the Dutton memorandum directed all federal agencies to establish ethics programs to familiarize their employees and officials with administration and criminal public ethics restrictions.

Fourth the Kennedy White House lobbied Congress to update the existing criminal conflict of interest statutes. On October 23, 1962, President Kennedy signed into law the **Bribery and Conflict of Interest Act of 1962** which consolidated the key criminal conflict of interest statutes between sections 201 and 209 of title 18 of the United States Code. To make it easier for federal agencies and departments to recruit part-time consultants, the new law exempted so-called "special government employees" from a number of key ethics restrictions. The new law also established new restrictions of lobbying of federal agencies and departments by former executive branch employees and officials and put in place a new financial conflict of interest prohibition.

On November 22, 1963, an assassin murdered President Kennedy as he traveled in a motorcade through Dallas, Texas. The ethics reforms adopted by the Kennedy White House laid the foundations for a new executive branch ethics program designed to protect public trust in the objectivity and impartiality of actions taken by executive branch employees and officials.

Related Entries: Bribery and Conflict of Interest Act of 1962; Gift Acceptance Prohibitions; Honorarium Restrictions; "Revolving Door" Restrictions

SUGGESTED READING: Robert Roberts, *White House Ethics: The History of the Politics of Conflict of Interest Regulation.* Westport, CT: Greenwood Press, 1988.

KOLTER, JOSEPH P. (September 3, 1926–). Representative from Pennsylvania, 1983–1993. *See* House Post Office Scandal

KOREAGATE INVESTIGATION. In late October 1976, the *Washington Post* disclosed an ongoing Justice Department investigation of alleged efforts by the South Korean government to funnel millions of dollars in cash and gifts to members of Congress. According to the allegation, in the early 1970s the South Korean government had developed the plan in an effort to prevent any future withdrawal of American troops from South Korea. Through 1977 and 1978, the investigation focused on the gift-giving practices of South Korean businessman Tongsun Park. The **Committee on Standards of Official Conduct** hired former Watergate special prosecutor **Leon Jaworski** to oversee the House investigation of a number of House members who had allegedly accepted campaign contributions and gifts from Tongsun Park.

On September 6, 1977, a federal **grand jury** indicted Park for mail fraud, bribery, failure to register as a foreign agent, and making illegal campaign contributions. The fact that Tongsun Park and other Koreagate figures lived in South Korea complicated both the criminal and congressional investigations. In February 1978 testimony before Congress, Tongsun Park admitted making a number of gifts to members of Congress but denied being an agent of the South Korean government. In March 1978 former Congressman Richard Hanna pleaded guilty to conspiracy to defraud the government. Hanna admitted to receiving some $200,000 from Tongsun Park between 1969 and 1975; he received a thirty-month sentence as part of the guilty plea.

In the end the Koreagate investigation resulted in the reprimand of three House members. On October 13, 1978, the full House voted to reprimand Representatives John McFall and Charles Wilson for failing to report campaign contributions from Park. The House also voted to reprimand Representative Charles Wilson for failing to disclose to the House ethics committee wedding gifts he received from Tongsun Park.

SUGGESTED READINGS: Charles R. Babcock, "Bringing Forth a Mouse, But an Honest One," *Washington Post*, October 9, 1978, A2; Congressional Quarterly, *Congressional Ethics: History, Facts, and Controversy*, Washington, DC: Congressional Quarterly, 1992, 58–59.

KRAFT, TIMOTHY. *See* Carter Administration Ethics Controversies; Independent Counsel Investigations

L

LA FOLLETTE, ROBERT MARION (June 14, 1855–June 18, 1925). U.S. Senator, 1906–1925.

Born in Primrose, Wisconsin, in 1855, Robert La Follette graduated from the University of Wisconsin in 1879. He then established a law practice in Madison, Wisconsin. From 1885 to 1901, La Follette served as a Republican member of the U.S. House of Representatives. In 1896 and 1898, he sought the Republican nomination for Wisconsin governor by advocating a progressive agenda of government reform and government regulation of big business. Faced with strong Republican opposition, Follette led a grassroots revolt against the Republican Party establishment. Despite strong Republican opposition, in 1900 Wisconsin voters elected La Follette as governor.

As Wisconsin governor, La Follette advocated the adoption of a direct primary to permit voters to go to the polls to select a party's candidate for a general election campaign. La Follette saw the direct primary as a way to break the power of party bosses who used the caucus convention system to control the selection of candidates. At La Follette's urging the Wisconsin legislature established a state commission to regulate railroad rates; it also established a civil service system for staffing the Wisconsin state government and increased state funding of public education.

Then, in 1904, Wisconsin voters elected Robert La Follette to the U.S. Senate. During his years in the Senate, La Follette supported government regulation of business and the rights of workers to join unions and engage in collective bargaining and campaign finance reform. Between 1917 and 1918, La Follette again demonstrated his independence by strongly opposing the involvement of the United States in World War I. His open opposition led to calls for expulsion from the Senate. However, in 1922 Wisconsin voters reelected him to the Senate.

In 1922 La Follette played a major role in uncovering the **Teapot Dome scandal**. During the spring of 1922, rumors began to circulate in Wyoming that the Interior Department had leased the Naval oil reserve at Teapot Dome, Wyoming, to oil tycoon Harry Sinclair. On April 15, 1922, Wyoming Senator John P. Kenrick introduced a resolution that demanded that Navy Secretary Edwin Denby and Interior Secretary **Albert Fall** provide the Senate with details regarding the alleged lease. The following week Senator La Follette introduced a second resolution demanding a full investigation of the Teapot Dome lease. President Warren G. Harding and Interior Secretary Fall vigorously defended the Teapot Dome lease as in the best interest of the United States. The vigorous defense mounted by Fall succeeded in delaying a congressional investigation. However, after the August 1923 death of President Harding the Teapot Dome conspiracy began to unravel.

In 1924 La Follette accepted the presidential nomination of the Progressive Party. He received 17 percent of the popular vote. Exhausted by the presidential campaign, La Follette died on June 18, 1925.

Related Entries: Campaign Finance Reform (Federal); Teapot Dome Scandal.

SUGGESTED READING: David Thelan, *Robert M. La Follette and the Insurgent Spirit*, Boston: Little, Brown, 1976.

LANCASTER, RALPH I., JR. *See* Independent Counsel Investigations

LANCE, BERT (June 3, 1931–). Director of Office of Management and Budget, 1977.

Shortly after his November 1978 presidential election victory, President-elect Jimmy Carter nominated Georgia banker and close friend Bert Lance to the important position of director of the Office of Management and Budget (OMB). Like other Carter nominees, Lance placed his National Bank of Georgia stock in a **blind trust** in order to satisfy demands by the Senate Governmental Affairs Committee responsible for confirming his appointment. Lance's blind trust agreement required his trustee to sell the bank stock by the end of 1977. In July 1977 President Carter asked the Senate Governmental Affairs Committee to allow Lance to modify his blind trust because of a sharp drop in the stock's value. If the committee required Lance to comply with the terms of the blind trust agreement, Lance would suffer a huge financial loss. The committee voted to permit Lance to delay the sale of his bank stock.

However, Lance's decision to request the stock divestiture extension led to new questions being raised regarding his financial affairs. On September 21, 1977, Lance resigned his position as the director of OMB to devote full time fighting allegations of improper banking practices. On May 23, 1979, an Atlanta, Georgia, federal **grand jury** indicted Lance and three of his business associates for illegally obtaining more than $20 million of loans from forty-one banks across the country and abroad. On May 1, 1980, a U.S. District Court jury in Atlanta, Georgia, acquitted Lance on nine counts of bank fraud. The judge declared a mistrial on the remaining three counts. The federal prosecutor subsequently declined to retry Bert Lance on the remaining counts.

Related Entry: Carter Administration Ethics Controversies

SUGGESTED READINGS: John F. Berry, "Lance Acquitted on Nine Counts; Mistrial on Three; Bert Lance Is Acquitted on 9 Counts," *Washington Post*, May 1, 1980, A1; Robert G. Kaiser, "Lance Denies Acts Were Illegal or Unethical; Lance Denies Banking Practices Were Unethical or Illegal; 'My Conscience Is Clear,' Budget Director Declares," *Washington Post*, September 16, 1977, A1; Bert Lance, *The Truth of the Matter: My Life In and Out of Politics*, New York: Summit Books, 1991.

LAVELLE, RITA M. (September 8, 1947–   ). Official, Environmental Protection Agency, 1981–1983.

In 1980 Congress established the Superfund program in order to fund the cleaning up of toxic waste sites across the United States. In November 1980 Republican presidential candidate Ronald Reagan defeated President Jimmy Carter in the 1980 presidential election. Through much of 1981 and the first half of 1982, Hugh Kaufman, a career Environmental Protection Agency (EPA) employee with the EPA's hazardous waste office, publicly complained about lax enforcement of the nation's hazardous waste laws by high-level Reagan appointees in the EPA. Within a short period of time, much of the criticism focused on EPA head Anne Gorsuch (Burford). Then, during the summer of 1982, Kaufman revealed that he had become the subject of an investigation by the EPA's Inspector General's Office. During fall 1982 the House Commerce and Energy Investigations Subcommittee, chaired by Representative John Dingell of Michigan, opened an investigation into the management of the Superfund program. In the course of the investigation, the subcommittee issued a subpoena for EPA's Superfund records. To the surprise of many legal observers, President Reagan acted on the recommendation of the Justice Department and directed EPA head Gorsuch not to turn over the subpoenaed documents on the grounds that the documents were protected by the doctrine of **executive privilege**. In an unprecedented action, the House cited Burford for contempt of Congress.

In December 1982 the House Science and Technology Subcommittee called Rita Lavelle to testify before the subcommittee on the administration of the Superfund program and the treatment of EPA whistle-blower Hugh Kaufman. During her testimony, Lavelle denied ever having expressed an interest in firing whistle-blower Kaufman. On February 7, 1983, President Reagan fired Lavelle after she refused to resign. Lavelle's dismissal did little to end the controversy over her administration of the Superfund program. On February 13, 1983, the House voted 413 to 0 to hold Lavelle in contempt of Congress for refusing to honor a subcommittee subpoena for Superfund documents. Yet, on July 22, 1983, a federal jury found Lavelle not guilty of contempt of Congress for refusing to testify regarding the Superfund program.

In August 1983 a second federal **grand jury** indicted Lavelle for perjury and obstructing a congressional investigation. On December 1, 1983, a U.S. District Court jury found Lavelle guilty of perjury and obstructing a congressional investigation while she managed the EPA's Superfund program. Lavelle received a six-month sentence. After failing to gain a reversal of her conviction, in 1985, Lavelle served five months of a six-month sentence.

Related Entry: Reagan Administration Ethics Controversies

SUGGESTED READINGS: Al Kamen, "Lavelle Found Guilty of Lying to House, Senate Committees," *Washington Post*, December 2, 1983, A1; Peter B. Levy, *Encyclopedia of the Reagan-Bush Years*, Westport, CT: Greenwood Press, 1996, 231–232; Lois Romono, "Rita Lavelle, Dumped; Swept Out of EPA, The 'Garbage Lady' Keeps Her Chin Up," *Washington Post*, March 5, 1983, C1.

LEWINSKY, MONICA (July 23, 1973–   ). White House intern, 1995–1996; Department of Defense public affairs assistant, 1996–1998.

Born on July 23, 1973, in San Francisco, California, Monica Lewinsky grew up in Brentwood and Beverly Hills, California. In July 1995, after graduating from college, Lewinsky began work as an intern in the office of the White House chief of staff. In November 1995 she obtained a paid position with the White House office of legislative affairs where she answered correspondence. According to Lewinsky's testimony, President Clinton and she began a sexual relationship on November 15, 1995, during the government shut-down. From November 1995 through March 1997, Lewinsky and President Clinton met alone several times in the White House Oval Office. In testimony before a federal grand jury, Lewinsky alleged that they shared several sexual encounters during these private meetings.

On April 5, 1996, Lewinsky's White House supervisors had her transferred to a public affairs position at the Pentagon because of concern that she spent too much time hanging around President Clinton. In her new position, Lewinsky became friends with **Linda Tripp** who had worked as a White House secretary during the Bush administration and for a short time during the Clinton administration. Lewinsky subsequently told independent counsel **Kenneth Starr** that she resumed having sexual contact with President Clinton during the early months of 1997. Lewinsky also subsequently told Starr that a few days before the May 27, 1997 Supreme Court decision in *Clinton v Jones*, President Clinton called Lewinsky to the White House to tell her that he was breaking off their sexual relationship. In the months following the meeting, President Clinton asked members of the White House staff to help find Lewinsky another job.

Late in September 1997, Tripp began to secretly tape phone conversations with Lewinsky in which Lewinsky discussed her alleged sexual relationship with Clinton. In November 1997, after inquiries failed to find Lewinsky a satisfactory position, Clinton asked close friend Vernon E. Jordan Jr. to help Lewinsky find a job in New York City.

In late October and November 1997, Tripp provided *Newsweek* reporter Michael Isikoff and lawyers representing Jones with the information she had secretly obtained. On December 5, 1997, lawyers representing Jones named Lewinsky as a potential witness. Then on January 7, 1998, Lewinsky signed an

Monica Lewinsky during a two-day book tour in Helsinki, Finland, April 4, 1999. AP/WIDE WORLD PHOTO

affidavit stating that she never had a sexual relationship with Clinton. During late December and early January, Vernon Jordan continued to help Lewinsky with her job search. In early January the Revlon Corporation offered Lewinsky a job, and on January 9, 1998, she accepted the position.

After a request by Attorney General **Janet Reno**, on January 16, 1998, a special three-judge federal appeals panel granted **independent counsel Kenneth Starr** the authority to investigate whether President Clinton violated any federal laws by trying to conceal his relationship with Lewinsky. On the same day, Starr and his deputies confronted Lewinsky about her alleged relationship with President Clinton. Between January 16 and the end of July 1998, Starr subpoenaed numerous witnesses to appear before the Monica Lewinsky **grand jury**. Throughout this period Starr sought to negotiate an immunity agreement with Lewinsky. Finally, on July 28, 1998, Starr and Lewinsky reached an immunity agreement which led to Lewinsky making a number of appearances before a federal grand jury regarding her alleged relationship with President Bill Clinton. Then on August 17, 1998, President Clinton testified before the Lewinsky grand jury by a closed circuit television hookup from the White House. In his testimony, Clinton acknowledged "inappropriate intimate contact" with Lewinsky; however, he refused to answer specific questions.

On September 9, 1998, Starr forwarded his report to the House of Representatives. The report listed eleven grounds for the impeachment of President Clinton. After stormy hearings before the House Judiciary Committee, on December 19, 1998, the House approved two Articles of Impeachment: perjury before the grand jury and obstruction of justice. In January and early February 1999, the Senate conducted Clinton's impeachment trial. Instead of calling witnesses before the Senate, the House impeachment managers and President Clinton's defense team reached an agreement to submit the videotaped testimony of **Sidney Blumenthal**, Monica Lewinsky, and Vernon Jordan. On February 12, 1999, the Senate found President Bill Clinton not guilty.

In March 2000, Monica Lewinsky stepped back into the national spotlight with the publication of her book *Monica's Story* written by Andrew Morton. Besides being interviewed by ABC's Barbara Walters Lewinsky undertook a book tour of several countries in Europe. With three other partners, Lewinsky then started The Real Monica Inc., in September 1999, which produced handbags designed by Lewinsky. In late 1999, Lewinsky entered into an endorsement deal with the diet company Jenny Craig. Published reports indicated that Lewinsky has used a significant percentage of the proceeds from her book, endorsement contract and handbag company to pay off some of her heavy legal fees resulting from Kenneth Starr's independent counsel inquiry and the impeachment of President Bill Clinton.

On January 20, 2001, the independent counsel ended his Monica Lewinsky investigation after President Clinton admitted he had made false statements with respect to his relationship with Lewinsky.

Related Entries: Impeachment Proceedings; Independent Counsel Investigations; Starr, Kenneth; Tripp, Linda

SUGGESTED READINGS: The Independent Counsel Report to Congress: Coverage by the News Hour with Jim Lehrer. URL: *http://www.pbs.org/newshour/starr-report/*; Andrew Morton, *Monica's Story*, New York: St. Martin's Press, 1999; Bob Woodward, *Shadow: Five Presidents and the Legacy of Watergate*, New York: Simon & Schuster, 1999.

LEWIS, CHARLES. *See* Center for Public Integrity

LIDDY, G. GORDON (November 30, 1930–   ). Conservative radio talk show host, author, and Watergate figure.

Angered by Daniel Ellsberg's release of the top secret **Pentagon Papers** to the *New York Times*, President Richard Nixon ordered White House aide **John Ehrlichman** to find a way to stop future leaks of top secret government information. Ehrlichman assigned responsibility for stopping the leaks to White House aides Egil Krogh and David Young. In 1971, White House aides hired former FBI agent and New York Republican activist G. Gordon Liddy as part of a new White House unit established to find the source of links. The unit came to be known as the "plumbers unit."

Then on September 4, 1971, G. Gordon Liddy and **E. Howard Hunt** directed the break-in of the Los Angeles, California, office of Lewis Fielding, Daniel

Special Agent George G. Liddy (now known as G.
Gordon Liddy). Still Picture Branch, National
Archives and Records Administration

Ellsberg's psychiatrist. Liddy and Hunt hired James W. McCord Jr., a former
CIA operative, and four Cuban exiles as members of their so-called plumbers
unit. White House officials approved the break-in as part of an effort to gather
information to discredit Ellsberg prior to his trial for illegally leaking the Pentagon Papers. A short time after the break-in, the White House disbanded the
so-called plumbers unit.

Between December 1971 and February 1972, former Attorney General and
Chairman of President Nixon's Committee to Re-Elect the President (CREEP)
John Mitchell hired Liddy and Hunt to go to work for CREEP. Early in 1972
Liddy proposed the establishment of a major campaign intelligence gathering
operation. CREEP also hired James McCord to serve as security coordinator.
Although Mitchell rejected a number of operations proposed by Liddy, he did
approve a limited campaign intelligence-gathering operation. On May 28, 1972,
Liddy and Hunt supervised the first break-in at the offices of the Democratic
National Committee (DNC) located in the **Watergate** complex. After the break-
in failed to produce the desired results, on June 17, 1972, Liddy and Hunt
supervised a second break-in of the DNC Watergate offices. However, police
caught McCord and four Cuban exiles inside the DNC headquarters. After find-

ing the names of Liddy and Hunt on the burglars, police arrested both men for planning the burglary. On January 30, 1973, a U.S. District Court jury found McCord and Liddy guilty. In an effort to get Liddy, McCord, and the other Watergate burglars to cooperate with the investigation, U.S. District Judge John Sirica sentenced Liddy and McCord to long prison sentences. Liddy received six to twenty years in federal prison. Shortly after the sentencing, McCord implicated **John Dean**, Mitchell, and other White House officials. On the other hand, Liddy refused to cooperate for the duration of the Watergate investigation.

When the dust from the Watergate scandal settled, Liddy served fifty-two months in federal prison. In April 1977 President Carter commuted his sentence to eight years. Liddy received a parole in September 1977. In 1980 Liddy published his autobiography, *Will*. Subsequently Liddy became a popular speaker on the college lecture circuit. In 1992 Liddy began a new career by hosting his own talk radio show.

Related Entries: Pentagon Papers; Watergate Scandal

SUGGESTED READINGS: *Current Biography*, New York: H. W. Wilson Company, 1980, 225–228; Howard Kurtz, "Gordon Liddy on Shooting from the Lip, Radio Host Denies Fueling the Lunatic Fringe," *Washington Post*, April 26, 1995, C01; Jeffrey Yorke, "Liddy vs. Limbaugh Nationwide?" *Washington Post*, December 1, 1992, C7.

LINCOLN, ABRAHAM (February 12, 1809–April 15, 1865). President of the United States, 1861–1865. *See* "Honest Abe"

LINCOLN BEDROOM FUND-RAISING CONTROVERSY. Early in 1995 President Bill Clinton and the Democratic National Committee agreed on a plan to raise tens of millions of dollars in **soft money** to pay for a blitz of early **issue ads** designed to raise Clinton's approval ratings during the 1996 presidential campaign. In 1979 the **Federal Election Commission** had issued rules permitting political parties to raise unlimited amounts of money for such so-called party-building activities as get out the vote and voter registration campaigns. By 1995 the DNC and RNC took the position that FEC regulations permitted the use of soft money to pay for issue ads.

In 1995 and 1996, President Clinton hosted 831 overnight guests at the White House. FEC reports indicated that one-third of the individuals made campaign contributions to the Clinton-Gore campaign or the Democratic National Committee. A number of other individuals spent the night in the Lincoln bedroom. In October 1996 **Common Cause**, the public interest lobby, filed a complaint with the FEC alleging that both the DNC and the RNC had violated federal law by spending soft money on issue ads. In February 1997 media inquiries forced the White House to release the list of White House overnight guests and a list of individuals who had attended White House coffees with President Clinton.

Later, Attorney General **Janet Reno** ruled that the White House overnights had not violated federal campaign fund-raising laws even though federal law prohibited campaign fund-raising on federal property. Attorney General Reno found that the fund-raising prohibition did not apply to fund-raising conducted in the private residence of the president. Then, in December 1998, the FEC voted that neither the DNC nor RNC had violated FEC regulations by using soft money to pay for issue ads during the 1996 presidential election campaign.

The Lincoln bedroom controversy brought home the growing emphasis of the Democratic and Republican Parties on raising so-called soft money.

Related Entries: Clinton Administration Ethics Controversies; Election of 1996; Federal Election Commission (FEC); Soft Money

SUGGESTED READINGS: Charles R. Babcock, "The Overnight Guests," *Washington Post*, February 27, 1997, A19; Roberto Suro, "FEC Lets '96 Campaigns Off on 'Issue Ads,' " *Washington Post*, December 11, 1998, A21.

LIVINGSTONE, CRAIG. *See* FBI Files Flap

LOBBYING. *See* Lobbying Disclosure Act of 1995; "Revolving Door" Restrictions

LOBBYING DISCLOSURE ACT OF 1995. In the 1980s and early 1990s, a series of congressional ethics controversies helped to build support for a revision of federal lobbying disclosure laws. Public interest organizations, such as **Common Cause** and **Public Citizen**, argued that the lax lobbying disclosure laws permitted special interests to spend hundreds of millions of dollars annually on lobbying members of Congress without having to disclose the subject of their lobbying activities and expenditures. On December 19, 1995, President Clinton signed into law the Lobbying Disclosure Act of 1995 (LDA). The act replaced the Federal Regulation of Lobbying Act of 1946. At the White House signing ceremony for the bill, President Clinton explained the importance of the legislation: "Until today, the rules governing lobbyists, virtually unchanged since 1946, have been more of a loophole than a law. . . . For the first time," continued the president, "this law requires professional lobbyists to disclose publicly who they are, for whom they work, what they're spending, and what bills they're trying to pass, kill or amend."

The Lobbying Disclosure Act of 1995 required lobbyists to file registration statements with the secretary of the Senate and the clerk of the U.S. House of Representatives. The act defined a lobbyist as any person or entity (1) employed for financial or other type of compensation; (2) which provided services that include more than one lobbying contact; and (3) which spent more than 20 percent of a person's or entity's time for a client or employer on lobbying activities during the six-month reporting period. Equally the act required individual lobbyists to file periodic reports on how much they received for lobbying and lobbying expenditures.

Besides expanding the number of individuals required to file as lobbyists, the Lobbying Disclosure Act required thousands of organizations to report what issues they lobbied the government about and how much they spent. Companies, organizations, and associations were required to register if they employed individuals as in-house lobbyists and expected to spend more than $20,500 on lobbying activities during a semiannual period. In addition LDA required lobbying firms to file separate registration statements for each client for lobbying activities expected to exceed $5,000 during a semiannual period.

A 1999 report by the nonprofit **Center for Responsive Politics**, which analyzed the lobbying reports for 1998, revealed that Washington lobbyists spent $1.42 billion. The report also revealed that the number of registered lobbyists "swelled to 20,512 by June 15, 1999."

Related Entry: "Revolving Door" Restrictions

SUGGESTED READINGS: Lobbying Disclosure Act Guidance, Office of the Clerk: United States House of Representatives. URL: *http://clerkweb.house.gov/lrc/pd/lobby/ guidance98.htm*; George D. Webster, "Understanding the Lobbying Disclosure Act," *Association Management* 48 (August 1996): 222–224.

M

MACY, JOHN W., JR. (April 6, 1917–). Chairman of the U.S. Civil Service Commission, 1961–1969.

Early in his administration, President John Kennedy appointed John Macy as chairman of the U.S. Civil Service Commission (CSC). Between 1950 and 1960, a series of high-profile ethics controversies involving members of the administrations of President Harry Truman and President Dwight David Eisenhower led to calls for a major overhaul of federal ethics regulations. In late January 1961, shortly after being sworn in as president of the United States, Kennedy appointed an ethics advisory panel to make recommendations on how to improve the effectiveness of the executive branch ethics program. After the November 1963 assassination of Kennedy, President Lyndon Johnson continued his ethics reform initiatives. From January 1961 through January 1969, John Macy played a key role in the drafting of a series of Kennedy and Johnson administration ethics directives.

In his 1971 book *Public Service: The Human Side of Government,* Macy described the purpose of these initiatives: "These ethics directives prohibited executive branch employees and officials (1) from accepting most gifts from donors affected by the actions of the employee or his agency, (2) from accepting compensation for lectures, articles, or public appearances related to the performance of official duties and (3) from engaging in outside employment incompatible with the performance of official duties."

In May 1965 President Johnson issued **Executive Order 11222** which established uniform ethics guidelines for millions of federal employees and officials. In an unprecedented action, Executive Order 11222 required thousands of presidential appointees and other high-level executive branch officials to file confidential financial disclosure statements. The order gave the chairman of the CSC the responsibility for reviewing the confidential financial disclosure statements of high-level presidential appointees for financial conflict of interest problems.

On January 20, 1969, Macy resigned as chairman of the CSC to become the first chairman of the federally funded Corporation for Public Broadcasting; he served there until 1972. During the administration of President Jimmy Carter, Macy served as the director of the Federal Emergency Management Corporation. On December 22, 1986, Macy died of a heart attack at his home in McLean, Virginia.

Related Entries: Executive Order 11222; Johnson Administration Ethics Reform Program; Kennedy Administration Ethics Reform Program

SUGGESTED READINGS: Bart Barnes, "John W. Macy Jr., Dies; Headed Civil Service in 1960s," *Washington Post*, December 24, 1986, B1; John Macy Jr., *Public Service: The Human Side of Government*, New York: Harper & Row, 1971.

MADISON GUARANTY SAVINGS AND LOAN. *See* McDougal, James; Whitewater Investigation

MAIL FRAUD STATUTE. Beginning in the late 1960s, **federal prosecutors** significantly increased the prosecution of local, state, and federal officials on public corruption charges. By the close of the 1970s, the Mail Fraud Statute, along with the **Hobbs Act** and False Statements Act, had become major tools in an expansion of federal efforts to crack down on state and local government corruption. The Mail Fraud Statute law prohibits anyone from using the mail or any interstate communications carrier in a scheme to defraud anyone of property. Aggressive federal prosecutors argued that when public officials used the mail to engage in "corrupt" activities which deprived citizens of honest government such conduct violated the federal mail fraud statute. In other words all citizens had an "intangible" property interest in honest government.

Through much of the 1980s, the majority of federal courts accepted this creative interpretation of the Mail Fraud Statute. However, the Supreme Court in the 1987 decision of *McNally v United States* held that the legislative history of the statute indicated that Congress had not intended to allow the prosecution of individuals for depriving citizens of the intangible right to honest government. The *McNally* decision sent shock waves through the federal law enforcement community. With remarkable speed, Congress, in 1998, amended the statute to make it a federal crime for any individual to deprive somebody of "the intangible right of honest services." The decision of Congress to broaden the scope of the Mail Fraud Statute permitted federal prosecutors to resume using the Mail Fraud Statute as the primary method of using federal law to hold accountable "corrupt" local, state, and federal officials. Through the 1990s federal prosecutors successfully used the statute in a significant number of public corruption prosecutions.

Related Entry: Federal Prosecutor

SUGGESTED READINGS: Robert Roberts and Marion T. Doss Jr., "The Federalization of 'Grass Roots' Corruption," *Spectrum* 66 (Winter 1993): 6–16; Barbara Vobejda, "Prosecutors May Regain Powerful Weapon; Mail-Fraud Provision in Drug Bill Seeks to Make It Easier to Win Corruption Cases," *Washington Post*, October 16, 1988, A4.

MARCECA, ANTHONY. *See* FBI Files Flap

MCCORMICK V UNITED STATES **500 U.S. 267 (1991).** As a member of the West Virginia House of Delegates, Robert McCormick advocated a program allowing graduates of foreign medical schools to practice in West Virginia while studying for the state medical licensing exam. In 1984 McCormick agreed to sponsor legislation to extend the life of the program and to grant medical licenses to graduates of foreign medical schools on the basis of their years of medical practice in West Virginia. During McCormick's 1984 reelection campaign, he allegedly received four cash payments from a lobbyist representing the group of foreign-trained doctors who had asked him to sponsor the legislation. McCormick did not report the payment as a political contribution or as income on his federal or state income tax forms.

Subsequently a federal **grand jury** indicted McCormick for extortion under the **Hobbs Act**. A West Virginia U.S. District Court jury then found McCormick guilty of a Hobbs Act violation. Prior to beginning deliberations, the U.S. District Court judge instructed the jury that the Hobbs Act did not require federal prosecutors to prove that McCormick had agreed to help obtain passage of the bill in return for the contribution. In other words the Hobbs Act did not require **federal prosecutors** to prove the existence of a quid pro quo. The U.S. Court of Appeals then upheld McCormick's conviction. In a decision ordering a new trial for McCormick, the Supreme Court found that the Court of Appeals had erred by not holding that a "quid pro quo is necessary for a conviction when an official receives a campaign contribution, regardless of whether it is a legitimate contribution." The *McCormick* decision made clear that proof of a quid pro quo is an essential element of any Hobbs Act prosecution.

Related Entries: Federal Prosecutor; Hobbs Act

SUGGESTED READINGS: Linda Greenhouse, "Supreme Court Roundup; Justices Limit Use of Extortion Law against Officials Getting Contributions," *New York Times*, May 24, 1991, 19; *McCormick v United States* (1991) *http://laws.findlaw.com/US/500/257.html*.

MCDOUGAL, JAMES (August 25, 1940–March 8, 1998). Former owner of Arkansas Madison Guaranty Savings and Loan; Whitewater investigation figure.

Between January 1994 and his March 1998 death, James McDougal became a key figure in the **Whitewater investigations** of special counsel **Robert B. Fiske Jr.** and independent counsel **Kenneth Starr**. During the late 1970s, Arkansas Governor Bill Clinton and **Hillary Rodham Clinton** joined with Arkansas friends Jim McDougal and **Susan McDougal** to establish the Whitewater Development Corporation. The partnership bought 230 acres in Marion County, Arkansas, for $202,000 to develop as vacation or retirement homes. After a brief period of service as a member of Governor Bill Clinton's administration and a failed bid for Congress, in 1982, Jim McDougal purchased a small savings and loan and transformed it into Madison Guaranty Savings and Loan Association. Like many savings and loans across the country, Madison Guaranty quickly grew but found itself in serious financial difficulties by 1986. In 1989, federal savings and loan regulators took control of Madison Guaranty. In 1990, a Little Rock, Arkansas, U.S. District Court jury acquitted McDougal on bank fraud charges.

Early in January 1994, Attorney General **Janet Reno** appointed New York lawyer Robert B. Fiske Jr. to serve as the Whitewater special counsel. Within a short time, Fiske's investigation began to focus upon a possible relationship between the failure of the Whitewater development and the collapse of Madison Guaranty. In early August 1996, a special three-judge federal appeals panel appointed Kenneth Starr as the Whitewater independent counsel. On August 17, 1995, a Little Rock, Arkansas, federal **grand jury** indicted James and Susan McDougal and Arkansas Governor Jim Guy Tucker for conspiring to illegally obtain $3 million in loans from an investment company operated by former Little Rock municipal judge **David Hale**. The Small Business Administration (SBA) had backed the loans. The McDougals subsequently used a portion of one of the loans to purchase a tract of land for the Whitewater Development Corporation. After a month-long trial, on May 26, 1996 a U.S. District Court jury convicted the McDougals and Tucker on multiple counts of fraud and conspiracy. After his conviction, James McDougal agreed to cooperate with Kenneth Starr's Whitewater investigation. In April 1997, McDougal began serving a three-year sentence. On March 8, 1998, he died at age 57 in a Texas federal correctional facility. Prior to his death, McDougal authored a book titled *Arkansas Mischief: The Birth of a National Scandal*.

Related Entries: Clinton Administration Ethics Controversies; McDougal, Susan; Starr, Kenneth; Whitewater Investigation

SUGGESTED READINGS: Lloyd Grove, "Jim McDougal Had His Way With Words; Only in Death Is He a Silent Partner," *Washington Post*, March 9, 1998, B1; "A McDougal Chronology," *Arkansas Democrat-Gazette*, March 9, 1998, A3.

MCDOUGAL, SUSAN (1956–   ). Partner in the Whitewater Development Corporation.

Between January 1994 and March 1999, Susan McDougal became a central figure in the **Whitewater investigations** of Justice Department special counsel **Robert Fiske Jr.** and later **independent counsel Kenneth Starr**. In 1978 Arkansas Attorney General Bill Clinton and **Hillary Rodham Clinton** joined in a partnership to develop some 230 acres of unimproved land near the White River located in the Arkansas Ozark Mountains. Later, the McDougals and Clintons established the Whitewater Development Corporation to manage the planned development of vacation and retirement homes. On August 17, 1995, a Little Rock, Arkansas, federal **grand jury** indicted **James McDougal**, his ex-wife Susan, and Arkansas Governor Jim Guy Tucker on multiple counts of illegally obtaining $3 million in loans backed by the Small Business Administration (SBA) from an investment company operated by former Little Rock, Arkansas, judge **David Hale**. The McDougals and Tucker had obtained the loans during the mid-1980s.

In the May 1996 trial, David Hale became the key witness in Kenneth Starr's prosecution of the McDougals and Jim Guy Tucker. Hale testified that in 1986 Arkansas Governor Bill Clinton pressured Hale to make the $300,000 loan to Susan McDougal. The McDougals used a portion of one of the loans to purchase land for the Whitewater Development Corporation. In videotaped testimony shown to the Little Rock, Arkansas, jury, Clinton denied ever having a conversation with David Hale about a loan for Susan McDougal. Despite President Clinton's testimony, on May 28, 1996, a U.S. District court jury found Governor Jim Guy Tucker and James and Susan McDougal guilty on numerous fraud and conspiracy counts related to illegally obtaining SBA loans. Susan McDougal received a two-year prison sentence for her part in the conspiracy.

After her conviction, Whitewater independent counsel Kenneth Starr called her before the Whitewater grand jury. In an effort to obtain McDougal's testimony regarding Clinton's possible involvement in the fraudulent loan scheme, Starr granted Susan McDougal immunity from prosecution for her grand jury testimony. Despite the grant of immunity, she refused to testify on the grounds that Starr wanted her to implicate President Clinton in wrongdoing. McDougal then spent eighteen months in jail for civil contempt. A Little Rock, Arkansas, U.S. District Judge ordered her release after concluding that continuing to hold McDougal in jail would not result in her testimony.

In May 1998, following her release, a Little Rock, Arkansas, federal grand jury indicted Susan McDougal on two felony counts of criminal contempt for continuing to refuse to testify before the Whitewater grand jury. On March 23, 1999, she took the stand in her criminal contempt trial. She testified that she had no knowledge of illegal activities by Bill Clinton. McDougal also testified that President Clinton had testified truthfully during her 1996 fraud trial. On April 12, 1999, a Little Rock, Arkansas, U.S. District Court jury found Susan McDougal not guilty on one count of obstruction of justice. The jury deadlocked on the two felony criminal contempt charges. On May 25, 1996, Kenneth Starr announced that he would not retry Susan McDougal on the contempt of court charges. In explaining his decision, Starr argued that the notoriety of McDougal and the Whitewater investigation made it impossible to find an impartial jury to consider the remaining criminal contempt charges.

On January 20, 2001, his last day in office, President Clinton pardoned Susan McDougal.

Related Entries: Clinton Administration Ethics Controversies; Starr, Kenneth; Whitewater Investigation

SUGGESTED READINGS: Roberto Suro and Leef Smith, "Starr Declines to Retry McDougal, Steele," *Washington Post*, May 26, 1999, A04; Linton Weeks, "McDougal Breaks Silence; Whitewater Figure Backs President," *Washington Post*, March 24, 1999, A1.

MCFARLANE, ROBERT C. (July 12, 1937–   ). National Security advisor to President Ronald Reagan, 1983–1985.

Robert C. McFarlane served as national security advisor to President Ronald Reagan from 1983 through 1985. Prior to being appointed, McFarlane had worked his way up through the military chain of command after graduating from the U.S. Naval Academy in 1958. During the 1970s McFarlane served as military assistant to Henry Kissinger, President Nixon's national security advisor, and Bret Scowcroft, President Ford's national security advisor. Between 1981 and 1982, McFarlane worked for Secretary of State Alexander Haig. Then, in 1982, McFarlane became the deputy assistant for national security affairs under President Reagan's National Security Advisor William Clark. When President Reagan named Clark as secretary of the interior after the resignation of **James Watt**, he also named McFarlane as his new national security advisor.

Upon assuming his new position, McFarlane found himself in the middle of a raging controversy over U.S. support for the Nicaraguan contras. Backed by the Central Intelligence Agency, the contras sought to overthrow the Sandinista government. In December 1982 Congress passed the Boland Amendment, prohibiting the United States from funding any operation directed at overthrowing the government of Nicaragua. Early in 1984 President Reagan directed McFarlane to find a way to keep the Nicaraguan contras alive. McFarlane delegated the task to Marine Lt. Col. **Oliver L. North**. Lt. Col. North subsequently developed a plan to raise money from foreign governments and wealthy Americans.

During 1985 McFarlane and CIA Director **William Casey** strongly advocated selling weapons to Iran in an effort to help to arrange the release of Americans being held hostage by pro-Iranian terrorists in Lebanon. After obtaining Reagan's approval for the arms for hostages deal, McFarlane and Casey placed North in charge of the operation. Despite the fact that McFarlane resigned as NSC advisor during December 1985, he remained in contact with North and the new national security advisor, Vice Admiral **John M. Poindexter**, regarding the progress of the arms for hostage operation. Throughout the period McFarlane took steps to conceal North's activities from Congress.

During December 1986 a special federal judicial panel appointed **Lawrence Walsh** as the Iran-contra **independent counsel**. On March 11, 1988, McFarlane pleaded guilty to four misdemeanor charges of withholding information from Congress about North's activities in support of the contras. As a condition of the guilty plea, McFarlane agreed to cooperate with Walsh's independent counsel investigation. Then on December 24, 1992, President George Bush pardoned McFarlane, former Secretary of Defense **Caspar Weinberger** and four other Iran-contra defendants.

Related Entries: Casey, William; Independent Counsel Investigations; Iran-Contra Scandal; North, Oliver; Tower, John; Walsh, Lawrence E.; Weinberger, Caspar Willard

SUGGESTED READINGS: Peter B. Levy, *Encyclopedia of the Reagan-Bush Years*, Westport, CT: Greenwood Press, 1996; Lawrence E. Walsh, *Iran-Contra: the Final Report* (1994), Lawrence Walsh, Contra Report–Chapter 1; *United States v Robert C. McFarlane*, URL: http://www.fas.org/irp/offdocs/walsh/chap_01.htm.

MCKAY, JAMES. *See* Independent Counsel Investigations; Nofziger, Lyn

MEESE, EDWIN, III. (December 2, 1931–   ). Counselor to President Reagan, 1981–1985; U.S. attorney general, 1985–1988.

Between 1981 and the end of 1988, Edwin Meese III served as counselor to President Ronald Reagan as attorney general of the United States. Prior to joining the White House staff, Meese had served as California Governor Reagan's chief of staff from 1969 to 1975. During Reagan's 1980 presidential campaign, Meese served as one of the top campaign advisors. After Reagan won the 1980 presidential election, he appointed Meese to the position of counselor to the president.

Meese's appointment to a key White House position surprised few. From 1981 through 1984, Meese served as a vocal spokesperson for the policies of the Reagan administration. He pushed Congress to enact large increases in defense spending, reduce the growth in spending for social programs, and to pass large tax cuts. Early in 1984 President Reagan nominated Meese for attorney general. His nomination faced immediate opposition from Democratic critics and from interest groups concerned about Meese's conservative views.

A short time after Meese's nomination, allegations surfaced that he might have helped a number of friends find jobs in the Reagan administration after these friends provided Meese with financial assistance to make the move from California to Washington, D.C. Critics focused on the apparent failure of Meese to disclose the alleged assistance on public financial disclosure statements required by the **Ethics in Government Act of 1978**. In an effort to resolve the controversy, Meese asked Attorney General William French Smith to request the appointment of an **independent counsel** to examine the allegations. Then a special three-judge federal appeals panel appointed Jacob Stein to serve as independent counsel. On September 24, 1984, Stein issued his final report which concluded that insufficient evidence existed. The report cleared the way for the Senate to confirm Meese as attorney general.

A short time after being confirmed, Meese found himself thrown in the middle of the Iran-contra investigation. In November 1986 media reports disclosed that the United States secretly sold weapons to Iran in an effort to obtain the release of Americans being held hostage by pro-Iranian terrorists operating out of Lebanon. Upon publication of the report, President Reagan directed Meese to conduct a full investigation. In a November 25, 1986, news conference, Attorney General Meese disclosed that National Security Council officials had diverted proceeds from the Iranian arms sales to support the contras. Meese reported that

President Reagan knew nothing about the diversion of profits from the arms sales to the Nicaraguan contras. He also announced the resignation of National Security Council official **John Poindexter** and the reassignment back to the Marines of Colonel **Oliver North**. President Reagan then announced the appointment of a commission, headed by former Senator **John Tower**, to conduct an independent review of the arms for hostages policy. After a preliminary Justice Department investigation, Meese requested the appointment of an independent counsel to determine whether any violations of criminal law had occurred. A special federal judicial panel appointed **Lawrence Walsh** to serve as the Iran-contra independent counsel.

By spring 1987 Meese found himself implicated in the growing **Wedtech scandal**. Reports alleged that in the early 1980s, White House counselor Meese had directed members of the White House staff to contact Defense Department officials on behalf of the Bronx, New York, Wedtech Corporation. Between 1983 and 1986, Wedtech obtained millions of dollars in military contracts under various programs designed to assist minority-owned companies in obtaining government contracts. In July 1998 James C. McKay issued his report on Attorney General Meese's involvement in the Wedtech scandal. The McKay report found insufficient evidence to prosecute Meese. However, McKay alleged that Meese had technically violated federal law by participating in discussions regarding the telecommunications industry and for failing to pay a few thousand dollars in capital taxes. In an angry response to McKay's report, Meese denied that he had violated federal law. Prior to the issuance of the McKay report, Meese had announced his intention to resign as attorney general.

Related Entries: Independent Counsel Investigations; Reagan Administration Ethics Controversies; Wedtech Scandal

SUGGESTED READINGS: "Excerpts from the McKay Report," *Washington Post*, July 19, 1988, A9; "Excerpts from the Response by Counsels for Meese," *Washington Post*, July 19, 1988, A10; Peter B. Levy, *Encyclopedia of the Reagan-Bush Years*, Westport, CT: Greenwood Press, 1996, 240–242.

MILLS, WILBUR (May 24, 1909–May 2, 1992). Member of the U.S. House of Representatives, 1939–1977.

Between January 3, 1939 and January 3, 1977, Wilbur Mills served as a representative from Arkansas. In the early 1960s, Mills became chairman of the powerful House Ways and Means Committee. On October 9, 1974, Washington, D.C., police stopped a car driven by Representative Mills for speeding. When the car stopped, a woman jumped out of the car and ran into the tidal basin. The woman turned out to be Fannie Fox, an Argentine striptease dancer. Despite the ensuing media coverage of the incident, Arkansas voters sent Wilbur Mills back to Congress during the 1974 election. After Mills's reelection, a photographer took a picture of Mills on stage with Fannie Fox after one of her performances. The incident led Mills to enter Bethesda Naval Hospital to receive treatment for alcoholism. The House Democratic caucus subsequently forced

Mills to give up his chairmanship of the Ways and Means Committee. He declined to run for reelection in 1976.

Coming a little more than a month after the August 1974 resignation of President Richard Nixon, the Wilbur Mills affairs came to symbolize a new willingness of the media to report on the private lives of public officials. Prior to the **Watergate scandal**, the mainstream media rarely reported on the sexual indiscretions of powerful Washington political figures.

SUGGESTED READING: Congressional Quarterly, *Congressional Ethics: History, Facts, and Controversy*, Washington, DC: Congressional Quarterly, 1992.

MITCHELL, JOHN (September 15, 1913–November 9, 1988). Attorney General of the United States, 1969–1972; Chairman, Committee to Re-Elect the President, 1972–1973.

John Mitchell served as attorney general of the United States from 1969 to 1972. Early in 1972 Mitchell resigned to chair President Richard Nixon's Committee to Re-Elect the President (CREEP). As chairman of CREEP, Mitchell allegedly approved the break-in of the offices of the Democratic National Committee located at the **Watergate** complex. Late in 1971 and early in 1972, CREEP hired **G. Gordon Liddy, E. Howard Hunt**, and James McCord to work in a new political intelligence unit. During the winter of 1972, Mitchell allegedly approved an intelligence gathering operation prepared by Liddy.

On June 17, 1972, police arrested McCord and four Cuban exiles inside the offices of the Democratic National Committee located in the Watergate complex. A short time later, police arrested Liddy and Hunt for directing the Watergate burglars. *Washington Post* reporters **Bob Woodward** and **Carl Bernstein** quickly determined that Liddy, Hunt, and McCord worked for CREEP. From June 1972 through 1973, Mitchell became a key figure in the Watergate cover-up. He allegedly participated in a White House conspiracy to prevent the FBI from tracing the money used to pay the Watergate burglars to campaign contributions made to CREEP. The money had been laundered through a Mexican bank.

On March 1, 1974, a federal **grand jury** indicted John Mitchell, **H. R. Haldeman, John Ehrlichman,** and **Charles Colson** on Watergate cover-up related charges. Later, a U.S. District Court jury convicted Haldeman, Ehrlichman, Colson, and Mitchell of obstruction of justice and perjury. Mitchell received a thirty-month to eight-year sentence. Throughout the Watergate years, he denied ever having authorized the Watergate break-in or having told President Nixon about his efforts to conceal the relationship of CREEP with the Watergate burglars. Mitchell served nineteen months at the minimum security federal prison at Maxwell Air Force Base in Alabama, and received a parole on January 20, 1979.

On November 9, 1988, former Attorney General John Mitchell died of a heart attack while walking home from work. Former President Nixon attended the funeral along with 300 mourners.

Related Entry: Watergate Scandal

SUGGESTED READING: *Current Biography* 50, New York: H. W. Wilson Company, January 1989: 62 (Obituary).

MORRIS, DICK (1948–   ). Political consultant.

The 1994 midterm congressional election saw the Republican Party gain control of the House of Representatives for the first time in forty years. After the Republican victory, many political observers concluded that President Bill Clinton faced an uphill battle to win reelection in 1996. Early in 1995 President Clinton contacted longtime political consultant Dick Morris for help. For close to two decades, Morris had provided Clinton with political advice. He helped Clinton win the 1978 Arkansas governorship. After Clinton lost his 1980 reelection bid, Morris helped Clinton make a political comeback by winning the 1982 election for Arkansas governor. Through the 1980s and early 1990s, Morris worked as a political consultant for both Republican and Democratic candidates. For example Morris worked for Senator Howard Metzenbaum, the Democratic senator from Ohio, and North Carolina Republican Senator Jesse Helms.

Clinton's decision to make Morris a top political advisor met with strong opposition from top White House aides. Despite the opposition Morris helped to craft a strategy for Clinton's comeback. A key element of the strategy involved the Democratic National Committee raising tens of millions of dollars to finance a media blitz to highlight the successes of the Clinton administration. Morris, Clinton, and the DNC sought to take full advantage of the FEC's **soft money** exemption which permitted political parties to raise unlimited amounts of so-called soft money for party-building activities such as voter registration and get out the vote campaigns. President Clinton, the DNC, and Morris believed that federal law permitted the DNC to spend soft money on **issue ads** designed to rebuild public support. Through 1995 and early 1996, President Clinton helped to raise millions of dollars in soft money contributions by hosting White House coffees with potential contributors and providing them with the opportunity to spend the night in the White House. The combined effect of the 1995 government shutdown, a growing economy, and the DNC media campaign succeeded in raising public confidence in President Clinton.

On August 29, 1996, Morris resigned as President Clinton's political consultant after the *Star* tabloid published a story revealing that he had had a long-term relationship with a prostitute. The story came in the middle of the Democratic presidential convention. Interestingly the Morris resignation had little impact on the convention or the Clinton 1996 reelection campaign. In 1997 Morris published *Behind the Oval Office: Winning the Presidency in the Nineties*. In the book Morris took the credit for saving President Clinton from certain political defeat. The Clinton White House did not respond positively to the Morris book. White House aides quickly made clear that President Clinton, not Dick Morris, deserved the credit for his own political comeback. Besides writing the book, Morris began a new career as a political commentator.

On January 21, 1998, the **Monica Lewinsky** scandal broke in the nation's headlines. On the same day, Dick Morris received a phone call from President Clinton. Later in testimony before the Lewinsky **grand jury**, Morris quoted the president as saying "with this girl, I didn't do what they said . . . but I did do something." At Clinton's request Morris then conducted a poll in an effort to measure how the public would react if the president admitted that he had lied under oath. After receiving the results, Morris testified that he told President Clinton that the majority of the public would support his impeachment if he told them he had lied under oath. In the aftermath of the Lewinsky scandal, Morris launched a new career as the host of a new Web site named Vote.com. He established the site to provide citizens with the opportunity to learn more about important public policy issues and to have their views forwarded through the Internet.

Related Entries: Election of 1996; Lewinsky, Monica

SUGGESTED READINGS: Howard Kurtz, "Dick Morris, Burning His Bridges; The Former Clinton Confidant Fires Off New Accusations." *Washington Post*, February 3, 1999, C01; Dick Morris, *Behind the Oval Office: Winning the Presidency in the Nineties*, New York: Random House, 1997.

MORRIS, NEWBOLD (February 2, 1902–April 1, 1966). Special Assistant to the Attorney General, 1951.

Between 1950 and the end of 1952, the Truman administration found itself forced to deal with a number of ethics controversies involving the Bureau of Internal Revenue, Reconstruction Finance Corporation (RFC), and White House aides. With the 1952 presidential election on the horizon, critics pressed President Truman to do something to demonstrate his commitment to ethics in government. Aides to President Truman floated a proposal to establish an independent three-member investigatory panel to conduct a governmentwide investigation of ethics problems in federal agencies and departments. Attorney General Howard J. McGrath strongly opposed the establishment of any independent body to conduct an investigation of possible criminal conduct by federal employees and officials.

Under intense White House pressure, Attorney General McGrath agreed to accept the appointment of a new special assistant to take responsibility for the Truman administration initiative to restore public trust in government. On February 1, 1952, President Truman appointed New York lawyer Newbold Morris as the special assistant to investigate "misconduct by employees of the Federal Government" and to "make recommendations to strengthen the integrity and efficiency of the entire administration of government functions."

Almost from the day of the announcement, it became clear that Attorney General McGrath had no intention of allowing Morris to conduct a large-scale investigation of misconduct in federal agencies and departments. Attorney General McGrath refused to provide Morris with the necessary funds to hire a staff large enough to conduct a meaningful investigation. Equally important Morris engaged in a number of actions that angered both members of Congress and the Truman White House. For instance Morris publicly announced his intention to send out 25,000 questionnaires to high-level federal officials requiring them to disclose all sources of income. On April 4, 1952, Attorney General McGrath dismissed Morris. On the same day, President Truman announced the resignation of Attorney General McGrath and the nomination of U.S. Federal Judge James P. McGranery as attorney general. Judge McGranery promptly announced that he would not appoint anyone to replace Morris. Surprisingly Morris's dismissal did not cause a major uproar in Congress or the press. In his brief time in Washington, he had made a number of enemies in Congress and few friends in the press.

After his dismissal Morris returned to law practice in New York. Late in 1952 he published a book entitled *Let the Chips Fall: My Battles with Corruption*. The book presented a colorful account of Morris's efforts to fight corruption in New York City and Washington. From 1960 to 1965, Morris served as city parks commissioner. He died on March 30, 1966.

Related Entry: Truman Administration Ethics Controversies

SUGGESTED READINGS: Andrew Dunar, *The Truman Scandals and the Politics of Morality*, Columbia: University of Missouri Press, 1984; "Newbold Morris," *Current Biography*, New York: H. W. Wilson Company, 1952; Newbold Morris, *Let the Chips Fall: My Battles with Corruption*, New York: Appleton-Century-Crofts, 1952.

MORRISON V OLSON, 487 U.S. 654 (1988). In 1978 Congress passed the **Ethics in Government Act**, which included a provision for the appointment of special prosecutors (**independent counsels**) to investigate allegations of criminal conduct by high-level executive branch officials, including the president of the United States. In an effort to guarantee the independence of independent counsel investigations, Congress required that the attorney general ask a special three-judge panel of the U.S. Court of Appeals for the District of Columbia to appoint a special prosecutor if a preliminary investigation by the attorney general found credible evidence of a possible criminal violation by a high-level executive branch official covered by the special prosecutor section of the Ethics Act.

In 1983 a major dispute erupted between Congress and President Reagan over congressional access to Environmental Protection Agency (EPA) documents dealing with the administration of the EPA's Superfund program. Congress had established the Superfund program to pay for the cleanup of toxic-waste sites across the United States. In the course of congressional investigations of the Superfund program, the EPA and the Reagan White House refused to supply Congress with certain documents under the doctrine of **executive privilege**. In the end allegations of mismanagement forced a number of high-level EPA officials to resign.

During the time of the dispute over the documents, Theodore Olson served as assistant attorney general and head of the Justice Department's Office of Legal Counsel. In 1985 the Democratic majority of the House Judiciary Committee issued a report alleging that Olson had provided a Judiciary subcommittee with false and misleading testimony regarding the executive privilege dispute. After a preliminary inquiry by the **Public Integrity Section of the Department of Justice**, the Justice Department requested the appointment of an independent counsel to investigate whether Olson misled Congress in his 1983 testimony. The special panel appointed Alexia Morrison to conduct the investigation.

In an unprecedented action, Olson brought suit challenging the constitutionality of the independent counsel provisions of the 1978 Ethics Act. He alleged that the provisions for the appointment of independent counsels violated the Constitution's separation of powers doctrine and argued that the Constitution required that an executive branch official appoint independent counsels. Instead the Ethics Act gave a special three-judge federal appeals panel the task of appointing and supervising independent counsels. Interestingly the Justice Department supported the position taken by Olson on the constitutionality of the independent counsel law.

In January 1988 a divided three-judge panel of the U.S. Court of Appeals for the District of Columbia found the independent counsel provisions of the Ethics Act unconstitutional. The decision put in jeopardy the conviction of former White House deputy chief of staff **Michael Deaver** and the conviction of former White House political director **Lyn Nofziger** on charges of illegal lobbying. Equally significant the decision placed in jeopardy the **Iran-contra** investigation of **Lawrence E. Walsh**. Independent counsel Olson immediately appealed the ruling. On June 29, 1988, the Supreme Court upheld the constitutionality of the independent counsel provisions of the Ethics Act by a vote of 7 to 1. The high court found that the provision requiring the attorney general to request the appointment of all independent counsels satisfied the Constitution's separation of powers doctrine. Finally, on August 26, 1988, independent counsel Morrison announced that she would not seek an indictment against Olson.

Related Entries: Ethics in Government Act of 1978; Independent Counsel Act

SUGGESTED READINGS: Al Kamen, "Court Upholds Independent Counsel Law," *Washington Post*, June 30, 1988, A1: Bill McAllister and Ruth Marcus, "Olson's Indictment Won't Be Sought; Counsel Ends 29-Month Probe of Ex-Assistant Attorney General," *Washington Post*, August 27, 1988, A1.

MUCKRAKER. Beginning in the late 1880s, a new generation of writers and journalists began to write articles and books exposing corporate misdeeds and political corruption. These writers and journalists came to be known as muckrakers. Many of the muckrakers argued that an unholy alliance between big business and politicians permitted powerful trusts to destroy actual or possible competitors and politicians to profit handsomely for looking the other way. A classic series of articles by Lincoln Steffens published in *McClure's Magazine* detailed the dismal conditions of those living and working in a number of large cities. Later compiled into *Shame of the Cities*, the articles and books written by Steffens and other muckrakers helped to give birth to the municipal reform movement.

Historians credit Theodore Roosevelt for coining the term muckraker in 1906. President Roosevelt had become enraged at a series of articles attacking the nation's meat inspection system. The articles revealed the terrible conditions at meat-packing plants. Upton Sinclair's book *The Jungle* had presented a devastating picture of the meat processing industry. The publication of the book led directly to the passage of the Pure Meat Act of 1906 which established a national meat inspection system. The impact of the muckrakers went far beyond simply angering President Theodore Roosevelt. From 1900 through 1920, often referred to as the Progressive era, the muckrakers helped to build public support for the enactment of a progressive reform agenda at the state and federal level. The reforms included open primaries and prohibitions on corporate campaign contributions.

Related Entries: Campaign Finance Reform (Federal); Campaign Finance Reform (State); La Follette, Robert

SUGGESTED READING: Arthur Link, *Progressivism*, Arlington Heights, IL: Harlan Davidson, 1983.

MULLIGAN LETTERS AFFAIR. *See* Blaine, James G.

N

NAST, THOMAS (1840–1902). Nineteenth-century political cartoonist.

Historians regard Thomas Nast as the father of political cartooning. In 1840 Nast arrived with his family from Pfalz, Germany; he grew up in New York City. At age fifteen Nast obtained a position with *Leslie's Weekly* which published his first cartoon attacking municipal corruption. Nast then went to work for the *New York Illustrated News*. In 1860 he traveled to England to draw an illustration of a heavyweight fight and then to Italy as a war correspondent. Returning to New York in 1862, Nast used his artist talents to cover the Civil War for the *News* and then for *Harper's Weekly Magazine*. By the end of the Civil War, Nast had become a household name in the North for his illustrations which championed the Union cause.

After the Civil War, Nast turned his attention to national, state, and local politics. From 1865 through the end of the 1880s, he drew political cartoons about New York City and national political figures, and he openly supported the election of a series of presidential candidates. Nast became best known for his crusade against **William Marcy Tweed**. Beginning in the 1830s, the Democratic political machine gradually took control of the New York City political system. Headquartered in **Tammany Hall**, the machine came to control city contracts, franchises, and jobs. By the early 1860s, Tweed gained control of the New York City Democratic Party. Popularly known as "Boss" Tweed, he and his cronies made tens of millions of dollars through various fraudulent schemes. Between 1869 and 1871, *Harper's Weekly* published a number of illustrations of Nast attacking "Boss" Tweed and the Tammany political machine. The Nast cartoons focused unwelcome attention on Tweed's activities, which ultimately led to Tweed's arrest and conviction on public corruption charges. Besides playing an instrumental role in bringing public attention to the corruption of the Tweed Ring, historians credit Nast with creating the Republican elephant and the Democratic donkey.

CIVIL SERVICE REFORM.

OFFICE-SEEKER. "St. Jackson, can't you save us? Can't *you* give us something?"

Cartoon by Thomas Nast, *Harper's Weekly*, March 31, 1877. Reproduced from the Collections of the LIBRARY OF CONGRESS

Between 1885 and 1900, Nast experienced a number of financial setbacks which left him with inadequate funds to support his family. In 1902 President Theodore Roosevelt, a longtime admirer of Nast's work, appointed Nast as consul general to Ecuador. The appointment permitted Nast to pay off his debts. However, late in December of 1902, Nast developed a fever and died at the age of sixty-two in Guayaquil, Ecuador.

Related Entries: Spoils System; Tammany Hall; Tweed, William Marcy

SUGGESTED READINGS: Lynda Pflueger, *Thomas Nast: Political Cartoonist*, Berkeley Heights, NJ: Enslow Publishers, 2000; Thomas Nast Home Page: URL: *http://www.buffnet.net/~starmist/nast/main.htm*.

NATIONAL PUBLICITY LAW ASSOCIATION. *See* Campaign Finance Reform (Federal)

NEW YORK CUSTOMS HOUSE. *See* Customs Collector Scandals

NIXON, RICHARD MILHOUS (January 9, 1913–April 22, 1994). President of the United States, 1969–1974. *See* "Checkers" Speech; Nixon Administration Ethics Controversies; Watergate Scandal

Vice President Spiro Agnew, California Governor Ronald Reagan, President Richard Nixon, and Attorney General John Mitchell at a January 24, 1971 meeting in the Oval Office. Nixon Presidential Materials Staff

NIXON ADMINISTRATION ETHICS CONTROVERSIES. Elected in November 1968 as the twenty-seventh president of the United States, Richard M. Nixon entered the White House distrustful of the media and even more distrustful of his political opponents. In 1960 when John F. Kennedy won the presidency, Nixon believed that Kennedy won as the direct result of massive voter fraud in a number of key states. In 1962 Nixon blamed negative media coverage for his loss of the election for California governor.

In late 1968 and early 1969, the Nixon transition faced considerable difficulty recruiting top flight executive talent to accept government positions. Although Nixon had won the presidential election, Democrats remained firmly in control of the House and Senate. As a result the Nixon transition expected that Senate Democrats would put Nixon nominees under a microscope. In January 1969 David M. Kennedy, Nixon's nominee for secretary of the treasury, resisted calls that he sell his bank stock in Continental Illinois Bank. Kennedy argued that the sale of his bank stock would subject him to unanticipated capital gain taxes. After difficult negotiations Kennedy agreed to place his bank stock in a trust and place control of the stock in the hands of an independent trustee.

Nixon's nominee for deputy secretary of defense, David Packard, faced a similar problem. The founder of Hewlett-Packard Corporation, a major defense contractor, Packard and family members controlled some $300 million in stock.

Instead of enforcing its policy of requiring high-level Defense Department nominees sell stock, the Senate Armed Services Committee permitted Packard to place his stock in a trust for the duration of his term in office.

By 1970, growing opposition to the Vietnam war led to the development of a siege mentality within the Nixon White House. The president and his White House aides devoted immense time and energy to develop plans to discredit political opponents. As part of this process, Nixon aides drew up the so-called "Enemies List" to identify individuals that should be targeted for intimidation. The Nixon White House made use of allies in the CIA, FBI, and IRS to spy on and intimidate individuals and groups perceived to be unfriendly to President Nixon and his policies. From the perspective of the Nixon White House, the 1971 leaking of the **Pentagon Papers** to the *New York Times* confirmed their worst fears. Daniel Ellsberg, an employee of the Rand Corporation, leaked the highly classified study of the history of U.S. involvement in Vietnam. After the Supreme Court refused to stop the *New York Times* from publishing the Pentagon Papers, President Nixon directed White House aide **John Ehrlichman** to find a way to plug future leaks.

Ehrlichman then directed White House aides to carry out President Nixon's directive. **G. Gordon Liddy, E. Howard Hunt**, and James McCord were hired as the core of the new unit. On September 3, 1971, the so-called White House plumbers unit broke into the Los Angeles, California, offices of Ellsberg's psychiatrist in an effort to find damaging information which the White House might use to discredit Ellsberg. Shortly after the break-in, the White House disbanded the plumbers unit.

Early in 1972 President Nixon asked Attorney General **John Mitchell** to chair the Committee to Re-Elect the President (CREEP). Despite Nixon's rising poll numbers, the Nixon White House and CREEP took a number of highly unethical and illegal steps to guarantee Nixon's reelection. Nixon White House aides set up a **"dirty tricks"** operation directed at disrupting the race for the Democratic presidential nomination. In addition, the Nixon White House and CREEP raised millions of dollars in illegal campaign contributions to finance Nixon's reelection campaign. And CREEP hired Liddy, Hunt, and McCord to gather campaign intelligence. On June 17, 1972, District of Columbia police arrested McCord and four Cuban exiles inside the **Watergate** offices of the Democratic National Committee.

In the midst of the Watergate scandal, **federal prosecutors** developed strong evidence that Vice President **Spiro Agnew** had taken kickbacks from government contractors while he served as Maryland's governor during the 1960s. Rather than face a long investigation and possible impeachment, in October 1973 Spiro Agnew resigned the vice presidency.

On August 8, 1974, President Nixon resigned a short time after the U.S. Supreme Court ordered him to turn over the Watergate tapes to **independent counsel Leon Jaworski**. On August 9, 1974, the *Washington Post* published an article by reporters **Bob Woodward** and **Carl Bernstein** entitled "A Passion for the Covert: The Response to the Threat of Discovery." Bernstein and Woodward painted a picture of a White House staffed by individuals only concerned with maintaining political power. "The President's men, as revealed on the tapes, shared the fearsome vision of their leader. . . . Willingly, even enthusiastically, they outdid each other with plans to 'screw' the White House enemies, to supplant the security functions of the FBI with a squad of White House vigilantes, to undermine the electoral process through disruption of the opposition party's primaries, to 'fix' mock elections in high schools, to smear the reputations of politicians and public servants of both parties and—finally—to undermine the administration of justice."

Related Entries: Colson, Charles W.; Cox, Archibald; Ehrlichman, John D.; Haldeman, H. R.; Hunt, E. Howard; Jaworski, Leon; Mitchell, John; Liddy, G. Gordon; Pentagon Papers; Saturday Night Massacre; Watergate Scandal

SUGGESTED READINGS: Thomas Bailey, *Presidential Saints and Sinners*, New York: Free Press, 1981. Carl Bernstein and Bob Woodward, "A Passion for the Covert: The Response to the Threat of Discovery," *Washington Post*, August 9, 1974, Special Section: The Nixon Years, p. 5.

NIXON V FITZGERALD, 457 U.S. 731 (1982). Late in 1968 Ernest Fitzgerald, a management analyst with the Department of the Air Force, testified before a congressional subcommittee about large cost overruns on the C5A transport plane. In January 1970 a Defense Department reorganization resulted in the elimination of Fitzgerald's job. After Fitzgerald lost his job, he sued President Richard Nixon and White House aides for pressuring the Air Force to dismiss him. Eventually Fitzgerald won the battle to get his job back. His suit against President Nixon continued through the early 1980s. In an effort to block Fitzgerald's suit, Nixon and former Nixon White House aides argued that the Constitution gave them absolute immunity from lawsuits.

On June 24, 1982, by a vote of 5 to 4, the Supreme Court held that the Constitution provided President Nixon with absolute immunity from civil suits for discretionary acts while he served as president. Prior to the Supreme Court decision, Nixon had agreed to pay Fitzgerald $142,000. The majority of the court argued that granting presidents absolute immunity from civil suits would not make future presidents more willing to violate the constitutional rights of citizens. According to the majority, any president who engaged in such conduct might subject himself or herself to impeachment, intense media scrutiny, and the anger of voters. In his dissent Justice Byron R. White criticized the majority opinion as "tragic" for placing the president above the law.

However, in the companion case of *Harlow v Fitzgerald*, 457 U.S. 1982 (1982), the court refused to extend absolute immunity from civil suits for violations of constitutional rights to aides in the Nixon White House. Instead the Constitution only provided Nixon aides with **qualified immunity** from suits alleging violations of constitutional rights. Although the high court refused to extend absolute immunity to White House aides, it did hold that before a federal court could hold a public official liable for monetary damages for violating an individual's constitutional rights, the court must find that the public official violated a "clearly established" constitutional or statutory right.

Related Entries: Absolute Official Immunity Doctrine; Qualified Official Immunity Doctrine

SUGGESTED READING: Fred Barbash, "Court Rules for Nixon, 5–4; Presidents Given Immunity from Suits," *Washington Post*, June 25, 1982, A1.

NOFZIGER, LYN (June 8, 1924–   ). Political consultant to President Reagan.

From the 1960s through the early 1980s, Lyn Nofziger worked for a series of Republican candidates for state and federal office. In 1966 Nofziger served as Ronald Reagan's press secretary during his campaign for governor of California and then as Governor Reagan's director of communications. He then served as a White House aide to President Richard Nixon from 1969 through 1974. Following President Nixon's August 8, 1974, resignation, Nofziger returned to California to work for a number of organizations that supported Reagan for president of the United States. In 1980 Nofziger served as Reagan's press secretary during his successful presidential campaign. Nofziger then joined the Reagan White House as the assistant to the president for political affairs.

In 1982 Nofziger left the Reagan White House to establish a Washington, D.C., public relations firm. Between 1982 and late 1986, Nofziger's transition from White House political consultant to public relations executive and lobbyist created little controversy. However, in November 1986 Nofziger found himself under investigation as part of the so-called **Wedtech** investigation. Originally known as the Welbilt Electronic Die Corporation, in the early 1980s the small Bronx, New York, company enlisted the help of Nofziger, members of Congress, and other Washington officials in an effort to obtain defense contracts. Wedtech applied for no-bid defense contracts under a program designed to help minority contractors obtain defense contracts. Between 1983 and 1986, Wedtech received some $250 million in no-bid defense department contracts. However, in 1987 the company went bankrupt after the Department of Defense ruled that Wedtech did not qualify for the no-bid contract program as a minority contractor.

In 1982 Wedtech had hired Nofziger to help obtain a no-bid contract from the army. According to subsequent testimony, in April 1982, while **Edwin Meese III** served as President Reagan's White House counselor, Nofziger sent Meese a letter about Wedtech's efforts to obtain a no-bid army contract. Meese friend and San Francisco, California, lawyer E. Bob Wallach also contacted Meese on behalf of Wedtech. On January 7, 1987, the Justice Department requested that a special three-judge federal judicial panel appoint an **independent counsel** to investigate whether Nofziger violated provisions of the **Ethics in Government Act of 1978** prohibiting former high-level executive branch officials from lobbying their former agencies for one year after leaving government employ. On February 2, 1987, a special federal judicial panel appointed James C. McKay to serve as the Nofziger independent counsel. On July 16, 1987, a federal **grand jury** indicted Nofziger on six counts of violating the Ethics Act one-year no-contract prohibition.

On February 11, 1988, a U.S. District Court jury convicted Nofziger of illegally lobbying senior White House aides on behalf of the Wedtech Corporation. On April 8, 1988, U.S. District Judge Thomas Flannery sentenced Nofziger to ninety days in prison and a $30,000 fine. Then on June 27, 1989, a federal appeals court, by a vote of 2 to 1, overturned Nofziger's conviction on the grounds that McKay had failed to prove that Nofziger knew his contacts violated the provisions of the 1978 Ethics Act. The Appeals Court found that the law required **federal prosecutors** to prove that Nofziger had knowledge of his violation, as well as proving that Nofziger improperly contacted high-level executive branch officials.

Related Entries: Meese, Edwin, III; Independent Counsel Investigations; Wedtech Scandal

SUGGESTED READINGS: George Lardner Jr., "McKay Reports Four 'Probable' Meese Offenses; Independent Counsel Points to Extenuating Circumstances," *Washington Post*, July 19, 1988, A1; George Lardner Jr., "Nofziger's Convictions Overturned; By 2–1, Conflict Law Is Ruled Ambiguous," *Washington Post*, June 28, 1989, A1.

NORTH, OLIVER (October 7, 1943–   ). Colonel, U.S. Marine Corps; staff member, National Security Council; Conservative talk show host.

In 1987 Marine Colonel and National Security Council staff member Oliver North became the center of the **Iran-contra scandal** which had its origins in efforts by the administration of President Ronald Reagan to prevent the further spread of communism. In 1982, with the strong support of President Reagan, CIA Director **William Casey** undertook a covert operation to support the Nicaraguan contras. The CIA secretly funneled funds and weapons to the group in an effort to prevent the Nicaraguan Sandinista government from supporting other communist revolutions in Central America. In December 1982 the House passed the Boland Amendment which prohibited the CIA or Defense Department from spending any federal funds to support the overthrow of the Nicaraguan government. From the perspective of the Reagan administration, the amendment threatened the survival of the Nicaraguan contras. During the same period, pro-Iranian terrorists took hostage a number of foreigners and Americans in Lebanon. The inability to free the hostages proved a great embarrassment to the Reagan administration.

In 1985, with the support of National Security Advisor **John Poindexter**, Oliver North developed a plan to sell arms to Iran in an effort to arrange the release of American hostages being held in Lebanon. North subsequently proposed using profits from the arms-for-hostages sales to fund the contras. Early in November 1986, media reports of the arms for hostages operation forced

Colonel Oliver North testifying at the Iran-Contra hearing. © Wally McNamee/CORBIS

Attorney General **Edwin Meese III** to request that a special three-judge panel appoint an **independent counsel** to investigate possible criminal conduct by individuals involved in the Iran-contra operation. The panel subsequently appointed **Lawrence Walsh** to serve as the Iran-contra independent counsel.

After receiving a grant of immunity from Congress, North appeared before the Iran-contra committee in July 1987. In nationally televised testimony, North defended the arms for hostages operation and the diversion of profits to the Nicaraguan contras. A federal **grand jury** subsequently indicted North for lying to Congress, destroying documents, and accepting an **illegal gratuity**. On May 4, 1989, a U.S. District Court jury found North guilty on all three counts. He received two years' probation, a $150,000 fine, and 1,200 hours of community service as a sentence. In 1990 a federal appeals court overturned North's conviction on the grounds that his testimony before Congress tainted the testimony of a number of witnesses who subsequently testified at North's trial.

In 1994 North challenged incumbent Democratic Senator Chuck Robb. Largely because of a split within the Republican Party, North lost his Senate race by a small margin. Republican Senator John Warner refused to support

North's candidacy because of the prior involvement in the Iran-contra affair. Instead Warner threw his support behind Marshall Coleman, who ran as an independent after failing to win the Republican Party Senate nomination.

Related Entries: Independent Counsel Investigations; Iran-Contra Scandal

SUGGESTED READINGS: Ben Bradlee Jr., *Guts and Glory: The Rise and Fall of Oliver North*, New York: D. I. Fine, 1988; Oliver North, *Under Fire: An American Story*, New York: HarperCollins, 1991.

O

OFFICE OF GOVERNMENT ETHICS. *See* U.S. Office of Government Ethics

OHIO GANG. In 1920 Republican Warren G. Harding won the presidential election after serving one term as a U.S. senator from Ohio. After his election President Harding appointed a number of individuals from Ohio to high-level executive branch offices. The members of the so-called Ohio gang included Attorney General **Harry Daugherty**, Comptroller of the Currency Daniel R. Crissinger, Director of the Mint Ed Scobey, Superintendent of Prisons Heber H. Votaw, and Head of the Veterans Bureau Colonel Charles R. Forbes. Early in August 1923, Harding died in San Francisco, California, after returning from a vacation trip to Alaska. Within a short time, a number of Harding's Ohio associates found themselves the subject of congressional and criminal public corruption investigations.

Related Entry: Harding Administration Scandals

SUGGESTED READING: Nathan Miller, *Stealing from America: A History of Corruption from Jamestown to Reagan*, New York: Paragon House, 1992.

OLSON, THEODORE. *See* Independent Counsel Investigations; *Morrison v Olson*; Reagan Administration Ethics Controversies

P

PACKWOOD, ROBERT (September 11, 1932–   ). U.S. Senator, 1969–1995.

Robert Packwood served as a Republican senator from Oregon from 1969 until his resignation from the Senate on October 1, 1995. During October 1992 a freelance reporter contacted the *Washington Post* regarding allegations that during Packwood's twenty-four years in the Senate he had made numerous improper sexual advances to former staff members and lobbyists. Official Washington found it exceptionally difficult to deal with the report. Throughout Packwood's time in the Senate, he had established an outstanding record as an advocate of women's rights. Coming shortly after his reelection to the Senate, Senator Packwood announced he would cooperate with a Senate Ethics Committee investigation of his treatment of female staff members and lobbyists.

To the great dismay of the Senate and members of the Senate Ethics Committee, it took more than two and one-half years to resolve the allegations of improper conduct. During the course of the investigation, the Senate Ethics Committee expanded the scope of its investigation to include an allegation that Senator Packwood improperly sought jobs for his former wife from lobbyists and others with an interest in legislation and that he tampered with his diaries after the Ethics Committee had requested they be turned over as part of the investigation. Through the early months of 1995, Packwood gave every indication he intended to fight for his Senate seat to the bitter end. However, on March 7, 1995, in a resignation speech to the Senate, Senator Packwood announced that he intended to resign on October 1, 1995. Instead of attacking his critics, Senator Packwood devoted his entire speech to a discussion of his successes during his twenty-seven years in the Senate.

SUGGESTED READINGS: Florence Graves and Charles E. Shepard, "Packwood Accused of Sexual Advances; Alleged Behavior Pattern Counters Image," *Washington Post*, November 22, 1992, A1; Senator Bob Packwood: Resignation Speech to Senate on March

7, 1995, Historical Documents, Resignation.com URL: *http://www.resignation.com/ historicaldocs/speech.phtml?id-23.*

PATERNITY CONTROVERSY AND GROVER CLEVELAND. *See* Election of 1884

PATRONAGE CRIMES. Beginning with the passage of the **Pendleton Act of 1883**, Congress enacted a series of laws directed at prohibiting traditional abuses related to the "**spoils system**." In 1939 Congress passed the Hatch Act in an effort to prohibit career federal employees from engaging in partisan political activities. For example section 607 of title 1 "prohibits anyone from soliciting or receiving a contribution for a federal election in any room, areas or building where federal employees are engaged in official duties." In 1993 President Bill Clinton signed into law major amendments to the Hatch Act which relaxed prohibitions on partisan political activities by federal employees and officials.

In the aftermath of Clinton's 1996 presidential election victory, the scope of federal patronage crimes became a mature legal and political issue. Critics of the 1996 fund-raising practices of the Democratic National Committee, President Clinton and Vice President Albert Gore alleged that both had violated the statutory prohibition against federal officials raising campaign funds from federal offices by making phone calls from the White House to potential campaign contributors. Critics also argued that President Clinton violated federal law by hosting campaign contributors in White House coffees and providing contributors with the opportunity to spend a night in the Lincoln bedroom.

In two controversial actions, Attorney General **Janet Reno** ruled that President Clinton had not violated federal law; also she refused to request the appointment of an **independent counsel** to investigate whether Vice President Gore violated federal law by making fund-raising calls from his government office, as well as his participation in a fund-raising event at a Buddhist Temple where a Democratic fund-raiser had collected thousands of dollars in illegal campaign contributions.

Related Entries: Clinton Administration Ethics Controversies; Election of 1996

SUGGESTED READINGS: Michael Hedges, "The Scope of Federal Election Offenses," *New York Law Journal*, June 3, 1997, 3; Roberto Suro and Lena H. Sun, "U.S. Set to Probe Gore Calls," *Washington Post*, September 4, 1997, A1.

PATRONAGE SYSTEM. *See* Spoils System

PEARSON, DANIEL S. *See* Brown, Ronald; Independent Counsel Investigations

PENDLETON ACT OF 1883. In 1883 Congress passed the Pendleton Act which established a new federal merit system. From the late 1860s through the passage of the act, the civil service reform movement worked to restrict the right of political parties and elected officials to appoint individuals to public jobs. Civil service reform advocates faced strong opposition from entrenched political machines that viewed patronage appointments as vital to the survival of their political parties. In July 1881 a disappointed office seeker shot President James Garfield who subsequently died from his wounds.

After Vice President **Chester A. Arthur** became president, supporters of the enactment of civil service reform legislation intensified their efforts. Somewhat surprisingly President Arthur, who had risen through Senator Roscoe Conkling's New York State political machine, threw his support behind the enactment of limited civil service reform legislation. Arthur's support proved crucial in overcoming strong opposition to reform legislation.

To oversee the implementation of the new merit system, the Pendleton Act provided for the establishment of an independent Civil Service Commission (CSC). The act directed the CSC to establish open competitive examinations for about 10 percent of the federal workforce and prohibited **political assessments** of civil service employees for political purposes. Equally important the act prohibited political fund-raising from federal buildings. Although the Pendleton Act did not end all **spoils system** appointments or political assessments, its passage represented the beginning of a long process which would extend the protection of merit systems to the vast majority of federal employees by the beginning of the 1930s.

Even before the passage of the Pendleton Act, the Republican Party significantly reduced reliance on political assessments for campaign funds. Instead the Republican Party sought direct campaign contributions from wealthy individuals and corporations. Through the 1890s criticism of direct corporate campaign contributions led to the birth of a movement to prohibit corporate campaign contributions and to require the disclosure of campaign contributions and expenditures.

Related Entries: Political Assessments; Spoils System

SUGGESTED READING: Frederick C. Mosher, *Democracy and Public Service*, New York: Oxford University Press, 1982.

PENTAGON PAPERS. In 1971, Daniel Ellsberg, a senior associate at the Massachusetts Institute of Technology's Center for International Studies, leaked the so-called Pentagon Papers to the *New York Times*. The 3,000-page Department of Defense study of the history of U.S. involvement in Vietnam painted a highly critical picture of U.S. involvement in Vietnam from the 1950s through the 1960s. At the direction of President Richard Nixon, Attorney General **John Mitchell** went into federal court to obtain an injunction to prevent the *New York Times* from publishing any other parts of the leaked report. After a U.S. District judge issued an injunction against further publication of the report, the *New York Times* appealed the decision to the Supreme Court. In the landmark case of *New York Times Co. v United States*, the Supreme Court, on June 30,

1971, ruled by a vote of 6 to 3 that the lower federal court had acted improperly by prohibiting the *New York Times* from publishing excerpts from the report. The decision sharply limited the authority of the federal courts to issue injunctions against the publication of controversial material by newspapers.

The leak of the Pentagon Papers and the Supreme Court decision infuriated President Nixon. Within a short time, he directed White House aide **John Ehrlichman** to find a way to plug future leaks. Later White House staff members hired **G. Gordon Liddy, E. Howard Hunt**, and James McCord, to work as a unit. Early in September 1971, the unit broke into the Los Angeles, California, office of Daniel Ellsberg's psychiatrist. The so-called plumbers unit conducted the burglary in an effort to obtain information that the White House might use to discredit Ellsberg before his criminal trial for leaking the Pentagon Papers. Shortly thereafter the White House disbanded the plumbers unit. Late in 1971 and early in 1972, President Nixon's Committee to Re-Elect the President (CREEP) hired Liddy, Hunt, and McCord to work for CREEP. On June 17, 1972, District of Columbia police arrested McCord along with four Cuban exiles inside the **Watergate** office of the Democratic National Committee. A short time later, police arrested Liddy and Hunt for overseeing the burglary. The ensuing attempts by the Nixon White House and CREEP to cover up their relationship to the burglars ultimately led to Nixon resigning the presidency on August 9, 1974.

Related Entries: Hunt, E. Howard; Liddy, G. Gordon; Watergate Scandal

SUGGESTED READING: Nathan Miller, *Stealing from America: A History of Corruption from Jamestown to Reagan*, New York: Paragon, 1992.

PINCHOT, GIFFORD (August 11, 1865–October 4, 1946). *See* Ballinger-Pinchot Affair

PLUMBERS UNIT. *See* Pentagon Papers; Watergate Scandal

POINDEXTER, JOHN MARLAN (August 12, 1936–). National Security Advisor 1985–1987.

In 1985 President Ronald Reagan appointed John Poindexter to the position of national security advisor. Prior to the appointment, Poindexter had served as deputy national security advisor to **Robert McFarlane**. Between 1982 and 1985, NSC staffer **Oliver North** and Robert McFarlane developed, gained approval, and implemented a plan to sell arms to Iran in an effort to gain the release of American hostages being held by pro-Iranian terrorists in Lebanon. In November 1986 news reports of the arms for hostages deal created an immediate crisis for the Reagan administration. On November 25, 1986, President Reagan dismissed

Poindexter and reassigned North back to the Marine Corps after Attorney General **Edwin Meese** reported to President Reagan that North and Poindexter had approved the diversion of profits from the Iranian arms sale to the Nicaraguan contras.

Following the preliminary report by Attorney General Meese, President Reagan appointed former Texas Senator **John Tower** to head a commission to review the **Iran-contra** affair. After completion of a preliminary Justice Department investigation, Attorney General Meese requested that a special three-judge federal appeals panel appoint an **independent counsel** to investigate. In December the panel appointed **Lawrence Walsh**.

In July 1987 after receiving immunity for his testimony, Poindexter appeared before Congress. In his testimony Poindexter took full responsibility for the diversion of the profits from the Iranian arms sale to the contras. Despite the grant of congressional immunity, a U.S. federal **grand jury** indicted Poindexter on a number of Iran-contra related charges. On April 7, 1990, a U.S. District Court jury convicted Poindexter of conspiracy, obstruction of justice, and perjury. He received a six-month jail term and a $250 fine. On November 16, 1991, the U.S. Court of Appeals for the District of Columbia reversed the conviction due to technical trial errors.

Related Entry: Iran-Contra Scandal

SUGGESTED READINGS: Michel Hedges, "Poindexter's Conviction Reversed," *Washington Times*, November 16, 1991, A1; Peter B. Levy, *Encyclopedia of the Reagan-Bush Years*, Westport, CT: Greenwood Press, 1996.

POLITICAL ACTION COMMITTEE. In 1944 the Congress of Industrial Organizations (CIO) formed the first political action committee to raise money for the reelection bid of President Franklin D. Roosevelt. Prior to the action, Congress had enacted legislation prohibiting both corporations and unions from making direct campaign contributions to federal candidates. In 1971 Congress passed the **Federal Election Campaign Act** which established comprehensive campaign finance disclosure requirements and new limits on campaign contributions to candidates in federal elections. In the aftermath of the **Watergate scandal**, Congress passed the **Federal Election Campaign Act Amendments of 1974** which established a $1,000 individual contribution limit to a candidate per election and a $5,000 contribution limit to a candidate per election for political action committees. Instead of reducing the amount of special interest campaign contributions, the 1974 FECA amendments contributed to the establishment of thousands of new political action committees during the remainder of the 1970s and then during the 1980s and 1990s. By the end of the 1980s, political action committees had become the most important source of **hard money** for candidates for federal office.

Related Entries: Campaign Finance Reform (Federal); Federal Election Campaign Act of 1971; Hard Money; Soft Money

SUGGESTED READINGS: Political Contributions by Political Action Committees, Center for Responsive Politics: *http://www.opensecrets.org/pacs/index.htm*; Larry Sabato, *PAC Power: Inside the World of Political Action Committees*, New York: Norton, 1990.

POLITICAL ASSESSMENTS. During the first half of the nineteenth century, the United States saw the growth of major political parties which learned to use political patronage as a way to strengthen their political machines. As the power of political parties and political machines grew, political affiliation became an accepted qualification for many government positions at the local, state, and federal level. Besides rewarding key supporters with government positions, political parties and political machines quickly began the practice of requiring government employees to contribute a portion of their public salaries to the political party or political machine controlling the government. Government employees who refused to make a contribution were fired. By the 1860s political assessments became a major source of revenue for the Republican and Democratic Parties.

Efforts to end political assessments at the local, state, and federal level faced strong opposition from major political parties and political machines. From 1869 through 1876, a series of public corruption scandals during the administration of President Ulysses S. Grant placed considerable pressure on Congress to prohibit political assessments. Shortly before the 1876 presidential election, Congress passed legislation "prohibiting executive officers and employees from requesting anything of value from other officers or employees for political purposes, or giving or receiving such." When President **Rutherford B. Hayes** took office in 1877, he issued an executive order to halt the practice of requiring federal employees to participate in partisan political activities and requiring employees to make campaign contributions. The Hayes executive order also reaffirmed the ban on political assessments.

The **Pendleton Act of 1883** included a number of provisions to protect members of the new federal merit system from being coerced to make political contributions and from being punished or fired for refusing to participate from partisan political activities. The law prohibited federal employees from asking other federal employees for campaign contributions. Equally important the law prohibited any person from soliciting a campaign contribution from inside a federal building. Despite effort by candidates for federal office to find a way around the new campaign fund-raising prohibitions, gradually the new rules took hold. From 1883 to 1910, the U.S. Civil Service Commission aggressively pursued complaints by federal employees of being forced to make campaign contributions or being punished for refusing to engage in partisan political activities. By the turn of the century, supporters of political reform turned their attention from the **spoils system** and civil service reform to **campaign finance reform**. The new reform campaign focused on prohibiting corporate political contributions to federal campaigns and requiring disclosure of campaign contributions and expenditures.

Related Entries: Patronage Crimes; Pendleton Act of 1883; Spoils System

SUGGESTED READINGS: Leonard D. White, *The Jacksonians*, New York: Free Press, 1965; Leonard D. White, *The Republican Era: 1869–1901*, New York: Macmillan Company, 1958; C. Vann Woodward, ed., *Responses of the Presidents to Charges of Misconduct*, New York: Delacorte Press, 1974.

POLITICS OF PERSONAL DESTRUCTION. At a $1,000-a-plate March 1994 Democratic fund-raiser, President Bill Clinton lashed out at his Republican critics. Clinton accused his Republican critics of being "committed to a politics of personal destruction." Throughout the Clinton presidency, supporters of President Clinton argued that critics of the Clinton presidency attempted to use the alleged ethical problems of President Clinton, **Hillary Rodham Clinton**, and members of the Clinton administration to overturn the 1992 and 1996 presidential election. President Clinton's strategy of blaming his ethical problems on political opponents succeeded in helping him maintain the support of those who voted for him in 1992 and 1996. More important the strategy proved essential in the Clinton White House campaign to defeat the effort by Republican members of Congress to have President Clinton removed from office as the result of his conduct in the **Monica Lewinsky** affair.

Related Entry: Clinton Administration Ethics Controversies

SUGGESTED READING: Ruth Marcus, "Clinton Angrily Denounces Republicans; Party Is 'Committed to Politics of Personal Destruction,' President Says," *Washington Post*, March 15, 1994, A1.

POWELL, ADAM CLAYTON (November 29, 1908–April 4, 1972). Representative from New York, 1945–1967 and 1969–1971.

During the 1960s Representative Adam Clayton Powell became one of the most controversial members of Congress. In 1958 a federal **grand jury** indicted Powell on tax evasion charges. Although a 1960 trial ended in a hung jury, the Internal Revenue Service subsequently forced Powell to pay some $27,833.17 in back taxes and penalties. Between 1960 and 1965, Powell became the subject of a number of civil suits alleging misconduct. Early in January 1967, a significant number of House members became extremely concerned about allegations that Powell repeatedly had the government pay for expensive trips which appeared to have little to do with congressional business. Instead of allowing Powell to take his seat in Congress, a majority of the House voted to delay Powell's swearing in until completion of an investigation of Powell's possible misuse of public funds. On March 1, 1967, by a vote of 307 to 116, the House voted to exclude Powell from the Ninetieth Congress.

Not unexpectedly Powell responded with anger to the House decision to refuse to seat him. He blamed the vote on racism in Congress. In an effort to force the House to seat him, Powell brought suit in federal court arguing that the Constitution required the House to seat him because he met all of the constitutional requirements for membership. While awaiting a decision, the governor of New York called a special election to fill the vacancy created by the

House decision to exclude Powell. Voters overwhelmingly voted to return Powell to the House. During the campaign Powell did not return to the New York City district to campaign. Earlier a New York court had held Powell in contempt of court for failing to comply with the terms of a civil judgment. Interestingly he decided not to attempt to take his House seat until the Supreme Court ruled on the constitutionality of the House decision.

On June 16, 1969, the Supreme Court ruled in *Powell v McCormack* that the Constitution prohibited the House from denying a seat to an individual who met all the constitutional requirements of House membership. In rendering the decision, the high court did not argue that the House lacked the authority to expel a member for misconduct or to impose other types of sanctions. However, the high court made it clear that the qualifications for membership in the House could only be changed through the passage and ratification of a constitutional amendment. On January 3, 1969, the House complied with the Supreme Court decision by seating Powell. However, the House stripped Powell of his seniority and fined him $25,000. The Supreme Court decision forced Congress to take a hard look at how it dealt with allegations of misconduct leveled against members of Congress. In direct response to the Powell controversy, the House, in 1967, established a new **Committee on Standards of Official Conduct**. The House also began the process of establishing a code of ethics for members. Powell's battle for his House seat took a heavy toll on Powell personally and on Powell's support within his congressional district. In 1970, Powell lost a primary contest for his House seat. On April 4, 1972 Powell died in Miami, Florida.

SUGGESTED READINGS: Charles V. Adams, *Adam Clayton Powell, Jr. The Political Biography of an American Dilemma*, New York: Atheneum, 1991; Congressional Quarterly, *Congressional Ethics*, 2nd. ed., Washington, DC: Congressional Quarterly, 1980,
153–155.

POWELL V MCCORMACK, **395 U.S. 486 (1969).** *See* Powell, Adam Clayton

PRESIDENTIAL ELECTION CAMPAIGN FUND ACT. *See* Public Financing of Presidential Elections

PRESIDENT'S COMMISSION ON FEDERAL ETHICS LAW REFORM. From January 1981 through January 1989, a number of major ethics controversies led to criminal investigations of high-level and former high-level officials who worked in the administration of President Ronald Reagan. Despite these **Reagan administration ethics controversies**, Vice President George Bush easily beat Democratic presidential nominee Michael Dukakis in the 1988 presidential election. Yet President-elect George Bush made it clear that he expected members of his administration to maintain the highest standards of personal and professional conduct.

On January 25, 1989, President Bush issued Executive Order 12668 which established the president's Commission on Federal Ethics Law Reform. Bush

President George Bush signing Executive Order 12668, Establishment of President's Commission on Federal Ethics Law Reform, January 26, 1989. George Bush Presidential Library

appointed former Federal Judge Malcolm R. Wilkey as chairman and former Carter administration Attorney General Griffen B. Bell as vice chairman. Other members of the Commission included Jan Baran, Lloyd N. Cutler, Fred Fisher Fielding, Harrison H. Schmitt, and R. James Woolsey. President Bush directed the Commission to take a "fresh look" at federal ethics standards and emphasized four key principles to guide the Commission. First "ethical standards for public servants must be exacting enough to ensure that the officials act with the utmost integrity and live up to the public's confidence in them." Second "standards must be fair, they must be objective and consistent with common sense." Third "the standards must be equitable all across the three branches of the federal government." Fourth "we cannot afford to have unreasonably restrictive requirements that discourage able citizens from entering public service."

On March 10, 1989, the Commission issued *To Serve with Honor: Report of the President's Commission on Federal Ethics Law Reform.* The Commission recommended prohibiting federal officials and employees in all three branches of the federal government from accepting all **honorariums** and that Congress enact a new restriction on former members of Congress and congressional employees from representing private parties in matters pending before it. At the same time, the Commission recommended that Congress enact legislation providing tax relief for federal officials required to sell financial assets in order to comply with conflict of interest restrictions. Equally important the Commission urged Congress to enact legislation granting all federal agencies and departments

gift acceptance authority. The provision would permit private sources to pay the travel and lodging expenses of federal employees and officials as long as such payments did not create conflict of interest problems.

President Bush subsequently submitted legislation to Congress designed to implement many of the Commission's recommendations. Lengthy negotiations with Congress led to the passage of the **Ethics Reform Act of 1989**. Specifically the act banned all federal employees and House members from accepting honorariums and permitted the director of the **United States Office of Government Ethics** to issue **certificates of divestiture** permitting federal employees and officials to defer paying capital gain taxes on financial assets sold in order to comply with ethics laws and regulations.

Related Entries: Bush Administration Ethics Reform Program; Certificate of Divestiture; Honorariums

SUGGESTED READINGS: President's Commission on Federal Ethics Law Reform, *To Serve with Honor: Report of the President's Commission on Federal Ethics Law Reform*, Washington, DC: The Commission, March 1989; Robert N. Roberts and Marion T. Doss, *From Watergate to Whitewater: The Public Integrity War*, Westport, CT: Praeger Press, 1997.

PROCUREMENT INTEGRITY ACT. During 1987 the Department of Justice opened a wide-ranging investigation into fraud by government defense contractors and consultants. The so-called **ill-wind investigation** led to the indictment and conviction of a number of defense consultants, defense department employees, former defense department officials, and defense contractors for illegally providing or obtaining nonpublic defense procurement information. In 1988, Congress enacted the original **Public Integrity Section** in response to the ill-wind investigation. In 1996 Congress rewrote the provisions of the Procurement Integrity Section.

First the 1996 act amendments prohibited federal government officials, former federal government officials, and government advisors from disclosing contractor bid or proposal information or source selection information to any unauthorized person. Second the act prohibited procurement officials from accepting anything over $20 from an employee, representative, or consultant of a company competing for a government contract. Third the act prohibited former government procurement officials from accepting compensation from defense contractors for a period of one year after leaving government if the former official had worked on or had significant involvement with a contract worth over $10,000,000 received by the defense contractor.

Related Entry: Ill-Wind Investigation

SUGGESTED READING: Kevin Power, "Mandating Integrity Is a Tricky Process," *Government Computer News*, October 30, 1989, 71–73.

PROGRESSIVE MOVEMENT. From 1890 through 1920, the progressive movement worked to address serious, economic, social, and political problems caused by the Industrial Revolution. Supporters of the movement focused much of their energy on gaining the enactment of reform designed to stop the concentration of economic power in the hands of a few large monopolies. The movement also sought to end the corrupt activities of party machines, to institute policies to preserve the nation's natural resources, to improve the living conditions of individuals forced to live in crowded slums, and to improve the working conditions of men, women, and children. Throughout the period a new generation of activist writers and journalists pushed the reform agenda of the progressive movement. **Muckraker** writers and journalists played a key role in building public support for the enactment of legislation designed to deal with the problems.

Legislative achievements of the progressive movement included the passage of the Sherman Antitrust Act of 1890 and the Pure Food and Drug Act of 1906. Progressive members of Congress also supported legislation establishing the Federal Reserve System (1913) and the Federal Trade Commission (1914). Through much of the progressive movement, Wisconsin Senator **Robert La Follette** led progressive members of the House and Senate. La Follette and other progressives strongly supported the passage and ratification of the Sixteenth Amendment which authorized the collection of a federal income tax.

Besides supporting increased government regulation of business, members of the progressive movement became strong supporters of **campaign finance reform**. Specifically they supported calls for legislation prohibiting corporate campaign contributions to federal candidates and the requirement that candidates disclose the sources of campaign funds. In 1907 Congress passed the **Tillman Act** which prohibited corporate contributions to candidates for federal office.

Related Entries: Campaign Finance Reform (Federal); Campaign Finance Reform (State); Muckraker

SUGGESTED READING: Richard Hofstadter, *The Progressive Movement: 1900–1915*, Englewood Cliffs, NJ: Prentice-Hall, 1963.

PUBLIC CITIZEN. In 1971 Ralph Nader founded Public Citizen to protect consumers from unsafe products and to lobby for safer energy sources and a cleaner environment. Public Citizen operates six divisions: Congress Watch lobbies Congress to protect consumer rights and to enact legislation to reduce the role of money in politics; the Health Research Group lobbies Congress for universal access to heath care and for safe foods, drugs, and medical devices; the Litigation Group brings lawsuits on behalf of citizens in an effort to protect the health, safety, and rights of consumers; the Critical Mass Energy Project lobbies to reduce the nation's reliance on nuclear and fossil fuels; the Global Trade Watch provides the American public with information on the impact of expanded international trade on jobs, the environment, and public health; and Buyers Up serves as a home heating-oil cooperative buying program.

In the aftermath of the presidential **election of 1996**, Public Citizen joined with other public interest groups to lobby Congress to enact new campaign finance reform legislation. In particular Public Citizen focused much of its criticism on the practice of the Democratic and Republican Parties of accepting millions of dollars in **soft money**. Despite intense lobbying by Public Citizen, **Common Cause**, and other good government groups, Congress failed to act on legislation restricting soft money contributions through the 2000 election year.

Related Entries: Campaign Finance Reform (Federal); Campaign Finance Reform (State)

SUGGESTED READINGS: Ruth Conniff, "Joan Claybrook," *The Progressive* 63 (March 1999): 33–37; Public Citizen: *http://www.citizen.org/*.

PUBLIC FINANCIAL DISCLOSURE. Today state and federal laws require many high-level officials to file complete annual financial disclosure statements. Public financial disclosure laws typically require high-level executive, judicial, and legislative branch officials to disclose their financial assets and the financial assets of immediate family members. In 1978 Congress passed the **Ethics in Government Act of 1978** which required high-level executive branch officials, members of Congress, and federal judges to file annual public financial disclosure statements. Many states have enacted similar laws.

Although good government reformers proposed public financial disclosure requirements during the early 1950s, it took the 1970s **Watergate scandal** to build sufficient public support for the passage of disclosure legislation. Supporters argue that they help to reassure the public that high-level public officials do not use their public positions to benefit themselves, family members, friends, or business associates; critics argue that they violate the privacy rights of public servants and may deter some individuals from accepting positions in government. Despite the criticism federal and state courts have upheld the right of public employers to require public employees and officials to file public financial disclosure statements.

To reduce the difficulty of complying, the Ethics in Government Act of 1978 permits federal officials required to file annual public disclosure statements to report assets and debts in broad categories.

Related Entry: Ethics in Government Act of 1978

SUGGESTED READINGS: Robert Roberts, *White House Ethics: The History of the Politics of Conflict of Interest Regulation*, Westport, CT: Greenwood Press, 1988; U.S. Office of Government Ethics, Financial Disclosure, URL: *http://www.usoge.gov/usoge003.html#disclosure*.

PUBLIC FINANCING OF PRESIDENTIAL ELECTIONS. On December 8, 1971, Congress passed legislation authorizing the establishment of a federal fund to finance presidential election campaigns. The Presidential Election Campaign Fund Act permitted taxpayers to authorize the Treasury to place $1 of their tax payment in the presidential campaign fund. Congress subsequently raised the check-off amount to $3. The check-off provision did not increase the tax liability of taxpayers. Congressional Democrats strongly supported the provision because of the serious difficulty the party had faced in raising campaign funds for the 1968 election. Although the Republican Party had experienced little difficulty raising presidential campaign contributions, President Richard Nixon signed the provision after Congress agreed to delay the use of the fund until the 1976 election.

From the passage of the Presidential Election Campaign Fund Act, the program has experienced considerable difficulty in persuading a significant number of taxpayers to authorize using their tax dollars for the presidential election funding program. Besides those taxpayers who did not support the public funding program, many taxpayers apparently believed that if they checked the deduction box they would pay more taxes. In fact the public financing provision did not take any money from taxpayers. The provision simply directed the Treasury Department to dedicate the amount to the presidential campaign fund. From the 1976 through the 1996 presidential elections, all Democrat and Republican presidential candidates agreed to accept federal campaign funds. In return federal law prohibited the campaigns from making direct campaign expenditures exceeding the amount from the presidential campaign fund.

The 1976 presidential campaign saw Democrat Jimmy Carter and Republican President **Gerald Ford** receive approximately $21,700,000 from the fund. The 1980 presidential campaign saw independent candidate John B. Anderson receive approximately $4,000,000 and Democrat President Jimmy Carter and Republican presidential candidate Ronald Reagan receive approximately $29,000,000 each from the fund. The 1984 presidential campaign saw Republican President Reagan and Democrat Walter Mondale receive approximately $40,000,000 each from the fund. The 1988 presidential campaign saw Republican Vice President George Bush and Democrat Michael Dukakis receive approximately $45,500,000 each from the fund. The 1992 presidential campaign saw Republican President George Bush and Democrat Bill Clinton receive approximately $55,000,000 each from the fund. The 1996 presidential election saw Democratic President Bill Clinton and Republican Bob Dole receive some $70,000,000 each in federal matching funds.

In 1979 the **Federal Election Commission (FEC)** issued new regulations which permitted political parties to raise unlimited amounts of so-called **soft money** for party-building activities such as get out to vote and voter registration campaigns. At the same time, FEC regulations prohibited the use of soft money to purchase campaign ads directly supporting the election of a presidential candidate. The 1996 presidential campaign revealed a major loophole in the soft money exception. Both major political parties argued that federal law and the First Amendment permitted them to spend soft money on **issue ads**. Through 1995 and the first half of 1996, the Democratic and Republican Parties raised tens of millions of dollars in soft money. President Clinton actively participated in a program to raise more than $40 million in soft money to finance a media blitz. Through the first half of 1996, the Democratic National Committee spent millions of dollars in soft money to pay for issue ads touting the successes of the Clinton administration. The Republican Party spent a smaller amount on similar types of issue ads.

During October 1996 **Common Cause**, the Washington-based public interest lobby, called on the FEC and the Department of Justice to launch a full-scale investigation of the misuse of soft money by both the Democratic and Republican National Committees. After conducting independent investigations, both the FEC and the Department of Justice declined to take action against either the Republican or Democratic Parties for illegally using soft money to support the election of Republican or Democratic candidates. In the aftermath of the 1996 election, legislative efforts to close the soft money loophole failed to overcome strong congressional opposition.

The 2000 election cycle saw both the Republican and Democratic Parties raise record amounts of soft money which both parties used to pay for issue ads during the 2000 presidential election campaign.

Related Entries: Federal Election Campaign Act of 1971; Federal Election Commission (FEC); Issue Ads; Soft Money

SUGGESTED READINGS: Anthony Corrado, *Paying for Presidents: Public Financing in National Elections*, Washington, DC: Brookings Institution, 1993; Federal Election Commission, *The Presidential Public Funding Program*, April 1993, URL: *http:// www.fec.gov/info/pfund.htm*; Fred Wertheimer, "Clinton's Subterfuge Is No Technicality," *Washington Post*, November 9, 1997, C1.

PUBLIC INTEGRITY BUREAUCRACY. A number of federal government agencies exercise responsibility for enforcing federal public integrity and campaign finance laws. These include the **Public Integrity Section of the Department of Justice**, U.S. attorneys' offices, the Federal Bureau of Investigation, Inspector General offices located in federal agencies and departments, the **United States Office of Government Ethics**, designated agency ethics officials (DAEOs), and the **Federal Election Commission**. In 1999 Congress allowed the **independent counsel** provisions of the **Ethics in Government Act of 1978** to expire.

Related Entries: Federal Election Commission (FEC); Federal Prosecutor; Public Integrity Section of the Department of Justice; U.S. Office of Government Ethics (USOGE)

SUGGESTED READING: Robert Roberts and Marion T. Doss, *From Watergate to Whitewater: The Public Integrity War*, Westport, CT: Praeger, 1997.

PUBLIC INTEGRITY SECTION OF THE DEPARTMENT OF JUSTICE. In 1976 in the aftermath of the **Watergate scandal**, the Department of Justice established the Public Integrity Section within the Justice Department's Criminal Division to oversee public corruption investigations of federal employees and officials, including the president of the United States. The Justice Department staffs the

Public Integrity Section with career **federal prosecutors**. From 1975 through the end of 1999, the Section became involved in a number of high-profile investigations of executive branch officials and members of Congress. For instance in 1980, the Public Integrity Section oversaw the **Abscam** sting. Historically the Section has worked closely with federal prosecutors employed by U.S. attorneys' offices around the country. Through the 1990s the Section assumed responsibility for establishing uniform prosecution guidelines for federal prosecutors pursuing public corruption investigations.

The special prosecutor (**independent counsel**) provisions of the **Ethics in Government Act of 1978** required that the attorney general conduct a preliminary inquiry regarding possible violations of criminal law by high-level executive branch officials. From 1979 through the summer of 1991 and from the summer of 1994 through June 1999, the Public Integrity Section conducted a number of preliminary special prosecutor and independent counsel inquiries which resulted in the attorney general requesting the appointment of a number of special prosecutors and independent counsels. By letting the independent counsel law expire at the end of June 1999, Congress recognized that the action returned to the Department of Justice and the attorney general responsibility for appointing future special counsels to investigate possible violations of criminal law by high-level federal officials. The action effectively turned back the clock to the situation that prevailed at the time of the Watergate scandal.

Related Entry: Independent Counsel Act

SUGGESTED READINGS: Robert Roberts and Marion T. Doss, *From Watergate to Whitewater: The Public Integrity War*, Westport, CT: Praeger, 1997; Roberto Suro, "Looking Inward at Justice; Reno to Back Department Role in Lieu of Independent Counsels," *Washington Post*, March 17, 1999, A25.

PUBLIC INTEGRITY WAR. Public integrity war is a term used by Professors Robert N. Roberts and Marion T. Doss in their 1997 book *From Watergate to Whitewater: The Public Integrity War*. Roberts and Doss argued that from the early 1950s through the **Whitewater** scandal of the 1990s, Republicans and Democrats used allegations of unethical or illegal conduct by members of opposing administrations to attempt to shift public opinion against their political opponents. Roberts and Doss also argued that the efforts to use political scandals for partisan political purposes changed few votes. Instead, they argue that the use of political scandals for partisan political purposes has made it increasingly difficult for voters to distinguish between actual wrongdoing by public officials and conduct blown out of proportion by partisan attacks.

Related Entry: Politics of Personal Destruction

SUGGESTED READING: Robert Roberts and Marion T. Doss, *From Watergate to Whitewater: The Public Integrity War*, Westport, CT: Praeger, 1997.

PUBLIC PRINTING SCANDALS. *See* Buchanan Administration Political Corruption Scandals

Q

QUALIFIED OFFICIAL IMMUNITY DOCTRINE. Through much of the twentieth century, courts provided the vast majority of local, state, and federal government employees with absolute immunity from civil suits alleging violations of statutory or constitutional rights. Federal and state courts justified the **absolute official immunity doctrine** on the grounds that permitting individuals to sue government employees and officials for money damages might make public employees and officials less willing to make the necessary discretionary decisions. Through the 1960s criticism of the doctrine intensified. Critics argued that the doctrine prevented citizens from collecting damages for violations of their rights by public employees and officials.

To the surprise of many constitutional scholars, the late 1960s and 1970s saw the Supreme Court issue a series of decisions that sharply limited the right of public officials to invoke the doctrine to prevent suits alleging violations of established civil rights. In these decisions the high court ruled that only a small number of public officials are entitled to absolute immunity from civil suits alleging violations of civil and constitutional rights. In the landmark case of *Nixon v Fitzgerald* (1982), the Supreme Court ruled that the Constitution prohibited a Defense Department employee from bringing a suit for money damages against former President Richard Nixon for ordering his firing for disclosing to Congress large cost overruns on a contract for a major military aircraft. On the other hand, in the companion case of *Harlow v Fitzgerald* (1982), the Supreme Court held that the Constitution only provided an aide to President Nixon qualified immunity from a suit for money damages for his involvement in the firing of the Defense Department employee.

During 1997 the Supreme Court again revisited the issue of presidential immunity. In the case of *Clinton v Jones*, the Supreme Court ruled that the Constitution did not prohibit a federal district court from considering the sexual harassment lawsuit of former Arkansas state employee **Paula Jones** against

President Bill Clinton. The suit alleged that during 1991, Clinton made improper sexual advances to Jones. The Supreme Court in *Clinton v Jones* held that the Constitution did not prohibit the Jones sexual harassment lawsuit from proceeding. In the aftermath of the Jones decision, a U.S. District Court judge required President Clinton to submit to questioning by attorneys representing Jones. During the questioning the attorneys representing Jones confronted Clinton with allegations of his relationship with former White House intern **Monica Lewinsky**.

Between January 16, 1997, and September 1998, **independent counsel Kenneth Starr** conducted a wide-ranging investigation into whether Clinton violated any federal laws in an effort to conceal his close personal relationship with Lewinsky.

Related Entries: Absolute Official Immunity Doctrine; *Clinton v Jones*; *Nixon v Fitzgerald*

SUGGESTED READING: Robert Roberts, "The Supreme Court and the Law of Public Service Ethics," *Public Integrity*, 1 (Winter 1999): 20–40.

R

RANDOLPH, EDMUND (August 10, 1753–September 12, 1813).

Born near Williamsburg, Virginia, in 1753, Edmund Randolph went on to serve as aide-de-camp to General George Washington and as a delegate to the Continental Congress from 1779 to 1782. While serving as governor of Virginia from 1786–1788, Randolph served as a delegate to the Federal Constitutional Convention. After the election of George Washington as the first president of the United States, Randolph served as Washington's attorney general from 1789 to 1793 and then secretary of state from 1794 to 1795.

Randolph became the subject of the first scandal involving a high-level official in a presidential administration. Despite the 1783 Treaty of Paris which brought to an end the Revolutionary War, Britain failed to live up to a number of provisions of the treaty. Specifically Britain refused to evaluate its forts along the Northwest territory, which effectively meant that Britain continued to control the lucrative fur trade. In addition British warships refused to respect the neutrality of American ships. After lengthy discussions the United States and Britain signed Jay's Treaty which sought to end the disputes.

During negotiations with Britain, Randolph opposed the treaty although all other members of Washington's cabinet supported the agreement. Randolph's opposition raised suspicion on the part of treaty supporters. Rumors began to circulate that representatives of the French government made payments to Randolph in an effort to persuade Washington and other members of Washington's administration to oppose the treaty. The French government viewed the treaty as a betrayal as the result of the assistance France had provided the colonists during the Revolutionary War. Consequently the idea that France might pay a member of Washington's cabinet to attempt to block the treaty seemed quite possible.

Despite any evidence supporting the truthfulness of the allegation, Randolph resigned as secretary of state after Washington confronted him with the alle-

Edmund Randolph. Reproduced from the Collections
of the LIBRARY OF CONGRESS

gation. After leaving Washington's cabinet, Randolph returned to private law
practice and devoted his energies to discrediting the allegations. The incident
did little to Randolph's popularity in his home state of Virginia.

SUGGESTED READING: C. Vann Woodward, ed., *Responses of the Presidents to
Charges of Misconduct*, New York: Delacorte, 1974.

RAY, ELIZABETH. *See* Hays, Wayne

RAY, ROBERT. *See* Independent Counsel Investigations; Starr, Kenneth

REAGAN, RONALD (February 6, 1911–   ). *See* Reagan Administration Ethics
Controversies

REAGAN ADMINISTRATION ETHICS CONTROVERSIES. From the beginning of the Reagan administration during January 1981 to end of President
Ronald Reagan's second term in January 1989, a number of members of the
Reagan administration found themselves subject to allegations of unethical or
illegal conduct. In addition to controversies surrounding the behavior of individual Reagan administration officials, the Reagan administration found itself

forced to deal with a number of ethics scandals which raised serious questions regarding the management of major federal policies or programs. Between 1981 and the end of the Reagan administration in 1989, over one hundred Reagan administration officials found themselves the subject of public ethics controversies. However, only a relatively few led to criminal prosecutions.

Beginning in 1982 the Environmental Protection Agency (EPA) faced intense criticism about its administration of the federal environmental law, including the Superfund program. Critics accused the EPA of not enforcing key environmental laws against corporate polluters. The ensuing battle over congressional access to EPA documents led to the dismissal of a number of EPA officials and the criminal prosecution and conviction of EPA official **Rita Lavelle**. The controversy also led to the 1986 appointment of Alexia Morrison as **independent counsel** to investigate whether Justice Department official Theodore Olson had not testified truthfully regarding the investigation of the EPA. In the 1989 Supreme Court decision of *Morrison v Olson*, the high court upheld the constitutionality of the independent counsel law.

Between 1984 and 1989, White House Counselor and Attorney General **Edwin Meese III** found himself the subject of two independent counsel investigations. Both ended with findings of insufficient evidence to support criminal prosecutions. In 1986 former Reagan White House Deputy Chief of Staff **Mike Deaver** found himself subject to an independent counsel investigation for allegedly violating postemployment lobbying restrictions. In December 1987 a U.S. District Court jury convicted Deaver of three counts of perjury, and he became the first individual convicted of a crime under the independent counsel law. Also in 1987 a federal **grand jury** indicted former Reagan White House aide and political consultant **Lyn Nofziger** of illegal lobbying. Convicted of illegal lobbying in 1988, during 1989 a federal appeals court overturned Nofziger's conviction.

Without question, the **Iran-contra** investigation created the most serious problems for the Reagan administration. From the beginning of the Reagan administration in 1981, President Reagan committed his administration to combating the spread of communism around the world. Equally important Reagan made clear that his administration would pursue terrorists anywhere in the world. Early in his first term, President Reagan directed the Central Intelligence Agency to assist anticommunist rebels in Nicaragua in their efforts to overthrow the communist government of the country. During the same period of time, pro-Iranian terrorists took captive a number of Americans in Lebanon.

After Congress passed legislation prohibiting the U.S. government from directly funding the contra rebels, President Reagan directed the National Security Council to find ways to keep the contras operating. President Reagan's National Security Advisor **Robert McFarlane** placed Marine Colonel **Oliver North** in charge of the secret operation. During December 1985 President Reagan approved a secret plan to sell arms to Iran in an effort to gain the release of hostages being held by pro-Iranian terrorists in Lebanon. The arms for hostages plan ran directly counter to Reagan's earlier promise not to deal with terrorists.

Besides coordinating the arms for hostages deal, North took profits from the transaction and used them to assist the contras.

When reports of the arms for hostages deal broke during November 1986, efforts by the Reagan White House to contain the damage failed. During December 1986 a special federal judicial panel appointed **Lawrence Walsh** to serve as the Iran-contra independent counsel. From December 1986 to the end of his investigation in 1994, Walsh vigorously pursued those involved in the arms for hostages deal and the diversion of profits to the contras.

Beginning in late 1987, the **ill-wind investigation** uncovered the practice of major defense contractors and defense consultants using their contacts with Defense Department procurement officials to obtain confidential information on defense contracts. And the 1988 **Wedtech** investigation raised serious questions regarding White House involvement in helping a Bronx company obtain tens of millions of dollars in no-bid defense contracts.

Related Entries: Deaver, Michael; Ill-Wind Investigation; Iran-Contra Scandal; Meese, Edwin, III; *Morrison v Olson*; Nofziger, Lyn; North, Oliver; Walsh, Lawrence E.; Wedtech Scandal

SUGGESTED READINGS: Peter B. Levy, *Encyclopedia of the Reagan-Bush Years*, Westport, CT: Greenwood Press, 1996; Robert Roberts and Marion T. Doss, *From Watergate to Whitewater: The Public Integrity War*, Westport, CT: Praeger, 1997.

RECONSTRUCTION FINANCE CORPORATION. *See* Truman Administration Ethics Controversies

RECUSAL AGREEMENT. When Congress passed the **Bribery and Conflict of Interest Act of 1962**, it enacted a new executive branch conflicting financial interest statute. Section 208 of title 18 of the United States Code prohibits any employee or official working for an executive branch agency or department from participating in any matter in which the employee or official has a financial interest. Interestingly the new financial conflict of interest prohibition did not require that an executive branch employee or official sell financial assets that created a financial conflict of interest. Between 1962 and the passage of the **Ethics in Government Act of 1978**, designated agency ethics officials (DAEOs) came to rely on the recusal agreement as the most common way to resolve financial conflict of interest problems. Under the provisions of a recusal agreement, the executive branch employee or official agreed not to participate personally and substantially in a matter in which they held a financial interest.

By 1989 concern over the effectiveness of the recusal agreements led Congress to include in the **Ethics Reform Act of 1989** a provision authorizing the director of the **U.S. Office of Government Ethics** to issue **certificates of divestiture**. Between the passage of the Ethics Reform Act of 1989 through the end of the 1990s, the director of OGE issued hundreds of certificates of divestiture permitting executive branch employees required to sell financial assets in order to comply with ethics rules to roll over capital gains into widely held financial instruments. The enactment of this provision significantly reduced the need for recusal agreements during the 1990s.

Related Entries: Bribery and Conflict of Interest Act of 1962; Certificate of Divestiture

SUGGESTED READING: Robert Roberts and Marion T. Doss, *From Watergate to Whitewater: The Public Integrity War.* Westport, CT: Praeger Press, 1997.

REHNQUIST, WILLIAM HUBBS (October 1, 1924–   ). Chief justice of the U.S. Supreme Court.

From 1969 to 1971, William Rehnquist served as President Nixon's assistant attorney general. Prior to joining the Department of Justice, Rehnquist had served as a law clerk to Supreme Court Justice Robert H. Jackson, and he practiced law in Phoenix, Arizona. Impressed by Rehnquist's conservative credentials, President Nixon nominated him as an associate justice of the Supreme Court. Despite considerable opposition to the nomination, the Senate confirmed Rehnquist. When Chief Justice Warren Burger announced his resignation, President Ronald Reagan nominated Rehnquist as chief justice. Again Rehnquist faced considerable opposition. On September 26, 1986, Rehnquist took the oath as chief justice from Chief Justice Burger.

Throughout his years on the Supreme Court, Justice Rehnquist has taken conservative positions on a wide range of constitutional and statutory issues that have come before the high court. Early in 1999 Rehnquist faced the responsibility of being the second chief justice in American history to preside over a Senate impeachment trial. On January 7, 1998, the Clinton impeachment trial opened. Throughout the monthlong impeachment trial, Chief Justice Rehnquist kept the proceedings moving along by requiring that the prosecution and defense comply with self-imposed time limitations. As a result the chief justice did not make any legal or constitutional rulings that had a significant impact upon the outcome of the proceedings. Unlike the March and April 1868 Senate impeachment trial of President Andrew Johnson, the impeachment trial of President Clinton produced few surprises. From the beginning of the trial, the House impeachment managers recognized that they had little hope of persuading the Senate to vote to remove Clinton from office. In the end, Chief Justice Rehnquist received high marks for his conduct of the impeachment proceedings.

Related Entry: Clinton Administration Ethics Controversies

SUGGESTED READINGS: Joan Biskupic, "Rehnquist Departs Trying Experience," *Washington Post*, February 13, 1999, A33; Richard Posner, *The Investigation, Impeachment and Trial of President Clinton*, Cambridge, MA: Harvard University Press, 1999.

RENO, JANET (July 21, 1938–   ). Attorney General of the United States, 1993–2001.

In late February 1992, President Bill Clinton nominated Miami, Florida, prosecutor Janet Reno as attorney general. Prior to the Reno nomination, controversies over the failure of Clinton attorney general nominees **Zoe Baird** and **Kimba Wood** to pay Social Security withholding taxes for domestic help forced the Clinton White House to withdraw their nomination. The Senate quickly confirmed Reno.

Within a short time of being confirmed, as Attorney General Reno found herself forced to explain what went wrong at Waco, Texas. On April 19, 1993, an FBI tear gas assault on the Branch-Davidians compound ended with the complex of the religious sect catching fire, resulting in the deaths of a large number of sect members including a number of children. Although Attorney General Reno took responsibility for a number of mistakes made by federal law enforcement agencies, President Clinton and the majority of members of Congress continued to back her.

In early 1994 the growing controversy over President Clinton's and **Hillary Rodham Clinton's** 1980s **Whitewater** land development led Clinton to ask Reno to name an independent investigator to probe the Clintons' involvement in the failed Whitewater Development Corporation. In January 1994 Reno named New York lawyer **Robert B. Fiske Jr**. as special counsel to investigate. In addition to investigating Whitewater, Reno gave Fiske the authority to investigate the July 1993 death of Deputy White House Counsel **Vincent Foster**.

During the early summer of 1994, President Clinton signed into law a reauthorization of the independent counsel law. Following a request by Attorney General Reno, a three-judge federal appeals panel appointed **Kenneth Starr** to serve as the Whitewater **independent counsel**. The decision not to appoint Robert Fiske Jr. to the position created considerable controversy.

The Whitewater controversy turned out to be only the first of a number of ethics controversies that required Attorney General Reno to consider the need for the appointment of independent counsels. Early in July 1994, Reno requested the appointment of an independent counsel to examine the financial affairs of Secretary of Commerce **Ronald Brown** for possible criminal wrongdoing. A special federal appeals panel subsequently appointed Miami attorney Daniel Pearson as independent counsel for the Ronald Brown investigation. On September 9, 1994, after a request by Attorney General Reno, a special three-judge appeals panel appointed Los Angeles, California, attorney Donald C. Smaltz to investigate whether Secretary of Agriculture **Mike Espy** violated any federal laws for allegedly accepting gifts from companies and individuals subject to regulation by the Department of Agriculture. Late in 1994 Secretary of Housing and Urban Development **Henry G. Cisneros** came under investigation for allegedly lying to the FBI regarding payments he made to a former mistress while Cisneros served as mayor of San Antonio, Texas. On May 24, 1995, at the request of Attorney General Reno, a special three-judge federal panel appointed Washington lawyer David M. Barrett to serve as the Cisneros independent counsel.

During mid-October 1996, **Common Cause**, the public interest lobby, accused both the Republican and Democratic parties of violating federal campaign finance laws by allegedly using tens of millions of dollars in **soft money** contributions to pay for **issue ads** to support the election of President Bill Clinton and Republican presidential candidate Bob Dole.

In the aftermath of Clinton's successful 1996 presidential election campaign, there were charges and countercharges regarding the campaign fund raising practices of the Clinton campaign. In late 1996, Attorney General Janet Reno established a Justice Department task force to investigate alleged campaign fund-raising abuses and to determine whether possible illegal conduct by high-level executive branch officials required the appointment of an independent counsel. During the first half of 1997, the investigation expanded to include allegations that the Clinton campaign accepted illegal foreign campaign contributions and that President Bill Clinton and Vice President Albert Gore might have violated federal law by making fund-raising calls from inside the White House. After finding that President Clinton had not violated fund-raising laws, in late November 1978 Reno found insufficient credible evidence of criminal conduct to request the appointment of an independent counsel to investigate possible illegal fund raising by Gore. And in late August 2000, Reno found insufficient evidence to appoint a Justice Department special counsel to investigate whether Gore might have made false statements regarding his participation in the controversial 1996 Buddhist temple fund-raising event. Attorney General Reno left responsibility for prosecuting any violations of federal campaign finance law during the 1996 presidential campaign in the hands of the Justice Department's campaign finance task force.

Related Entry: Clinton Administration Ethics Controversies

SUGGESTED READINGS: David Johnston, "Reno Ends Inquiry into Fund-Raising by Vice President," *New York Times*, November 25, 1998, A1; David Johnston, "Reno Rejects Outside Inquiry on Clinton for Campaign Ads," *New York Times*, December 8, 1998, A1; Larry Rohter, "Woman in the News: Clinton Picks Miami Woman, Veteran State Prosecutor to Be His Attorney General," *New York Times*, February 12, 1993, A1.

RESOLUTION TRUST CORPORATION. *See* Whitewater Investigation

"REVOLVING DOOR" RESTRICTIONS. From the 1870s through the end of the twentieth century, public ethics experts have worried about former government employees going to work as lobbyists for private parties. Critics of the so-called "revolving door" argue that former government employees leave government with information that may give their new employers an unfair advantage when dealing with government agencies. In addition critics argue that government employees may give former government employees preferential treatment because of long-standing friendships or an effort by government employees to improve their opportunity for lucrative employment after leaving government service.

Congress passed the first restriction on former federal government employees representing private parties with respect to matters pending before a federal government agency or department during the early 1870s. The new statute prohibited former members of Congress and former executive branch officials from helping private individuals prosecute claims against the United States. Although the Congress periodically updated the revolving door restrictions from 1872 through the 1950s, federal law enforcement agencies rarely attempted to enforce the restrictions. Through the 1950s concern increased over lobbying by former government officials. On the other hand, critics of revolving door restrictions argued that unreasonable restrictions might make it much more difficult for the government to recruit essential professional and technical employees and officials.

Concern over the effectiveness of public service ethics led the Kennedy administration to lobby for major changes in federal ethics regulation between 1961 and 1963. As part of the reform program, Congress passed the **Bribery and Conflict of Interest Act of 1962**. Enactment of a new revolving door statute constituted a major feature of the new ethics law. Section 207 of title 18 of the United States Code established two new restrictions. One prohibition placed a lifetime ban on former executive branch employees and officials representing anyone before a federal agency or department with respect to any particular matter in which the former employee or official had participated personally and substantially while working in the government. Supporters of the so-called new "switching side" prohibition argued that the prohibition would help to prevent former government employees from using confidential information and their government contacts to help their new employers. In addition to the lifetime switching sides ban, the new ethics law included a second two-year ban on former executive branch officials representing anyone before a government agency with respect to matters under the employee's official responsibility during their period of government service.

Through the remainder of the 1960s, good government groups and the media devoted little attention to the lobbying activities of former government employees. The situation changed significantly during the 1970s. A number of new public interest organizations started a campaign to place much tighter restrictions on the lobbying activities of former government employees and officials. Groups such as **Common Cause** and Ralph Nader's **Public Citizen** argued that many federal regulatory agencies hired too many individuals who had previously worked for regulated industries. Equally important these groups argued that a significant number of employees and officials had left regulatory agencies to work for companies they previously had responsibility for regulating. According to these groups, the revolving door of regulators back and forth between regulatory agencies and regulated industries created an environment where regulatory agencies often served the interests of regulated industries rather than the public interest. Although many scholars found little evidence to support this view of regulatory behavior, the theory of "regulatory capture" received considerable attention in the media.

The **Watergate scandal** and the subsequent effort to tighten federal ethics rules provided critics of the revolving door with the opportunity to persuade Congress to tighten the 1962 restrictions. During the 1976 presidential campaign, Democratic presidential candidate Jimmy Carter expressed strong support for tightening restrictions on lobbying by former executive branch employees and officials. With the strong support of President Carter, Congress included new revolving door restrictions as part of the **Ethics in Government Act of 1978**. Of these restrictions the so-called one-year cooling off period constituted the most significant change in the law. For the first time, federal law prohibited former executive branch employees and officials from contacting anyone in their former government agencies with respect to specific matters they had not previously dealt with while working in government.

Between 1981 and 1989, former members of the administration of President Ronald Reagan found themselves subject to intense scrutiny after leaving the government to become well-paid lobbyists. Former Reagan Deputy Chief of Staff **Mike Deaver** and former Reagan political advisor **Lyn Nofziger** found themselves subject to **independent counsel investigations** and criminal prosecutions resulting from allegations that they violated the new one-year cooling off period. The Deaver and Nofziger investigations and prosecutions led to calls for even tighter revolving door restrictions. Although Congress passed tighter restrictions in 1988, President Reagan vetoed the legislation after Vice President George Bush won the 1988 presidential election. After long and often heated negotiations, President Bush signed the **Ethics Reform Act of 1989** which for the first time subjected former members of Congress to revolving door restrictions. At the same time, the Ethics Reform Act tightened the one-year no-contact ban enacted as part of the Ethics in Government Act of 1978.

Related Entries: Ethics in Government Act of 1978; Ethics Reform Act of 1989

SUGGESTED READINGS: Robert Roberts, *White House Ethics: The Politics of the History of Conflict of Interest Regulation*, Westport, CT: Greenwood Press, 1988; Robert Roberts and Marion T. Doss, *From Watergate to Whitewater: The Public Integrity War*, Westport, CT: Praeger, 1997; U.S. Office of Government Ethics: Postemployment restrictions. URL: *http://www.usoge.gov*.

RICE, DONNA. *See* Hart, Gary

RICHARDSON, ELLIOT (July 20, 1920–December 31, 1999). Attorney General of the United States, 1973.

Elliot Richardson was one of the key figures in the 1970s **Watergate scandal**. After serving as the attorney general and lieutenant governor of Massachusetts, Richardson served as President Richard Nixon's secretary of health, education, and welfare; secretary of defense; and undersecretary of state between 1969 and 1973. Early in 1972 Attorney General **John Mitchell** resigned as attorney general to become chairman of President Nixon's 1972 presidential reelection cam-

President Nixon meeting with Attorney General Elliot Richardson (at left) and FBI Director-Designate Clarence H. Kelly, July 7, 1973. Nixon Presidential Materials Staff

paign. Nixon then nominated and the Senate confirmed Richard Kleindienst as attorney general. On June 17, 1972, District of Columbia police arrested James McCord and four Cuban exiles inside the **Watergate** offices of the Democratic National Committee. A short time later, police arrested **G. Gordon Liddy** and **E. Howard Hunt** for overseeing the operation.

On July 16, 1973, the Watergate scandal took a dramatic turn. Former White House aide and Administrator of the Federal Aviation Administration **Alexander Butterfield** testified before the **Senate Watergate Committee** that President Nixon operated a secret taping system in the White House Oval Office. The revelation sent shock waves through official Washington. Earlier Dean had testified before the Watergate Committee alleging a conspiracy by President Nixon, members of the White House staff, and officials of CREEP to cover up White House and CREEP involvement with the Watergate burglars. After President Nixon refused to voluntarily turn over the tapes to either the Watergate Committee or Cox, the Senate Watergate Committee and Cox issued subpoenas for the tapes.

Through the summer and early fall of 1973, President Nixon refused to turn over the tapes. He argued that the doctrine of **executive privilege** protected the tapes from disclosure. Then on October 20, 1973, Nixon ordered Attorney General Richardson to fire Cox. To Nixon's surprise Richardson resigned rather than carry out the order. Associate Attorney General William Ruckelshaus also resigned for the same reason. After Richardson and Ruckelshaus refused to carry out Nixon's order, he appointed Solicitor General **Robert Bork** as acting attorney general. Bork then carried out Nixon's order to fire Cox.

The so-called **Saturday Night Massacre** only served to fuel speculation that President Nixon had something to hide. Nixon then named **Leon Jaworski** as the second Watergate special counsel, and Jaworski immediately resumed efforts to force President Nixon to hand over the White House tapes. On July 24, 1974, the Supreme Court in *United States v Nixon* ordered President Nixon to hand over the White House tapes to Jaworski.

After resigning as attorney general, Richardson became a fellow at the Woodrow Wilson Center for Scholars. In 1975 President **Gerald Ford** appointed Richardson as ambassador to Britain. In 1976 and 1977, Richardson served as Ford's secretary of commerce, and from 1977 through 1980, he served as President Jimmy Carter's representative to the Law of the Sea Conference in Washington. From 1980 until 1992, Richardson served as a partner in the Washington office of the New York law firm of Milbank, Tweed, Hadley & McCloy. On December 31, 1999, Richardson died at age seventy-nine during a visit to relatives in Massachusetts.

Related Entries: Bork, Robert; Cox, Archibald; Saturday Night Massacre; Watergate Scandal

SUGGESTED READINGS: Bart Barnes, "Elliot Richardson Dies at 79: 1973 Resignation as Attorney General Shocked the Nation," *Washington Post*, January 1, 2000, B7; Elliot Richardson, *Reflections of a Radical Moderate*, New York: Pantheon Books, 1996.

ROBB, CHARLES (June 26, 1939–   ). Governor of Virginia, 1982–1986; U.S. Senator, 1986–   .

After he served as governor of Virginia from 1982 to 1986, Virginia voters elected Charles Robb to the U.S. Senate in 1988. In April 1991 former Miss Virginia-USA, Tanquil "Tai" Collins of Roanoke, alleged that she had an extramarital affair with Robb while he served as governor of Virginia. Also in 1991 reports surfaced that members of Robb's governor's office had obtained illegal tapes of a 1988 cellular phone call between Governor Doug Wilder and a political supporter, not a member of Robb's staff. Later three Robb aides resigned as a result of the controversy, and one individual pleaded guilty to illegally taping the calls. On January 12, 1993, a federal **grand jury** declined to indict with respect to the illegal taping of Governor Doug Wilder.

In 1992 Robb ran for reelection against Republican senatorial nominee **Oliver North**. In an election contest that saw millions of dollars in campaign ads attacking both the characters of Charles Robb and Oliver North, incumbent Senator Robb won reelection by a narrow margin.

Related Entry: Ruff, Charles

SUGGESTED READING: Patricia Edmonds, "No Reason to Indict Robb, Grand Jury Says," *USA Today*, January 13, 1993, 3A.

RODINO, PETER (June 7, 1909–). Member of Congress, D-N.J., 1949–1989.

Peter Rodino graduated from the New Jersey Law School in 1937 and entered the practice of law. He enlisted in the U.S. Army during March 1941. Rodino received numerous awards for military service in North Africa and Italy. Voters in Newark, New Jersey, first elected Rodino to Congress in 1948 as a New Jersey Democrat. He became a strong supporter of the New Deal, Fair Deal, and Great Society programs of the Roosevelt, Truman, and Johnson administrations.

In 1974 Peter Rodino became a national figure as chairman of the House Judiciary Committee. During winter, spring, and early summer of 1974, the House Judiciary considered a number of articles of impeachment against President Richard Nixon resulting from the **Watergate** break-in and cover-up. In late July 1974, the House Judiciary Committee voted three articles of impeachment against President Nixon. On August 9, 1974, Nixon resigned before the full House could take a vote on the articles of impeachment.

Historians give House Judiciary Chairman Rodino much of the credit for building a consensus on the House Judiciary Committee for Nixon's impeachment. In 1974 House Democrats held a significant majority on the House Judiciary Committee. Equally important the committee included a number of moderate Republicans who kept an open mind to allegations leveled against a president of their own party. After forty years in the House, Rodino declined to run for reelection in 1988.

Related Entries: Impeachment Proceedings; Watergate Scandal

SUGGESTED READING: Clifford D. May, "After 40 Years Making the Law, Rodino Now Teaches It," *New York Times*, January 27, 1989, B1.

ROOSEVELT, THEODORE (October 27, 1858–January 6, 1919). President of the United States, 1901–1909. *See* Election of 1904; Muckraker; Tillman Act

ROSTENKOWSKI, DAN (January 2, 1928–). Democratic representative from Illinois, 1959–1995.

First elected to Congress in 1958, Representative Dan Rostenkowski rose to become the chairman of the powerful House Ways and Means Committee. During 1993 Rostenkowski became the subject of an investigation related to alleged corruption in the **House Post Office**. In May 1994 a federal **grand jury** indicted Rostenkowski for allegedly using the House Post Office to exchange stamps paid for with public funds for cash and for allegedly paying salaries to individuals who rarely showed up for work at his Illinois District office. In November 1994 Rostenkowski lost his reelection bid. On April 9, 1996, he pleaded guilty to two counts of mail fraud. However, Rostenkowski denied ever having used the House Post Office to exchange stamps for cash. As part of his plea agreement, Rostenkowski spent fifteen months in a federal correctional facility.

In his defense Rostenkowski maintained that **federal prosecutors** singled him out because of his position in Congress. He argued that many other members of Congress had engaged in similar conduct without facing criminal prosecution. On the other hand, federal prosecutors maintained that Rostenkowski violated the public trust by using public funds to pay individuals who did little or no work and for using public funds to buy gifts for private individuals.

President Clinton pardoned Rostenkowski in December 2000, after Rostenkowski had finished serving his sentence.

Related Entry: House Post Office Scandal

SUGGESTED READING: Toni Locy, "Rostenkowski Fraud Plea Brings 17-Month Sentence; Former Ways and Means Chief Fined $100,000," *Washington Post*, April 10, 1996, A01.

ROTA, ROBERT V. *See* House Post Office Scandal

RUFF, CHARLES (1940–2000). Watergate special prosecutor; Justice Department lawyer; White House Counsel, 1997–1999; Washington lawyer.

Regarded as one of the most respected lawyers in Washington, D.C., Ruff graduated from Columbia University Law School in 1963. He then received a Ford Foundation grant to teach law in Liberia where he contracted Guillain-Barre syndrome while teaching in Liberia. The disease left his legs paralyzed. After **Leon Jaworski** resigned in 1975 as **Watergate** prosecutor, Ruff became the third Watergate **special prosecutor**. Ruff successfully prosecuted former Attorney General **John Mitchell** for his involvement in the Watergate cover-up. As the U.S. attorney for the District of Columbia during the late 1970s and early 1980s, Ruff prosecuted members of Congress on public corruption charges and John Hinckley for attempting to assassinate President Ronald Reagan.

Between 1982 and 1995, Ruff worked as a private Washington, D.C., lawyer. In 1991 Senator Charles Robb (D-Va.) became the subject of a criminal investigation over whether Robb illegally obtained transcripts of a cell phone call of Virginia governor L. Douglas Wilder. Senator Robb hired Ruff to represent him in the matter. Early in 1993 a federal **grand jury** declined to indict Senator Robb for distributing transcripts of the Wilder phone call. Legal observers credited Ruff with helping Senator Robb to avoid the criminal indictment. In 1995 Ruff left his law firm to become corporation counsel for the District of Columbia.

In 1997 Ruff accepted the position of President Bill Clinton's White House counsel. Early in January 1998, Ruff found himself in the midst of the **Monica Lewinsky** investigation. From January through August 1998, Ruff coordinated the White House response to **independent counsel Kenneth Starr's** Monica Lewinsky investigation. During that period Ruff battled Starr over whether Starr had the authority to call certain members of the White House staff and members of the Secret Service to testify before the Lewinsky federal grand jury. During fall 1998 Ruff appeared before the House Judiciary Committee as it considered

Articles of Impeachment against President Clinton. Although Ruff conceded that President Clinton may have engaged in inappropriate conduct, he argued that Clinton had not committed any impeachable offenses. After the House Judiciary Committee and full House voted to impeach Clinton, Ruff helped to present his defense at the Senate impeachment trial. Clinton was acquitted on the charges of perjury and obstruction of justice.

During the summer of 1999, Charles Ruff resigned as White House counsel to return to private law practice. He died in an accident in late 2000.

Related Entries: Clinton Administration Ethics Controversies; Impeachment Proceedings; Lewinsky, Monica; Robb, Charles; Watergate Scandal

SUGGESTED READING: "For the Defense: Thirty Years after Prosecuting One President, Charles Ruff Tries to Save Another," *People Weekly*, February 1, 1999, 59–60.

S

SALARY SUPPLEMENTATION PROHIBITION. When Congress passed the **Bribery and Conflict of Interest Act of 1962**, it continued the ban on executive branch employees and officials accepting salary supplements from nonfederal sources. Congress initially enacted the salary supplementation ban in 1917 after concern developed over major foundations paying the salaries of federal employees employed by the Department of Interior's Bureau of Education. Supporters of the 1917 salary supplementation ban argued that federal employees who had their salaries paid for by private foundations might feel greater loyalty to the private foundations than to federal agencies and departments.

The new law placed the salary supplementation ban at section 209 of title 18 of the United States Code. At the urging of the Kennedy White House, Congress modified the salary supplementation ban by making clear the ban did not prohibit federal employees and officials from accepting payments from bona fide retirement or pension plans. Congress agreed to the modification in order to remove a possible barrier to the recruitment of professional and technical personnel by federal agencies and departments.

From 1962 through the 1980s, the Department of Justice broadly interpreted the scope of the salary supplementation prohibition. Besides prohibiting payments to executive branch employees and officials after they became a federal employee, the Justice Department ruled that the salary supplementation ban prohibited individuals planning to accept federal positions to accept severance payments from employers designed to ease their transition into federal service. The interpretation significantly complicated the recruitment of executives from private companies by prohibiting corporations from providing executives with substantial severance packages as an incentive for their executives to take positions in federal government agencies and departments. Despite the sweeping nature of this interpretation, no one challenged the interpretation through much of the 1980s.

Early in 1982 Boeing Corporation provided a number of employees who had accepted Defense Department positions with large severance payments in an effort to make it easier for the employees to accept the government positions. The Boeing employees received the severance payments before they began work with the federal government. In 1986 the Justice Department brought suit against the former Boeing employees and Boeing Corporation for violating the salary supplementation prohibition. The civil suit sought to require Boeing and the employees to turn over the severance payments they had received to the federal government. Criminal proceedings had not been pursued because the statute of limitations had expired. In the 1990 case of *Crandon v United States*, the Supreme Court ruled that the salary supplementation ban did not prohibit severance payments made before individuals entered a federal agency or department. In the aftermath of the *Crandon* decision, Congress did not move to amend the salary supplementation prohibition.

Related Entries: Bribery and Conflict of Interest Act of 1962; *Crandon v United States*

SUGGESTED READINGS: Linda Greenhouse, "Boeing Wins Plea on Severance Pay," *New York Times*, February 28, 1990, A21; Robert Roberts, *White House Ethics: The History of the Politics of Conflict of Interest Regulation*, Westport, CT: Greenwood Press, 1988.

"SATURDAY NIGHT MASSACRE." On May 19, 1973, **Archibald Cox** accepted the appointment offered by Attorney General **Elliot Richardson** to serve as the **Watergate** special counsel. From 1961 to 1965, Cox had served as solicitor general of the United States, the third highest position in the Justice Department. In July 1973 **Alexander Butterfield** testified before the **Senate Watergate Committee** that President Nixon had ordered the installation of a system to record his conversations in the White House Oval Office. Shortly after the revelation, Cox and the Senate Watergate Committee requested access to the tapes. President Nixon subsequently invoked the doctrine of **executive privilege** to deny access to the tapes, whereupon both Cox and the Committee issued subpoenas to acquire them.

On October 20, 1973, President Richard Nixon ordered Attorney General Richardson to fire Cox. Earlier Cox had rejected a compromise offer by the Nixon White House which would have provided Cox access to edited transcripts of some of the tapes. Instead of carrying out President Nixon's order, first Richardson and then Deputy Attorney General William Ruckelshaus resigned. Following the resignations, President Nixon appointed Solicitor General **Robert Bork** as acting attorney general. Bork then carried out Nixon's order to fire Cox. Nixon directed the Department of Justice to continue the investigation after Cox's dismissal.

Nixon badly underestimated congressional, media, and public reaction to Cox's dismissal. His action soon became known as the "Saturday Night Massacre." Within a short time, congressional and public reaction forced Nixon to name another special prosecutor. Houston attorney **Leon Jaworski** became the second Watergate special prosecutor. Jaworski soon made it clear that he intended to continue to pursue access to the White House tapes. In the July 1974 case of *United States v Nixon*, the Supreme Court ordered Nixon to deliver the White House tapes to Jaworski. The argument of executive privilege was rejected. On August 9, 1974, President Nixon became the first individual to resign from the presidency.

Largely due to Nixon's dismissal of Cox, Congress included a provision providing for the appointment of **special prosecutors** (**independent counsels**) by a special three-judge federal appeals panel in the **Ethics in Government Act of 1978**.

Related Entries: Bork, Robert; Ethics in Government Act of 1978; Independent Counsel Act; Jaworski, Leon; Richardson, Elliott; *United States v Nixon*; Watergate Scandal

SUGGESTED READINGS: Carroll Kilpatrick, "Nixon Forces Firing of Cox; Richardson, Ruckelshaus Quit: President Abolishes Prosecutor's Office; FBI Seals Records," *Washington Post*, October 21, 1973, A01; George Lardner Jr., "Cox Is Chosen as Special Prosecutor: Democrat Served under Kennedy as Solicitor General," *Washington Post*, May 19, 1973, A1.

SCHURZ, CARL (March 2, 1829–May 14, 1906). Political reformer; Secretary of the Interior, 1877–1881.

Carl Schurz migrated to the United States in 1852 after being forced to flee Germany because of his political activities. Schurz settled in Wisconsin where he became an influential member of the new Republican Party. After helping Abraham Lincoln win the 1960 presidential election, Lincoln appointed Schurz to serve as minister to Spain. Schurz returned to the United States in 1862 and received a commission as a brigadier general in the Union army. Following the Civil War, Schurz became a correspondent for the *New York Tribune*. After being elected as a senator from Missouri, he played a major role in establishing a liberal wing of the Republican Party. Schurz and other liberals fought against corruption and the expansion of the **spoils system** during President Ulysses S. Grant's first term as president. In 1872 liberal Republicans bolted from the Republican Party to support Democratic Party presidential nominee Horace Greeley for president. Despite the split in the Republican Party, in 1872 President Grant easily won reelection.

In 1876 a badly split Republican Party nominated Ohio Republican Governor **Rutherford B. Hayes** as their presidential candidate. Although Hayes lost the popular vote, the House elected him president after Democratic Party candidate Samuel Tilden failed to win the majority of electoral votes. In 1877 President Hayes nominated Schurz to serve as secretary of the interior. From 1877 through 1881, Schurz made major strides in eliminating corruption in the Interior Department and the Bureau of Indian Affairs.

From the end of the 1860s through the turn of the century, Schurz became a vocal supporter of civil service reform as a way to end the spoils system. During 1883 he played a major role in lobbying Congress to pass the **Pendleton Act** or the Civil Service Reform Act of 1883. From 1892 through 1901, Schurz served as the president of the National Civil Service Reform League. Historians regard him as one of the most influential reform figures from the Civil War to the beginning of the twentieth century.

Related Entries: Hayes, Rutherford B.; Pendleton Act of 1883

SUGGESTED READING: Hans Louis Trefousse, *Carl Schurz, a Biography*, New York: Fordham University Press, 1998.

SEGAL, ELI J. *See* Independent Counsel Investigations

SENATE COMMITTEE ON STANDARDS AND CONDUCT. In 1964 the Senate voted to establish the bipartisan Committee on Standards and Conduct after the majority of senators expressed displeasure over the handling of the **Bobby Baker** affair by the Senate Rules and Administration Committee. Prior to the eruption of the 1964 scandal, Baker had served as an aide to Senate Majority Leader Lyndon Johnson and as secretary to the Senate. He had become the subject of a Senate and subsequent criminal investigation over the alleged use of his Senate position to promote his private business interests.

From 1964 through 1976, the Senate Committee on Standards and Conduct conducted a number of high-profile investigations of alleged misconduct by members of the Senate, including Senator **Thomas J. Dodd**.

Related Entry: Senate Select Committee on Ethics

SUGGESTED READING: Congressional Quarterly, *Congressional Ethics: History, Facts, and Controversy*, Washington, DC: Congressional Quarterly, 1992.

SENATE IMPEACHMENT TRIALS. *See* Impeachment Proceedings

SENATE SELECT COMMITTEE ON ETHICS. During 1977 the Senate voted to change the name **Senate Committee on Standards and Conduct** to the Senate Select Committee on Ethics. From its establishment in 1977 through the early 1990s, the Senate Select Committee on Ethics conducted a number of high-profile ethics investigations. In 1979 the Committee voted to denounce Georgia Senator Herman E. Talmadge for financial misconduct. On August 24, 1981, the Senate Select Committee on Ethics recommended that the Senate expel Williams for his conduct. On March 11, 1982, Senator Harrison Williams resigned after it became clear that the Senate would indeed vote to expel him. A U.S. District Court jury had earlier convicted Senator Williams for accepting bribes in relation to the FBI's 1980 **Abscam** investigation. On July 25, 1990, the Senate voted to denounce Senator David Durenberger for financial impropriety on the basis of a recommendation of the Senate Select Committee on Ethics. During

1989 and 1990, the Committee conducted the highly publicized **Keating Five** investigation. Then, on September 6, 1995, the Senate Ethics Committee voted unanimously to recommend expulsion for Senator **Robert Packwood** for sexual and official misconduct. On September 7, 1995, Packwood announced he would resign in response to the Senate Ethics Committee recommendation for his expulsion.

Related Entries: Abscam Investigation; Keating Five Affair; Packwood, Robert

SUGGESTED READING: Congressional Quarterly, *Congressional Ethics: History, Facts, and Controversy*, Washington, DC: Congressional Quarterly, 1992.

SENATE WATERGATE COMMITTEE (SENATE SELECT COMMITTEE TO IN-VESTIGATE CAMPAIGN PRACTICES). During the spring and summer of 1973, the Senate Select Committee to Investigate Campaign Practices conducted televised hearings to investigate allegations that President Richard Nixon's Committee to Re-Elect the President (CREEP) had engaged in a number of unlawful campaign practices during the 1992 Nixon presidential campaign. The Senate Watergate Committee sought to determine whether the CREEP had violated the campaign fund-raising and campaign disclosure requirements of the **Federal Election Campaign Finance Act of 1971**. The Committee also sought to investigate allegations that the Nixon reelection campaign had engaged in a number of **dirty tricks** directed at disrupting the Democratic presidential primary and general election campaign. Instead of focusing on alleged campaign fund-raising abuses, the Senate Watergate Committee soon directed their attention to the possible role of CREEP and the Nixon White House with the June 17, 1972, break-in of the offices of the Democratic National Committee located in the **Watergate** complex. From June 17, 1972, through May 1973, *Washington Post* reporters **Bob Woodward** and **Carl Bernstein** had written a series of stories disclosing the relationship between the Watergate burglars, CREEP, and the White House.

Chaired by North Carolina Senator **Sam Ervin**, the Senate Watergate Committee began televised hearings in May 1973. Between May and early July, a series of witnesses testified about the activities of Nixon's 1972 reelection campaign, the Watergate break-in, and subsequent efforts by the White House to conceal its relationship with the Watergate burglars. In July 1973 former White House Counsel **John Dean** provided the Senate Watergate Committee with a detailed account of alleged White House efforts to cover up testimony implicating high-level White House officials in the cover-up of the Watergate break-in. Dean's testimony implicated President Nixon, former Attorney General **John Mitchell**, and a number of White House aides. Former White House aides **John Ehrlichman** and **H. R. Haldeman** denied any White House involvement in the Watergate break-in, as well as the existence of any cover-up.

A turning point in the Senate Watergate hearings took place when former

White House aide and current Administrator of the Federal Aviation Administration **Alexander Butterfield** revealed that President Nixon operated a White House taping system. The Senate Committee quickly realized that any existing tapes might permit the Committee to confirm or discredit the testimony of Dean and other Watergate witnesses. To prevent both special prosecutor **Archibald Cox** and the Senate Watergate Committee from gaining access to the Watergate tapes, President Nixon invoked the doctrine of **executive privilege**. In late July 1974, the Supreme Court in *United States v Nixon* ordered Nixon to turn over the White House tapes to **Special Prosecutor** Cox. Shortly after turning over the tapes, on August 9, 1974, Richard Nixon resigned the presidency.

Over the summer of 1973, the members of the Senate Watergate Committee became household names. Besides Sam Ervin (D-N.C.), other Watergate Committee members included Howard H. Baker Jr. (R-Tenn.), Herman E. Talmadge (D-Ga.), Daniel K. Inouye (D-Hawaii), Joseph M. Montaya (D-N.M.), Edward J. Gurney (R-Fla.), and Lowell P. Weicker (R-Conn.). Historians credit the Senate Watergate Committee with playing a major role in uncovering efforts by the Nixon White House to cover up administration involvement in the Watergate break-in and other illegal conduct prior to and during the 1972 presidential campaign.

Related Entries: Ervin, Sam; Watergate Scandal

SUGGESTED READING: Samuel Dash, *Inside the Ervin Committee—The Untold Story of Watergate*, New York: Random House, 1976.

SEYMOUR, WHITNEY NORTH, JR. *See* Deaver, Michael; Independent Counsel Investigations

SILVERMAN, LEON. *See* Donovan, Raymond; Independent Counsel Investigations

SINCLAIR, HARRY F. *See* Teapot Dome Scandal

SOFT MONEY. The **Federal Election Commission (FEC)** defines soft money as "funds raised and/or spent outside the limitations and prohibitions of the FECA. Sometimes called non federal funds, soft money often includes corporate and/or labor treasury funds, and individual contributions in excess of the federal limits, which cannot legally be used in connection with federal elections, but can be used for other purposes." Not until the passage of the **Federal Election Campaign Act of 1971 (FECA)** did Congress place meaningful restrictions on campaign contributions to candidates for federal office. However, the 1971 FECA followed by the 1974 and 1976 amendments placed sharp limits on campaign contributions to political parties for so-called party-building activities. Through the 1970s the Democratic and Republican Parties complained that campaign contribution restrictions prevented them from raising enough money to conduct traditional party-building activities such as get out the vote and voter registration programs.

In response to the complaints, the FEC, in 1979, issued new rules permitting political parties to raise unlimited amounts of money for traditional party-building activities. Beginning in the early 1980s, both the Republicans and Democrats moved to take full advantage of the soft money exception. For example the Democratic National Party raised $31,356,076 in soft money during 1992 and $101,905,186 during 1996, and the Republican National Committee raised $35,936,945 in soft money during 1992 and $113,127,016 during 1996. Republican and Democratic House and Senatorial Campaign Committees raised additional soft money during 1996.

The mid-1990s saw a significant expansion in the use of soft money by both the Republican and Democratic Parties. Instead of limiting the use of soft money to party-building activities, both major political parties argued that federal law permitted them to spend soft money to pay for so-called **issue ads**. In contrast to traditional campaign ads supporting the election of a particular individual, issue ads do not advocate the election of specific candidates but take a position on various public policy issues. For example as part of a plan to flood the air waves with issue ads touting the policy initiatives of the Clinton presidency, in 1995 and early 1996 the Democratic National Committee raised over $40 million in soft money to pay for a spring 1996 media blitz. As part of the fund-raising program, President Clinton hosted numerous events at the White House for potential soft money contributors. The DNC gave campaign contributors and potential campaign contributors the opportunity to attend White House coffees, and some contributors had the opportunity to spend the night in the White House Lincoln bedroom.

Although FEC rules permitted political parties to use soft money to pay for issue ads, they required that political parties use **hard money**—campaign contributions subject to the FECA's contribution limits—to pay part of the cost of running the issue ads. In other words, the FEC required political parties to use a mix of hard and soft money to pay the cost of running issue ads during a federal campaign.

Late in October 1996, **Common Cause**, the public interest lobby, filed a complaint with the FEC alleging that both the Republican and Democratic Parties had violated the FECA by using soft money for partisan political activities. In December 1998 the FEC held that neither the Republican nor Democratic Parties violated FECA regulations by spending millions of dollars of soft money on issue ads during the 1996 presidential election campaign. The FEC ruling did not prevent various reform groups from calling for the passage of legislation to close the soft money loophole. Senators John McCain and Russell Feingold authored campaign finance legislation designed to close the loophole. Although the McCain/Feingold bill initially received considerable support, supporters of soft money restrictions proved able to overcome strong opposition.

Related Entries: Campaign Finance Reform (Federal); Election of 1996; Federal Election Campaign Act of 1971; Federal Election Commission (FEC); Lincoln Bedroom Fund-raising Controversy

SUGGESTED READINGS: Charles R. Babcock and Ruth Marcus, "A Hard-Charging Flood of 'Soft Money'; With Bigger Donations, Parties Taking Larger and Different Roles," *Washington Post*, October 24, 1996, A01; Susan B. Glasser, "Funding Finds a New Use," *Washington Post*, October 17, 1999, A16; Ruth Marcus, "Hidden Assets; Flood of Secret Money Erodes Election Limits," *Washington Post*, May 15, 2000, A01.

SPECIAL PROSECUTOR. Today, the term special prosecutor is most closely associated with the **Watergate scandal**. Long before the Watergate scandal, state courts, governors and Presidents appointed so-called special prosecutors or special counsels to assure the independence of certain types of criminal investigations. For instance, in 1924 President Calvin Coolidge nominated Own J. Roberts and Atlee Pomerene as special counsels to investigate the **Teapot Dome** scandal. Like other local, state and federal prosecutors, special prosecutors typically have the authority to convene a **grand jury**, to subpoena witnesses and to prosecute individuals suspected of criminal violations.

In April 1973 Attorney General **Elliot Richardson** appointed Harvard law professor **Archibald Cox** to serve as a Department of Justice special counsel to investigate the June 1972 break-in at the Watergate headquarters of the Democratic National Committee. In October 1973 President Richard Nixon ordered Cox's dismissal. The so-called **Saturday Night Massacre** led Congress to include a provision for the appointment of independent special prosecutors in the Ethics in Government Act of 1978.

The act required the attorney general to conduct a preliminary investigation into whether credible evidence existed to request that a special three-judge panel of the D.C. Court of Appeals appoint a special prosecutor to investigate further. In 1982 Congress changed the name of special prosecutor to **independent counsel** when it voted to extend the independent investigation provisions of the Ethics Act. Then in December 1992, Congress allowed the independent counsel law to expire in large measure as the result of displeasure with the length of independent counsel **Lawrence Walsh**'s **Iran-contra** investigation.

In January 1994 Attorney General **Janet Reno** appointed **Robert Fiske Jr**. to serve as the Justice Department's **Whitewater** special prosecutor. Late in June 1994, President Bill Clinton signed into law a bill renewing the independent counsel law. In the aftermath of Clinton's January/February Senate **impeachment** trial, Congress again allowed the independent counsel law to expire at the end of June 1999. With the expiration, Attorney General Reno assumed responsibility for making future appointments of special counsels.

Related Entries: Ethics in Government Act of 1978; Watergate Scandal; Whitewater Investigation

SUGGESTED READING: Katy J. Harriger, *Independent Justice: The Special Prosecutor in American Politics*, 2nd ed., Lawrence: University of Kansas Press, 2000.

Cartoon by Thomas Nast showing Andrew Jackson astride a pig. © Bettmann/CORBIS

SPOILS SYSTEM. Beginning in the 1820s, growing political parties significantly increased the practice of using political affiliation as a major consideration in the selection of government employees. By the end of the 1830s, major political parties had put in place spoils systems to reward loyal supporters and as part of a much larger system to raise campaign funds. Although historians give President Andrew Jackson credit for extending the spoils system to the federal government, he simply expanded the practice of using political affiliation as a way to reward political supports. However, President Jackson effectively defended the practice by putting forward the theory of "rotation-in-office." He argued that the spoils system provided average citizens with the opportunity to serve the public and then return to their homes.

From the 1830s through the early 1880s, the spoils system thrived. A series of Democratic and Republican presidents made frequent use of the power of appointment to strengthen party control over federal agencies and departments and to provide the parties with a source of campaign funds through the use of **political assessments**. Although protests against the spoils system began as far back as the 1830s, the protests gave way to the birth of an organized civil service reform movement during the 1850s. By the 1860s the civil service reform movement established a strong foothold in the United States. Supporters of the enactment of civil service reform argued that patronage appointments contributed to corruption in government by attracting to government individuals more interested in lining their pockets than serving the public. In 1883, President **Chester Arthur** signed into law the **Pendleton Act** which established a new federal merit system. Arthur became president after a disgruntled office seeker assassinated President James Garfield during the summer of 1881.

The passage of the Pendleton Act did not bring to an immediate end the executive branch spoils system. The Pendleton Act only covered 10 percent of the employees working for federal agencies and departments. From 1883 through the end of the 1930s, through a series of presidential directives and legislation passed by Congress, the majority of federal employees received merit system protection.

Related Entries: Patronage Crimes; Pendleton Act of 1883; Political Assessments

SUGGESTED READING: Frederick Mosher, *Democracy and Public Service*, New York: Oxford University Press, 1982.

STARR, KENNETH (July 21, 1948–   ). Former Federal Court of Appeals judge; Whitewater independent counsel, 1994–1999.

On August 5, 1994, a special three-judge federal panel appointed Kenneth Starr to serve as the **Whitewater independent counsel**. The appointment created an immediate controversy. In January 1994, Attorney General **Janet Reno** had appointed New York lawyer **Robert B. Fiske Jr.** as the Justice Department's Whitewater special counsel. During late June 1994, Congress passed and President Bill Clinton signed into law a reauthorization of the independent counsel law. Largely in response to growing unhappiness over the effectiveness of the law brought about by **Lawrence Walsh**'s **Iran-contra** investigation, Congress had allowed the independent counsel law to expire in 1991.

Critics to the Starr appointment pointed to his close ties to the Reagan and Bush administrations. After serving on the U.S. Court of Appeals for the D.C. Circuit from 1983 to 1989, Starr served as U.S. solicitor general from 1989 to 1993. After the election of Clinton as president, Starr returned to private practice.

From August 1994 until his October 1999 resignation, Starr saw his Whitewater investigation expand to include additional investigations of the July 1993 death of Deputy White House Counsel **Vincent Foster**, the spring 1993 **Travel Office firings**, the summer 1994 **FBI files flap**, and the 1998 **Monica Lewinsky** affair. A special three-judge appeals panel later appointed Robert W. Ray, a career federal prosecutor, to replace Starr as the Whitewater independent counsel.

Related Entries: Clinton Administration Ethics Controversies; FBI Files Flap; Foster, Vincent; Impeachment Proceedings; Independent Counsel Investigations; Lewinsky, Monica; Travel Office Firings; Whitewater Investigation

Kenneth Starr testifying before the House Judiciary Committee's impeachment hearing for President Bill Clinton, November 19, 1998. AP/WIDE WORLD PHOTO

SUGGESTED READINGS: Nancy E. Roman, "Starr Hailed as Fair, Moderate," *Washington Times*, August 6, 1994, A6; Susan Schmidt and Michael Weisskopf, *Truth at Any Cost: Ken Starr and the Unmaking of Bill Clinton*, New York: HarperCollins, 2000.

STARR REPORT. On September 9, 1998, **Whitewater independent counsel Kenneth Starr** delivered to the House of Representatives a 453-page report that argued eleven grounds existed for the impeachment of President Bill Clinton as the result of actions taken by Clinton to conceal his relationship with former White House intern **Monica Lewinsky**. The report included a graphic account of Clinton's alleged personal relationship with Lewinsky. On September 12, 1998, the House Judiciary Committee placed on the Internet the Starr Report which contained a number of graphic accounts of alleged sexual conduct between Clinton and Lewinsky inside the Oval Office suite. In the report Starr argued that Clinton's testimony at his **Paula Jones** deposition and Lewinsky **grand jury** and his actions in concealing his relationship to Lewinsky constituted perjury and obstruction of justice.

To Starr's surprise the content of the report received as much attention as the issue of whether Clinton violated the federal perjury and obstruction of justice statutes. Many observers questioned Starr's judgment for including such graphic details of the alleged sexual acts between Clinton and Lewinsky. Starr subsequently explained that he had not expected that the House Judiciary Committee would place the entire report on the Internet. Starr also explained that he had no choice but to report the graphic details of the alleged relationship between

Clinton and Lewinsky because Clinton had denied certain types of sexual acts during his deposition in the *Jones* case and refused to answer specific questions regarding his conduct before the federal grand jury.

Related Entries: Clinton Administration Ethics Controversies; Lewinsky, Monica

SUGGESTED READING: Office of the Independent Counsel, *The Report of the Independent Counsel to the House of Representatives*, Washington, DC: Office of the Independent Counsel, 1998.

STEIN, JACOB. *See* Independent Counsel Investigations; Meese, Edwin, III; Reagan Administration Ethics Controversies

STINGS, PUBLIC CORRUPTION. In the aftermath of the **Watergate scandal**, the Federal Bureau of Investigation significantly increased resources directed to pursuing public corruption investigations. Prior to the Watergate scandal, the FBI conducted few undercover public corruption operations. After Watergate, the FBI reconsidered its position on undercover stings designed to test the willingness of public officials to accept bribes. Undercover public corruption stings involve FBI agents posing as individuals interested in purchasing favors from public officials. The 1980 **Abscam investigation** used an undercover sting to catch on videotape four members of the House of Representatives and one U.S. senator accepting cash to help an FBI agent posing as an Arab sheik with immigration problems. Through the 1980s and 1990s, the FBI conducted a number of public corruption stings which resulted in the arrest and conviction of a number of state and local government officials on public corruption charges.

Critics of stings argue that the FBI should not target public officials without evidence of possible illegal conduct by those officials. Supporters argue that the honest public officials have nothing to fear from undercover stings. Like stings directed at other types of criminal activity, stings constitute an effective law enforcement tool for uncovering "corrupt" public officials.

Related Entry: Abscam Investigation

SUGGESTED READING: Ronald J. Ostrow, "FBI Goes from Skeptic to True Believers in Sting Technique," *Los Angeles Times*, October 2, 1988, Part 1, 3, c. 1.

SUNUNU, JOHN HENRY (July 2, 1939–   ). Chief of Staff to President Bush, 1989–1991; counselor to President Bush, 1991–1992.

Early in 1989 President George Bush named former New Hampshire Governor John Sununu as his chief of staff. In late April 1991, the *Washington Post* published a report alleging that Sununu had used military aircraft for some sixty trips during the preceding two years. In addition the article alleged that Sununu had used military aircraft to conduct personal business and for partisan political activities. The White House subsequently reported that Sununu had taken seventy-seven trips on military aircraft. Some of the trips were back to his home

John Sununu (far right) with President George Bush, December 20, 1989.
George Bush Presidential Library

state of New Hampshire. Sununu maintained that all of his trips on military
aircraft had involved official business. Later reports then alleged that Sununu
had used a government car to travel from Washington to New York to attend a
stamp auction, and he had taken free rides on corporate airplanes.

The **Ethics Reform Act of 1989** had given all federal agencies and departments **gift acceptance** authority. However, the gift acceptance authority provisions of the act did not permit federal employees and officials to solicit free
travel from nonfederal sources. On July 1, 1991, Sununu apologized to President
Bush for the controversy surrounding his travel. After the apology Bush expressed his full support for Sununu. On December 3, 1991, Sununu submitted
his letter of resignation. In his letter he explained that with the 1992 presidential
election approaching, he did not want to become a political issue. Consequently
Sununu found it necessary to step aside as chief of staff to assume the position
of counselor to the President.

The Sununu travel affair led the Bush White House to put in place tighter
restrictions on White House employees and officials using military aircraft for
travel and on the acceptance of free travel from private sources.

Related Entry: Bush Administration Ethics Controversies

SUGGESTED READING: Robert N. Roberts and Marion T. Doss, Jr., *From Watergate
to Whitewater: The Public Integrity War*, Westport, CT: Praeger, 1997.

T

TAMMANY HALL. During the Revolutionary War, Tammany societies grew up in the Northeastern region of the country. Founders named the new societies after a Delaware Indian chief whom folklore held to have welcomed William Penn to America. By 1789 only one society remained active in New York City. The New York City Tammany Society had their headquarters in Tammany Hall. During the 1830s the society assumed control over the New York City Democratic Party and eventually became the most powerful political organization in New York City. In the late 1850s, **William Marcy Tweed** (Boss Tweed) became the undisputed leader of the New York City Democratic political machine. Tweed and his associates used their power to loot the city treasury of tens of millions of dollars and to obtain millions of dollars in bribes and kickbacks from individuals and businesses seeking business franchises.

Related Entries: Nast, Thomas; Tweed, William Marcy

SUGGESTED READING: Thomas H. Johnson, *The Oxford Companion to American History*, New York: Oxford University Press, 1966.

TEAPOT DOME SCANDAL. In 1920 voters elected Ohio U.S. Senator Warren G. Harding as president of the United States. During 1921 Secretary of the Interior **Albert B. Fall** proposed to Secretary of the Navy **Edwin Denby** that the Navy Department transfer control of naval oil field reserves at Teapot Dome, Wyoming, and Elk Hills, California. Fall subsequently convinced Denby and President Harding that the Interior Department would do a better job managing all of the nation's oil reserves. In 1922 Secretary Fall quietly leased the Teapot Dome oil reserves to oil developer Harry F. Sinclair and the Elk Hills, California, oil fields to Edward L. Doheny. When word of the leases leaked, a number of senators demanded a full investigation. Through 1922 and much of 1923, Fall, Denby, and President Harding denied any wrongdoing and argued that the leases served the best interests of the United States.

"Tammany Hall Is Going to the Inauguration, News They Can't Help Themselves." Cartoon by Thomas Nast, *Harper's Weekly*, February 21, 1885. Reproduced from the Collections of the LIBRARY OF CONGRESS

Through 1923 pressure mounted for a full and independent investigation. On August 2, 1923, President Harding died in San Francisco, California. Harding's death made Vice President Calvin Coolidge president. By early 1924 President Coolidge had obtained the resignations of Fall and Denby. Coolidge then proceeded to nominate well-respected Owen Roberts and former Democratic senator Atlee Pomerene as Justice Department **special prosecutors**. The investigation turned up strong evidence that Fall had received large amounts of money from Sinclair and Doheny.

From early 1924 through 1929, the Teapot Dome investigations dragged on. In a series of controversial trials, both U.S. District Court juries acquitted Doheny and Sinclair of bribing Fall to obtain the oil leases. However, a U.S. District Court jury subsequently convicted Sinclair of contempt of Congress for refusing to testify before the Senate. Despite the earlier verdicts finding Doheny and Sinclair innocent, in 1929 a U.S. District Court jury found Fall guilty. After Fall failed to have his guilty verdict overturned, he became the first individual who

Oil wells near Teapot Dome, Wyoming. Still Picture Branch, National Archives and Records Administration

had previously served in a Cabinet position to serve time in jail. Interestingly, in 1927 the Supreme Court in *Mammoth Oil Co. v United States*, 275 U.S. 13 (1927) upheld the authority of the United States to cancel the Teapot Dome oil and gas lease with Mammoth Oil Co.

Related Entries: Denby, Edwin L.; Fall, Albert B.; Harding Administration Scandals

SUGGESTED READING: Nathan Miller, *Stealing from America: A History of Corruption from Jamestown to Reagan*, New York, Paragon House, 1992.

THOMAS, CLARENCE (June 23, 1948–   ). Supreme Court Justice, 1991–   .

In the summer of 1991, President George Bush nominated African American U.S. Court of Appeals Judge Clarence Thomas to the U.S. Supreme Court. President Bush made the nomination after the resignation of African American Justice Thurgood Marshall. Prior to joining the Court of Appeals, Thomas had served as assistant secretary for civil rights in the Department of Education and was head of the Equal Employment Opportunity Commission during the Reagan and Bush administrations. In 1990 President Bush had nominated Thomas to the Court of Appeals.

The Thomas nomination produced immediate opposition from liberals concerned about Thomas's conservative views on a number of important legal and constitutional issues. After several days of hearings before the Senate Judiciary

Committee, it appeared that the Senate would confirm Thomas's nomination. At this point University of Oklahoma Law School professor **Anita Hill** contacted opponents to the Thomas nomination. In subsequent nationally televised testimony, Anita Hill alleged that Thomas had made a number of graphic sexual statements to Hill while she worked with him in the Department of Education and the Equal Employment Opportunity Commission. In a blistering response, Thomas denied every allegation. The Senate subsequently voted 52 to 48 to confirm Clarence Thomas as an associate justice of the U.S. Supreme Court. In the years following the Thomas confirmation battle, neither Hill nor Thomas backed away from their Senate testimony.

Related Entry: Hill, Anita

SUGGESTED READING: Jane Flax, *The American Dream in Black and White: The Clarence Thomas Hearings*, Ithaca, NY: Cornell University Press, 1999.

THOMPSON, LARRY. *See* HUD Scandal; Independent Counsel Investigations

TILLMAN ACT. The 1904 presidential election saw voters reelect President Theodore Roosevelt. Despite the fact that Roosevelt received a landslide election victory, he and the National Republican Party faced intense criticism for accepting millions of dollars in corporate campaign contributions. Critics of the 1904 Roosevelt presidential campaign alleged that in return for the campaign contributions, that Republican Party officials and President Roosevelt agreed not to continue effort to break up major trusts. Although a subsequent congressional investigation did not find any evidence that the Roosevelt campaign had accepted bribes, the congressional investigation did give birth to a movement to limit corporate campaign contributions to federal campaigns. Supporters of campaign contribution restrictions established the National Publicity Law Association to lobby for restrictions on campaign contributions to federal campaigns.

On December 5, 1905, in an effort to distance himself from the abuses associated with his 1904 presidential campaign, President Theodore Roosevelt proposed to prohibit corporations from making campaign contributions to any federal campaign. On January 26, 1907, Congress passed the Tillman Act which prohibited all corporations and any national bank from making any campaign contribution to the campaign for anyone running for federal office. However, the Tillman Act did not require candidates for federal office to disclose campaign contributions. In 1910 Congress passed legislation requiring House candidates to file with the clerk of the House the name and address of each individual making a campaign contribution of over $100 or more. In 1911 Congress passed legislation requiring Senate candidates to provide similar information to the Senate. Historians regard the Tillman Act as the first major law enacted by Congress designed to regulate campaign contributions to federal campaigns.

Related Entry: Campaign Finance Reform (Federal)

SUGGESTED READING: Congressional Quarterly, *Congressional Ethics*, Washington, DC: Congressional Quarterly, 1977.

President Ronald Reagan receiving Tower Commission Report. Courtesy
Ronald Reagan Library

TOWER, JOHN (September 29, 1925–April 5, 1991). U.S. senator, 1961–1985.
From 1961 through January 1985, John Tower served as Republican senator
from Texas. In late November 1987, President Ronald Reagan appointed Tower
to chair the President's Special Review Board (Tower Commission) to investigate the Reagan administration's decision to sell arms to Iran in an effort to
obtain the release of Americans being held hostage by pro-Iranian terrorists in
Beirut, Lebanon. In late February 1987, the Commission released its report. The
report found that the decision to sell arms to Iran contradicted U.S. counterter-
rorism policies, that employees and officials of the National Security Council
(NSC) had supervised the contra war in Nicaragua from 1985 through 1987,
and that NSC officials had taken steps to cover up the Iranian arms sales and
the subsequent diversion of profits from the arms sales to the contras. However,
the Tower Commission report did little to clarify whether President Reagan,
Vice President George Bush, and other high-level Reagan administration officials knew and approved the diversion of profits from the Iranian arms sales to
the Nicaraguan contras.
    Early in 1989 President Bush nominated Tower as secretary of defense. Al-
though it initially appeared that Tower would receive strong Senate support,
critics of the Tower nomination raised the issue of whether Tower's reputation
for heavy drinking disqualified him. Largely as the result of the allegations, the
Senate rejected Tower's confirmation by a 53 to 47 vote in early March 1989.
On April 5, 1991, John Tower died in a plane crash near Brunswick, Georgia.

314   TOWER COMMISSION

Related Entries: Bush Administration Ethics Controversies; Iran-Contra Scandal

SUGGESTED READING: "Principal Conclusions of the Tower Commission Report, the Tower Commission Report," *Washington Post*, February 27, 1987, A10.

TOWER COMMISSION. *See* Tower, John

TRAVEL OFFICE FIRINGS. On May 19, 1993, citing gross financial mismanagement, the White House announced the firing of seven members of the White House Travel Office. Within days of the announcement, a controversy developed over the reasons for the firing and alleged misuse of the FBI to support the White House action. On July 2, 1993, the White House issued an internal report sharply criticizing a number of high-level White House aides for their involvement in the firing of the staff of the White House Travel Office. The report recommended the rehiring of five Travel Office employees who had not exercised managerial responsibilities. A federal **grand jury** subsequently indicted Billy Ray Dale, the director of the White House Travel Office, on embezzlement charges. On November, 16, 1995, a U.S. District Court jury found Dale not guilty on all counts.

On January 17, 1996, former White House aide David Watkins testified before a House committee investigating the Travel Office firing that he felt pressure from **Hillary Rodham Clinton** and Deputy White House Counsel **Vincent Foster** to fire the Travel Office staff. Prior to and after Watkins' House testimony, Hillary Clinton denied ever having pressured Watkins to fire the White House Travel Office staff. After a request by Attorney General **Janet Reno**, on March 22, 1996, a special three-judge appeals panel granted **independent counsel Kenneth Starr** authority to investigate whether Watkins had lied about Hillary's role in the White House Travel Office firings. The investigation also provided Starr with the authority to determine whether Hillary Clinton or other White House officials might have lied to federal investigators regarding their role in the Travel Office firings. On October 19, 1999, Robert W. Ray took over the Whitewater and Travel Office investigations from Starr. On June 22, 2000, Robert Ray ended his Travel Office investigation by declining to seek an indictment against Mrs. Clinton for making false statements regarding her involvement in the matter.

Related Entries: Clinton Administration Ethics Controversies; Independent Counsel Investigations

SUGGESTED READINGS: Ann Devroy, "Longtime Travel Staff Given Walking Papers," *Washington Post*, May 20, 1993, A1; Ann Devroy, "Travel Aides' Firing Called Staff Error; Internal Review Raps Clinton Officials," *Washington Post*, July 2, 1993, A1; Toni Locy, "Ex-Aide Tells of Pressure for Travel Office Firings," *Washington Post*, January 18, 1996, A6; Toni Locy, "Starr Given Authority to Wide Probe; At Issue Are Accounts of Travel Office Firings," *Washington Post*, March 23, 1996, A1.

TRIPP, LINDA (1954–   ). Public Affairs Officer, Department of Defense.
From January 1998 through the end of President Bill Clinton's Senate im-

peachment trial during February of 1999, Linda Tripp became a central figure in **independent counsel Kenneth Starr**'s investigation of Clinton's relationship with **Monica Lewinsky**.

Beginning in 1972 Tripp accompanied her husband on various military assignments in Europe and the United States. In 1990 she obtained a secretarial position in the White House of President George Bush. After the election of Clinton as president, Tripp continued to work in the White House. During August 1994, White House officials notified her that she would need to find another position, and they helped her to find a position at the Pentagon. In April 1996 White House officials transferred Lewinsky to the Pentagon because of growing concern over the amount of time she spent around President Clinton. Lewinsky was assigned to the same office as Tripp.

Within a short time of going to work at the Pentagon, Lewinsky and Tripp became close friends. Lewinsky then began to tell Tripp about her personal relationship with President Clinton. Early in fall 1997, Tripp contacted Lucianne Goldberg, a New York City literary agent. Tripp expressed to Goldberg an interest in writing a book on her experiences while working for the Bush and Clinton administrations. When told of Lewinsky's story, Goldberg recommended that Tripp tape her conversations with Lewinsky. From the fall of 1997 through late 1998, Tripp taped hundreds of hours of conversations.

In October 1997 an unidentified individual contacted lawyers representing **Paula Jones** in her sexual harassment lawsuit against President Clinton about the alleged relationship between Lewinsky and the president. Tripp then met with a reporter for *Newsweek* to discuss the possible Lewinsky-Clinton affair. On January 12, 1997, Tripp delivered tapes of her conversations with Lewinsky to Starr. On January 16, 1998, a special three-judge federal appeals panel granted Starr the authority to investigate whether President Clinton violated federal law in his effort to conceal his relationship with Lewinsky. On the same day, Tripp met with a member of Jones's legal team. At this meeting Tripp provided the attorney with detailed information regarding the alleged relationship between Lewinsky and Clinton. The Jones legal team used the information provided by Tripp on January 17, 1998, in their deposition of President Clinton.

Within a short time of handing over the tapes to Starr, Tripp became the subject of a Maryland criminal investigation by the Maryland state prosecutor and the Howard County, Maryland, state attorney. The investigation involved whether Tripp violated a Maryland law that made it a crime to record telephone conversations without the consent of all parties.

Starr spent much of 1998 attempting to verify the allegations on the Tripp tapes and to negotiate an immunity agreement with Lewinsky. Early in September 1998, Starr forwarded to Congress a detailed report which concluded that Clinton had committed impeachable offenses during his efforts to conceal his relationship with Lewinsky to lawyers representing Jones, as well as his own independent counsel investigation. In December 1998 the House Judiciary Committee and the full House voted to impeach Clinton. In February 1998 the Senate voted to acquit the president for perjury and for obstruction of justice before a federal **grand jury**.

On July 30, 1999, a Maryland grand jury indicted Tripp on criminal charges of illegal wiretapping. Her representatives responded with anger to the indictment decision. Tripp became the only individual involved in the Clinton-Lewinsky investigation to be indicted for their conduct.

On July 30, 1999, a Maryland grand jury indicted Tripp on criminal charges of illegal wiretapping. Her representatives responded with anger to the indictment decision. Tripp became the only individual involved in the Clinton-Lewinsky investigation to be indicted for his or her conduct. Then on May 24, 2000, Maryland State Prosecutor Stephen Montanarelli announced the dropping of the state's case against Tripp. The decision came after a decision of a Howard County Circuit Court blocking testimony from Monica Lewinsky. The judge found that information provided by Tripp under a grant of immunity from independent counsel Kenneth Starr had "tainted" Lewinsky's testimony. Without Lewinsky's testimony, the Maryland prosecutor could not authenticate Tripp's recordings.

Related Entries: Lewinsky, Monica; Starr, Kenneth

SUGGESTED READINGS: Dana Priest and Renee Sanchez, "Once-Trusted Aide at Heart of It All," *Washington Post*, January 23, 1998, A22; Michael E. Ruane and Fredrick Kunkle, "Md. Drops Linda Tripp Prosecution; Judge Had Left State with 'Nowhere to Go,' " *Washington Post*, May 25, 2000, A1; Saundra Torry and Raja Mishra, "Tripp Indicted on Charges of Wiretapping," *Washington Post*, July 31, 1999, A1.

TRUMAN, HARRY S. (May 8, 1884–December 26, 1972). President of the United States, 1945–1952. *See* Truman Administration Ethics Controversies

TRUMAN ADMINISTRATION ETHICS CONTROVERSIES. Between 1947 and the end of 1952, President Harry S. Truman faced a series of ethics problems that raised serious questions regarding the ability of the federal government to prevent special interests from exerting undue influence on government decision makers.

In 1947 a number of Truman administration officials faced criticism for making large profits from stock speculation. Although subsequent investigations failed to produce any evidence, the allegations led many Americans to believe that government officials profited handsomely from access to nonpublic financial information.

Allegations surrounding the conduct of President Truman's military aide, Brigadier General **Harry H. Vaughan**, also plagued the Truman administration. Between 1947 and 1951, Vaughan faced allegations that he allowed friends to use their relationship with him as a way of lining up clients interested in obtaining government business. The most famous incident involved a friend of

President Truman meets with attorney general nominee Judge James P. McGranery, April 4, 1952. National Park Service Photograph-Rowe/Harry S. Truman Library

Vaughan's who provided Vaughan, President Truman, and a number of high-level Truman administration officials with free deep freezers. Despite calls that President Truman dismiss Vaughan, Truman stood behind his friend through the end of his administration in 1953.

The Reconstruction Finance Corporation (RFC) and **Bureau of Internal Revenue** controversies proved equally serious for the Truman White House. In 1950 allegations swirled over a number of bad loans made by the RFC. A February 1951 Senate report blamed the loan defaults on mismanagement and political favoritism. In 1951 and 1952, allegations surfaced that Bureau of Internal Revenue employees and officials of the Justice Department Tax Division had demanded payments from delinquent taxpayers in return for resolving their tax problems. The controversy would result in the dismissal of a number of Bureau of Internal Revenue employees and subsequently force the Truman White House and Congress to reorganize to Bureau of Internal Revenue.

By late 1951 the growing Bureau of Internal Revenue (BIR) placed great pressure on the Truman White House to appoint a special prosecutor or counsel to investigate the matter. In January 1992 Attorney General Howard McGrath appointed New York lawyer **Newbold Morris** as his special assistant to search out corruption in the federal government. Morris and McGrath proved unable to cooperate on anything. McGrath viewed the appointment of Morris as a direct threat to the independence of the Justice Department, and Morris regarded McGrath as an obstacle to cleaning up rampant corruption in federal agencies and departments. Never given the resources of freedom to conduct a thorough investigation, on April 3, 1952, Attorney General McGrath dismissed Morris. On the same day, McGrath resigned. The next day President Truman nominated Judge James P. McGranery as the new attorney general. The Morris controversy did little to help the Truman administration deal with its tarnished reputation.

In addition to facing strong criticism from Republican critics, liberal members of Truman's Democratic Party saw the alleged scandals as evidence that Truman had not done enough to prevent powerful special interests from influencing the formulation and implementation of federal policy. The 1952 presidential election saw the Republican Party attempt to turn the so-called Truman scandals into a major campaign issue although political historians generally attribute Republican presidential candidate Dwight David Eisenhower's victory to his World War II war record rather than to the Truman scandals.

Related Entries: Bureau of Internal Revenue Scandal; Vaughan, Harry H.

SUGGESTED READING: Andrew Dunar, *The Truman Scandals and the Politics of Morality*, Columbia: University of Missouri Press, 1984.

TWEED, WILLIAM MARCY (April 3, 1823–April 12, 1878). New York City political boss; member of New York State Legislature.

After 1857 William Marcy Tweed became the political boss of the New York City political machine commonly known as the **Tammany Hall** political machine. The political machine made tens of millions of dollars on fraudulent city contracts and by demanding payments from private businesses seeking city services and business. Elected to the New York State Senate in 1868, after 1870 Tweed experienced a rapid decline in his political fortunes. Tweed and the Tammany political machine maintained power by helping new immigrants to New York City find housing and employment. In return the Tweed ring and Tammany Hall demanded political loyalty.

By the end of the 1860s, growing concern over rising taxes and the exploding cost of running New York City led to the birth of a reform movement directed at ousting Tweed. In 1866 New York City lawyer Samuel J. Tilden became chairman of the state Democratic Party. Largely as the result of the efforts of Tilden, political cartoonist **Thomas Nast**, and the publication of evidence of widespread graft by New York City newspapers, Tweed received a twelve-year prison sentence on public corruption charges in 1871. Tweed temporarily escaped prison by fleeing to Spain. After being extradited back to New York,

"Tweed-Le-Dee and Tilden Dum." Cartoon by Thomas Nast, *Harper's Weekly*, July 1, 1876. Reproduced from the Collections of the LIBRARY OF CONGRESS

Tweed died in prison in 1876. Tweed's death, however, did not mean the end of Tammany Hall. Operating out of Tammany Hall, the Democratic political machine continued to control New York City politics for decades to come.

Related Entry: Nast, Thomas

SUGGESTED READING: William Alan Bales, *Tiger in the Streets*, New York: Dodd, Mead, 1962.

U.S. ATTORNEYS. *See* Federal Prosecutor

U.S. OFFICE OF GOVERNMENT ETHICS (USOGE). The **Ethics in Government Act of 1978** established the Office of Government Ethics to oversee the management of the federal executive branch ethics program. However, the Ethics Act left the day-to-day management of agency ethics programs in the hands of Designated Agency Ethics Officials (DAEOs). To help maintain the effectiveness of agency ethics programs, USOGE conducts an extensive program of training workshops for DAEOs and interested federal agency employees and officials. The Office of Government Ethics also has the authority to issue regulations interpreting a number of criminal conflict of interest statues. For instance USOGE has issued lengthy regulations providing former federal employees with guidance regarding the restrictions on lobbying by former federal employees and officials.

In 1989, President George Bush issued **Executive Order 12674**, Principles of Ethical Conduct for Government Officers and Employees. The Bush ethics directive required USOGE to issue new standards of conduct for federal employees and officials. In 1991 USOGE issued over sixty pages of new ethics guidelines governing a wide range of government ethics issues such as acceptance of gifts, outside employment, misuse of nonpublic government information, and financial conflicts of interest.

In addition to overseeing the executive branch ethics education program, USOGE reviews the annual public financial disclosure statements of presidential appointees subject to Senate confirmation for financial conflict of interest problems. To resolve the financial conflict of interest problems of executive branch employees and officials, federal law gives the USOGE the authority to approve the creation of **blind trusts**. In 1989 Congress passed the **Ethics Reform Act** which included a provision for the issuance of **certificates of divestiture** by the director of the Office of Government Ethics. Under the provision federal employees and officials are required to sell financial assets in order to comply with federal ethics regulations; they are permitted to roll over any capital gains resulting from a forced sale of a financial asset into a widely held financial instrument if issued a certificate of divestiture by the director of USOGE.

However, the Ethics in Government Act of 1978 did not give the USOGE the authority to investigate allegations of criminal misconduct by federal agencies and officials. After the passage of the 1978 Ethics Act, responsibility for criminal investigations remained with the **Public Integrity Section of the Department of Justice**, U.S. attorneys, and **independent counsels**. At the end of June 1999, Congress allowed the independent counsel provision of the Ethics Act to go out of existence.

Related Entries: Certificate of Divestiture; Ethics in Government Act of 1978; Public Financial Disclosure

SUGGESTED READINGS: Robert Roberts, *White House Ethics: The History of the Politics of Federal Conflict of Interest Regulation*, Westport, CT: Greenwood Press, 1988. Robert N. Roberts and Marion T. Doss, Jr., *From Watergate to Whitewater: The Public Integrity War*, Westport, CT: Praeger, 1997. OGE Home Page, URL: *www.usoge.gov*.

UNITED STATES V MISSISSIPPI VALLEY GENERATING COMPANY, 364 U.S. 520 (1961).

On January 9, 1961, the Supreme Court reversed a decision by the U.S. Court of Claims awarding Mississippi Valley Generating Company millions of dollars in damages for the cancellation of a contract for the construction of a power plant to free up power for the Atomic Energy Commission. The decision brought to an end the so-called **Dixon-Yates** controversy. In a broadly worded opinion, Chief Justice Earl Warren ruled that President Eisenhower legally ordered cancellation of the contract because of the appearance of a conflict of interest.

In 1953 the Bureau of the Budget entered into a contract with a Memphis, Tennessee, area power company for the construction of a new power plant. Under the arrangement the new power company would sell power to the City of Memphis. Relieved of the responsibility of meeting the power needs of Memphis, the federally owned Tennessee Valley Authority could then meet the growing power needs of the Atomic Energy Commission. The new power company was named the Mississippi Valley Generating Company. Critics of the contract saw it as an effort by the Eisenhower administration to begin dismantling the government-owned Tennessee Valley Authority. During February 1955 congressional critics of the contract learned that Adolpe Wenzell, a vice president with First Boston Corporation, had worked as an unpaid consultant to the Bureau of the Budget during the time the Bureau negotiated the Dixon-Yates contract. After the Bureau negotiated, First Boston received the contract to finance the construction of the new power plant.

On July 11, 1955, President Eisenhower announced his decision to cancel the contract. Mississippi Valley Generating Company then sued the U.S. government for the cancellation fee provided for under the terms of the contract. In June 1956 the U.S. Court of Claims ordered the government to pay Mississippi Valley Generating Company $1.87 million. The *Mississippi Valley Generating Company* decision helped to persuade President John F. Kennedy of the need to reform the executive branch ethics system. The Kennedy White House subsequently issued a number of ethics directives designed to eliminate confusion regarding executive branch ethics rules and to prevent federal employees and officials from becoming involved in situations that might raise questions regarding the objectivity or impartiality of actions taken by government employees and officials.

Related Entries: Dixon-Yates Affair; Eisenhower Administration Ethics Controversies

SUGGESTED READINGS: Robert N. Roberts, *White House Ethics: History of the Politics of Conflict of Interest Regulation*, Westport, CT: Greenwood Press, 1988; *United States v Mississippi Valley Generating Company* (1961) *http://laws.findlaw.com/364/520.html.*

UNITED STATES V NATIONAL TREASURY EMPLOYEES UNION, 513 U.S. 454 (1995).

As part of the provisions of the **Ethics Reform Act of 1989**, the law prohibited members of the House from keeping any **honorariums** received for speaking engagements, writing articles, or attending conferences. The law required members to donate any honorariums they received to charity. For reasons difficult to understand, the Ethics Reform Act included a provision prohibiting all executive branch employees from accepting all honorariums. From 1961 through the passage of the Ethics Reform Act, federal ethics rules prohibited executive branch employees from accepting honorariums for giving speeches, writing articles, or attending events related to their official duties. Federal ethics rules also prohibited executive branch employees from accepting honorariums from individuals or corporations regulated by the employee's agency or doing business with the employee's agency. Other than these restrictions, federal ethics rules permitted most executive branch employees to accept honorariums for giving speeches, writing articles, or attending conferences unrelated to the performance of their official duties.

Not unexpectedly federal employees responded in anger to the congressional action. After efforts to persuade Congress to exempt career federal employees from the new honorarium ban failed, the National Treasury Employee's Union brought suit seeking to overturn the ban on the grounds that it violated the First Amendment rights of federal employees and officials. The Union argued the ban would deter many federal employees from writing articles or giving speeches, and as a result, the prohibition had a constitutional chilling effect on the First Amendment freedom of speech rights of federal employees.

In a decision that caught many court watchers off guard, the Supreme Court struck the part of the honorarium ban that applied to most career federal employees. It left intact the prohibition that applied to presidential appointees and nominees. The court found that the prohibition violated the First Amendment rights of the majority of classified federal employees. The decision did not abolish all honorarium restrictions on classified federal employees and officials; it simply abolished the absolute ban on all executive branch employees and officials established by the Ethics Reform Act.

Related Entries: Ethics Reform Act of 1989; Honorarium Restrictions

SUGGESTED READINGS: Joan Biskupic, "Court Allows Honoraria for Federal Rank and File," *Washington Post*, February 23, 1995, A01; *United States v National Treasury Employees Union*, URL: *http://laws.findlaw.com/US/000/u10314.html*.

UNITED STATES V NIXON, 418 U.S. 683 (1974). On July 13, 1973, White House aide **Alexander Butterfield** told the **Senate Watergate Committee** of the existence of a White House taping system. During July 1973 the White House notified the Committee and **special prosecutor Archibald Cox** that President Nixon refused to turn over the White House tapes. Both the Committee and Cox immediately issued subpoenas for the tapes. The action touched off a battle over whether a court could require a president to turn over the tapes. On October 20, 1973, President Nixon ordered Attorney General **Elliot Richardson** to fire Cox. Rather than carrying out Nixon's order, both Richardson and Deputy Attorney General William Ruckelshaus resigned. Acting Attorney General **Robert Bork** then fired Cox. Congressional, media, and public reaction to the so-called **Saturday Night Massacre** forced President Nixon to appoint a new Watergate special prosecutor. **Leon Jaworski** became the second Watergate special prosecutor.

Prior to Cox's dismissal, President Nixon had invoked the doctrine of **executive privilege** as the ground for refusing to turn over the Watergate tapes to **Independent Counsel** Cox and the Senate Watergate Committee. After receiving the appointment as the second Watergate special prosecutor, Jaworski continued the effort to force President Nixon to turn over the Watergate tapes. On July 24, 1974, the Supreme Court ordered Nixon to hand over the tapes. The court rejected the White House argument that the doctrine of executive privilege placed an absolute ban on the disclosure of the tapes. Instead the high court found that Jaworski had made a compelling argument for obtaining access to the tapes as part of a legitimate criminal investigation that overrode the national interest in keeping the personal conversations of a president confidential while he/she occupied the Oval Office. In other words the court held that the doctrine of executive privilege did protect from subpoena certain types of information held within the White House such as noncriminal conversations involving foreign affairs and national security.

On August 9, 1974, President Nixon resigned the presidency.

Related Entries: Cox, Archibald; Executive Privilege Doctrine; Jaworski, Leon; Senate Watergate Committee; Watergate Scandal

SUGGESTED READINGS: John P. MacKenzie, "Court Orders Nixon to Yield Tapes; President Promises to Comply Fully: Justices Reject Privilege Claim in 8-to-0 Ruling," *Washington Post*, Thursday, July 25, 1974, A01; *United States v Nixon*, URL: *http:// laws.findlaw.com/US/418/683.html*.

UNITED STATES V SUN-DIAMOND GROWERS OF CALIFORNIA, No. 98–131 (1999).

At the urging of the Kennedy White House, Congress passed the **Bribery and Conflict of Interest Act of 1962**. Besides updating a number of federal conflict of interest laws, the law revamped the federal bribery statute. The new bribery statute included two bribery offenses. The first offense dealt with the typical bribery situation where a federal employee accepts something of value from an individual after agreeing to do something in return for the payment. In addition to the so-called quid pro quo prohibition, Congress included a second unnamed bribery offense. Over time federal prosecutors began referring to the statute as the **illegal gratuity statute**.

The statute prohibits federal employees and officials from accepting anything of value from a nonfederal source "for or because of the performance of an official act." In contrast to the first bribery statute, the statute does not contain a quid pro quo element of the offense. Because of the major difference between the first and second bribery offense, from the early 1970s through the 1990s, **federal prosecutors** found it much easier to convict federal employees and officials of accepting an illegal gratuity than of accepting a bribe. During the 1980s and 1990s, federal prosecutors attempted to convince the federal courts that the statute prohibited private individuals and corporations from providing federal employees and officials with valuable gifts as a way to show their appreciation for their performance as a federal employee or official.

During August 1994 Secretary of Agriculture **Mike Espy** resigned after reports that he received thousands of dollars of gifts from Tyson Corporation and a number of other private sources. After a request by Attorney General **Janet Reno**, a special federal judicial panel appointed Donald Smaltz to investigate whether Espy violated any federal criminal laws by accepting the gifts. Independent Counsel Smaltz obtained the indictment of Mike Espy for the acceptance of illegal gratuities. Smaltz also obtained indictments against a small number of corporations and individuals for providing Espy with illegal gratuities. Although Tyson Foods pleaded guilty to providing Espy with illegal gratuities, Espy maintained his innocence, and Sun-Diamond Growers Cooperative of California argued that it had not violated the illegal gratuity statute when the cooperative allegedly provided Espy with $2,295 in U.S. Open tickets, $2,427 in luggage, $665 in meals, and a framed print and crystal bowl worth $554.

During December 1998 a federal jury found Espy not guilty on multiple counts of accepting illegal gratuities while serving as secretary of agriculture between 1993 and August 1994. On April 27, 1999, the Supreme Court upheld a decision of a federal Court of Appeals overturning the conviction of Sun-Diamond Growers of California. In reaching its decision, the Supreme Court found that the type of private hospitality provided by Sun-Diamond Growers did not constitute illegal gratuities. The decision constituted a significant defeat for Smaltz and significantly narrowed the scope of the illegal gratuity statute.

Related Entries: Espy, Mike; Illegal Gratuity Statute

SUGGESTED READINGS: Joan Biskupic, "High Court Narrows Law on Gratuities in Espy Case; Prosecutors Must Tie Gifts to Official Acts," *Washington Post*, April 28, 1999, A01; *United States v Sun-Diamond Growers of California*, URL: *http://laws. findlaw.com/US/000/98–131.html*.

V

VAUGHAN, HARRY H. (November 23, 1893–May 21, 1981). Brigadier general and military aide to President Harry S. Truman.

Harry Truman and Harry Vaughan first met in 1917 at Fort Still, Oklahoma, as lieutenants in the field artillery. After the end of World War I, Vaughan and Truman renewed their friendship as National Guard officers at Fort Riley, Kansas. When Truman ran for the Senate in 1940, Vaughan served as treasurer for the campaign. During 1941 Vaughan briefly served as Senator Truman's executive assistant. Vaughan again went on active duty and served as provost marshal in Australia until he broke his back in a plane crash. After returning to Washington to recover from his injuries, in 1943 Vaughan received a posting to the Senate Armed Services Committee subcommittee, chaired by Truman, and he was given the responsibility for investigating procurement fraud. When voters elected Truman as vice president in 1944, Vaughan was named as his military aide. Vaughan later became the military aide to President Truman.

Between 1947 and the end of the Truman administration in 1953, Vaughan became the subject of a number of allegations accusing him of using his position in the White House to help friends obtain clients for their businesses. Many of the allegations came from powerful Washington columnist Drew Pearson. The first controversy erupted during January 1947, when Drew Pearson attacked Vaughan for his relationship with Missouri friend John F. Maragon. Through 1945 and into 1946, Maragon became a frequent visitor to Vaughan's White House office. On occasion Maragon received business calls at Vaughan's office. With the help of Vaughn, Maragon obtained a position with the U.S. mission to Greece in 1946. The mission had responsibility for monitoring the Greek elections. At the time Greek communists were attempting to take over the government. Although the appointment did not give Maragon any policy-making authority, critics alleged that Maragon attempted to exert his influence.

As soon as the controversy over Maragon had calmed down, Walter Winchell,

Harry H. Vaughan. National Park Service Photograph-Rowe/Harry S. Truman Library

another reporter and Truman critic, broadcast a story indicating that Colonel Juan Peron, the dictator of Argentina, planned to award Vaughan a medal. In a February 1949 speech before the Reserve Officers Association, President Truman made it clear that he would not allow radio and newspaper stories to drive Vaughan from office. "I want you to distinctly understand," stressed Truman, "that any s.o.b. who thinks he can cause anyone of these people to be discharged by me by some smart aleck statement over the air or in the paper, has another thing coming."

However, the so-called "five-percenter" scandal proved much more serious for General Vaughan and President Truman. During the summer of 1949, the *New York Herald Tribune* published a story about the activities of Vaughan's friend James V. Hunt. Hunt operated a Washington, D.C., consulting business where he solicited clients interested in obtaining government contracts. Hunt was also a paid government consultant. Clients paid Hunt a monthly fee and agreed to pay Hunt 5 percent of any contract he received. According to the story, Hunt claimed to be a close friend of Harry Vaughan and a number of other high-level government officials as part of his sales pitch to sign up clients. Many of the so-called five percenters signed up clients by arguing that they had little hope of obtaining government contracts without the help of a well-connected Washington insider.

During the summer of 1949, the Senate Investigations Subcommittee of the

Committee on Expenditures in the Executive Departments opened an investigation into the role of five percenters. Chaired by Senator Clyde R. Hoey, D-N.C., the Hoey Committee spent much of its time investigating Vaughan and whether he received any payment for helping friends. During the course of the investigation, the subcommittee learned that in late 1945, a friend of Harry Vaughan sent Vaughan, Mrs. Harry Truman, and several other high-level administration officials deep freezers after Vaughan had told his friend that Mrs. Truman had been unable to obtain one. The story of the deep freezer preoccupied Washington and the nation for a number of weeks. Yet the investigation failed to develop any evidence that Vaughan had received anything for helping out his friends. In the end Vaughan remained Truman's military aide until the last day of the administration.

Related Entry: Truman Administration Ethics Controversies

SUGGESTED READINGS: Andrew Dunar, *The Truman Scandals and the Politics of Morality*, Columbia: University of Missouri Press, 1984; "Harry H. Vaughan, Major General Who Was an Aide to Truman, Dies," *New York Times*, May 22, 1981, B6.

W

WALSH, LAWRENCE E. (January 8, 1912–). Independent Counsel, Iran-contra investigation, 1986–1994.

In December 1986 a special federal judicial appeals panel named Lawrence Walsh as the **independent counsel** for the **Iran-contra scandal**. From December 1986 through much of 1994, Walsh pursued an aggressive investigation of the events surrounding the decision of President Reagan to authorize the sale of arms to Iran in an effort to obtain the release of Americans being held hostage by pro-Iranian terrorists operating inside Lebanon. The investigation also dealt with the apparent diversion of Iranian payments for the weapons to assist the Nicaraguan contras in their effort to overthrow the elected communist Sandinista government of Nicaragua.

From the beginning the Walsh investigation found itself the center of a political firestorm. Despite the vigorous opposition of **Independent Counsel** Walsh, the Senate voted to grant key Iran-contra figures immunity in order to obtain their testimony. By taking this action, the Senate placed in serious jeopardy any prosecutions of individuals who testified before the committee. Subsequent events proved Walsh correct. After Walsh successfully prosecuted Marine Colonel **Oliver North** for lying to Congress and accepting an **illegal gratuity**, the Federal Court of Appeals for the District of Columbia reversed North's convictions on the grounds that witnesses Walsh had used to convict North had watched parts of his televised congressional Iran-contra testimony. The Appeals Court also reversed the Iran-contra conviction of former National Security Council Advisor Admiral **John Poindexter**. Besides the convictions of North and Poindexter, Walsh obtained a number of other Iran-contra related guilty pleas and convictions.

By 1991 polls indicated that the majority of the American people had grown tired of the Iran-contra investigation. Equally important the length and cost of the Iran-contra investigation helped to increase opposition to the renewal of the

Iran-Contra Independent Counsel Lawrence E. Walsh at a January 14, 1994 news conference for the final Iran-Contra report release. AP/WIDE WORLD PHOTO

independent counsel law. Despite the harsh criticism of his investigation, Walsh persisted through the end of both the Reagan and Bush administrations.

In June 1992 a federal **grand jury** indicted former Reagan administration Secretary of Defense **Caspar Weinberger** on five felony counts of lying to Congress on matters related to the Iran-contra affair. The indictment enraged President George Bush and many Republican and Democratic members of Congress. Both Secretary of State George Shultz and Weinberger had opposed the plan for the sale of arms to Iran when first proposed. On Christmas Eve of 1992, President Bush pardoned Weinberger and a number of other individuals found guilty of Iran-contra related offenses. During November 1992 President George Bush lost the presidential election to Arkansas Governor Bill Clinton. In July 1994 Walsh filed his final Iran-contra report which sharply criticized President Reagan and President Bush for their alleged involvement in the approval of the arms for hostages policy.

Related Entries: Iran-contra Scandal; North, Oliver; Poindexter, John Marlan; Reagan Administration Ethics Controversies; Weinberger, Caspar Willard

SUGGESTED READING: Lawrence E. Walsh, *Iran-Contra: The Final Report,* New York: Times Books, 1994.

Watergate Complex. FOIA and Special Access Records, National Archives and Records Administration

WATERGATE SCANDAL. On August 9, 1974, President Richard Nixon re-signed as president of the United States. From the June 17, 1972, break-in at the Watergate offices of the Democratic National Committee (DNC), President Nixon and a number of White House aides struggled to conceal the relationship between the White House, the Committee to Re-Elect the President (CREEP), and the Watergate burglars. Over time the Watergate scandal evolved into an investigation of an unprecedented abuse of power by a president, White House aides, and a presidential campaign committee. For better or for worse, the Watergate scandal ushered in a new era of intense scrutiny of the public and private lives of public officials and led to the enactment of a series of new laws directed at protecting trust in government.

Most historians trace the beginning of the Watergate scandal to the June 1971 publication of the so-called **Pentagon Papers** by the *New York Times*. Rand Corporation employee Daniel Ellsberg leaked the highly critical Defense Department report on U.S. involvement in the Vietnam War. Angered by the leaks of sensitive information to the press, President Nixon ordered White House aide **John Ehrlichman** to find a way to stop leaks of classified and sensitive information. In response to Ehrlichman's directive, White House aides hired former FBI special agent **G. Gordon Liddy** and former CIA operatives **E. Howard Hunt** and James McCord for the new unit. The unit came to be known as the plumbers unit. On September 3, 1971, members of the unit burglarized the

Presidential advisers H. R. Haldeman and John D. Ehrlichman. Nixon
Presidential Materials Staff

offices of Ellsberg's psychiatrist in an effort to obtain information that the White
House might use to discredit Ellsberg prior to his criminal trial for leaking the
Pentagon Papers. Shortly after the break-in, the White House disbanded the
plumbers unit.

Besides the break-in, the approach of the 1972 presidential campaign saw the
establishment of CREEP. Attorney General **John Mitchell** resigned and took
the job as chairman of President Nixon's reelection campaign. During this time
the Nixon White House hatched a plan to disrupt the 1972 Democratic presidential primary campaign. With the full approval of White House Chief of Staff
H. R. Haldeman, White House aide Dwight Chapin hired Donald Segretti to
conduct a number of **"dirty tricks"** on candidates for the Democratic presidential nomination. During the primary campaign, Segretti distributed forged
campaign literature, including a letter accusing former Vice President Hubert
Humphrey of having used prostitutes provided by lobbyists.

Late in 1971 and early 1972, CREEP hired Liddy, Hunt, and McCord to
operate a new political intelligence unit. Although considerable controversy continues over who approved the break-in at the Democratic National Committee
offices located in the Watergate complex, Liddy and his team planned and carried out two break-ins. On June 17, 1972, District of Columbia police arrested
McCord and four Cuban exiles inside the office of the DNC. A short time later,
police arrested Liddy and Hunt for their involvement. Both the CREEP and the
Nixon White House immediately denied any involvement.

Between June 17, 1972, through spring 1973, President Nixon, members of

President Richard Nixon leaves the White
House after his resignation, August 9, 1974.
© Owen Franken/CORBIS

his White House staff, and CREEP attempted to contain the damage from the break-in. However, *Washington Post* reporters **Bob Woodward** and **Carl Bernstein** persistently pursued the relationship between the Watergate burglars and the Nixon administration. On January 30, 1973, a U.S. District Court jury convicted McCord and Liddy of breaking into and illegally wiretapping the Democratic National Committee headquarters. In February 1973 the Senate voted to establish a Select Committee on Presidential Campaign Activities. And in March 1973, in an effort to get the Watergate burglars to disclose who approved the operation, U.S. District Judge John Sirica sentenced the burglars to long prison sentences. McCord implicated John Mitchell and other White House officials in the burglary. On April 30, 1973, White House aides Haldeman and Ehrlichman resigned. The White House also announced the dismissal of White House Counsel **John Dean** and the resignation of Attorney General Richard Kleindienst. On May 19, 1973, Attorney General nominee **Elliot Richardson** announced the appointment of **Archibald Cox** as the Watergate **special prosecutor**.

During the late spring and summer of 1973, the **Senate Watergate Committee** held extensive hearings into President Nixon's 1972 presidential campaign. In June 1973 testimony, Dean implicated Nixon in the Watergate cover-up. In early July 1973, former White House aide **Alexander Butterfield** revealed to the Senate Watergate Committee the existence of a White House taping system. Later in July 1973, Mitchell and Haldeman both denied participating in any cover-up and that anyone told President Nixon. Late in July 1973, President Nixon invoked the doctrine of **executive privilege** to refuse to turn over the tapes to the Senate Watergate Committee and to Cox. On October 20, 1973, Nixon ordered Richardson to fire Cox. Both Attorney General Richardson and Deputy Attorney General William Ruckelshaus resigned rather than carry out Nixon's order. Acting Attorney General **Robert Bork** then dismissed Cox.

On November 1, 1973, President Nixon appointed **Leon Jaworski** as the second Watergate **special prosecutor**. Jaworski continued the effort to require Nixon to turn over the Watergate tapes. On March 1, 1974, a federal **grand jury** indicted Mitchell, Haldeman, Ehrlichman, **Charles Colson**, Robert C. Mardian, Kenneth W. Parkinson, and Gordon Strachen for actions related to the Watergate cover-up. The grand jury named President Nixon as an unindicted coconspirator. On July 24, 1974, the Supreme Court issued a unanimous opinion that directed President Nixon to turn over sixty-four taped conversations to Jaworski. On July 27, 1973, the House Judiciary Committee passed the first of three articles of impeachment. On August 9, 1973, Nixon resigned the presidency. On September 8, 1974, President **Gerald Ford** announced his pardon of former President Richard Nixon.

Related Entries: Bernstein, Carl; Colson, Charles W.; Cox, Archibald; Dean, John; Ehrlichman, John D.; Ervin, Sam; Ford, Gerald R.; Haldeman, H. R.; Jaworski, Leon; Liddy, G. Gordon; Mitchell, John; Richardson, Elliot; *United States v Nixon*; Woodward, Bob

SUGGESTED READING: Bob Woodward and Carl Bernstein, *All the President's Men*, New York: Simon & Schuster, 1974.

WATERGATE-ERA REFORMS. The **Watergate scandal** and the subsequent August 1974 resignation of President Richard Nixon helped to build public and congressional support for the enactment of a number of good government reforms. First Congress passed the **Federal Election Campaign Act of 1974** in an effort to close a number of major loopholes in the 1971 FECA law. The Watergate investigation had disclosed widespread illegal campaign fund-raising by President Nixon's Committee to Re-Elect the President (CREEP). The 1974 amendments established lower campaign contribution limits for individuals and **political action committees** (PACs). In addition the amendments established a new **Federal Election Commission** to oversee enforcement of the new federal campaign finance law.

During 1977 the House and Senate adopted new ethics codes which tightened standard of conduct regulations governing the acceptance of honorariums, fees, gifts, and outside earned income. Equally significant the new code required members to file annual public financial disclosure statements. During October 1978 Congress passed the **Ethics in Government Act of 1978**. The act required public financial disclosure by high-level federal officials in all three branches of the federal government. In addition the act strengthened existing **"revolving door"** restrictions on former high-level executive branch officials contacting other officials in executive branch agencies and departments. The act established a complex mechanism for appointing **special prosecutors (independent counsels)** to investigate allegations of criminal conduct involving high-level executive branch officials. Finally the Ethics Act delegated to the new Office of Government Ethics responsibility for overseeing the executive branch ethics program.

Related Entries: Carter Administration Ethics Reform Program; Ethics in Government Act of 1978; Federal Election Campaign Act Amendments of 1974; Federal Election Campaign Act Amendments of 1976; U.S. Office of Government Ethics

SUGGESTED READING: Bob Woodward, *Shadow: Five Presidents and the Legacy of Watergate*, New York: Simon & Schuster, 1999.

WATT, JAMES GAIUS (January 31, 1938–   ). Secretary of Interior, 1981–1983.
   James Watt served as President Ronald Reagan's secretary of interior from 1981 until his 1983 resignation. Watt left the Interior Department as the result of a major controversy over the environmental policies of the Reagan administration. After leaving the Interior Department, Watt became a government consultant and lobbyist.
   In 1989 a major scandal erupted over the management of the Department of Housing and Urban Development (HUD). Critics alleged that HUD had awarded grants and low-income loan guarantees to landlords and developers on the basis of their political connections with HUD officials rather than on the basis of merit. A three-judge federal appeals panel subsequently appointed Arlin Adams as the HUD **independent counsel**. On February 22, 1995, Adams obtained a twenty-five-count indictment against Watt. The indictments alleged that Watt lied to Congress and a federal **grand jury** regarding his contacts with HUD officials on behalf of private clients seeking HUD housing funds. Watt vigorously denied having lied to Congress or a federal grand jury regarding his lobbying activities. On January 2, 1996, Watt pleaded guilty to a misdemeanor charge of attempting to mislead a federal grand jury investigating influence peddling in HUD during the Reagan administration. Despite Watt's guilty plea, many legal observers saw the plea as a victory for Watt and a major defeat for independent counsel Larry Thompson who had taken over the independent counsel investigation from Adams.
   Related Entries: HUD Scandal; Independent Counsel Investigations; Reagan Administration Ethics Controversies

SUGGESTED READING: Toni Locy, "Watt Pleads to Misdemeanor in HUD Case; Ex-Interior Secretary Originally Indicted on 25 Felony Counts," *Washington Post*, January 3, 1996, A1.

WEDTECH SCANDAL. In 1979 the Wedtech Company, a small Bronx, New York, company, hired the law firm of Biaggi & Ehrlich to help the company obtain government contracts set aside for minority-owned businesses. In May 1982 Wedtech employed the services of **Lyn Nofziger**, a former member of President Reagan's White House staff, to help the company obtain army contracts under a program designed to help minority-owned businesses. In an effort to cut through Army red tape, Nofziger wrote deputy White House Counsel **Edwin Meese** regarding an army contract. Meese subsequently helped to arrange a White House meeting where Wedtech officials, representatives of the army, and Small Business Administration officials worked out an agreement where Wedtech received a $27.7 million no-bid contract to build small gasoline engines. Between 1982 and 1987, Wedtech received hundreds of millions of dollars in no-bid army and navy contracts.

In 1986 questions arose whether Wedtech should have received the contracts under the minority set-aside program. Within months of the beginning of the investigation, Wedtech went bankrupt. In February 1987 four Wedtech officials pleaded guilty to various contract-related offenses. The officials alleged that they made payoffs to government officials in order to obtain help in obtaining government contracts. In February 1987 a special three-judge appeals panel appointed James McKay as an **independent counsel** to investigate whether Nofziger violated federal law. After receiving the appointment as the Wedtech independent counsel, McKay received permission to investigate whether Meese violated any federal laws by directing White House staff members to contact the department of defense on behalf of Wedtech.

A federal **grand jury** subsequently indicted Nofziger for violating the one-year waiting period. He was subsequently convicted. Then in July 1988, McKay issued his final report on Meese's conduct. McKay found insufficient credible evidence to prosecute Meese. However, the McKay report stated that Meese probably had violated federal law by failing to pay a few thousand dollars in capital gains taxes in 1985 and by taking part in decisions regarding the telecommunications industry despite the fact that Meese technically owned a small amount of stock in telephone companies. These two issues had nothing to do with Meese's alleged involvement with Wedtech. In 1989 the U.S. Court of Appeals for the District of Columbia overturned Nofziger's conviction on the grounds that McKay had failed to prove that Nofziger had knowingly violated the one-year no contact ban.

Besides the investigations of Nofziger and Meese, the New York U.S. attorney's office pursued an investigation and prosecutions of New York Democrat Representative Robert Garcia and San Francisco lawyer E. Robert Wallach. Although U.S. District Court juries convicted Wallach in 1989 of taking illegal payments and Representative Garcia of extorting a no-interest loan from Wedtech, in September 1993 the New York U.S. attorney's office dropped charges against Wallach and former Representative Garcia after a U.S. Court of Appeals reversed Wallach's and Garcia's convictions.

Related Entries: Independent Counsel Investigations; Meese, Edwin, III; Nofziger, Lyn; Reagan Administration Ethics Controversies

SUGGESTED READING: Robert Roberts and Marion T. Doss, *From Watergate to Whitewater: The Public Integrity War*, Westport, CT: Praeger, 1997.

WEINBERGER, CASPAR WILLARD (August 18, 1917–   ). Secretary of health and human services, 1970–1975; secretary of defense, 1981–1987.

Caspar Weinberger first came to Washington in 1969 to serve as President Nixon's secretary of health and human resources. After resigning, Weinberger returned to private business in California. After Ronald Reagan won the 1980 presidential election, he recruited Weinberger for the position of secretary of defense. Between January 1981 and 1987, Weinberger presided over one of the largest defense build-ups in American history.

On December 19, 1986, a three-judge appellate panel appointed **Lawrence Walsh** to serve as the **Iran-contra independent counsel**. Walsh received the authority to investigate whether diversion of profits from the sale of arms to Iran to the Nicaraguan contras violated any federal laws and whether Reagan administration officials lied to Congress and federal investigators regarding their involvement in policy decisions to sell arms to Iran in an effort to gain the release of hostages being held by pro-Iranian terrorists in Lebanon. Interestingly Weinberger had been one of the few Reagan administration officials who had strongly opposed the proposal to sell arms to Iran in an effort to obtain release of American hostages.

On June 16, 1992, a federal **grand jury** indicted former Secretary of Defense Weinberger for allegedly obstructing the congressional Iran-contra investigation by concealing hundreds of pages of Iran-contra related notes which he took. Weinberger vigorously denied that he had intentionally concealed any documents requested by Walsh. On December 24, 1992, President Bush pardoned former Weinberger and five other Iran-contra figures after he lost the 1992 presidential election to Arkansas Governor Bill Clinton. In sharp contrast to President **Gerald Ford**'s 1974 pardon of former President Richard Nixon, the Bush pardons created little controversy.

Related Entries: Iran-contra Scandal; Walsh, Lawrence E.

SUGGESTED READING: "Text of President Bush's Statement on the Pardon of Weinberger and Others," *New York Times*, December 25, 1992, A 22.

WHISKEY RING. In 1874 President Ulysses S. Grant appointed **Benjamin H. Bristow** as secretary of the treasury. Bristow took his mandate to clean up the Treasury Department seriously. Shortly after taking over, he audited tax records that indicated that the Treasury Department had failed to collect taxes on millions of gallons of whiskey. Early in 1875 Bristow and Solicitor of the Treasury Bluford Wilson undertook a secret operation to determine the reason for the shortfall in excise tax receipts. Through 1875 the investigation uncovered a massive conspiracy by whiskey distillers, federal revenue agents, and others to avoid paying millions of dollars in federal excise taxes on distilled spirits.

The Great Whiskey Ring trial, *United States v Babcock*, February 26, 1876. Reproduced from the Collections of the LIBRARY OF CONGRESS

After tariffs federal excise taxes constituted the second most important revenue source for the federal government.

During 1875 and early 1876, federal **grand juries** indicted some 350 individuals on fraud charges, including General John A. McDonald, supervisor of revenue for Missouri and a number of other states. Even more alarming the investigation led to the arrest of **General Orville E. Babcock**, President Grant's secretary. In July 1875 Bristow told President Grant of the alleged involvement of Orville Babcock with the Whiskey Ring. According to Grant historian William B. Hesseltine, Grant subsequently wrote "Let no guilty man escape, if it can be avoided. Be especially vigilant . . . against all who insinuate that they have high influence to protect, or to protect them."

Early in February 1875, Babcock went on trial in St. Louis, Missouri. As part of Babcock's defense, Babcock's lawyers introduced the written testimony of President Ulysses S. Grant who allowed himself to undergo questioning in Washington, D.C. In his testimony, President Grant vouched for Babcock's character. Without Grant's testimony a strong likelihood existed that the U.S. District Court jury would convict Babcock. Instead, the jury found Babcock innocent of all charges on February 28, 1876.

Not unexpectedly Bristow's insistence on vigorously pursuing the Whiskey Ring investigation made him as many enemies as friends. Many Republicans saw Bristow's campaign as causing severe damage to the Republican chances for winning the presidency in 1876. After Babcock's acquittal, Bristow's relationship with Grant quickly deteriorated. The Grant White House made clear to Bristow that he should leave the administration. After submitting his resignation, Bristow set his sights on the White House. Looking for a candidate who might take government reform seriously, many reform-minded Republicans supported his candidacy at the 1876 Republican convention. Yet Bristow had made too many enemies to win the nomination. In the end a badly split Republican Party nominated Ohio governor **Rutherford B. Hayes** as their presidential nominee. Hayes went on to win the disputed election of 1876.

Related Entries: Babcock, General Orville E.; Bristow, Benjamin Helm; Election of 1876; Grant Administration Ethics Controversies

SUGGESTED READING: C. Vann Woodward, ed., *Responses of Presidents to Charges of Misconduct*, New York: Delacorte Press, 1974.

WHITEWATER INVESTIGATION. During 1978, then–Arkansas Attorney General Bill Clinton and **Hillary Rodham Clinton** entered into a partnership with friends **James B. McDougal** and **Susan McDougal** to develop a tract of land in Marion County, Arkansas, located along the White River. The Clintons and McDougals borrowed $203,000 to buy land. Later, they would establish the Whitewater Development Corporation with the purpose of developing the land for retirement or vacation homes. In November 1978, Arkansas voters elected Bill Clinton as governor. In 1980, Clinton lost his bid for reelection, but in 1982, Arkansas voters again elected him as governor.

During the early 1980s, James McDougal joined with a number of other individuals to enter the banking business. In 1982, McDougal bought a small savings and loan which he renamed Madison Guaranty Savings and Loan. From 1982 through 1984, Madison Guaranty grew rapidly. By 1984, state regulators expressed concern over the financial stability of the savings and loan. During 1985, in an effort to resolve regulatory concerns, James McDougal hired Hillary Rodham Clinton and the Rose Law Firm to represent Madison Guaranty before state regulators. In 1986, Madison's board of directors removed James Mc-Dougal as president, but he remained the owner of Madison Guaranty. In 1989, the company collapsed as a result of a series of bad loans and general misman-agement. The failure of Madison Guaranty cost federal taxpayers over $60 million. In 1990, a Little Rock, Arkansas, U.S. District Court jury found McDougal not guilty of fraud related to the management of a real estate subsidiary of Madison Guaranty. In 1992, the Clintons sold their remaining interest in White-water to the McDougals for $1,000.

On March 8, 1992, the *New York Times* published a story that detailed the history of the Whitewater land development which raised questions regarding whether the failure of the Whitewater development might have contributed to the failure of Madison Guaranty. Coming in the midst of Clinton's primary campaign to win the Democratic presidential nomination, his campaign quickly commissioned a report that indicated that the Clintons had lost some $60,000 on the Whitewater development. In September 1992, the Resolution Trust Cor-

President Jimmy Carter meets Arkansas Governor Bill Clinton, December 1, 1978. Jimmy Carter Library

poration (RTC) asked the Justice Department to investigate whether the Clintons might have benefitted from illegal activities at Madison Guaranty. In November 1992, Bill Clinton won the presidential election in a three-way race with Vice President George Bush and Reform Party candidate Ross Perot.

From January through June 1993, media interest in Whitewater waned. However, in July 1993, Deputy White House Counsel **Vincent Foster** committed suicide in a Washington, D.C., area park. While a partner in the Little Rock, Arkansas, Rose Law Firm, Foster handled many of the Clintons' legal matters. Through the remainder of 1993, pressure intensified on Attorney General **Janet Reno** to appoint a special counsel to investigate the Whitewater matter. In January 1994, Attorney General Reno appointed New York lawyer **Robert B. Fiske Jr.** as the Justice Department's special counsel for the Whitewater matter in an effort to resolve continuing doubts regarding the death of Vincent Foster. Shortly after beginning this investigation, Attorney General Reno gave Fiske the authority to review the circumstances surrounding Foster's death. In March 1994, Associate Attorney General **Webster Hubbell** resigned as the result of allegations regarding his billing practices while he served as a partner in the Rose Law Firm. During early spring 1994, Fiske issued a report that confirmed Vincent Foster's suicide. Late in June 1994, Congress passed and President Clinton signed into law a new **independent counsel** law.

Early in August 1994, a special three-judge federal appeals panel appointed **Kenneth Starr** as the Whitewater independent counsel. Largely because Starr had served as solicitor general during the Bush administration, the Starr appointment faced considerable criticism. Through the remainder of 1994 and 1995, he conducted an intense review of the Whitewater Development Corporation and the failure of Madison Guaranty. In 1995, a federal grand jury indicted James and Susan McDougal and Arkansas Governor Jim Guy Tucker for obtaining $3 million in fraudulent Small Business Administration (SBA) loans from a financial management company operated by former Little Rock, Arkansas, municipal judge **David Hale**. Hale operated a private investment company that specialized in helping disadvantaged business owners obtain loans backed by the Small Business Administration. The indictment alleged that the McDougals and Tucker did not qualify as disadvantaged business owners eligible for SBA-backed small business loans. During 1994, Hale pleaded guilty to using his company to make fraudulent SBA backed loans. Hale received a twenty-eight-month prison sentence after agreeing to cooperate with Starr's Whitewater investigation.

On January 4, 1996, White House officials found Hillary Clinton's Rose Law Firm billing records in a White House book room located in the Clintons' private residence. The records indicated that Mrs. Clinton had performed sixty hours of legal work for James McDougal's Madison Guaranty Savings and Loan during 1985 and 1986. Independent Counsel Starr had subpoenaed the billing records two years earlier. After discovery of the records, Starr began an inquiry into whether Hillary Rodham Clinton lied about the location of the billing records. Throughout the Whitewater investigation, she denied having any knowledge regarding the location of the billing records.

In a May 1996, Little Rock, Arkansas, U.S. District Court trial David Hale testified that during the mid-1980s Arkansas Governor Bill Clinton pressured him to make a fraudulent $300,000 loan to Susan McDougal's marketing company. In videotaped testimony, President Clinton denied ever asking Hale to loan any money to Susan McDougal. On May 26, a U.S. District Court jury convicted Tucker and the McDougals on illegally obtaining $3 million of SBA backed loans from Hale Capital Management.

Through the remainder of Starr's Whitewater investigation, he proved unsuccessful in finding evidence to confirm Hale's allegation or to seek an indictment of Hillary Rodham Clinton for giving false testimony regarding her involvement with the Whitewater development and Madison Guaranty Savings and Loan. After Starr resigned as the Whitewater independent counsel, a special federal appeals panel appointed Robert W. Ray as the Whitewater independent counsel in October 1999. Between August 1994 and September 30, 1999, Kenneth Starr and Robert Ray spent $52,344,649 on various Clinton administration probes.

On September 20, 2000, Ray issued his final Whitewater report. He announced that the Whitewater investigation had failed to develop sufficient evidence to indict and convict the Clintons for illegal activities related to the failed land development. In addition, Ray announced that insufficient evidence existed to indict or convict Hillary Rodham Clinton for the disappearance of her Rose Law Firm billing records. He also announced that insufficient evidence existed to indict and convict either Bill Clinton or Hillary Rodham Clinton for making false statements regarding the Whitewater development. However, Ray did note that fourteen convictions had resulted from the Whitewater investigation, including former Associate Attorney General Webster Hubbell, Arkansas Governor Jim Guy Tucker, and James and Susan McDougal.

Related Entries: Clinton Administration Ethics Controversies; Fiske, Robert, Jr.; Hale, David; Independent Counsel Investigations; McDougal, Susan; Starr, Kenneth

SUGGESTED READINGS: Bill Miller, "Probe of Clintons' Land Deal Is Closed," *Washington Post*, September 21, 2000, A1; Robert Roberts and Marion T. Doss, *From Watergate to Whitewater: The Public Integrity War*, Westport, CT: Praeger, 1997.

WOOD, KIMBA (1944–   ). New York City judge.

In early February 1993, President Bill Clinton nominated New York City Judge Kimba Wood as attorney general. A short time after the announcement of Wood's nomination, she withdrew her name from consideration. Like earlier Clinton Attorney General nominee **Zoe Baird**, Wood admitted that she had failed to pay Social Security taxes for a nonresident alien employed as a nanny. After the failed Baird and Wood nominations, President Clinton nominated and the Senate confirmed Miami, Florida, prosecutor **Janet Reno** as attorney general.

In July 1993 Deputy White House Counsel **Vincent Foster** committed suicide. The investigation into the suicide revealed that Foster blamed himself for the embarrassment to the Clinton administration caused by the Zoe Baird and Kimba Wood confirmation controversies.

Related Entry: Clinton Administration Ethics Controversies

SUGGESTED READINGS: Richard L. Berke, "Clinton Chooses New York Judge for Justice Post," *New York Times*, February 5, 1993, A1; Jerry Seper and Paul Bedard, " 'Baird Problem' Forces Wood Out," *Washington Times*, February 6, 1993, A1.

WOODWARD, BOB (March 26, 1943–   ). Author; political commentator; *Washington Post* reporter.

Bob Woodward was a *Washington Post* reporter who, along with **Carl Bernstein**, was credited with uncovering the relationship behind the burglary inside the Democratic National Committee headquarters located in the Washington, D.C., **Watergate** complex. On June 19, 1972, Woodward and Bernstein began a long series of stories which ultimately established a direct link between the Watergate burglars, the Committee to Re-Elect the President (CREEP), and the White House. Over the following months, Woodward and Bernstein established that former Attorney General and Chairman of CREEP **John Mitchell** controlled a slush fund used to pay the Watergate burglars and that CREEP employees had conducted a number of operations to sabotage the campaigns of potential Democratic opponents. Woodward and Bernstein also uncovered efforts by the Nixon White House and CREEP to conceal their relationship with the Watergate burglars.

Woodward and Bernstein subsequently credited much of the information they used in their stories to "Deep Throat"—an anonymous source. Long after the August 1974 resignation of President Richard Nixon, Woodward and Bernstein refused to identify "Deep Throat." During 1974 they published *All the President's Men*, which was written based on their Watergate experience. The book became an instant best-seller that was then made into a movie starring Robert Redford and Dustin Hoffman.

Between 1974 and the year 2000, Bob Woodward authored a series of non-fiction books. *The Final Days* (coauthored with Carl Bernstein) dealt with President Nixon's final days in the White House. Published in 1994 *The Agenda* presented a behind-the-scenes description of efforts by the new Clinton White House to persuade Congress to adopt national health care reform and Clinton's controversial budget. Woodward followed *The Agenda* with *The Choice*, a book that provided an inside account of the 1996 presidential campaign. In 1999 Woodward published *Shadow: Five Presidents and the Legacy of Watergate*.

Related Entries: Bernstein, Carl; Watergate Scandal

SUGGESTED READINGS: Bob Woodward and Carl Bernstein, *All the President's Men*, New York: Simon & Schuster, 1974; Bob Woodward, *Shadow: Five Presidents and the Legacy of Watergate*, New York: Simon & Schuster, 1974.

WRIGHT, JIM (December 22, 1922–   ). Speaker of the House of Representatives.

During the spring of 1988, Representative **Newt Gingrich** (R-Ga.) filed an ethics complaint with the **Committee on Standards of Official Conduct** which alleged that Democratic Speaker of the House Jim Wright (D-Tex.) had violated House ethics rules in his personal financial dealings. Later, **Common Cause**, the Washington, D.C.–based good government lobby, also demanded a full investigation of the allegations. On June 8, 1988, Speaker Wright told the press that he welcomed a full inquiry by the Committee on Standards of Official Conduct.

The most serious charges involved allegations that Wright violated House earned income limits and **gift acceptance prohibitions** by arranging the bulk sales of Wright's book, *Reflections of a Public Man*, and by accepting favors from a Texas developer. Besides traditional outlets Wright supporters had sold the book at numerous political rallies. In addition a number of lobbyists had purchased large numbers of copies. Wright had received a 55 percent royalty on each book sold, which critics attacked as exceptionally high. Wright ultimately earned approximately $55,000 in royalties.

On April 17, 1989, after a ten-month investigation, the Committee on Standards of Official Conduct charged Speaker Wright with accepting improper gifts from the developer and using a bulk sales scheme to get around outside earned income limitations. Then on May 31, 1989, Speaker Wright announced to the full House his intention to resign. He used the opportunity to blast the political climate of Washington which had made destroying the reputation of honest public officials a spectator sport. "It is intolerable that qualified members of the executive and legislative branches are resigning because of the ambiguities and the confusion surrounding the ethics laws and because of their own consequent vulnerability to personal attack. That's a shame. It is happening." Wright then went on to blame his situation on "self-appointed vigilantes carrying out personal vendettas against members of the other party." He resigned as Speaker on June 6, 1989 and left the House on June 30, 1989.

The Wright affair put further pressure on Congress to tighten ethics rules to avoid a repeat of the situation that might have contributed to Speaker Wright running afoul of House ethics rules.

During the late 1980s, a large percentage of House members felt they deserved a substantial pay increase. However, many feared a strong voter backlash if they voted it for themselves. Through much of 1989, the House leadership urged President George Bush to support a governmentwide pay increase. Bush made it quite clear that he did not intend to support a large congressional pay increase unless the House and Senate agreed to prohibit their members from accepting **honorariums**. After considerable arm twisting, the House agreed to prohibit members from accepting any honorariums for the personal use of House members. Consequently when Congress passed and President Bush signed into law the **Ethics Reform Act of 1989**, it included a substantial pay increase for House members. At the same time, the law prohibited House members from accepting any honorarium.

To the dismay of the Democratic congressional leadership, the Wright resignation and the subsequent passage of the Ethics Reform Act did not bring to an end embarrassing congressional ethics scandals. Between 1990 and the November 1994 congressional midterm elections, the **Keating Five, House Banking**, and **House Post Office** scandals further tarnished the reputation of Congress.

Related Entry: Honorarium Restrictions

SUGGESTED READINGS: Congressional Quarterly, *Congressional Ethics: History, Facts, and Controversy*, Washington, DC: Congressional Quarterly, 1992; Jim Wright, Text of Speaker of the House Jim Wright's Resignation Speech delivered on May 31, 1989. URL: *http://www.resignation.com/historicaldocs/speech.phtml?id=66.*

WRIGHT, SUSAN WEBBER (August 22, 1948–   ). U.S. Federal District Judge.

On May 6, 1994, former Arkansas state employee **Paula Jones** filed a federal civil rights suit against President Bill Clinton. The suit alleged that in 1991 Clinton had made unlawful sexual advances to Jones in a Little Rock, Arkansas, hotel room. Later assigned the case, U.S. Federal District Court Judge Susan Webber Wright would preside over the Paula Jones case from May 1994 through the settlement of the case in September 1998.

After Judge Wright ruled in December 1994 that the Constitution provided President Clinton with immunity from suit while he remained in the White House, Jones took the issue to the U.S. Supreme Court. On May 28, 1997, the Supreme Court ruled in *Jones v Clinton* that the Constitution did not prohibit Jones's lawsuit from proceeding because the alleged illegal acts took place before Clinton became president. The high court, however, granted Judge Wright considerable discretion in the scheduling of any pretrial depositions or a subsequent trial.

On January 17, 1998, Clinton traveled to the offices of his lawyer **Robert Bennett** in Washington, D.C., to participate in a videotaped deposition for lawyers representing Jones. During the deposition attorneys representing Jones asked President Clinton numerous questions regarding his alleged relationship with former White House intern and employee **Monica Lewinsky**. Prior to the deposition, Lewinsky had submitted a deposition to Jones's lawyers denying ever having sexual relations with Clinton. In response to the questions, Clinton testified that he neither had been alone with or had had a sexual relationship with Lewinsky. Judge Wright preceded over the deposition. A day earlier **independent counsel Kenneth Starr** had received permission from a special three-judge federal appeals panel to expand his **Whitewater** investigation to include whether Clinton might have violated federal law in his effort to conceal his relationship with Monica Lewinsky.

Then on April 2, 1998, Judge Wright dismissed the Jones lawsuit on the grounds the president's alleged conduct did not constitute sexual assault and that Jones had failed to produce any evidence that Clinton or his associates had punished Jones for allegedly rebuffing Clinton's sexual advance. On April 17, 1998, Jones announced her intention to appeal the dismissal of her sexual harassment lawsuit. On November 13, 1998, Jones and Clinton reached an agreement to settle. Clinton agree to pay Jones $850,000. As part of the settlement, Clinton did not admit any wrongdoing. In December 1998 the House voted to impeach Clinton for perjury and obstruction of justice. In February 1999 he was acquitted on both charges.

However, the Senate action did not end Clinton's legal problems. On April 13, 1999, Judge Wright found Clinton in contempt of court for giving "false, misleading and evasive answers that were designed to obstruct the judicial process" in his January 1999 Jones deposition. On July 30, 1999, Judge Wright ordered Clinton to pay Jones's lawyers $90,000.

Related Entries: Impeachment Proceedings; Jones, Paula

SUGGESTED READING: Roberto Suro and Joan Biskupic, "Judge Finds Clinton in Contempt of Court; Wright Says Answers in Jones Civil Suit Were 'Designed to Obstruct,' " *Washington Post*, April 13, 1999, A1.

INDEX

Page references in **bold type** indicate main entries in the encyclopedia.

ethics for federal employees and officials, 70–71; and gift acceptance prohibitions, 154; and honorarium restrictions, 178; and Kennedy administration ethics reform program, 223

Executive Order 11222, Prescribing Standards of Ethical Conduct for Government Officers and Employees, **126–127**; and appearance of impropriety rule, 7; and Bush ethics reform program, 39; and codes of ethics for federal employees and officials, 71; and confidential financial disclosure, 127; and designated agency ethics officials, 122, 308; and Executive Order 10939, 125–126; and financial conflict of interest prohibitions, 143; and honorarium restrictions, 178; and Johnson administration ethics reform program, 211; and John Macy, 237–238

Executive Order 12674, Principles of Ethical Conduct for Government Officers and Employees, **127–129**; and appearance of impropriety rule, 8; and Bush administration ethics reform program, 39; and codes of ethics for federal employees and officials, 71; and Executive Order 11222, 127; and honorarium restrictions, 179; and the President's Commission on Federal Ethics Law Reform, 270; and U.S. Office of Government Ethics, 321

Executive Order 12731, Principles of Ethical Conduct for Government Officers and Employees, **129**. See also Executive Order 12674

Executive Order 12834, Ethical Commitments by Executive Branch Appointees, **126–127**. See also "Revolving door" restrictions

Executive privilege doctrine, **130–131**; and Sidney Blumenthal, 26; and Archibald Cox, 83; and Leon Jaworski, 207; and Rita Lavelle, 229; and Nixon's White House tapes, 41, 83, 279, 296; and "Saturday Night Massacre," 296; and Senate Watergate Committee, 300; and Kenneth Starr, 26; and *United*

States v Nixon, 324; and Watergate scandal, 336

Fall, Albert, **133–134**; and Edwin Denby, 96; and Harding administration ethics controversies, 169; and Robert La Follette, 227–228; and Teapot Dome scandal, 309–311

False Statements Accountability Act of 1996, **134–135**

False Statements Act. See False Statements Accountability Act of 1996

FBI files flap, 66, **135–136**

Federal Bureau of Investigation (FBI), 1–2, 135–136, 276, 306

Federal campaign finance reform. See Campaign finance reform (federal)

Federal Election Campaign Act Amendments of 1974, **137–138**; and *Buckley v Valeo*, 35; and campaign finance reform (federal), 48; and Federal Election Commission, 139; and hard money, 166; and independent political expenditures, 198; and soft money, 300

Federal Election Campaign Act Amendments of 1976, **138**; and *Buckley v Valeo*, 35; and campaign finance reform (federal), 48; and Federal Election Commission, 139; and independent political expenditures, 198

Federal Election Campaign Act of 1971 (FECA), **138–139**; and campaign finance reform (federal), 48; and hard money, 166; and independent political expenditures, 198; and Senate Watergate Committee, 299; and Watergate scandal, 334

Federal Election Commission (FEC), **139–140**; and Federal Election Campaign Act Amendments of 1974, 137; and Federal Election Campaign Act Amendments of 1976, 138; and Presidential Election Campaign Fund Act, 274–275; and soft money, 301

Federal financial conflict of interest prohibitions. See Financial conflict of interest prohibitions

Federal prosecution of public corruption:

About the Author

ROBERT NORTH ROBERTS has taught in the Department of Political Science at James Madison University since 1982. He is author of *White House Ethics: The Politics of the History of Federal Conflict of Interest Regulation* and co-authored with Professor Marion T. Doss, *From Watergate to Whitewater: The Public Integrity War*. Professor Roberts, author of numerous articles on public service, received from the Ethics Section of the American Society for Public Administration the Ethics Scholarship Award for the Best Article published in 1999 for "The Supreme Court and the Law of Public Service Ethics," which appeared in *Public Integrity* (Winter, 1999).